Translations of Greek Tragedy in the Work of Ezra Pound

Bloomsbury Studies in Classical Reception

Bloomsbury Studies in Classical Reception presents scholarly monographs offering new and innovative research and debate to students and scholars in the reception of Classical Studies. Each volume will explore the appropriation, reconceptualization and recontextualization of various aspects of the Graeco-Roman world and its culture, looking at the impact of the ancient world on modernity. Research will also cover reception within antiquity, the theory and practice of translation, and reception theory.

Also available in the Series:

Ancient Magic and the Supernatural in the Modern Visual and Performing Arts, edited by Filippo Carlà & Irene Berti

Ancient Greek Myth in World Fiction since 1989, edited by Justine McConnell & Edith Hall

Antipodean Antiquities, edited by Marguerite Johnson

Classics in Extremis, edited by Edmund Richardson

Frankenstein and its Classics, edited by Jesse Weiner, Benjamin Eldon Stevens & Brett M. Rogers

Greek and Roman Classics in the British Struggle for Social Reform, edited by Henry Stead & Edith Hall

Homer's Iliad and the Trojan War: Dialogues on Tradition, Jan Haywood & Naoíse Mac Sweeney

Imagining Xerxes, Emma Bridges

Julius Caesar's Self-Created Image and Its Dramatic Afterlife, Miryana Dimitrova

Once and Future Antiquities in Science Fiction and Fantasy, edited by Brett M. Rogers & Benjamin Eldon Stevens

Ovid's Myth of Pygmalion on Screen, Paula James

Reading Poetry, Writing Genre, edited by Silvio Bär & Emily Hauser

The Codex Fori Mussolini, Han Lamers and Bettina Reitz-Joosse

The Classics in Modernist Translation, edited by Miranda Hickman and Lynn Kozak

The Gentle, Jealous God, Simon Perris

Victorian Classical Burlesques, Laura Monrós-Gaspar

Victorian Epic Burlesques, Rachel Bryant Davies

Translations of Greek Tragedy in the Work of Ezra Pound

Peter Liebregts

BLOOMSBURY ACADEMIC
LONDON • NEW YORK • OXFORD • NEW DELHI • SYDNEY

BLOOMSBURY ACADEMIC
Bloomsbury Publishing Plc
50 Bedford Square, London, WC1B 3DP, UK
1385 Broadway, New York, NY 10018, USA
29 Earlsfort Terrace, Dublin 2, Ireland

BLOOMSBURY, BLOOMSBURY ACADEMIC and the Diana logo are trademarks of Bloomsbury Publishing Plc

First published in Great Britain 2019
Paperback edition published 2021

Copyright © Peter Liebregts, 2019

Peter Liebregts has asserted his right under the Copyright, Designs and Patents Act, 1988, to be identified as Author of this work.

For legal purposes the Acknowledgements on p. ix constitute an extension of this copyright page.

Cover design: Terry Woodley
Cover image © Stage and cavea of ancient ruins of Greek Theatre, Syracuse, Sicily. kpzfoto/Alamy Stock Photo

All rights reserved. No part of this publication may be reproduced or transmitted in any form or by any means, electronic or mechanical, including photocopying, recording, or any information storage or retrieval system, without prior permission in writing from the publishers.

Bloomsbury Publishing Plc does not have any control over, or responsibility for, any third-party websites referred to or in this book. All internet addresses given in this book were correct at the time of going to press. The author and publisher regret any inconvenience caused if addresses have changed or sites have ceased to exist, but can accept no responsibility for any such changes.

A catalogue record for this book is available from the British Library.

Library of Congress Cataloging-in-Publication Data
Names: Liebregts, P. Th. M. G., author.
Title: Translations of Greek tragedy in the work of Ezra Pound / Peter Liebregts.
Description: London ; New York, NY : Bloomsbury Academic, 2019. | Series: Bloomsbury studies in classical reception | Includes bibliographical references and index.
Identifiers: LCCN 2019010452| ISBN 9781350084155 (hb) | ISBN 9781350084179 (ebook) | ISBN 9781350084162 (PDF)
Subjects: LCSH: Pound, Ezra, 1885–1972–Criticism and interpretation. | Pound, Ezra, 1885–1972–Knowledge–Language and languages. | Greek language–Translating into English–History–20th century. | Greek drama (Tragedy)–Translations into English–History and criticism. | Sophocles–Translations into English–History and criticism. | Aeschylus–Translations into English–History and criticism.
Classification: LCC PS3531.O82 Z73835 2019 | DDC 811/.52—dc23
LC record available at https://lccn.loc.gov/2019010452

ISBN: HB: 978-1-3500-8415-5
PB: 978-1-3501-9134-1
ePDF: 978-1-3500-8416-2
eBook: 978-1-3500-8417-9

Series: Bloomsbury Studies in Classical Reception

Typeset by RefineCatch Limited, Bungay, Suffolk

To find out more about our authors and books visit www.bloomsbury.com and sign up for our newsletters.

Contents

Preface ... vi
Acknowledgements ... ix
Notes on the Text ... xi
List of Abbreviations ... xii

1 Translation, Metrics and Greek Tragedy ... 1
2 Ezra Pound and Aeschylus ... 21
3 Ezra Pound and Sophocles ... 47
4 Sophocles, Pound and *Elektra* I ... 67
5 Sophocles, Pound and *Elektra* II ... 97
6 Sophocles, Pound and *Elektra* III ... 123
7 *Women of Trachis* – Introduction ... 153
8 Sophocles, Pound and *Women of Trachis* I ... 173
9 Sophocles, Pound and *Women of Trachis* II ... 209

Bibliography ... 249
Index ... 255

Preface

The picture on the cover of this book is of the Greek theatre near Siracusa on Sicily, built in the fifth century BCE and renovated in the Roman period. In January 1925 Ezra Pound and William Butler Yeats visited the site, and in his essay 'Hell' (1934) the American poet recalled that Yeats wanted him to speak some verse aloud to test out the acoustics. The Irish poet was annoyed when Pound 'bellowed' Sappho's Greek ode to Aphrodite, but he explained his refusal to 'spout English poesy' by claiming that 'English verse wasn't CUT'. This anecdote is but one of many telling examples of Pound's admiration for what he regarded as the unsurpassed musical and rhythmic quality of classical Greek poetry, which throughout his life he would champion as a model to emulate in English.

This monograph aims to offer a detailed, at times line-by-line, from Greek to English philological analysis of Ezra Pound's translations of Greek tragedy, while contextualizing these versions with regard to the poet's biography and his work, particularly *The Cantos*. The key texts are Pound's renderings of Aeschylus' *Agamemnon* and Sophocles' *Elektra* and *Trachiniae*. In the case of the last two plays, this book will show on the basis of my own cribs of the Greek and through comparison with English translations by F. Storr and by Richard Jebb, both used by Pound, how Pound's versions came about. This analysis will include material that has not as yet been published or has been understudied, particularly Pound's annotations to his Loeb edition of Sophocles (now in his personal library at Brunnenburg), his unpublished correspondence with scholars such as F. R. Earp and Rudd Fleming, as well as manuscript versions of the plays, and other as yet unpublished drafts and texts.

Chapter 1, 'Translation, Metrics, and Greek Tragedy', deals with the question of the extent of Ezra Pound's knowledge of classical Greek, his views on existing translations from the Greek, and what, in his perspective, a translation should be like. This chapter also discusses Pound's changing views on the relationship between poetry and the dramatic element in Greek tragedy, with a particular focus on his interest in *melopoeia* and Greek metrics in relation to English poetry. The first chapter thus contextualizes what will be one of the claims of this book, namely, that Pound's renderings are based on a careful reading of the Greek source texts, which will become clear in the detailed analyses presented in the subsequent chapters.

Chapter 2, 'Ezra Pound and Aeschylus', offers a detailed look at Pound's interest in the Greek playwright. It begins with a discussion of his two essays on Aeschylus published in *The Egoist* in early 1919, with a focus on what Pound considered the 'touchstones' of the *Agamemnon*. Given his high praise for this play, the chapter offers a philological analysis of Pound's attempt at rendering the beginning of the *Agamemnon*, and concludes with a discussion of Pound's use of Aeschylus in *The Cantos*, showing how there is a continuous appropriation of his writings until the late 1950s, especially of the *Oresteia*.

Chapter 3, 'Ezra Pound and Sophocles', opens with an as yet unpublished text from the Beinecke library, which is not a translation but rather a spoof on Sophocles' *Oedipus Rex*, which can be seen as a bridge between Pound's attempt at the *Agamemnon* and his later work on Sophocles. It then deals with the influence of the work of the classicist F. R. Earp, especially his book *The Style of Sophocles* (1944), followed by a discussion of Pound's collaboration with Rudd Fleming in translating *Elektra*. The chapter ends with possible reasons why Pound was so attracted to *Elektra* and *Trachiniae*, and not to the other Sophoclean plays.

In Chapter 4. 'Pound, Sophocles, and *Elektra* I', we will first take a look at scholarly approaches to Sophocles' *Elektra*, with a particular focus on Jebb's edition and Earp's book on Sophocles, as these were available to Pound, and on a contemporary discussion by H. Kitto in *Greek Tragedy* (1939), before taking a look at Pound's method of translating the play. The remainder of the chapter offers a detailed philological analysis of Pound's rendering of Sophocles' *Elektra* ll. 1–250.

This analysis is continued in Chapters 5 and 6, 'Pound, Sophocles, and *Elektra* II' and 'Pound, Sophocles, and *Elektra* III', dealing with ll. 251–1057 and ll. 1058–1510, respectively. Together these three chapters make clear how Pound's work on the play is related to the Pisan Cantos and his 1950s work on Confucius. By providing the original Greek with a transliteration followed by a crib, the reader can assess in detail the extent of the relation between Sophocles and Pound's, at times idiosyncratic, version. The analysis also discusses the musical interplay in Pound's version between the Greek and his rendering. Special attention is paid to the lyrical sections of the play. Furthermore, these chapters also take into account changes made from typescript to published version, Fleming's comments and suggestions, and Pound's annotations in his Loeb edition. By offering this (on occasion line-by-line) analysis, the chapters provide an in-depth discussion of Pound's perspective on the play, and on the characters involved. Chapter 6 ends with a coda discussing Pound's use of *Elektra* in Canto 90.

Chapter 7, '*Women of Trachis* – Introduction', surveys scholarly approaches to Sophocles' *Trachiniae* and examines Pound's methods of translation. It also includes a discussion of why Pound had such an interest in what, for a long time, was Sophocles' least studied play, and relates this interest to the poet's knowledge of Japanese Noh as well as his work on *The Cantos*. The chapter also makes use of the unpublished correspondence between F. R. Earp and Pound on the problems of translating Sophocles and the *Trachiniae* in particular.

Chapters 8 and 9 ('Sophocles, Pound, and *Women of Trachis* I'; 'Sophocles, Pound, and Women of *Trachis* II') present a detailed philological analysis of Pound's rendering of Sophocles' *Trachiniae* ll. 1–632 and ll. 633–1278, respectively, using the same method as sketched in the overview of the translation of the *Elektra* in Chapter 4. It discusses Pound's version in comparison to literal translations of the Greek as well as to the translations by Storr and Jebb. The analysis also incorporates the correspondence with F. R. Earp. As the analysis demonstrates, Pound seems to have been far more confident in rendering his second Greek play, and his deviations and stylistic choices were determined by a more extreme personal interpretation of the *Trachiniae*. The second half of Pound's version makes clear how much of his work on Sophocles was related to his ongoing work on *The Cantos*, with its dominant themes of love and divine enlightenment, especially seen in the poet's rendering of the Exodos, centring on the word 'splendour', which for Pound had strong Neoplatonic connotations.

Acknowledgements

During my work on this book I have greatly benefited in conversation and correspondence from the spirit of collegial exchange which characterizes the global community of Pound scholars. My debt to them as friends and experts is enormous, and I especially wish to thank Catherine Paul and Dave Cappella for their support and so many wonderful get-togethers throughout the years ever since we first met at Rapallo in 2005. The Ezra Pound International Conferences have always been stimulating sites for lively and enlightening discussions, and they would not be the same without the Poundians I have met throughout the years, particularly Anderson Araujo, Bernard Dew, David ten Eyck, Justin Kishbaugh, Galateia Demetriou, Mark Byron, Ron Smith, Viorica Patea, Demetres Tryphonopoulos, Ron Bush, Ken Haynes, Akitoshi Nagahata, Richard Parker, Walter Baumann, Bill Pratt, Roxana Preda, John Gery, Biljana Obradovic, Sean Pryor, Réka Mihálka, Stephen Wilson, Massimo Bacigalupo, Ira Nadel, Svetlana Ehtee, Andy Trevathan, Krista Rascoe, Eloisa Bressan, Rhett Forman, and Claudio Sansone. Special thanks are due to Alec Marsh whose work on (political) Pound in the 1950s has greatly helped me in contextualizing my findings. Alec also selflessly made a last-minute trip to Princeton on my behalf to check on archival material. I also thank David Moody, not only for his magisterial biography of Pound, but also for his advice in the various stages of writing my book.

I wish to thank my colleagues at the English Department at Leiden University for continuing to make my academic environment a pleasant and stimulating one, particularly Jan Frans van Dijkhuizen, Michael Newton, and Evert Jan van Leeuwen. Thank you to Katinka Zeven and Lettie Dorst for their suggestions about translational matters.

I owe an enormous debt of gratitude to the Pound Estate and New Directions in New York for their generosity in allowing me to use so much published and unpublished Pound material. I greatly appreciate all the help and advice offered by Chris Wait of New Directions. Most of all I am grateful to Mary de Rachewiltz who allowed me to consult Pound's library at Schloss Brunnenburg in Dorf Tyrol, and I have fond memories of our long discussions over afternoon tea. Her lifelong support for the study of Pound's work has been essential for all Poundian scholars, while she also has a great love for the Greek language. I therefore dedicate this book to her.

Studying Pound includes delving into archives, and I thank the staff at Yale University's Beinecke Library for their assistance and friendly service, especially Mary Ellen Budney. My thanks also go to Isabel Planton of Indiana University's Lilly Library, and AnnaLee Pauls of Princeton University's Department of Rare Books and Special Collections. In reproducing unpublished material from these archives, all reasonable efforts have been made to trace relevant copyright holders, and I would be happy to hear from any in the future.

One section of Chapter 2 has been published in a different form as 'Wrestling with Verbiage: Ezra Pound, Thomas Stanley and Aeschylus', in *Ezra Pound and London: New Perspectives*, ed. Walter Baumann and William Pratt (AMS Press 2015). I wish to acknowledge my debt to the people at Bloomsbury responsible for seeing this book come to fruition, notably David Avital, Alice Wright, Emma Payne, and Lily Mac Mahon. I also thank Andrew Devine for his careful copy-editing of the text. My thanks too to the anonymous reviewers of this manuscript, whose perceptive comments greatly helped.

I am deeply grateful, as always, to my daughter Niki for making me understand the meaning of the phrase 'It all coheres'. Finally, I thank Irene, for many reasons. She offered invaluable advice in drawing up the book proposal which I submitted to Bloomsbury, and gave detailed and insightful feedback on the typescript. For the other reasons I adhere to Sigismondo Malatesta's motto *tempus loquendi, tempus tacendi*.

Notes on the Text

In all cases where Pound's manuscripts, typescripts or letters are quoted, no attempt has been made to standardize spelling or punctuation. Editorial explanations are given within square brackets. I have retained Pound's inconsistencies in his transliterations of the Greek. In my own transliterations, I have used ē for the letter ēta, ō for ōmega, dz voor zēta, x for xi (pronounced as 'ks'), and ch for chi.

Unless indicated otherwise, all translations from Latin and Greek are my own.

Abbreviations

Works by Pound

ABCR	*ABC of Reading*. London: Faber, 1961
C	*The Cantos*. New York: New Directions, 1998. All references to *The Cantos* are followed by the Canto number and page number in this edition, separated by a slash. For example: (98/704)
CON	*Confucius: The Unwobbling Pivot, The Great Digest, The Analects*. New York: New Directions, 1969
E	*Sophocles: Elektra*, a version by Ezra Pound and Rudd Fleming, edited and annotated by Richard Reid, London: Faber, 1990
GB	*Gaudier-Brzeska: A Memoir*. New York: New Directions, 1970
GK	*Guide to Kulchur*. London: Peter Owen, 1952
LE	*Literary Essays of Ezra Pound*, ed. T. S. Eliot. London: Faber, 1954
P	*Personae: The Shorter Poems*, ed. Lea Baechler and A. Walton Litz. New York: New Directions, 1990
SL	*Selected Letters 1907–1941*, ed. D. D. Paige. New York: New Directions, 1971
SP	*Selected Prose 1909–1965*, ed. William Cookson. London: Faber, 1973
SR	*The Spirit of Romance*. London: Peter Owen, 1952 (rev. edn of 1910)
T	*Translations*. London: Faber, 1970
WT	*Sophocles: Women of Trachis*. London: Faber, 1969

Archival materials

Beinecke   Ezra Pound Papers (YCAL MSS 43), Yale Collection of American Literature, Beinecke Rare Book and Manuscript Library. All references to material in this collection are followed by box and folder numbers. For example: (Beinecke 70/3125).

Lilly   Ezra Pound MSS., II, Manuscripts Department, The Lilly Library, Indiana University, Bloomington, Indiana. The Pound/Fleming correspondence is in Box 5. All references are given as 'Lilly'.

Princeton   Ezra Pound Translations of Greek Drama (C0301); Manuscripts Division, Department of Rare Books and Special Collections, Princeton University Library. All references to material in this collection are followed by box and folder numbers. For example: (Princeton 1/13).

1

Translation, Metrics and Greek Tragedy

Introduction

Throughout his life Ezra Pound fostered an unwavering love and admiration for Greek classical poetry, as evidenced by the many comments in his critical prose, the quotations and allusions in his poetic output, and his translations of what he regarded as key texts. However, his own statements about the extent of his knowledge of Greek, such as his claims in 'Translators of Greek' (1920) that he probably was not 'the sole creature who has been well taught his Latin and very ill-taught his Greek' (*LE* 249), and in a 1935 letter to the classicist W. H. D. Rouse that he was 'Too god damn iggurunt of *Greek*' to translate the *Odyssey* (*SL* 274), have had considerable influence on the way his translations from the Greek classics have been received and assessed. This depreciation is strengthened by Pound's, at times rather dismissive, statements about linguistic expertise, as in this letter to Iris Barry of 24 August 1916:

> Really one DON'T need to know a language. One NEEDS, damn well needs, to know the few hundred words in the few really good poems that any language has in it. It is better to know [Sappho's] POIKILOTHRON by heart than to be able to read Thucydides without trouble.
>
> SL 93

Such statements are part of Pound's life-long dismissive attitude towards academics obsessed with philological minutiae at the cost of aesthetic appreciation of a text. Driven by his intention to read the best that literature had to offer, Pound showed that when armed with a crib in one language he was quite capable of resolving some of the difficulties in another. However, he did not always take the time to consider every detail in order to establish a correct interpretation. Edward Marsh, co-editor of the first Georgian anthology in 1912, recalled in his memoir *A Number of People* (1939) that Pound seemed 'to be like the character in George Eliot who "knew Latin" in general, but was apt to be defeated by any particular piece of Latin' (Marsh 328). Consequently, opinion on Pound's knowledge of Greek has been divided. Michael Reck, one of Pound's close friends during the 1950s, claimed that the poet's Greek was not extensive, and that Pound had to rely greatly on the bilingual Loeb Classical Library translations (Reck 118), whereas James Laughlin, Pound's American publisher, has stated that the poet actually did have a fair knowledge of Greek, but that the accents posed a problem (Laughlin 8).

Paradoxically, both accounts are probably true. Most people who studied ancient Greek when young, would agree that mastering the language takes far more effort than learning Latin, and despite the more intense labour, one tends to forget Greek more easily after a short period than Latin after a very long while. As his drafts and annotations show, when Pound began translating Sophocles' *Elektra* at the beginning of 1949, he struggled sometimes with some of the most elemental of semantic, morphological and syntactic matters. Pound confessed to two visitors to St Elizabeths in the 1950s that 'My Greek is still not as good as I want it' (Norman 444), and he exclaimed while reading Plotinus for Canto 105, drafted in 1956, that he would 'have to learn a little Greek to keep up with this' (105/770), since, as he said to another visitor in 1957, he was 'an old man that never learned his Greek properly' (Rattray 344). Whatever Pound's mastery of Greek may have been at any given time, either in his or others' views, he apparently never experienced the ease and swiftness of comprehension which helped him to enjoy his study of Latin texts.

An additional reason for the generally negative reception of Pound's Greek translations relates to his idiosyncratic notions about the nature and function of translation. In order to assess these, we need to look briefly at the history of translation and discuss some of the main approaches in Translation Studies that help us to analyse his work.

The art of translation

Debates about translations in Pound's time were still very much dominated by the 'word-for-word' versus the 'sense-for-sense' approach. This distinction, going back as far as Cicero and St Jerome, had determined thinking about translation for centuries, and had generated such famous contributions as John Dryden's categorization of translations as 'metaphrase' (literal translation), 'paraphrase' (sense-for-sense), and 'imitation', where translation becomes so free that the result is more of an adaptation. In his preface to his anthology of Ovid's *Epistles*

(1680), Dryden prefers the paraphrase in which the author takes moderate freedoms in rendering the meaning of the source text. In his view, metaphrasing versions lack readability, while imitations make the original too subservient to the translator's own personality and literary ambition, as the translator 'assumes the liberty not only to vary from the words and sense, but to forsake them both as he sees occasion: and taking only some general hints from the Original, to run division on the ground-work, as he pleases' (Dryden 38). As George Steiner has rightly noted, Dryden thus gave the word 'imitation' a negative twist, but twentieth-century poets like Ezra Pound and Robert Lowell would adopt its use 'with a positive inflection' (Steiner 268).

A major step in theorizing about translation was made by Friedrich Schleiermacher in 1813 with his *Über die verschiedenen Methoden des Übersetzens* ('On the different methods of translating'), in which he moved beyond the 'literal versus free' debate by claiming that a translator must choose between two methods. Either he must bring the reader close to the author of the source text by emphasizing the 'strangeness' or 'otherness' of the original through an 'alienating' translation, or, on the contrary, make the source text more understandable for a reader in the target language by 'naturalizing' it. In an alienating translation the source text is to be rendered in such a way that it has to be understood on its own terms, with the source language and the characteristics of the original text determining the nature of the translation.

This distinction between 'alienating' and 'naturalizing' translations had an enormous influence and can be seen, for example, in the distinction drawn by Lawrence Venuti in the 1990s between 'foreignization' and 'domestication' (or 'acculturation'). Venuti criticized many Anglo-American translations for making their translators 'invisible', with source texts domesticated into 'readable' or 'transparent' target texts to the extent that any possible difficulty for the reader was smoothed out and the translation reads like a product of the target culture. In contrast, a foreignizing translation should choose an estranging style to emphasize and respect the cultural otherness of the source text. One may do this, for example, by sticking closely to the syntax of the original, or by translating source text words and phrases literally, by deliberately employing archaisms.

Venuti has noted how the history of modern translation theory can be regarded 'as a set of changing relationships between the relative autonomy of the translated text and two other categories: equivalence and function' (Venuti 2012, 5). Equivalence may encompass such notions as fidelity, accuracy or adequacy, terms used to describe the connection of a translation to its source text, making the latter the focus of attention. Function refers to the aims and effects of a translation, and is used to study how the translated text is connected to the target culture.

Equivalence came to the fore in the 1960s and 1970s in the work of the Biblical scholar Eugene Nida, who discarded the old terms 'free' and 'literal' in favour of two types of equivalence, formal and dynamic, and so introducing a more reader-oriented approach. Formal equivalence occurs when the target text corresponds to the form of the source text, as when, for example, two words are translated as two words, or a phrase is rendered literally, or the translation closely follows the textual pattern of the source text. This close approximation to the source text turns such translations into what Nida calls 'gloss translations', often accompanied by scholarly footnotes. They are geared towards readers who want to gain the closest possible access to the original, short of reading it in the source language. Dynamic equivalence aims for 'the principle of equivalent effect', that is, 'the relationship between receptor and message should be substantially the same as that which existed between the original receptors and the message' (Nida 144). The target text tries to find the closest natural equivalents of elements used in the source text, and thus the lexicon, the grammar and cultural references may all be adapted to produce an autonomous and 'natural' translation.

It is evident that this dynamic equivalence is in fact a functional equivalence, and thus may be linked to other receptor-oriented approaches to translation, such as the so-called *skopos* theory. Scholars like Hans Vermeer and Katharina Reiss in the 1980s introduced the notion of *skopos* (Greek for 'aim' or 'purpose') to analyse how the purpose of a translation determines the chosen method in producing the target text (Bassnett 83–84). This accounts for the possibility that one source text may give rise to very different translations, as a translator may make any adjustment that they deem appropriate. The result should be a functionally adequate target text, with adequacy replacing full equivalence as the measure of the translational action, as a translation does not need to be equivalent to the source text if that is not its prime purpose.

As Susan Bassnett has noted, many Victorian translators were concerned with the need 'to convey the remoteness of the original in time and place' (Bassnett 76). She gives as examples William Morris's deliberately archaic and obscure translations of Virgil, Homer and the Norse sagas, which stress the strangeness and foreignness of the source texts, and Thomas Carlyle's renderings from German. The reader was brought to the source text through a foreignizing translation made by experts and scholars, who made transparency of style subservient to their attempt to instil in the reader the right appreciation of the original. Of course, there were notable exceptions such as Edward Fitzgerald who with his version of *The Rubaiyat of Omar Khayyam* (1858) aimed to produce a more natural translation of the original, although a reason for his doing so was his belief that he could improve upon what he regarded as inferior elements of the source text.

Pound as translator

At the turn of the twentieth century, such Victorian practices of 'literalness, archaizing, pedantry and the production of a text of second-rate literary merit' (Bassnett 81) continued to dominate much of the discussion in English on translation. Pound's translational work clashed with these nineteenth-century notions. With any translation or adaptation, he wanted to reproduce the original as a living work, and to 'make new' the source texts of those writers who he believed could have a revitalizing effect on modern writing. Pound appropriated and translated (parts of) works which he regarded as important because of their techniques, historical value, and universal message. As such, the act of translation for Pound is simultaneously one of criticism, interpretation, creative transposition and original creation, with no systematic and consistent approach, as each text is perceived as making its own demands and each translation is meant to serve its own *skopos*.

This is why throughout his career Pound employed a great variety of translational strategies for his translations, producing such different target texts as 'The Seafarer' or the Chinese poems in *Cathay*. In his translations, then, Pound is constantly slipping through translational theoretical nets, as he will use whatever means available to show the ongoing relevance of these originals and to make the personae of the translated texts speak with a voice from an older and different source culture and at the same time as a contemporary. In his versions the 'literary' is more important than the 'literal', and Pound claimed for himself the freedom to render the original in any way he saw fit in order to preserve its relevance for modern times. For example, in *Homage to Sextus Propertius* we see Pound combining Dryden's three categories at will, with the poet naturalizing and foreignizing throughout the text, juxtaposing archaisms and contemporary colloquialisms, with occasional occurrences of phonemic and metrical translations, and mixing formal and dynamic equivalence. At times Pound recognized in texts by other writers a 'ready-made' description of a congenial experience, and saw in their works aspects of his own self already expressed. As such, by evoking the dead poet as a living presence and by 'making new' their texts, his translations could serve as 'masks of the self' (*GB* 85). In this way Pound's versions of original texts became permeated by the strong verbal presence of his own personality, with the result that the distinction between 'original work' and '(creative) translation' became blurred.

Most of Pound's early literary criticism and observations about translation deal with poetry as the highest form of literature. With regard to the Greek classics, Homer is unquestionably Pound's favourite, and it is significant that in its 'final' version *The Cantos* opens, as a sort of homage, with a rendering (in an imitation of Anglo-Saxon poetry) of a Renaissance Latin translation of a passage of Book 11 of the *Odyssey*. Canto 1 makes clear how Pound made no firm distinction between original writing and translation, which is why his canon of the classics also included the latter, because, as he stated in *How to Read* (1929), 'English literature lives on translation, it is fed by translation; every new exuberance, every new heave is stimulated by translation, every allegedly great age is an age of translations' (*LE* 34–35).

However, Pound's praise of classical translations restricted itself to renderings from the Latin, such as the *Aeneid* by Gavin Douglas (1474–1522), and the *Metamorphoses* (1567) by Arthur Golding, which he even called 'the most beautiful book in the language' (*ABCR* 127). Although Pound appreciated certain parts of George Chapman's *Odyssey* or Alexander Pope's *Iliad*, he did not include translations from the Greek in his canon as in his view there was 'no satisfactory translation of any Greek author' (*LE* 35). In a letter to Iris Barry of July 1916, he advised her, if she could not read Greek poetry in the original, to use Latin translations, as most English translations are 'hopeless' (*SL* 87). It is an opinion he held on to for a long time, as this statement from 1942 in 'A Visiting Card' attests: 'Practically no one has succeeded in producing satisfactory English translations from the Greek: only a few fragments have come through successfully' (*SP* 294).

Pound and Greek tragedy

It may well be that the existing translations determined Pound's at first rather negative view of Greek tragedy. He greatly disliked the work of Gilbert Murray (1866–1957), Regius Professor of Greek at Oxford from 1908 to 1936, and one of the most popular translators of Greek drama of the twentieth century. Pound voiced his criticism most strongly in *Guide to Kulchur* (1938):

> There are, to the best of my knowledge, no translations of these plays that an awakened man can read without deadly boredom.
>
> Eliot's internment of Murray might have been the last word: 'erected a barrier between Euripides and the reader more impassable than the greek language'.
>
> GK 92

Here Pound paraphrases T. S. Eliot's statement in 'Euripides and Professor Murray', published in *The Sacred Wood* in 1920, that 'Professor Murray has simply interposed between Euripides and ourselves a barrier more impenetrable than the Greek language' (Eliot 1969, 75). A few paragraphs later Eliot had concluded:

> It is to be hoped that we may be grateful to Professor Murray and his friends for what they have done, while we endeavour to neutralize Professor Murray's influence upon Greek literature and English language in his translations by making better translations. The choruses from Euripides by H. D. are, allowing for errors and even occasional omissions of difficult passages, much nearer to both Greek and English than Mr. Murray's.
>
> ibid. 77

Eliot's problem with Murray's language was that he 'almost habitually uses two words where the Greek language requires one' (ibid. 73–74). Pound wholeheartedly agreed with this, as apparent from his statement in *Guide to Kulchur* that the poet Hilda Doolittle in her version of Euripides' *Ion* (1937) 'pared down as much as the Genevan pacifist [Murray] has upholstered and straw-filled' (*GK* 93).

Pound also did not think very highly of the translations of Sophocles by the classical scholar Sir Richard C. Jebb (1841–1905), who had edited the playwright's work between 1883 and 1896 in seven volumes, later reissued in an edition with the Greek and English translation on facing pages, with a full commentary. Jebb's edition not only gives reasonably accurate renderings of the originals, but its notes made the edition a standard scholarly work. The translations were published separately in 1905 by Cambridge University Press as *The Tragedies of Sophocles, Translated into English Verse*, a copy of which can still be found in Pound's library at Brunnenburg (with no annotations or traces of reading whatsoever). In his 'Translators of Greek', Pound noted that 'Sophocles falls to Jebb and does not appear satisfactory' (*LE* 269). His statement in a letter to Iris Barry of August 1916 that he has 'looked at a bad trans. of Sophocles' (*SL* 95) is most likely a reference to Jebb's version of the *Oedipus Rex*.[1]

In another letter to Iris Barry of August 1916, Pound wrote that he was 'probably suspicious' of Greek drama:

> People keep on assuring me that it is excellent despite the fact that too many people have praised it. STILL there has been a lot of rhetoric spent on it. And I admit the opening of *Prometheus* (Aeschylus') is impressive. (Then the play goes to pot.) Also I like the remarks about Xerxes making a mess of {illegible} in another Aeschylean play, forget the name. Some choruses annoy me. Moralizing nonentities making remarks on the pleasures of a chaste hymeneal relation, etc. etc. Statements to the effect that Prudence is always more discreet than rashness, and other such brilliant propositions.
>
> I think it would probably be easier to fake a play by Sophocles than a novel by Stendhal, apart from the versification.
>
> SL 94[2]

The title of the play which Pound 'forgot' is *The Persians*, a play about the defeat of the Persians by the Greeks at the battle of Salamis in 480 BCE. Aeschylus presents King Xerxes' mother Atossa as eagerly awaiting news from the expedition against Greece, and, after a long speech by a messenger informing her in detail of the defeat and an appearance by the ghost of Xerxes' father Darius castigating his son for his *hubris*, Xerxes himself arrives on stage, where he in a lyrical dialogue with the Chorus laments the Greek victory. The passage Pound refers to in his letter is most likely part of the choral ode following the dialogue between Atossa and the messenger, namely ll. 548–57, in which the Chorus denounces Xerxes' failed expedition, and contrasts it to his father's military exploits ten years earlier:

> νῦν γὰρ δὴ πρόπασα μὲν στένει γαῖ᾽
> Ἀσιὰς ἐκκενουμένα.
> Ξέρξης μὲν ἄγαγεν, ποποῖ,
> Ξέρξης δ᾽ ἀπώλεσεν, τοτοῖ,
> Ξέρξης δὲ πάντ᾽ ἐπέσπε δυσφρόνως
> βαρίδεσσι ποντίαις.
> τίπτε Δαρεῖος μὲν οὕ-
> τω τότ᾽ ἀβλαβὴς ἐπῆν
> τόξαρχος πολιήταις,
> Σουσίδαις φίλος ἄκτωρ; (edn Weir Smyth)
>
> *nun gar dē propasa men stenei gai'*
> *Asias ekkenoumena.*
> *Xerxēs men agagen, popoi,*

Xerxēs d'apōlesen, totoi,
Xerxēs de pant'epespe dusphronōs
baridessi pontiais.
tipte Dareios men hou-
tō tot'ablabēs epēn
toxarchos poliētais,
Sousidais philos aktōr?

For now the whole emptied land
of Asia groans.
Xerxes led them – shame!
Xerxes destroyed them – woe!
Xerxes did everything unwisely
with his sea-going vessels.
Why was Dareios then
so without harm,
the lord of the bow for his citizens,
the beloved leader for the people of Susa?

my trl

Pound may well have been attracted to this passage because of the anaphoric condemnation of both Xerxes and the enormous and senseless loss of life, a rhetorical effect he would himself employ in the anti-Great War poem IV of *Hugh Selwyn Mauberley* (1920; *P* 187–88). The tricolon may also have reminded him of the pun on Helen's name in Aeschylus' *Agamemnon* (which he would use in *The Cantos*). Pound concluded in his letter to Barry that, although he is 'too damd ignorant to talk intelligently about the Greek drama', he still 'mistrust[s] it, *dona ferentes*, etc' (*SL* 94).

This generally negative attitude recurs in *How to Read* (1929) and *ABC of Reading* (1934). In *How to Read*, Pound sees in the Greek tragedians a decline from Homer, upon whom they were very much dependent for their effects: 'their "charge", at its highest potential, depends so often, and so greatly on their being able to count on their audience's knowledge of the *Iliad*' (*LE* 27). And in *ABC of Reading*, after repeating this claim, he adds that the poetry of Greek drama is not of the same quality as lyric poetry, because the language has been made subservient to the action:

> Ultimately, I suppose, any man with decent literary curiosity will read the *Agamemnon* of Aeschylus, but if he has seriously considered drama as a means of expression he will see that whereas the medium of poetry is WORDS, the medium of drama is people moving about on a stage and using words. That is,

the words are only a part of the medium and the gaps between them, or deficiencies in their meaning, can be made up by 'action'.

People who have given the matter dispassionate and careful attention are fairly convinced that the maximum charge of verbal meaning cannot be used on the stage, save for very brief instants.

Pound finds the poetry of Greek drama failing:

> Taken as READING MATTER, I do NOT believe that the Greek dramatists are up to Homer. Even Aeschylus is rhetorical. Even in the Agamemnon there are quantities of words which do not function as reading matter. I.E., are not necessary to our understanding of the subject.
>
> ABCR 46–47

Ultimately, then, for Pound the key to Greek poetic literature, which includes drama, is not form but language, as is also clear made clear in his discussion on the notion of 'form' in 'Dr Williams' Position' (1928), in which he notes:

> consider the number of very important chunks of world-literature in which form, major form, is remarkable mainly for absence.
>
> There is a corking plot to the *Iliad*, but it is not told us in the poem or at least not in the parts of the poem known to history as The Iliad. It would be hard to find a worse justification of the theories of dramatic construction than the *Prometheus* of Aeschylus....
>
> The component of these great works and *the* indispensable component is texture.
>
> LE 394–95

All of this may well explain why Pound in his early criticism on occasion would praise Aeschylus and Sophocles for their style, while denouncing tragedy in general. In his letter to Iris Barry of 29 August 1916, Pound is quite outspoken on this matter: 'Certainly the whole Oedipus story is a darn silly lot of buncombe – used as a peg for some very magnificent phrases. Superbly used' (*SL* 95). This praise for Sophocles' poetic artistry concurs with other early (Imagist) expressions of admiration for the playwright's style: in the poem 'Ité' (1913) Pound praised the 'hard Sophoclean light' (*P* 86), in a letter of January 1915 the 'Sophoclean severity' (*SL* 50), and in *How to Read* he referred to the 'Sophoclean economy' (*LE* 36, n.1). Of course, Pound would later change his mind about Sophocles the *dramatist* during his stay at St Elizabeths.

Greek drama for Pound seemed to consist only of Aeschylus and Sophocles, as he hardly ever referred to Euripides throughout his writings, and never offered any in-depth analysis of the contents or style of that playwright's work. Pound in the *Little Review* of November 1918 praised H. D.'s translation from Euripides, 'Choruses from *Iphigeneia in Aulis*', but was not 'convinced one can approach the Greek drama via Euripides', despite the fact that H. D.'s renderings are superior to 'windy and verbose translators', such as Robert Browning, 'if, via Homer and Aeschylus one has contracted an interest in the Atreidae' (Pound 1918, 16). This statement implies that Pound felt that H. D. had wasted her skills, as Euripides for him was a minor talent in comparison to Aeschylus and Sophocles. Eliot agreed with him, as his essay 'Euripides and Professor Murray' makes clear: 'H. D. and the other poets of the "Poets' Translation Series" have so far done no more than pick up some of the more romantic crumbs of Greek literature' (Eliot 1969, 77).

It may well be that in their assessment of Euripides both Eliot and Pound were (indirectly) influenced by Friedrich Nietzsche's *The Birth of Tragedy* (1872), translated into English in 1909, in which Nietzsche described Euripides as inferior to the other two Greek playwrights, and even saw him as the destroyer of tragedy for having substituted naturalism and rationalism for the primitive energy of myth.[3] Moreover, in Victorian England many scholars and poets preferred Aeschylus and Sophocles to Euripides, who seemed less poetic, and whose plays, filled with debates about controversial issues, seemed less able to live up to the ideal of Greece as championed by, for example, Matthew Arnold.[4] Yet this modernity of Euripides was also the cause of his increasing popularity at the beginning of the twentieth century, not least because of Gilbert Murray, who was tireless in promoting his favourite author, and presented the Greek playwright in *Euripides and his Age* (1913) as a champion of contemporary causes (like an ancient G. B. Shaw or Henrik Ibsen). This connection between Murray and Euripides may have been the major reason for Eliot and Pound's dislike of the Athenian dramatist.

Still, Euripides may have been vital in Pound's discovery of the *poetry* of Greek drama. As a young student at the University of Pennsylvania, Pound played the part of one of the fifteen maidens in the chorus of an undergraduate production of Euripides' *Iphigenia Among the Taurians* in Greek, presented by the Department of Greek in April 1903, with especially composed music. William Carlos Williams later recalled that Pound, wearing a blond wig, 'waved his arms about and heaved his massive breasts in ecstasies of extreme emotion' (Williams 1951, 57). Given Pound's mediocre academic results, this may have been the most remarkable event of his sophomore year at Penn. Yet this exposure to the sounds and rhythms of Greek may have led to the only positive mention of Euripides in his work, namely, his recommendation of the

Greek playwright in 'The Tradition' in *Poetry* of December 1913 as a possible model for free verse.

This brings us to another reason why Pound admired Greek literature, aside from its mythopoeic quality, namely the fact that he valued ancient Greek poetry and drama especially for what he called its *melopoeia*, defined in *How to Read* as a kind of poetry 'wherein the words are charged, over and above their plain meaning, with some musical property, which directs the bearing or trend of that meaning' (*LE* 25). *Melopoeia* or 'poetry as music', then, represents a perfect aesthetic marriage between sound and sense, which in Greek is enhanced by the wide range of complicated metrical patterns, the study of which could expand the possibilities of English verse.

Pound and classical metres

The matter of Pound's prosody in relation to classical metrics is one of the recurrent and still not fully resolved issues in Poundian scholarship. Starting points are usually the observation that Pound wanted to break the dominance of the iambic pentameter in English verse, and that for this purpose he studied the prosodic techniques of other languages, such as Old English, Latin, Greek, Provençal and Chinese. Most scholars will agree with Barry Edwards' general claim that no single system can account for the great variety of Pound's verse (Edwards 31), but even when we confine ourselves to the poet's treatment of quantitative classical metrics, scholars are not in agreement as to what extent and with what degree of success Pound understood and adapted Greek metrics.[5]

In English poetry, metre is based on natural stress, not on syllable length or quantity, whereas Greek and Latin poetry is quantitative, in which rhythm is determined by the alternation of long and short vowels, and quantity means the duration of pronunciation. There are rules to determine the length of the vowels, and Greek metrics offers several possibilities to change vowel length. For example, in Homer's dactylic hexameter a naturally unstressed short-vowel syllable becomes metrically stressed when followed by two consonants. Furthermore, in Greek metrics substitution may take place (which allows, for example, two short syllables to be substituted for a long one). This allows duration in Greek metrics to either coincide with or play against natural stress or natural duration, unlike in English verse where metre is always determined by stress and natural speech patterns. Another major difference between Greek and English, apart from the first having a far wider range of polysyllabic words, is the fact that as an inflected language Greek allows for a much freer distribution of words over a line since the grammatical function of the words remains the same, regardless of their placement, whereas an English poet is constrained by the demands of intelligible syntax.

This brief survey demonstrates the difficulties inherent in creating English quantitative verse after the model of classical metrics. Users of classical patterns generally make stress represent quantity, so English poetry in classical metres uses the alternation of stressed and unstressed syllables to imitate the long and short syllables of Greek. However, despite attempts by English poets throughout the centuries to imitate classical metres, 'a purely quantitative meter is impossible in English. Unlike Greek or Latin, English has neither fixed quantities, existing in nature or defined by rules of grammar, nor metrical convention which, by artificial and traditional means, can create rhythms out of long and short syllables' (Gross 32).

What did Pound himself think about the potential of classical metrics for writing English verse? As Stephen Adams has argued, Pound 'was motivated in part by a desire to counteract the stress-timed nature of [English]. He learned to delight in releasing quasi-syllable timed Greek patterns in counter-motion, so that much of the originality of his lyrical rhythms arises from the unusual collocations of syllables – especially adjacent stresses – that seem designed to stretch or squeeze normally equivalent time intervals and to prevent traditional English metrical patterns from taking hold' (Adams 63). In fact, most of Pound's mature poetry uses as its basis rhythm, not metre. He claimed with regard to rhythm in his introduction to *The Sonnets and Ballate of Guido Cavalcanti* (1912) that

> The perception of the intellect is given in the word, that of the emotions in the cadence. It is only, then, in perfect rhythm joined to the perfect word that the twofold vision can be recorded...It is the poet's business that this correspondence be exact, i.e. that it be the emotion which surrounds the thought expressed.
>
> T 23–24

Given the importance of rhythm, Pound advocated that a poet should master 'all known forms and systems of metric' in order to enhance feeling for its various possibilities in English. In this respect, one of the available alternatives for the tradition of accentual-syllabic metrics in English poetry could be found in Greek poetry. It is not for nothing that Pound used Greek to coin the term *melopoeia*, because for him, as he noted in *ABC of Reading*, 'the maximum of *melopoeia* is reached in Greek' (42).

Pound was not alone in his enthusiasm for what he regarded as the *melopoeia* of Greek verse, as already from the late eighteenth century onward poets found in Greek prosodies new ways of dealing with English metre, and to 'praise Greek for its musicality' became 'commonplace' (Haynes 130).[6] Some Greek metres, such as the Sapphic, were directly adopted, as in Algernon Swinburne's 'Sapphics' (1866), while one can find many attempts to transpose Homer's dactylic hexameter. At the same time, there were endless discussions in Victorian England about the (im)possibility of quantitative verse in English.

Nineteenth-century prosodic theory accepted some (contested) notions that are now obsolete, such as the anacrusis or putative unstressed first syllable before the first foot, which does not count in the scansion of the poem. Other concepts were that of the paeon (a foot of four syllables with one long syllable, in any of the four possible positions), and that of logaoedic verse, which referred to metrical combinations of dactyls with trochees or iambs. Although such concepts were largely based on a misunderstanding of Greek metrics, they allowed poets to experiment with the possibilities of verse, and such metrical units became especially popular when dealing with topics related to antiquity. This may account for the fact that readers of English poetry may hear 'metrical echoes of Greek poetry', but in fact most of the time these poems do not 'imitate specific Greek metres; they are examples of metrical invention by poets who trained their ear of Greek poetry' (Haynes 137), such as Pound. In a letter to Iris Barry of August 1916, he wrote:

> we don't *know* that the Greeks didn't ruin their stuff by rocking-horse reading. Though I can't believe they did. At any rate, early Greek *can* be read with wonderful music.
>
> *SL* 95

Actually, we do not know how ancient Greek sounded. Nowadays we use stress to pronounce it, but when the accents were introduced in the second century BCE, these connoted a sort of musical pitch rather than stress. It is only later that accents came to indicate stress. Pound admitted in 'How to Write' (1930) that he does not know 'whether I read the *Odyssey* as the Homeric Greeks read it', but for 'the purpose of enjoying its rhythm, it does not matter one tittle whether one reads it with philologic correctness; what matters is getting from it a fecund and exciting rhythmic sensation' (Pound 1996, 93). Therefore, as Pound argued in *How to Read*, one should study the musicality of Greek poetry since 'the *melopoeia* can be appreciated by a foreigner with a sensitive ear, even though he be ignorant of the language in which the poem is written'. This is why he referred to Euripides in 'The Tradition' (1913), in which he claimed that 'it is vaguely possible that the light of *vers libre* might spread some faint aurora upon [the] cerebral tissues' of 'the earnest upholder of conventional imbecility' if he were to turn 'to the works of Euripides, or in particular to such passages as *Hippolytus* 1268 *et Seq.*, or to *Alkestis* 266 *et seq.*, or idem 455 *et seq.*, or to *Phoenissae* 1030 *et circa*, or to almost any notable Greek chorus' (*LE* 93). If one looks up these passages from Greek tragedy, it becomes evident that what attracted Pound to Greek metrics was the freedom it offered to the poet.

Lines 1268–82 of Euripides' *Hippolytus*, for example, part of a lyrical ode to Aphrodite, have as their basic rhythm the *dochmius*, a typically tragic metre with the scheme (× – – × –, in which × = short, and – = long). The dochmius can be heard in 'the wise kangaroos'. This basic metre knows several variations as any of the three long syllables may be resolved into two short ones, each of the two short syllables may be replaced by a long one, and a long one may replace one short. Thus eight of the nine lines of *Hippolytus* ll. 1268–76 begin with a dochmius in variations (and the ninth with a choriamb × – – ×), demonstrating the freedom the poet has in varying upon the rhythm:

(1268) × – – × – – × × – × –
(1269) × – – × –
(1270) × – × – × × – × × –
(1271) × – – × –
(1272) × – – × – × – – – –
(1273) – × × × × – –
(1274) – – × – – – × × – × × –
(1275) – × × – × –
(1276) – × × –

This passage is 'free', as no later strophe rhythmically matches it (Powell 11).

Alkestis 266–72, Pound's second example, is part of a dialogue in which Alcestis is singing her lines in iambics; this passage shows the great freedom in the use of iambic metre, as it employs various metrical units:

(266) × × × × × – – [ithyphallic [– × – × – –] resolved]
(267) – × – × – × – [lecythion]
(268) – × × – – [extended choriamb = adonean]
(269) × × – × – – × – × – – [anacrusis + iambic metron + ithyphallic]
(270) × × × – × × – [dodrans = choriamb + iamb]
(271) – × × – – – – – [choriambic dimeter]
(272) – – × – × × × × × × – – [catalectic iambic trimester, resolved]

Alkestis 455–75 is an even more complicated example of this procedure, while Pound probably referred to line 1030 of Euripides' *Phoenissae* because it supplied him with the most extreme example of 'Greek *vers libre*'. The line is a variation on the iambic dimeter, (× – × – | × – × –). Because many iambs may be resolved, a *tribrachys* or three short vowels in succession, can occur regularly, and thus we see four perfect *tribracheis* in line 1030, in which the entire dimeter is resolved:

epheres, epheres achea patridi
× × × × × × × × × × ×

These examples demonstrate why Pound believed Greek to be 'a storehouse of wonderful rhythms, possibly impracticable rhythms' (*SL* 87), and why he 'prize[d] the Greek more for the movement of the words, rhythm, perhaps than for anything else' (ibid. 91).

Still, although Pound experimented with the melopoeic possibilities of Greek patterns in English by employing duration to distinguish between first and second stresses, and by being attentive to the relative weight of long and short syllables, he had to admit that it was 'practically impossible to transfer or translate [*melopoeia*] from one language into another, save perhaps by divine accident, and for half a line at a time' (*LE* 25). This concurs with what he observed in the *Dial* of December 1920 in 'The Island of Paris':

> the 'laws' of Greek quantitative prosody do not correspond with an English reality. No one has succeeded in writing satisfactory English quantitative verse, according to these 'rules', though, on the other hand, no English poet has seriously tried to write quantitative verse without by this effort improving his cadence.
>
> Pound 1920, 637

Given this difficulty, Pound did not advocate imitating classical metres in English, but, as he stated in 'Re Vers Libre' (1917), 'progress lies rather in an attempt to approximate classical quantitative meters (NOT to copy them)' (*LE* 13). He himself only published a few poems directly based on a Greek metric pattern, all to be found in the 1912 volume *Ripostes*. 'Apparuit' (*P* 64–65) is Pound's only poem (almost) successfully employing the Sapphic stanza, while another poem, 'The Return' (*P* 69–70), uses as its basic metrical unit the choriamb (– × × –), and ends with an adonic (– × × – ˆ, where the last syllable may be either short or long), which also ends any Sapphic stanza. By using the choriamb in 'The Return' as a rhythmic constant with a variable number of syllables in between occurrences, Pound gives the poem a metrical unity but at the same time he is free to create *vers libre*. The poem shows, therefore, how one might reinstate the Greek art of *melopoeia* in English poetry, whether in original work or in translation.

However, this should not be done mechanically. Pound in 'A Few Don'ts' (1913) explicitly warned the reader to 'Consider the discrepancies between the actual writing of the Greek poets and dramatists, and the theories of the Graeco-Roman grammarians, concocted to explain their metres' (*LE* 4). And in 'The Tradition', in which he discussed *vers libre* in relation to Greek poetry, Pound claimed that 'the Melic poets ... composed to the feel of the thing, to the cadence ... [and were not] much influenced by discussions held in Alexandria some centuries after their deaths' (*LE* 92–93). Pound here refers to the fact that after the classical period (fifth century BCE), the composition and practice of singing poetry became less understood, so that Alexandrian philologists developed elaborate theoretical systems that enabled them to divide and analyse the poetical texts into metrical units. Yet these systems tended to treat the relationship between the words and music of Greek lyric in a rather mechanical manner. Pound's view on this is perhaps best summed up in *ABC of Reading*, where he noted that the Greek dramatists 'arrived at chorus forms which are to all extents "free", though a superstructure of nomenclature has been gummed on to them by analysers whom neither Aeschylus nor Euripides would ever have bothered to read'. These 'nomenclatures were probably invented by people who had never LISTENED to verse' (*ABCR* 204).

Pound thus rejected what he saw as the Alexandrian 'counting' of feet and syllables in favour of a more 'gut-feeling' approach for the rhythm of a poem. Verse should be written according to the poet's feeling for the cadence of words in patterns instead of adhering to strict laws of metrical distribution. As Pound noted in 'The Tradition':

> No one is so foolish as to suppose that a musician using 'four four' time is compelled to use always four quarter notes in each bar, or in 'seven-eights' time to use even seven eighth notes uniformly in each bar. He may use one ½, one ¼ and one ⅛ rest, or any such combination as he may happen to choose or find fitting. To apply this musical truism to verse is to employ *vers libre*.
>
> *LE* 93

This is not to say that one should reject all traditional English versification, as Pound warned in 'Re Vers Libre': 'I think one should write *vers libre* only when one "must", that is to say, only when the "thing" builds up a rhythm more beautiful than that of set metres, or more real, more a part of the emotion of the "thing", more germane, intimate, interpretative than the measure of regular accentual verse; a rhythm which discontents one with set iambic or set anapestic' (*LE* 12).

Pound, then, wants poets to create for each poem or passage its own intuitive and expressive rhythm. He himself often does not adopt fixed metres for lines on end, but uses certain recurrent rhythmic accentual-syllabic patterns or units, which resemble or can be circumscribed as Greek metrical units. Here one cannot but agree with Polten's acute observation: 'While [Pound's] verse does not strictly follow these [classical] meters in every syllable, the meters appear and reappear as key points of reference against which the rhythms of Pound's individual lines define themselves' (Polten 267). What makes Pound's verse so free, then, is the fact that he can set up a rhythmic metrical pattern and then undo it, against reader's expectations, allowing him to set off the beat of a line against its natural stress. Rhythm for Pound is not only determined by the number of beats per line, but also includes the duration of the intervals between those beats. The result is not a total recreation of Greek quantitative metre, but verse that has freed itself from imposed English metrical constraints.

However important the study of Greek metrics and rhythm was to Pound, his notion of *melopoeia* also included the 'soundscape' and diction used. *Melos*, as he stated in *I Gather the Limbs of Osiris* (1911–12) is 'the union of words, rhythm, and music (i.e. that part of music which we do not perceive as rhythm)' (*SP* 27). The totality of *melos*, then, for Pound consisted not only of the rhythm but also of musical effects such as assonance, consonance, and alliteration. As he wrote in the 1950s to Mary Barnard seeking his advice on how to translate Greek texts:

> THE JOB of the writer of verse is to get the LIVE language AND the prosody simultaneously. Prosody: articulation of the total sound of a poem (not bits of certain shapes gummed together.)
>
> Barnard 282

All of this should be considered not only when reading and writing poetic texts, but also when translating them. In the following chapter we will look at Pound's first great attempt at tackling and appreciating Greek drama in his use of Aeschylus, and particularly the *Agamemnon*.

Notes

1 Yet Pound in *The Spirit of Romance* (1910) did use Jebb's translation of the first choral ode of Sophocles' *Oedipus at Colonus* (ll. 668–93), a well-known passage

celebrating the beauty of the Attic *deme* of Colonus, given here as evidence that classical texts can include 'romantic' elements (*SR* 13–14).

2 Cp. 'Paris Letter' in the *Dial* of March 1923: 'Poetry is immortal, drama isn't. The Antigone of Sophocles contains great antitheses. It also contains stucco. The Greek sophistry about the irreplaceability of the brother for example' (Pound 1923, 278).

3 On Pound's knowledge of Nietzsche, see Liebregts 2004, 395–96 n. 56.

4 See Micheline, 3–51.

5 See, for example, Powell 1979, who sees quantitative Greek prosody as central to Pound's poetic output; this is severely qualified by Edwards 1998. For other discussions, see Polten 2017, 265–66 n. 9.

6 For an excellent general discussion of nineteenth-century poets adapting Greek prosody, see Haynes 2003, 130–37.

2

Ezra Pound and Aeschylus

Aeschylus (ca. 525–456 BCE), the earliest of the surviving three tragic poets, may be credited with having invented drama. According to Aristotle's *Poetics*, he was the first Athenian playwright to use a second actor, whereas previously performances had employed a single actor and a chorus. He was the author of between seventy and ninety plays, only seven of which have survived (although his authorship of *Prometheus Bound* is disputed), including the only extant trilogy, the *Oresteia* (consisting of *Agamemnon*, *Choephoroi* ['Libation Bearers'], and *Eumenides*).

Pound began to study Aeschylus in detail between 1918 and 1922. This is clear from four pieces of evidence. First, in *The Egoist* of January–February and that of March–April, 1919, Pound published two essays on Aeschylus to conclude his 'Hellenist Series', which appeared in six instalments between August 1918 and March 1919. The first part of 'Aeschylus' focused on the *Agamemnon* and would become part of the larger essay 'Translators of Greek', published one year later in *Instigations* (1920), while the second essay dealt with *Prometheus Bound*.

Secondly, Pound made an (unpublished) translation of the opening of the *Agamemnon*, which he dated in a letter written in 1934 to T.S. Eliot as '1919 or thereabouts' (Beinecke 66/2859). Thirdly, in the early Cantos 5, 7, and 8 (which later would become Canto 2), we find several quotations from Aeschylus' *Agamemnon*, while in an autograph note for Canto 5 at the Pound Archive in the Beinecke Library, one may find a passage not included in the published version, and which contains quotations from *Prometheus Bound* as well as *Agamemnon*. Cantos 5 to 7 were written in 1919, while the early Canto 8 was composed at the beginning of 1922.

And lastly, in the second stanza of 'E.P.: Ode Pour L'Élection de Son Sepulchre' (*P* 185), the opening poem of *Hugh Selwyn Mauberley* (1920), Pound mentions 'Capaneus', one of the Seven against Thebes, that is, one of the leaders of an army headed by Polyneikes in his struggle with his brother Eteokles for control of Thebes. In Aeschylus' play *Seven Against Thebes* ll. 423–50, Capaneus is prevented by Zeus from invading Thebes after his provocative boast that even the god could not stop him from entering the city. He was consequently killed by a thunderbolt. Admittedly, Pound already knew of Capaneus through Dante, as he had offered in *The Spirit of Romance* (1910) an analysis of *Inferno* XIV.43–72, which argues that Capaneus is a man 'unrelenting in his defiance of the supreme power' (*SR* 132). Still, the reference in *Mauberley* may well have been triggered by Pound's study of Aeschylus.

Pound's 1919 essays on Aeschylus

In the first of the two Aeschylus essays, Pound starts by commending the usefulness of Latin cribs to study Homer in the original Greek, and then vehemently exclaims: 'A search for Aeschylus in English is deadly, accursed, mind-rending' (*LE* 267). Pound notes that there is 'no English translation before 1777, a couple in the 1820s, more in the middle of the century, since 1880 past counting, and no promising names in the list' (268). He especially dismisses Robert Browning's (in)famous version of the *Agamemnon* (1877) for the attempt to reproduce as much as possible the word order of the original. This is why Pound returns 'thankfully' to the Samuel Butler reprint (1809–16) of Thomas Stanley's eight-volume edition of Aeschylus with Latin translations, which he had bought at a second-hand stall in December 1916.[1] This dismissive attitude towards modern translations in English is consistent with those outlined in Chapter 1.

Sir Thomas Stanley (1625–78) is known for two main contributions to classical scholarship. First, his *History of Philosophy* (1655–62) was for a long time the authoritative account of classical thought. Secondly, he produced a ground-breaking edition of the text of Aeschylus, with a Latin translation and commentary, in 1663, which was not only revolutionary in that it included a wealth of historical, literary and philosophical explanations alongside its philological explications, but the Latin translation was also an attempt at making Aeschylus more accessible to a larger (albeit scholarly) audience.

Still, it would take a considerable amount of time before the English would come to appreciate Aeschylus, which may have to do with the fact that there was no translation into English until 1773, when one of his plays appeared complete (Thomas Morell's *Prometheus*), while the first translation of all the plays by Robert Potter was published in 1777 (referred to by Pound in 'Aeschylus' without mentioning Potter's name). Given Aeschylus' reputation as a sublime and visionary poet, who composed in very lyrical language, he would only come to receive more attention and popularity in the Romantic age. After the 1820s, as Pound rightly claimed, there was a steady flow of translations, both of the entire oeuvre as well as of individual plays, with the *Agamemnon* and *Prometheus Bound* being the two most popular ones.

Prometheus was also Pound's personal favourite, although he admired the *Agamemnon* as Aeschylus' finest achievement. In this respect it is interesting to note that *Prometheus* was translated by Elizabeth Barrett Browning in 1833 (and revised in 1850) in a very readable version. The same cannot be said of the already mentioned notorious rendering by Robert Browning of the *Agamemnon*, in which he tried to stay as close as possible to the word formation and syntax of the original Greek, while adapting Aeschylus' fondness for compound polysyllabic adjectives and elliptical phrasing. The result was a version which at times distorts the English language beyond recognition, and produced the famous quip by the classical scholar W. B. Stanford that it is a good thing that we have the Greek Aeschylus to explain what Browning meant in English.

This brings us to Pound's assessment of Stanley and Browning in his 1919 essay 'Aeschylus', in which he rejects any translation which uses unnatural and stilted speech as this would turn the audience away from the actual to the theatrical. One of Pound's 'touchstones' for any good translation of Aeschylus are the lines from the *Agamemnon* where Klytaimnestra comments on her murder of her husband. They are given here in the original Greek:

>   οὗτός ἐστιν Ἀγαμέμνων, ἐμὸς
>   πόσις, νεκρὸς δέ, τῆσδε δεξιᾶς χερὸς,
>   ἔργον, δικαίας τέκτονος. τάδ' ὧδ' ἔχει.
>
> Ag. ll. 1404–06; Greek text Sommerstein

>   *houtos estin Agamemnōn, emos*
>   *posis, nekros de, tēsde dexiās cheros,*
>   *ergon, dikaias tektonos. tad' hōd' echei.*

> 'This is Agamemnon, my husband, a corpse, the work of this right hand, the maker of justice. That's how it is.'
>
> my trl

These phrases were for Pound luminous details representing Aeschylus' poetic craft, and he would quote these lines or parts of them throughout his writings. Thus we may find the last words of Klytaimnestra's speech after she has killed her husband, 'τάδ' ὧδ' ἔχει', at the very end of Canto 58, one of the Chinese Cantos, where Pound concludes the description of a family feud with her words (58/323). And Pound quotes the exact same phrase in Greek in *Guide to Kulchur* when he praises Thomas Hardy for his economy of language (*GK* 285).

In 'Aeschylus', Pound juxtaposes the renderings of this very passage by Thomas Stanley and Robert Browning:

> 'Hicce est Agamemnon, maritus
> Meus, hac dextra mortuus,
> Facinus justae artificis. Haec ita se habent.'

We turn to Browning and find:

> '——— this man is Agamemnon,
> My husband, dead, the work of this right hand here,
> Aye, of a just artificer: so things are'.

To the infinite advantage of the Latin, and the complete explanation of why Browning's Aeschylus, to say nothing of forty translations of Aeschylus, is unreadable.

LE 270

In Pound's eyes, Stanley's Latin has the virtue of bringing the reader in close 'contact with the force of a great original'. It may well be that for Pound Klytaimnestra's speech became a touchstone because of Stanley's remarks in his commentary on Aeschylus' particular style. Stanley mentions Aeschylus's grandiloquence, but notes that on occasion he can also be extremely restrained for effectiveness, as in Klytaimnestra's speech over Agamemnon's dead body, where *breviloquentia* gives each word its own weight (Stanley 880). It is evident that Pound would have concurred with this view, as it matched his own ideal of concision in poetry. This is clearly why he feels no further need to offer a philological or linguistic justification of his dismissal of Browning. Interestingly enough, he himself then gives what he calls a 'bungling translation' in which *tēsde dexiās cheros,/ ergon dikaias tektonos* is rendered as 'Dead by this hand, / And a good job.' In a sense, his version is indeed 'bungling', as the word 'good' may retain the 'rightness' of the action, but could also be read as reflecting Klytaimnestra's feelings how well the murder was executed, which is not in the original. In a note, Pound added: 'In 1934, one would emend the last lines to: "I did it. That's how it is"' (*LE* 270). Although this version is rather free, it is an attempt to retain the 'dental soundscape' of the original, even more than in Pound's earlier rendering. As we will see, Pound would quote the same phrases as well as Aeschylus' Greek and Stanley's Latin rendering from memory in Canto 82.

Another Aeschylean touchstone for Pound is the passage containing the famous pun on 'Helen' in *Agamemnon* 689–90, 'ἑλέναυς, ἕλανδρος, ἑλέπτολις' (*helenaus, helandros, heleptolis*), 'ship-wrecking, man-killing, city-destroying', which Pound used in Cantos 2 and 7. Canto 7 opens with a reference to Eleanor of Aquitaine, 'Eleanor, (she spoiled in a British climate) / Ἕλανδρος and Ἑλέπτολις' (7/24), and Pound even gives the full tricolon in Greek on the next page of the Canto. Eleanor of Aquitaine, wife of Louis VII of France and later of Henry II of England, was allegedly the cause of the Hundred Years' War. By using the Aeschylean pun Pound linked Eleanor to Helen, thus underlining the major theme of metamorphosis of *The Cantos* by presenting both women as actualizations of the archetypal idea of the *femme fatale*, as well as of the notion of the 'repeat in history'.

When, in December 1921, Pound had published *Poems 1918–21* which included Cantos 4–7, he continued to work on what was then Canto 8, which subsequently appeared in *The Dial* in May 1922. This early Canto 8 again included a link between Helen and Eleanor, a variation on the line from Canto 7: 'Eleanor, ἑλέναυς and ἑλέπτολις!' (2/6). However, dissatisfied with this version, Pound revised it and then designated it as Canto 2, probably because it is closely linked in various ways to Canto 1 through, for example, the Homeric connection supplied by Odysseus in Canto 1 and Helen in Canto 2, and the translation of the passage about the elders from *Iliad* Book III, who are looking at Helen and commenting on the pernicious consequences of her beauty. This reassignment makes clear that Pound associated the theme of fatal consequences for the desire of beauty and the material in Cantos 4 to 8 with the Trojan war and the *Agamemnon*. Further evidence of this may be found in Canto 46, where Pound summarized the moral lesson of his epic poem up to that point by giving us the opposing forces of good and evil as Amor and Usura, respectively. The latter is presented as that which destroys men, cities and nations, with Pound using once again the Aeschylean pun:

> 19 years on this case/first case. I have set down part of
> The Evidence. Part/commune sepulchrum
> Aurum est commune sepulchrum. Usura, commune sepulchrum.
> helandros   kai heleptolis   kai helarxe.
> Hic Geryon est. Hic hyperusura.
>
>   46/234–35

Usury here is called 'man-killing', 'city-destroying', and, through a Greek neologism created by Pound on the same pattern by combining *hel-* (ἑλ-) with *archē* (ἀρχή), 'government-wrecking'. (Pound would later in Canto 78 (502) again associate Helen with usury, and with Mussolini's failed attempts to reform the economy.)

In his discussion of this Aeschylean touchstone in his 1919 essay, Pound does not give us the Greek text, but offers us Stanley's rendition followed by his own translation. In order to appreciate these Latin and English renderings, I first give a literal translation with the Greek text in transliteration:

> to the spear-bride [*tan dorigambron*] contended by two [*amphineikē*],
> Helen [*Helenan*]? For fitting <that name> [*epei prepontōs*]
> ship-wrecking [*helenaus*], man-killing [*helandros*], city-
> destroying [*heleptolis*] from the delicate [*ek tōn habropēnōn*]
> curtains [*prokalummatōn*] she sailed [*epleuse*]
> with the breeze of giant Zephyrus [*Zephuron gigantos aurai*].
>
> ll. 687–92

Stanley's version reads:

> 'In bellam nuptam
> Autricemque contentionum, Helenam?
> Quippe quae congruenter
> Perditrix navium, perditrix virorum, perditrix urbium,
> E delicates
> Thalami ornamentis navigavit
> Zephyri terrigenae aura.'
>
> LE 272

Although Pound highly appreciates Stanley's Latin version, it must be said that Stanley here loses the specific reference to the spear in his *bellam nuptam*, 'married to war', and apparently sees no other option but to translate the pun on Helen and *helein* ('to capture', to 'kill' or 'destroy') through a triple *perditrix*, 'she who destroys', losing both the homophonic sound as well as the concision of the original Greek. Furthermore, Stanley adds to the image of the delicate curtains the word *thalami* to indicate the bedroom or marriage bed, and takes *gigantos* to mean 'Titan' and thus 'earth-born' (*terrigenae*). The rendering by Pound, with an eye on both the Greek and Stanley's translation, is more concise while giving the pun on Helen as well in depicting the image of the room, but it loses the mythological reference to Zephyrus:

'War-wed, author of strife,
Fitly Helen, destroyer of ships, of men,
Destroyer of cities,
From delicate-curtained room
Sped by land breezes.'

LE 272

Pound's rendering of *autricemque contentionum* as 'author of strife' may remind us of similar 'literalist-homonymic' strategies used in *Homage to Sextus Propertius*. But he then offers a slightly revised version which substitutes 'contested' ('Ἀμφινεικῆ') for 'author of strife' (ibid.).

Pound continues with a rendering of ll. 694–99, which again I give first in a literal translation with transliteration:

and many men [*poluandroi te*], shield-carrying hunters [*pheraspides kunagoi*],
on the invisible trail [*kat'ichnos aphanton*] of oar-blades [*platān*],
after they had landed on [*kelsantōn ep'*] Simois' [*Simoentos*]
leafy [*aexiphullous*] banks [*aktas*],
because of bloody Strife [*di' Erin haimatoessan*].

Pound gives us Stanley's Latin followed by his own first version:

'Et numerosi scutiferi,
Venatores secundum vestigia,
Remorum inapparentia
Appulerunt ad Simoentis ripas
Foliis abundantes
Ob jurgiu cruentum.'

'Swift the shields on your track,
Oars on the unseen traces,
And leafy Simois
Gone red with blood.'

LE 272

While Stanley really serves as a crib here, Pound has brilliantly condensed and at the same time expanded on both the Greek and Latin by emphasizing the 'hunt for Helen' through the phrases 'on your track' and 'unseen traces', while gaining speed by deleting the *venatores*, 'hunters', referring metonymically to them by the shields (and one may detect echoes of his 'Greek' poem 'The Return' here). The last two lines are an excellent example of Poundian compression for effectiveness:

'the banks of the Simois abundant with leaves' are given as 'leafy Simois'. Stanley's *ob iurgium cruentum*, 'because of bloody strife', which actually refers to the whole Greek expedition, which originates in the role played by Eris (Strife) in the Judgment of Paris, is vividly rendered as 'gone red with blood' and linked directly to the river Simois. In his second version, Pound compressed this even further to 'Red leaves in Simois!' (*LE* 273), which seems less effective (and even suggests a sort of New England autumnal setting). Pound's essay on 'Aeschylus' thus offers us an excellent insight into the poet's detailed study of the Greek playwright.

The sixth and concluding part of the 'Hellenist Series', published in *The Egoist* of March–April 1919, was not included in the essay 'Translators of Greek'. This may have to do with its rather rambling set of observations on the classics and how to study them. Interestingly enough, however, it includes a rather nuanced evaluation of Aeschylus, and a more positive attitude than the one we find later in *ABC of Reading*. Although Pound again argues that Aeschylus is 'rhetorical', he also praises him, even when compared to Homer:

> It may be argued, though not quite fairly or conclusively, that the Greek dramatists are a decadence from Homer. But the plainer passages of Aeschylus are untouchable, even as writing, and he obviously knew certain things about his art which were unknown to Homer (or to Peisistratus).
>
> Pound 1919, 25

This statement makes clear, just as the first essay does, why Pound would be particularly interested in the Greek playwright at this time. The second half of the second essay is taken up by the translation of the opening (ll. 1–45) of Aeschylus' *Prometheus Bound* in Italian by Felice Bellotti, published in 1821, which in Pound's view has not 'utterly ruined' this 'stupendous opening', while there is not anything 'in English which greatly improves on the hack-work in Bohn' (Pound 1919, 25). This is a reference to the Classical Library by the British publisher Henry George Bohn, who from 1846 onward published editions of standard works and translations targeted at a mass market. In 1849 Bohn published *The Tragedies of Aeschylus*, translated with critical and illustrative notes and an introduction by Theodore Alois Buckley. Pound may have felt that this second essay did not add much to what he had already said about Aeschylus in his earlier instalment, and therefore decided to leave it out of 'Translators of Greek'.

Ronald Bush has emphasized the importance of the essays on Aeschylus in his analysis of the evolution of Pound's style while working on *The Cantos*. He argues that Pound gradually began to have his reservations about Fenollosa's ideas about Chinese ideograms. As is well-known, Pound had studied the notebooks on Chinese poetry and Japanese Noh drama by the oriental scholar Ernest Fenollosa (1853–1908), left to Pound by his widow. He edited and published in 1919 Fenollosa's essay *The Chinese Written Character as a Medium for Poetry*, which claimed that Chinese characters pictorially represent their original meanings, and that ideograms are able to express abstract notions by combining particular characters. The famous example (actually made up by Fenollosa) is that the ideogram for 'red' has juxtaposed the signs for 'rose', 'iron rust', 'cherry' and 'flamingo'.

This notion underlies Pound's 'ideogrammic method' in his poetry after 1914, including *The Cantos*, in which he combines different particular facts or elements to evoke a generalization and suggest an abstract theme. However, Fenollosa's essay also claimed that in language only transitive verbs express energy and power, whereas predicates and the use of copula only petrify a language. Bush argues that 'Pound began to see that poetry did not need the actual presence of verbs so much as a syntax that could incorporate their action and relate it to other actions' (179). In order to cope with the (subjective) presentation of his (objective) material in *The Cantos*, Pound adapted from Henry James his late discursive style, with its use of involutions and participial constructions, through which the characters actively ponder the issues at hand. Yet the poet also wanted to have the mythical scope lacking in James and, according to Bush, he found this in Aeschylus.

Pound in his essay 'Aeschylus' claims that the obscurity of the playwright's language lies in the fact that he, too, at his stage in literary history was trying to find words for his personal thoughts, for which as yet there was no set language. This accounts for his difficult syntax as he is trying to forge connections:

> One might almost say that Aeschylus' Greek is agglutinative, that his general drive, especially in choruses, is merely to remind the audience of the events of the Trojan war; that syntax is subordinate, and duly subordinated, left out, that he is not austere, but often even verbose after a fashion.
>
> LE 273

Pound, then, derived from Aeschylus 'a syntax designed to connect grammatically disparate but related facets of racial memory' (Bush 176), with 'its tangled complexities' and 'interwoven clauses' drawing 'together elements of past and present, history and myth'. Bush concludes that Aeschylus' 'agglutinative' syntax provided Pound with a technique that was 'able to "mirror" his narrator's sensibility and "pierce into" historical awareness "not yet current, not yet worn into phrase"' (181–82).

Although I agree with Bush about Pound's reservations with regard to some of Fenollosa's ideas, perhaps his analysis is too limited in crediting Aeschylus alone for making Pound arrive at his new technique of syntax, as he already knew from his earlier reading of Greek poetry that one of its hallmarks was its employment of parataxis or coordination, next to hypotaxis or subordination. After all, in his early Imagist poems, Pound had already experimented with juxtaposition without explicit connection, thus coordinating images or lines of verse instead of subordinating them. It is true that Pound between 1914 and 1918 turned from Greek to Chinese models due to Fenollosa's notion of the ideogram, but his reading of Aeschylus at the end of the Great War may have reminded him of his earlier use of Greek parataxis. This now offered him in the composition of his expansive and expanding poem the possibility to present mental relationships through appositions without connective verbs or conjunctions, and thus put the ideogrammic notions of Fenollosa into practice on an even bigger scale.

Pound's translation of the *Agamemnon*

A major reason why Pound turned to Aeschylus around 1918–19 may well be that the Great War had shown him the darker sides of humanity and civilization, and Aeschylus' depiction of the treacherous homecoming of Agamemnon after the Trojan War in a world of disorder and disillusionment must have struck a chord. Indeed, we may hear an Aeschylean echo in poem IV of *Hugh Selwyn Mauberley*, a denunciation of the futility of war after which soldiers 'came home, home to a lie / home to many deceits / home to old lies and new infamy' (*P* 188).

Pound's interest in the *Agamemnon* sparked his interest in translating the play, perhaps strengthened by Eliot's claim in 'Euripides and Professor Murray' (1920) that H. D. and other modern poets had only picked up 'some of the more romantic crumbs of Greek literature; none of them has yet shown himself competent to attack the *Agamemnon*' (Eliot 1969, 77). Thus for Eliot, Aeschylus' play represented the pinnacle of Greek tragedy, as it did for Pound, who stated in his 'Paris Letter' in the *Dial* of March 1923, that 'The Agamemnon drives one to admiration; it is a great work, it probably knocks the spots off other Greek plays. The Prometheus Bound has an opening situation and trails off into nothing, et cetera' (Pound 1923, 277). We find a similar sentiment in *Guide to Kulchur*: 'If one greek play can claim pre-eminence over the best dozen others (which it probably cannot) that play wd. be the *Agamemnon*' (*GK* 92).

When exactly Pound made his attempt at rendering the *Agamemnon* is unclear. In his 'Paris Letter' of March 1923, Pound recalls how '[y]ears ago' he gave Eliot a copy of Aeschylus' play and asked him to translate it. Apparently, Eliot kept this text for a while, but 'at the end of three or four years nothing had happened', so then Pound 'grew impatient' and thought he 'would have a shot at it' (Pound 1923, 277). Donald Gallup believes Pound may have approached Eliot already in 1916, which would date Pound's own attempt around 1919–20 (Gallup 117). However, in a later (conflicting) account in *Guide to Kulchur*, Pound writes that after his request, Eliot 'sat on it for eight months or some longer period', after which Pound took over (*GK* 92).

Some light on the issue may be thrown by looking at the correspondence between Eliot and Pound in the early 1920s. In a letter of 24 December 1921 (according to Paige, editor of Pound's letter) or 24 January 1922 (according to Eliot and Haughton, editors of Eliot's letter), Pound thanked T. S. Eliot for 'the Aggymemnon' (*SL* 170), which may refer to the return of the Greek copy he had lent him. Eliot replied on 26 January 1922 that he 'would have sent Aeschule before but have in bed with flu' (*SL* 171).[2] That same month Pound wrote to Eliot that 'Aeschylus not so good as I had hoped, but haven't time to improve him, yet' (ibid.). Here Pound may have been referring to his translation, not to the Greek original, in the light of Eliot ending a letter of 12 March 1922 with 'Best sympathies to D. and enquiries after Agamemnon' (Eliot 2009, 643). This would place Pound's attempt at the beginning of 1922, at the time he was also working on Canto 8. This exchange of letters in combination with the passage from the *Dial* would then suggest that it was in 1919–20 that Pound had asked Eliot for a translation, which is why he later may have confused matters of chronology when he dated his own attempt at '1919 or thereabouts' at the bottom of a typescript copy of his rendering attached to a 1934 letter to T.S. Eliot, now in the Beinecke library:

13 GiuGN [1934]
Dear Possum/
   In KOrekting the epreuves for my sassays/ and in exCAvatin' the Aggymenon fer to KOrekt it/ I finds the enc/ speaking of blank or damatic verse/ and mebbe as it wuz done before I leff [....]

Beinecke 66/2859

This typescript copy confirms Pound's description of his stylistic approach in rendering the *Agamemnon* in his 'Paris Letter' of March 1923:

I tried every possible dodge, making the watchman a negro, and giving him a *fihn Géoogiah voyce*; making the chorus talk cockney, et cetera. This is a usual form of evasion in modern drama. Ibsen makes his people provincial, Chekhov also, the Irish theatre talks dialect, to get a 'language.' In the Agamemnon there is simply too much stuff that doesn't function; you put it in and the thing goes dead, you start omitting it, and the remains are insufficient.

Pound 1923, 277

It also aligns with his late reflections on the translation in *Guide to Kulchur*:

> I twisted, turned, tried every ellipsis and elimination. I made the watchman talk nigger, and by the time you had taken out the remplissage, there was no play left on one's page.
>
> There was magnificence; there was SENSE of play, the beacon telegraph stuff is incomparable. Nobody but a fanatic like myself wd. have the crust to insist that the greek writers were on the down grade AFTER Homer. But the translation is unreadable. No one with a theatric imagination can conceive it holding now as a stage play IF you leave in all the verbiage. But as an entity it stands rock-like.

GK 92–93

The typescript copy is titled 'Opening for an Agamemnon', and not, as Donald Gallup's 1986 edition of the text has it, 'An Opening for *Agamemnon*' (Gallup 118). Pound's title clearly underlines how he regarded his version as both an attempt and as a 'criticism by translation'. The typescript reads as follows:

[p.1] 'OPENING FOR AN AGAMEMNON'
Concierge:
    Dey keep me up hyear lak a dawg
        teh bark at de consterlations,
    I'm a watchman, I am;
    That is to say: I was,
    Dey don' take much watchin' from the outside,
    But de ole lady has had <u>some</u> vacation . . .
        Do I get paid for this job?
    Yaas! Gawd, he goin' to pay for it;
    You watch deh lights, on de islands, for
    The GREAT men are acomin' hoam, special
    Despatches,
        And do I sleep?
        (<u>looks over the balcony and lies down</u>
        <u>under edge of the parapet</u>.)
    When dey come, I make a hullaballoo,
    And get de ole lady out of bed, and de glad
    Hand ready for massa! When dey get de city

 (Yaas, WHEN!)
> (starts crapshootin')

 When I throw triple sixes.
> (sleeps.)

EMERGE KLYTAIMNESTRA:
  The Greeks are IN!

[p.2]
Voice: Whaa'?
Klyt: The greeks are IN!
Voice: Whaat?
Klyt: Troy! Do you get me!

Members of Chorus. (1. by the door, starts weeping).
   2. They ain't hurried theirselves!
   3. Did you dream it?

Klyt: Not likely.
   4. Oo told yuh? deh hobo?
   5. Yes? And when did they do it?
Klyt: Last night!
   3. Yes, somebody run 'ome teh tell her.
   4. Some runner!
Klyt: <u>(leads him up the steps and shows him the beacon lights</u>.)
   Ida, Hermaeus, Lemnos, Mt Athos, Hellespont,
   Picea (yellow light) Euripus, Mesapidi,
   Gorgopin, Mt Aegiplanctus,
      Ain't you never heard of the TELEgraph!
   Saronica, Arachnaeus, and home sweet home;
   The House of Atreus.
   Atreus, that's the workin' of it, there's
   Another way round, two or three.
   Besides, there was a chap come through,
   Said it 'ud be about this time.
   There's a mix up in Troy town tonight, a salad
   There is, and some dressin', some racket!
   Atrocities?
   What cher mean? Don't they always do it? What's
   A war for anyhow?
    What 'ud they done to us, anyhow?

Chorus:	That's talkin'
	'Gott mit uns' is my motto.
Parson:	Let us give thanks unto Jupiter
	King of gods, for the beautiful evening, and for
	Our victory over the Trojans,
	Let us express our gratitude, that Paris has
	Been punished for his sins, and his immoralities,
	And for killing Achilles.

EP. (1919 or thereabouts) Beinecke 66/2859

Pound's rendering indeed changed Aeschylus' highly rhetorical language into what he deplorably called 'nigger and cockney', that is, living speech, while using every possible ellipsis and elimination.[3] Pound's fragment thus only has fifty-six lines of speech for what in the original Greek amounts to 366 lines, its most important deletion being the entire Parodos (*Ag*. ll. 40–263) in which the Chorus describes the Trojan expedition and gives the famous address to Zeus.[4] However, these mere statistics do not as yet reveal what Pound actually managed to add to this very shortened text, which we will now discuss in detail.

The opening speech by the Watchman, termed 'Concierge' by Pound, which has seventeen lines for the original thirty-nine, immediately makes clear what one can expect in this version characterized by condensation and humorous addition. A literal translation of this opening reads:

> I beg the gods to give me release from my toils, the yearlong watch, during which I have been lying on my elbows like a dog on top of the roof of the house of the Atreidae, and come to know the assembly of stars of the night, and the bright potentates, conspicuous in the sky, which bring winter and summer to mortals, whenever they rise and whenever they fall.
>
> *Ag*. ll. 1–7

Pound condenses this to two lines ('Dey keep me up ... consterlations') before the Concierge alludes to the queen's adultery ('But de ole lady has had <u>some</u> vacation'), a theme Aeschylus' Watchman refers to only at the end of his speech (*Ag*. ll. 36–39).

In the original the Watchman, who first is afraid of falling asleep, suddenly sees the beacon, knows that Troy has fallen, and becomes very excited. His mistress Klytaimnestra should now 'raise herself from her bed, as quickly as possible' (*Ag*. ll. 26–27), and raise an *ololugmos*, 'a loud cry of triumph'. The Watchman also expects to be rewarded for his efforts. In Pound's version, however, the Concierge, who is also afraid of succumbing to sleep, actually falls asleep at the end of his speech and thus never sees the beacon! For him, the fall of Troy is still only a possibility in the future, and he can only imagine what he would do were it to happen.

Pound also gives the *ololugmos* to his Concierge, although he retains the original statement that the soldier hopes to clasp his master's 'well-loved hand in this hand of mine' (*Ag*. ll. 34–35), rendered as 'de glad hand ready for massa', an example of Pound's 'nigger and cockney'. In the original the fire of the beacons indicates the Greek victory, presented by Aeschylus through a gaming metaphor of the throwing of the dice in which the beacon-watching has resulted in a winning triple six for the Watchman, as he can now expect a reward for his services (*Ag*. l. 32). Pound's rendering, however, suggests that Troy will not fall until the Concierge has thrown a lucky hand in his game of crap-shooting. One can only speculate as to why Pound would offer such a radically deviating version of this opening speech. The throwing of the dice to determine the siege of the city might suggest the uncertainty of the fortunes of war, or even the decisive power of the underlings to bring about the success of 'The GREAT men'. The Concierge's falling asleep not only makes him human, and cuts down the grand tragedy to human size, but also emphasizes the indifference of the common man to the fate of his leaders (thereby reversing the situation common in classical tragedy).

A good example of Pound's extreme choices in striving for concision and emotional, compact speech is his version of the dialogue between Klytaimnestra and the chorus in which she informs the people about the fall of Troy. The original reads in translation:

> Klyt. Just as the proverb says, may the morning born from its mother <Night> be a messenger of good news! You will hear about a joy greater than hope: the Argives have captured the city of Priam!
> Chorus. What are you saying? Your words escaped me, as they are so incredible.
> Klyt. That Troy now is the Achaeans': am I saying this clearly?
>
> *Ag*. ll. 264–269

In Pound's hands this becomes a rather lapidary sort of dialogue:

> EMERGE KLYTAIMNESTRA:
>   The Greeks are IN!
> Voice: Whaa'?
> Klyt: The greeks are IN!
> Voice: Whaat?
> Klyt: Troy! Do you get me!

Pound had singled out l. 269 of the *Agamemnon* in his essay 'Aeschylus' to comment on the difficulty of rendering the pace of the action. Having quoted the original Greek, Τροίαν Ἀχαιῶν οὖσαν [*Troian Achaiōn ousan*], Pound offered Dante Gabriel Rossetti's phrase from the poem 'Troy Town' (1869), '"Troy's down, tall Troy's on fire"', which he prefers to Browning's '"Troia the Achaioi hold"', because the latter cannot be 'shouted uncontrolledly and hysterically'. He himself offers the excellent 'Troy is the Greeks', but admits that this would sound ambiguous on stage, and should thus be rendered as '"Know that our men are in Ilion."' (*LE* 267–68) – hence 'The Greeks are IN!'

Pound here adds a touch of humour by inserting a line not in the original, namely, a comment by the chorus: 'They ain't hurried theirselves!'. In his rendering of the dialogue following, he brings Aeschylus' high-flowing poetry down to earth:

> Ch. And what is it that convinces you? Have you some proof of these things?
> Klyt. Of course I have – unless a god has deceived us.
> Ch. Are you in awe of a persuasive dream-vision?
> Klyt. I wouldn't accept the vision of a slumbering mind.
> Ch. Maybe some wingless rumour has gone to your head?
>
> *Ag.* ll. 272–75

In Pound's hands this comes out as follows:

> 3. Did you dream it?
> Klyt: Not likely.
> 4. Oo told yuh? deh hobo?

Having thus condensed the seventeen lines of dialogue between Klytaimnestra and the Chorus (*Ag.* ll. 264–280) to the utmost minimum of speech, Pound then offers his version of the Queen's 'beacon speech', in which she explains how the signal from Troy had reached Mycenae.[5] The thirty-six lines (*Ag.* ll. 281–316) are cut down to six, but idiosyncratically so: Pound only gives the names of the mountains on which beacons had been placed, before adding 'Ain't you never heard of the TELegraph!' After this Pound takes extreme licence with the original by sarcastically juxtaposing 'The House of Atreus' with 'home sweet home'. Klytaimnestra's evocation of the festivities as well as of the suffering in Troy (*Ag.* ll. 320–350), in which the voices of the victors and the conquered mingle, is very freely rendered, ending with a pun on 'Atreus':

> There's a mix up in Troy town tonight, a salad
> There is, and some dressin', some racket!
> Atrocities?

Klytaimnestra hopes that the Greeks will not forget to pray to the gods in thanks before starting to plunder. The chorus in the Greek original shares the Queen's prudence:

> Lady, like a sensible man, you have spoken wisely, and having heard your trustworthy proof, I am preparing to address the gods in a proper manner, because a highly-prized reward has been given for our sufferings.
>
> *Ag.* ll. 351–54

Pound, on the other hand, replaces Klytaimnestra's prudence with a generalizing depiction of self-justification on the part of any victor in any war:

> Atrocities?
> What cher mean? Don't they always do it? What's
> A war for anyhow?
> What 'ud they done to us, anyhow?

He then reduces the Chorus' response to 'That's talkin' / "Gott mit uns" is my motto', thereby replacing Aeschylus' grandiloquence with his own brevity, also changing the sentiment in the process.

The introductory stanza (*Ag.* ll. 355–66) of the Chorus' *stasimon* in the original, in which they offer a thanksgiving to Zeus, is the last part rendered by Pound through the voice of a 'Parson'. He probably never finished his translation because he was unable to overcome the dilemma expressed in *Guide to Kulchur*: 'No one with a theatric imagination can conceive [the *Agamemnon*] holding now as a stage play IF you leave in all the verbiage' (*GK* 93).

Pound's translational strategy with regard to the *Agamemnon* was taken up thirty years later by Dallam Simpson, also known as Dallam Flynn, a correspondent and visitor to St Elizabeths. On Pound's advice he started in 1948 a magazine in Texas, *Four Pages*, to distribute the teachings of his master, resulting in fifteen issues between January 1948 and January 1951, with contributions from W. C. Williams, Robert Duncan, Basil Bunting, and Pound himself (anonymously). In the 1950s Simpson became a preacher in Texas, where he would give racist sermons, and was involved in right-wing and segregationist groups.[6] Simpson's rendering of the opening of the *Agamemnon* was included in Pound's anthology *Confucius to Cummings* (1964). It offers us the first 121 lines of the original, and stays far closer to the Greek text than Pound did, using quatrains rhyming abab with a free number of syllables per line. However, Pound's influence is immediately noticeable not only in the dividing up of the choral songs to individual members, designated as Bureaucrats, but especially in the Watchman's speech, which uses the 'nigger and cockney' Pound had tried to adopt in his version. Indeed, when Simpson sent Pound his version in a letter of October 27, 1955, he acknowledged that 'the negro dialect idea was yours' (Beinecke 48/2135). Simpson's opening stanza reads:

> Fo' a yeah or mo' on this roof I'se layed,
> Lik a shif'less houn'dog watchin' stars,
> Lawd in the morn' an at night I'se prayed,
> Fo' mah massa's return frum the Trojun wars.
>
> Pound 1964, 19

In Simpson's version, however, the Watchman does not fall asleep but sees the signal fire, and he exclaims: 'O! lemme tell missy to stir her fat,/ Fo' Troytown's down an massa's won' (ibid.). In contrast, the Bureaucrats are given an aristocratic mock-British tone.

Pound's use of the *Agamemnon* in *The Cantos*

Apart from his attempt at translation, Pound's post-war interest in the *Agamemnon* is reflected in his work on the Cantos between 1919 and 1922. Canto 4, published more or less in its current form in October 1919, opens with an image of the destruction of Troy, while the first half of the Canto deals with tales of lust, sexual violation and murder. The main body of the Canto consists of juxtapositions of four Greek-Provençal narratives (Itys, Guillems da Cabestanh, Actaeon, and Pierre Vidal), all of them moral fables dealing with men who are encapsulated by lust for sensible beauty. Leon Surette has rightly stated that the connection between the opening image and these tales may have been suggested by the *Agamemnon* (Surette 28–29). The Greek tragedy reminded Pound that it was sheer lust that drove Helen and Paris to Troy, thus causing the destruction of the city, while the war also made Klytaimnestra have an affair with Aigisthos and murder her husband on his return. In Canto 5 Pound provides a further Provençal parallel to the Paris-Helen-Menelaus triangle, namely the tale of Pieire de Maensac from Auvergne, the troubadour who carried the wife of Bernart de Tierci off to a castle of the Dauphin d'Auvergne, an act that resulted in an unsuccessful war begun by the husband who wished to regain her (5/18).[7]

The link between Troy and violence as the result of lust and murder in Canto 5 is also forged through an explicit use of Aeschylus' *Agamemnon*. Immediately after the parallel drawn between Troy and Auvergnat, the poem continues with the line 'John Borgia is bathed at last' (5/18), which introduces a verse paragraph in which Pound juxtaposes two murders of the Italian Renaissance with Agamemnon's death (Terrell 19).[8] The first is that of Giovanni Borgia, murdered by Lorenzino di Medici in 1497. Pound's line refers to the fact that Giovanni Borgia's body was thrown into the Tiber, a fate which connects him with Agamemnon, who was murdered in his bath. The second murder is that of Alessandro di Medici, duke of Florence, in 1537, again by Lorenzino, Alessandro's nephew. Pound connects the two killings through the use of two conflated lines from *Agamemnon* 1344–45 in the original Greek: 'Σίγα μαλ' αὖθις δευτέραν!' [*Siga mal' authis deuteran*] (5/19), which mean 'Silence, once again a second time'. In the Greek play, the first word forms part of a line spoken by the Chorus, who hear that Agamemnon is being murdered in his bath by Klytaimnestra and her lover Aigisthos: σῖγα· τίς πληγὴν αὐτεῖ καιρίως οὐτασμένος; [*siga; tis plēgēn autei kairiōs outasmenos?*], 'Silence! Who's that screaming that he is being struck by a deadly blow?'. The other three words in Pound's line are taken from the line that follows, spoken by Agamemnon: ὤμοι μάλ' αὖθις δευτέραν πεπληγμένος [*ōmoi mal' authis deuteran peplēgmenos*], 'Aaagh, me again, I have been struck a second blow'. Pound apparently deliberately conflated these lines in order to not only denote a repeat in history, but also to juxtapose the two murders (while the 'doubleness' is later literally emphasized in the Canto by the repetition of a double 'Σίγα, σίγα' (5/19)). Pound creates a further connection between the murders in ancient Greece and Renaissance Italy by letting Lorenzino address his uncle Alessandro as '"Dog-eye!!"' (ibid.), a reference to Achilles' description of Agamemnon in *Iliad* I.159 and 225 as κυνῶπα [*kunōpa*] and κυνὸς ὄμματ' ἔχων [*kunos ommat' echōn*], 'dog-eyed' and 'dog-faced'.

The Ezra Pound Papers at the Beinecke Library contain an autograph note for Canto 5, which was not included in the final version, and which gives further evidence for both Pound's interest in the *Agamemnon* as well as his admiration for the opening of Aeschylus' *Prometheus Bound*:

> ? Prometheus urges us, across the stage
> 'and I am willing and then unwilling'
> rings the great line
> ἄκοντα σ' ακον [=ἄκων]
>   δυσλύτοις χαλκεύμασι
>
>   The paid seat stiffens

>   as Menelaus
>   hunts bright images
> ruled by a form
>   a film drawn of air
> Helena was here
> Ἰώ, ἰώ δῶμα…
> ἰώ λέχος καὶ στίβοι φιλάνορες
>
> (Beinecke 70/3125)

The question mark suggests that Pound was uncertain whether the 'great line' is spoken by Prometheus, and rightly so, as actually these words are delivered in the opening speech by Hephaestus when he admits to Prometheus that he does not dare to defy Zeus and thus has no other choice but to chain the demigod to the rock: 'I, just as unwilling as you are, [will nail you] with metal bonds hard to undo' (ll. 19-20). What Pound may have found attractive about the line is its implicit contrast to Prometheus' defiance and refusal to submit to Zeus' power (which accords with Pound's reference to Capaneus in *Hugh Selwyn Mauberley*). The second Greek quotation in this unpublished fragment stems from the *Agamemnon*, where the chorus evokes the image of Helen entering Troy, which elicits a prophecy by the seers picturing Menelaus after Helen's departure as wandering aimlessly through his palace: 'Alas for the house [*Iō, iō dōma*], alas for the house and its chiefs! Alas for the bed and the traces of a loving wife! [*iō lechos kai stiboi philanores*]' (*Ag.* 410–11). When we look at the passage in full, it is clear that Pound in his lines before the Greek quotation has condensed the Chorus's depiction:

> One can see the silent and dishonoured, neither reviling nor praying for those who left; because of his longing for her who is overseas, he will think a phantom is ruling the house. The charm of beautiful statues becomes hateful to the husband: as they have no eyes, all their grace is lost.
>
> Sorrowful imaginings, seen in dreams, are present, bringing an empty delight; for it is empty when one sees what seems to be desirable, and then the vision slipping aside through one's arms is gone, never afterwards accompanying on wings the paths of sleep.
>
> *Ag.* ll. 412–26

Although Pound's autograph passage, which would have fitted neatly into the presentation of love triangles in Canto 5, was never used, it is of relevance because it shows us to what extent Pound was involved in reading Aeschylus while composing the early Cantos.

In another unpublished fragment, to be used for Canto 21 and written in 1924, Pound again referred to Agamemnon:

And could you, wrote Mr. Jefferson,
        find me a gardener
Who can play the French horn;
                you in a civilized country
(Burgundy) where these things doubtless exist,
We like music of an evening.

And coming back to the cabin (Sambo) unexpectedly
Dinah having company, Sambo,
        (Dinah, who dat in you' bed)
St[r]uck unexpectedly.
        Mah glory, Gawd my glory,
    boh, you dun cut Massa Washin'tun .
George died of a hemorage, that is, throat trouble
At Mt Vernon,
        and they put up a symbolic monument,
AGAMEMNON.

Beinecke 71/3194[9]

In his extensive analysis and contextualization of this draft, Alec Marsh has observed that an expanded version of the Jefferson passage appears in Canto 21 (21/97), the first Canto to introduce an American historical theme, but that the Washington passage, 'with its phallic joke and minstrelized African Americans', has completely disappeared (Marsh 2000, 125–26).

Two elements are of importance here. First, the imagined murder of Washington by a jealous slave because the former president has been found *in flagrante delicto* with his wife, is here linked to Agamemnon. Note the Aeschylean word 'St[r]uck' which Pound had also used in Canto 5 to describe a murder. This underscores the violence on which state power is founded. Secondly, Marsh has connected this fragment that employs 'black voice' to the stereotypical appropriation that Toni Morrison in *Playing in the Dark* (1992) has called 'American-Africanism', that is, the construction of 'a nonwhite, Africanlike (or Africanist) presence or persona' in American literature as a means to reflect on Americanness and slavery, with 'the myth of blackness' as 'the silenced but pervasive original background of American culture'.

This accounts for the ambiguity of the rejected passage, as it is very problematic in terms of its racist approach to language, but it also shows awareness of the darker sides of American history and its 'legacy of slavery, racism and forbidden sexuality' (Marsh 2000, 127–28). The reason why Pound may have used the 'Afro-American' dialect is his belief that African Americans have retained the authentic and original American speech; their language has not been tainted by 'impure racial politics', and thus opposes 'the official version of United States history' (ibid. 130–31). At the same time Pound uses the 'black voice' here and in his rendering of the Watchman's speech in opposition to what he regarded as the deadening 'translationese' of contemporary versions of the Greek classics.

In his later published Cantos, such as Canto 58, Pound would continue to use Aeschylus. The *Agamemnon* is a presence permeating the Pisan Cantos, a sequence balancing between despair and the hope for restoration of order. Thus Canto 82 on its opening page has a reference to the Watchman's words at the opening of the play, in the original Greek, Stanley's Latin translation and Pound's own rendering:

> "On the Atreides' roof"
> "like a dog ... and a good job
> ΕΜΟΣ ΠΟΣΙΣ ... ΧΕΡΟΣ
> hac dextera mortus
> dead by this hand (82/543)

Pound precedes these quotations with an anecdote about Algernon Swinburne, who in October 1869 nearly drowned when swimming off the coast of Normandy. He was saved by some French fishermen to whom the poet started reciting Victor Hugo. Pound substituted Hugo with Aeschylus, perhaps due to faulty memory or, more likely, because Swinburne with his love of the classics and his florid, adjectival style with its compound words connoted the Greek playwright. Moreover, Swinburne's attempts to revive the classics, to make 'them new', can thus be linked to Pound's own attempts at translating Klytaimnestra's boast over Agamemnon's body in his 1919 essay on Aeschylus, and at reviving the *Agamemnon* through his version of the Prologue in an idiosyncratic African-American dialect. Pound may have been reminded of this abandoned translation in the DTC in Pisa where he found himself among African-American prisoners, whose presence constitute one of the backgrounds of the Pisan Cantos.

Furthermore, the Watchman's situation becomes connected to Pound's own predicament at Pisa, watching and waiting for a resolution. This theme recurs in the course of the Canto which reflects on justice, the justification of violence, and the notion of just war, symbolized here by the siege of Troy:

> there are no righteous wars in 'The Spring and Autumn'
> that is, perfectly right on one side or the other
> total right on either side of the battle line
> and the news is a long time moving
> a long time in arriving
> thru the impenetrable
> crystalline, indestructible
> ignorance of locality
> The news was quicker in Troy's time
> a match on Cnidos, a glow worm on Mitylene
>
> 82/545

Here the poet's comparison of his own plight with that of the Mycenean watchman, who is watching the news about the fall of Troy through the chain of beacon fires spreading the message, is concluded in favour of the latter.

Pound in Canto 77 also invokes the prophetess Cassandra who foresaw the destruction of Troy as well as the death of Agamemnon, but who due to a curse by Apollo was never believed by anyone and regarded as mad. In *Agamemnon* ll. 1072–1330 she offers an extended vision of violence and murder before she enters the palace, where she and Agamemnon will be killed. Pound addresses her at the end of Canto 77: 'the wind mad as Cassandra/ who was as sane as the lot of 'em' (77/495), lines that are picked up at the opening of the next Canto:

> Cassandra, your eyes are like tigers,
> with no word written in them
> You also have I carried to nowhere
> to an ill house and there is
> no end to the journey.
>
> 78/497; cp. 502

In 'Translators of Greek', Pound had offered several selections from Stanley's Latin renderings of Cassandra's speech – it is likely that Stanley's version of her exclamation in l. 1097, 'Ah! Quo me tandem duxisti? Ad qualem domum?' (*LE* 271; 'ah, to where have you brought me? To what sort of house?'), is referred to by Pound in Canto 78: 'You also have I carried to nowhere/ to an ill house' (78/497). In a complex interplay, then, Pound seems to have used the Watchman's prologue as an expression of his hope for the termination of his own uncertain waiting for an outcome of the war in

1945, and Cassandra as an image of his own prophecies in *The Cantos* and over Italian radio during the war years, and his consequent removal off the metaphoric stage, ending up at the 'ill house' of the DTC at Pisa (and later St Elizabeths).[10]

No wonder then that at the end of Canto 82 the poet longs for rest, to be provided by Mother Earth. He now desires a 'connubium terrae' (82/546), a mystic marriage with the earth, a 'ΧΘΟΝΙΟΣ, mysterium'. In between these two phrases there is the Greek phrase 'ἔφατα πόσις ἐμός' [*ephata posis emos*], 'my husband said'. At first this seems to be another quotation from Klytaimnestra's speech from the *Agamemnon*, but only the last two words can be linked to that Greek text, already used earlier in this Canto. These words now have become the subject of the verb 'to speak'. The resulting Greek phrase, coined by Pound, underlines how the man guilty of violence and death, himself the victim of retributive killing, now hopes to find redemption.

The bloodshed running through the *Agamemnon*, destroying so many lives, is finally overcome in the paradisal Canto 91 in *Section: Rock-Drill* (Cantos 85–95), which is concerned with vision and with love as an intellectual and moral instigation. In this Canto, which has the last reference to Agamemnon in Pound's poem, the depths of the sea (of material reality) are associated with a woman's eyes, offering either destruction or salvation. When Sir Francis Drake looks into the eyes of Queen Elizabeth I, he sees both 'splendour and wreckage/ in that clarity' (91/631). This is why Pound once again uses ''Ἑλέναυς' (632), and lets Drake see 'in the Queen's eye the reflection' of 'Ra-Set over crystal … moving' (632). Drake thus uses his reason to overcome his personal feelings of lust that may lead to ruin, and to attain the benevolent intellect that will offer him the victory of the 'splendours of paradise' as well as the defeat of the Spanish Armada:

> He asked not
> nor wavered, seeing, nor had fear of the wood-queen, Artemis
> that is Diana
> nor had killed save by the hunting rite,
> sanctus.
>
> 91/632

Drake, then, is unlike the lustful Actaeon or impious Agamemnon, who appears in Canto 89 in the lines: 'Judge Marshall, father of war/ Agamemnon killed that stag, against hunting rites' (89/622). This reference is taken from Pound's version of Sophocles' *Elektra* (see Chapter 6), and denotes how Agamemnon evoked Artemis's anger for having killed one of her deer, an act of impiety, as a result of which he was asked to sacrifice his daughter Iphigeneia after his fleet had been unable to sail to Troy because of lack of wind. This stresses again how for Pound the *Agamemnon* was essentially a play about lust and violence.

It may not surprise us, then, that in *Rock-Drill*, a section concerned with order and justice as the formative elements of any *paradiso terrestre*, Pound would turn to the last part of Aeschylus' trilogy, the *Eumenides*, where the cycle of vengeance and blood is broken by the establishment of civilized law through Athena, goddess of reason. The Eumenides are the former Erinyes or Furies who in Greek religious thought are divine elemental powers who pursue any mortal who has committed a murder or perjury, or who has violated the sacred respect the young have to pay to the aged, hosts to their guests, state officials to their suppliants, and children to their parents. They threaten particularly the murderer of relatives with madness and death. The Furies play a leading role in the *Eumenides* in which they pursue Orestes for the killing of his mother. Athena manages to soothe them by suggesting that they take up residence in a grotto at Athens where they will receive sacrifices, libations and other ritual honours in worship of their power. The Erinyes agree and are henceforth known as the 'Eumenides' or 'Kindly Ones'.[11] In place of vengeance killings and taking the law into one's own hands, Athens will now have a court of law to determine guilt or innocence and any course of legal action with regard to murder.

Having referred to this in Canto 85 as 'Jury trial was in Athens' (85/579), Pound uses another extended allusion in Canto 86, in a context praising enlightened civilizations, such as the Chinese second dynasty of Shang (1766–1121 BCE). Here Pound presents the beginning of jury trial in Western civilization:

> Ἀθάνα broke tie,
> That is 6 jurors against 6 jurors
>   needed Ἀθάνα.
> Right, all of it, was under Shang
>   save what came in Athens.
>
> 86/591

The very same image is used in Canto 89 after Pound's definition of law, a central principle in *The Cantos*:

> "Neither by force nor by fraud, that there be
> no coercion, either by force or by fraud,
>   That is law's purpose, or should be.
> Ἀθήνη swung the hung jury
>
> 89/621

The arc of retributive killing to the formation of a judicial system as depicted in Aeschylus' trilogy may well be the reason why Pound in *Guide to Kulchur* placed the Greek dramatists alongside Homer's *Odyssey*. Both texts represent for him the 'rise of sense of civic responsibility' (*GK* 352).

Notes

1. See Pound 2010, 385. In 'Aeschylus', Pound described the edition in detail (*LE* 269). For a fuller discussion of Pound and Stanley, see Liebregts 2015, 97–99.
2. Cp. Eliot 2009, 628–29.
3. For a discussion of the racist language, see the next chapter.
4. That Pound knew the passage about Zeus is evident from his lengthy discussion of Aristotle's *Nicomachean Ethics*, with its idiosyncratic philological commentary, in *Guide to Kulchur*. Pound notes in connection with the Greek text of *Ethics* VI.xii.10 that the '"*hotidepote*" of the greek is easy to slide over. But I seem to recall a dramatist's (wasn't it) "Zeus whoever he is?"' (*GK* 329) – a reference to *Agamemnon* l. 160, Ζεὺς ὅστις ποτ' ἐστίν [*Zeus hostis pot' estin*], the opening of Aeschylus' famous Ode to the king of the gods.
5. Incidentally, Pound at the end of 'Aeschylus' stated that the 1909 translation of the *Oresteia* by E. D. A. Morshead (1849–1912) 'is bearable in Clytemnestra's description of the beacons' (*LE* 274).
6. On Simpson, see Marsh 2000, 138 and 141 n. 8; and Moody, 268 and 291–92.
7. Pound later in Canto 23 'revised' or 'corrected' the parallel since the castle in Auvergnat, unlike Troy, was not destroyed, nor was De Tierci's wife returned to him. However, he did retain the link to Troy as the verse paragraph following the depiction of Pieire de Maensac starts with 'And that was when Troy was down, all right/ superbo Ilion …' (23/109).
8. Also see the online *The Cantos Project*: http://thecantosproject.ed.ac.uk/.
9. Quoted in Marsh 2000, 125.
10. Here I disagree with Stergiopoulou 2015, 94, who aligns Agamemnon with Mussolini.
11. There is an early reference to the Eumenides in the poem 'Anima Sola' (Pound 1977, 19-21), published in *A Lume Spento* (1908).

3

Ezra Pound and Sophocles

When Pound enclosed his rendering of the *Agamemnon* in a letter to T. S. Eliot in June 1934, he addressed him, as he often did, as 'Possum'. Pound's well-known nickname for Eliot and his comment in *Guide to Kulchur* four years later that he had tried in his *Agamemnon* to let 'the watchman talk nigger' (*GK* 93) require explanation. An as yet not rightly identified and still unpublished piece of writing, now in the Beinecke Library, may serve as a link between Pound's early interest in Aeschylus and his later work on Sophocles, as well as explaining why he adopted this mode of speech.

Both '(Old) Possum' and Pound's name for himself, 'Brer Rabbit', were taken from Joel Chandler Harris' *Uncle Remus* stories, which were based on Harris's personal experience of having listened to the stories told to him by the African Americans in the slave quarters in Eatonton, Georgia. The stories, which employed a dialect reflective of the Afro-American oral tradition, were published from 1876 onward in various newspapers and magazines across the United States. *Uncle Remus: His Songs and His Sayings*, a collection of plantation fables published in 1880, became a best-seller, and made Harris a national celebrity. They featured Brer Rabbit, a trickster hero who uses his intelligence to overcome adversity. Harris would write nine books of Uncle Remus stories in total, three of which were published after his death in 1908. They were immensely popular among both black and white people in the United States, but also found a wide readership in Great Britain. In the late 1950s Pound would read the Uncle Remus Stories of Brer Rabbit to his grandchildren at Brunnenburg, 'doing the voices with immense enjoyment' (Moody 445–46).

In their correspondence, Pound and Eliot used an Uncle Remus-inspired dialect for humorous and mocking purposes, and for intimate references to incidents and persons, while also, on occasion, using such speech in their poetic and dramatic writings. Michael North has argued how the dialect of *Uncle Remus* was particularly important to them because in their Modernist attack on literary propriety, it 'offered itself as a natural alternative to more conventional speech, superior precisely to the degree to which it failed to approximate grammatical correctness'. In this way it was a means to deconstruct 'the privilege that the standard enjoyed' (North i).[1] According to North, Pound saw the use of black speech as 'the most prominent prior challenge to the dominance of received linguistic forms' (ibid. 78). As we have seen, this is was the purpose of its employment by Pound in his *Agamemnon*, but it was Eliot who with *Sweeney Agonistes* or 'Fragments of an Aristophanic Melodrama', published in 1926–27, managed to produce what Pound had failed to do, 'the combination of Greek classics and black dialect' (ibid. 87). After the publication of *Sweeney*, Eliot would stop using this 'Possum' voice, but Pound continued to be the Brer Rabbit fighting cultural homogeneity and conformity, and widening the linguistic possibilities and registers of Anglophone literature by employing mixtures of the great variety of British English, American English and global versions of English, from highbrow literary speech to slang. Pound would still use 'black dialect' elsewhere as in, for example, his translation of some of the folksier poems of the Confucian Odes.

In a letter to Eliot of 28 March 1935, in which he talked about translation, Pound included a poem which would be a 'li'l hard on Brid. and Co., tryin so hard, but still true enough to be stingy' (*SL* 272).

> SONG FER THE MUSES' GARDEN
> Ez PO and Possum
> Have picked all the blossom,
> Let all the others
> Run back to their mothers
>   Fer a boye's bes' friend iz hiz Oedipus,
>   A boy's best friend is his Oedipus.
>
> *SL* 270

In referring to 'Brid. and Co.', Pound is denouncing the poet Robert Bridges, who in the 1920s had wanted to 'purify' the English language, and as a member of the Society for Pure English, founded in 1919, had pointed to the hazardous influence of 'other-speaking races', which included Americans (North 80). The poem can be read as subverting this claim of exclusivity.

Pound's poem may be linked to an undated typescript in Box 138 of the Ezra Pound Papers at the Beinecke Library. This contains various translations from French, Italian, Latin and Greek, including Folder 6070 marked as '[Translation from Greek]: typescript n.d.'. This text is not a translation from an actual Greek text, but an imagined scene from *Oedipus Rex*, written in Pound's version of the

Uncle Remus dialect. It consists of two pages of typescript, with some corrections in red, and a pencilled note in the margin of the first page: 'Oedipus as Brer devil heard it.' Two pencil marks on the same page read 'agon' and 'antagon', that is, 'agonist' and 'antagonist', thus indicating that the text is a dramatic dialogue in the Greek manner. Pound situates his scene at the end of Sophocles' play, when Oedipus has blinded himself after having discovered the truth of his marriage to his mother.

The typescript reads:

[Page one]
As Oedipus, streatching forth his and:
                               Ahw mih pooah pooah cheeildren!!
ek . . .
CHORUS   . . . oo zee th doctor? (whaaat? we'll aint they
all in traable?)   ees goin to cuah them ee iz
Dew yew know wot EE's DONE (?whaaat? tasty bit er filth
this ere . . .
       fawncy bit er filth this ere;

       wots ee bloindid himself fowh?
            go on Bill, donchu know, there's
a bit er dirt here. Wot you mean durt? ees ad is ma eee
as.
       gewan . . .
                gewan, taint possible. gewan eee cant do that
       you cant do that there ere // I tell you ee as ee had is
ma, that s wot th old bloke with th whiskers said.
               wot does ee know about it.
yew are iggerunt donchu know th story?

Edopus conplex/ OO zee. that's wot i been explaining to ye th
       ole evening but yur that igurnut.

What did he put his eyes out for then? because he's
remorseful. Remorseful?
       For that bit of dirt eee done er.
       Done oo? I tell you is ma.
Ow, so that's what they call the Edipus complex. Fine bit of
dirt this is.

[Page two]
Sayve us
      gorblime ee must be in a bad waye//
ss h   thats th steowry.

I can smell a sopt of bother somewhere.

    Tiresias///
        Chorus / That's torn it, eees spilt th beans
    proper this time.

Beinecke 138/6070

In Sophocles' original, the Chorus is told by a messenger that Iocaste has committed suicide, and that Oedipus has blinded himself (*Oedipus Rex* ll. 1231–96). When Oedipus re-appears on the stage, the Chorus engages in a dialogue with the king (ll. 1297–1415). They lament his fate, while Oedipus regrets the decisions he made in the past. Then Creon enters and commands Oedipus to go inside, but Oedipus pleads to be banished together with his daughters (ll. 1416–75). When they too appear on the stage, Oedipus in a monologue takes pity on them (ll. 1476–1514). The play ends with a dialogue between Oedipus and Creon (ll. 1515–1523), with the latter ordering the king to leave. As always in a Greek tragedy, the Chorus offers a few lines reflecting on what has happened and summarizing the moral message, in this case a meditation of how deep the mighty have fallen, and the well-known advice never to call anyone happy until the day of death (ll. 1524–30).

In his version, Pound has deviated from the original plot. He begins, like Sophocles, with Oedipus entering and taking pity on his children, but then it becomes clear that part of the Chorus (referred to as 'Bill') does not know what has happened and why the king has blinded himself. The other part informs them that this was caused by a 'tasty bit of filth', as Oedipus 'has had his mother'. Bill reacts shocked: 'you cannot do that here', but apparently those in the know insist it is true as they have been informed by 'the old bloke with the whiskers', clearly a reference to the seer Tiresias. They then introduce the (anachronistic) term '[O]Edipus complex', and explain that Oedipus blinded himself out of remorse for having slept with his mother. The other half of the chorus which had been 'ignorant', finally understands what a 'Fine bit of dirt this is', and all agree with Tiresias at the end that Oedipus 'spilt the beans proper this time'.

In this dramatic dialogue, Pound used ordinary speech and colloquial expressions in a mixture of Afro-American, Anglo-Irish, and Cockney English:

'pooah' (poor), 'cuah' (cure), 'bloindid' (blinded), 'ees ad is ma eee as' (he had his ma he has), 'gewan' (go on), 'gorblime' (cor blimey, as in 'may God blind me', which fits the context). The text thus is meant to represent the reaction of 'common' people to the tragic event (in line with the speech of the Watchman in the *Agamemnon*). The fact that part of the Chorus is referred to as 'Bill' may be related to Pound's essay 'Aeschylus':

> As for the word-sense and phrase-sense, we still hear workmen and peasants and metropolitan bus-riders repeating the simplest sentences three and four times, back and forth between interlocutors: trying to get the sense 'I sez to Bill, I'm goin' to 'Arrow' or some other such subtlety from one occiput into another.
> 'You sez to Bill, etc.',
> 'Yus, I sez.... Etc.'
>
> LE 269

Pound's Oedipus fragment is clearly not meant as a serious piece of writing. This may well have to do with the fact that Pound never liked the *Oedipus Rex* that much, as outlined in Chapter 1. In a letter of 29 August 1916 to Iris Barry, he stated that 'the whole Oedipus story is a darn silly lot of buncombe' (SL 95). As a letter of October 1956 testifies, Pound stuck to this conviction throughout his life: 'FED-up-us [Oedipus] bores me to hell an gone' (Pound 1994, 17). When Thomas Cole, the editor/publisher of the poetry magazine *Imagi*, presented Pound with a copy of Dudley Fitts and Robert Fitzgerald's newly translated *Oedipus Rex* (1949), Pound said he had no use for it (Cole 56).

The typescript of Pound's spoof of Sophocles has no date. I suggest that it originates from the mid to late 1930s, a period in which Pound was reminded of his 'black' *Agamemnon* by sending it to Eliot in June 1934, followed by the short Oedipus poem a year later, and his reflections on his version of Aeschylus in *Guide to Kulchur*. Moreover, as Leah Flack has shown, in 1934 Pound approached the British classicist W. H. D. Rouse (1863–1950), co-founder and editor of the Loeb Classical Library, to translate the *Odyssey* in a plain prose translation. From their correspondence between 1934–1937, we may learn that Pound persuaded Rouse not to go in for verbal fidelity, but to attempt to render the sense and atmosphere of the original, and to produce a '*fresh*' and '*new*' translation (SL 275).[2] 'Pound insisted that Rouse render all of Homer's characters in a colloquial language relying heavily on slang and local dialects' (Flack 137–38). Rouse did adopt a 'playful approach' in his *The Story of Odysseus* (London, 1937), exemplified by the Cyclops becoming 'Goggle-eyes'; by Ino telling Odysseus: 'Poor Odysseus! You're odd-I-see, true to your name!'; and Poseidon exclaiming: 'Damn it all, the gods have changed their minds about Odysseus, as soon as I was out of the way!'³ Pound, however, felt that Rouse was too 'British' to be able to use live speech, and that perhaps only an American would have the linguistic vitality he was looking for (Flack 139).

Sophocles at St Elizabeths

After his claim in *Guide to Kulchur* (1938) that with the Greek tragedians we see the 'rise of sense of civic responsibility' (*GK* 352), Pound's renewed and more positive appreciation of Greek tragedy, and more particularly of Sophocles, deepened a few years after he had been sent to St Elizabeths Hospital for the Criminally Insane in Washington, DC, in December 1945. Accused of treason for actions during the war, in which he had delivered radio speeches that were deemed anti-American, and having spent six months of imprisonment in the army Disciplinary Training Center (DTC) at Pisa, Pound was flown to Washington in November 1945. Pound escaped trial and a possible death sentence because of his lawyer's plea of insanity, which was convincing enough for the jury to find him 'of unsound mind' at a hearing in February 1946.⁴ This resulted in Pound's stay in St Elizabeths for more than twelve years until his official discharge in May 1958.

Apart from the publication of *The Pisan Cantos* in July 1948, the first half of Pound's period at St Elizabeths is marked by his work on four Confucian texts and two plays by Sophocles. That he perceived a link between them is evident from a note on the left bottom corner of the typescript title page of *Women of Trachis*: 'Kung 551–479/ Σοφοκλες 495–406' (Princeton 1/13). In 1946 Pound began making drafts of his versions of the 305 Confucian Odes, which he published in 1954 as *The Classic Anthology Defined by Confucius*. In 1947 Pound published both *The Unwobbling Pivot* and *The Great Digest* (*Ta Hio*), having already typed up these texts in Pisa (Italian versions had appeared during the war). They emphasize self-knowledge and self-discipline as the basis of order, as do *The Analects*, Pound's rendition of which appeared in 1950 in the *Hudson Review*. Pound's Confucianism with its set of practical ethical rules and emphasis on man's social responsibilities is at the heart of his *Weltanschauung* and underlies the greater part of his work from the 1920s onward.

Pound's *Pisan Cantos* were awarded the Bollingen Prize for Poetry in February 1949, and it is around this time that Pound returned to Sophocles by taking up the *Elektra*. This was part of a larger re-appreciation of the Greek dramatists, as may be attested by a letter to William Carlos Williams of 13 October 1949, quoted in *Paterson*, in which he urged Williams to 're read *all* the Gk tragedies in/ Loeb' (Williams 1992, 138). Pound's high regard for Sophocles during his St Elizabeths years is evident in a letter of 14 October 1953, in which he stated that if people 'had read Dant and Sophokl they / wd not stand FILTH at the top' (Pound 1994, 228).[5] Eventually Pound would prefer Sophocles to Aeschylus. Guy Davenport reports in 1953 that when Pound was asked if *ABC of Reading* needed 'revision because of later considerations, Pound replied that he would give Sophocles the place Aeschylus has in the text' (Davenport 33, n. 2). This confirms what Pound wrote to John Espey in a letter of 3 March 1955: 'Having looked at Aeschylus, and thrown him at TSE [=T.S. Eliot] ... I HAD swallowed the superstition that gk/ stage declined Aesch/ Soph and Gib. Murray/ whereas what I had taken for latin virtue is 'all' (so far as I now see) there in Soph' (Beinecke 15/691). This positive reassessment also occurs in the 'Publisher's Note' to *Confucius to Cummings* (1964), in which it is said that Pound claimed

> he had swallowed the idea that Aeschylus represented the acme of Greek drama, and, neglecting Sophokles, had thought certain qualities found in the best Latin were of Latin origin ... The emendation of his proportionate estimate of authors in world literature accessible to him can be summarized, then, in his phrase, as 'dress (in the military sense) on Sophokles.'
>
> Pound 1964, xi

Pound came to prefer Sophocles (ca. 496–406 BCE) over Aeschylus, most likely because Sophocles' style generally is less grandiloquent than that of Aeschylus, while his diction is more elevated than that of Euripides. As such, Sophocles is the dramatist with a better balance between realistic depiction, mythopoeic imagination and poetic expression.

From Sophocles' output of 123 plays only seven survived, all taking their subject matter from heroic myth. After Aeschylus had introduced a second actor, Sophocles introduced a third, and focused more on the portrayal of character. Fundamental to all his plays, as P. E. Easterling has noted, is 'the same two-sided view of man, in which his heroic splendor is matched by his utter vulnerability to circumstance'. Alongside 'man's potentiality for greatness are set his helplessness and mortality ... caught in the infinite web of circumstances outside his control, limited by time ... by his passions which impede his judgment or undermine his will, always liable to destroy himself and others through failure – or unwillingness – to understand' (Easterling 1989, 47–48). Sophocles was also unanimously praised by ancient critics for his 'honeyed' style.

Pound and F. R. Earp

According to Guy Davenport, two books by the British classical scholar F. R. Earp (1871–1955), *The Style of Sophocles* (1944) and *The Style of Aeschylus* (1948), were partly responsible for Pound's re-appreciation of Sophocles at the cost of Aeschylus (Davenport 33, n. 2). Earp criticized many translators of Greek tragedy for having used a uniform style in rendering the playwrights, thereby failing to see how the dramatists varied their style throughout their career. His studies attempt to redress this by a careful and formal analysis of the styles of Greek drama, aiming to highlight the excellence of its poetry.[6]

In spite of Davenport's contention, it is unclear whether Pound read both of Earp's books. A letter of 3 April 1953 by Earp in his unpublished correspondence with Pound in 1953–54,[7] demonstrates that Pound admired the Sophocles volume. Earp thanked Pound in a letter of 11 May, claiming that if he had enjoyed his work, 'you must know more Greek than you admit, for I warned my Greekless against buying it. But of course to be interested in style is half the battle, & very few people are'. Earp promised to send Pound a copy of his book on Aeschylus, observing that Pound would find it 'easier than the Sophocles, for I have enlarged on various things that interest me' (Beinecke 14/646). As is evident from Earp's response to a letter by Pound of 24 May, the poet himself had been unable to find a copy, but Earp sent him the 'only ... one left' at the Cambridge University Press (letter of 24 August). We do not know if Pound actually read Earp's book on Aeschylus. We can establish, however, that Pound was still interested in Aeschylus in 1953, as he asked Earp a question about a papyrus. This question is most likely related to the publication in 1952 of the so-called Oxyrhynchus Papyrus 2256, which contained a fragment which could be used as evidence that Aeschylus' *Suppliants* was not the earliest of his surviving plays, as had previously been the scholarly consensus. Pound's letter has been lost, but apparently he asked for a scholarly explanation, as evinced by Earp's lengthy didactic response in a letter of 11 May 1953:

> I'll try to answer your question as to what the papyrus says as briefly as I can.
>
> It contains a fragment of the didascalia, i.e. notices which were inscribed in Athens after the competition with tragedies, giving the names of the poets who had won 1st, 2nd, or 3rd prize. It is to them that we owe our scanty knowledge of the dates of Greek plays. Later on they were copied from the marble by those interested in the history of Greek drama, & cropt up sometimes in MSS & elsewhere, as in this bit of papyrus. This fragment does not mention the Supplices by name, but only the Danaides, of which the Suppl. has always been assumed

to be part. That assumption is natural enough, for there is no other legend known about the <u>Danaides</u> which could be made into a trilogy. But on the other hand there is no telling what will fire the imagination of a poet. A normal man would not find much in the legend of Prometheus, but Aeschylus made a trilogy of it.

As to the date of the play, the fragment states that Sophocles was competing that year, & he was nearly 40 years younger than Aeschylus: so it can't be an early play by Aeschylus.

There is <u>also</u> a date, given, as usual at Athens, by mentioning the Archon Eponymous of the year. And the first two letters of the name have survived in the fragment, but experts in chronology say that the only one who will fit the name was archon in 463 BC. Even if they are wrong, the mention of Sophocles shows that it cannot have been an early play of Aeschylus, unless he produced a play at that date which he had written long before. But that is hardly likely.

Beinecke 14/646

Such an informed response explains why Pound in 1953 stated, according to Guy Davenport, that Earp is 'the only man who knows anything about Greek' (Davenport 33 n. 2). What may have influenced his appraisal was that Earp, like Pound, did not have a high regard for Euripides, calling him 'not such an artist in language' and thus 'easier to translate' (Letter of 29 June 1953; Beinecke 14/646). Furthermore, he shared Pound's dislike for Gilbert Murray, as this passage from a letter of 29 May 1954, attests: 'I don't like Gilbert Murray's translations much but his translations from Euripides are the best, chiefly because they have rather the same kind of mind' (ibid.). And in a later letter of 7 August, Earp acidly notes: 'There was a boom in England in Euripides at the end of the last century & the beginning of this. He suited the ideas of the time, but as I did not share them, I preferred Aeschylus & Sophocles. I notice that Gilbert Murray appeals specially to women' (ibid.).

In *The Style of Sophocles* Earp presents Sophocles as the greatest Athenian tragedian, who has a style 'so surpassingly good' that it 'makes the style of nearly all other poets, even the greatest, seem a kind of fumbling' (Earp 1). The aim of his book is to account for this greatness, which in his view shows a development from a partly conventional style still filled with Aeschylean ὄγκος [*onkos*] or 'grandiloquence' (consisting of, among other things, compounds and periphrases) to a late style which is more individual, natural and, in the words of Plutarch (*Moralia* 79B), ἠθικώτατόν [*ēthikōtaton*], 'most expressive of character' (Earp 12). Throughout his career Sophocles is able to mix the 'elevated' and the colloquial. Earp analyses the development of his style by focusing on Sophocles' use of words uniquely used by him or as adopted from Homer and Aeschylus, while also paying attention to figures of speech (simile, metaphor, antithesis, and anaphora), and metrical techniques. Earp also devotes a few pages to what Pound called the *melopoeia*, as 'half of the beauty of poetry depends on the sound'. However, Earp notes that 'our ears cannot estimate the effect of the Greek accent', and thus we are unable to assess whether the effects we feel were actually intended by the poet. Still, we may 'feel keenly the beauty of sound in some Greek poetry' (Earp 144). In the case of Sophocles, it is obvious that, aside from the rhythm, alliteration and assonance are elements in producing the musical effect. As we will see, Earp's book had some influence on Pound's versions of the *Trachiniae* and the *Elektra*. Moreover, Pound corresponded with Earp about Greek drama and his translations between April 1953 and September 1954, and these letters, thus far unstudied, shed some light on the poet's work on Sophocles.

Pound and Rudd Fleming

Another scholarly figure who influenced Pound's translations was Rudd Fleming (1909–1991). Fleming held a doctorate in comparative literature from Cornell University and was appointed as a professor of English at Maryland University in 1945. Fluent in French, German, Italian, Latin, and ancient Greek, he was deeply interested in Greek drama. Fleming would visit Pound almost every week with his wife Mary ('Polly') through most of the St Elizabeth's years from January 1949 onward. In a letter of July 1951 Pound described the friendship as one between 'a highly cultured couple of enthusiasts fer kulchur and greek drama' (Pound 1998, 70). According to Michael Reck, Fleming and Pound 'would discuss Greek things, which were his passion. But toward the end of Mr. Pound's Elizabethan Age there ensued the inevitable "coolness." Perhaps the root of it was Fleming's obtuseness concerning the Ezraic economic theories, but Pound was heard muttering about "sterile Hellenism"' (Reck 105–106). Yet before this happened, Pound with the help of Fleming would translate Sophocles' *Elektra*. The collaboration consisted of Pound first typing a version, which they then discussed during visiting hours at St Elizabeths, with Fleming then incorporating all the changes in a fair copy typed out by him.

As his correspondence with Pound demonstrates, Fleming shared his great interest in the *melopoeia* of Greek poetry, as one of his early letters, written on 19 January 1949, attests:

> I'm very anxious lest my inability to visit you this afternoon should break off our enterprise with the Greek plays. Of course, it might not come to much. But I have been practicing <u>Electra</u> and <u>Oedipus Tyrannus</u> aloud with the help of a recording machine, and although the Greek still sounds pretty soggy in most places, there are occasional spots which make me hopeful. If we could get together in the presence of these plays and try out speeches here and there or, for that matter, read through a whole play, you could probably show me whether or not I am on the right track into this everlasting business of the Greek tragedies.
>
> Lilly[8]

In a letter of 19 February 1949, Fleming wrote that with his next visit he would bring a copy of Gustave Reese's *Music in the Middle Ages, with an Introduction on the Music of Ancient Times*, noting: 'But musicians are impatient to pry the Greek music off the words, which is fine for alleluias and perhaps for love songs, but what is wanted for the Greek plays is not song but *mask* for the voice – or so it seems to me' (ibid.). On 6 June 1949, Fleming reported that he

> was still working on pronunciation of Trachiniae and there is a good deal of progress (I got a crick in my back swinging to the metronome); but I can't translate it. Translations are no good, except as ponies, unless the tone of their language could conceivably have generated, or been in at the birth of, their idea and content. In your Electra and, I think maybe, in Seven Against Thebes there is a language idea at work; but the closer I get to what I think are the actual Greek rhythmic constructions, the more non-plussed I become. But I got to the foot of this impossible mountain after rejecting an awful lot of other things and I guess I am going to try to climb it. Your genius and inexhaustible kindness have been an absolutely extraordinary help (!).
>
> ibid.

Fleming also tried out Homeric pronunciation, as is evident from a letter of 19 June 1950, in which he wrote that he was 'having another whack at Greek pronunciation', and was trying to get 'the description of Achilles' shield by heart', mixing it in his 'auditory imagination' with Pound's Canto 81 (ibid.). As his student Carlo Parcelli later recalled, much of Fleming's teaching focused on the auditory qualities of the texts he discussed. When dealing with Homer, Fleming 'would simply launch into the *Odyssey* in the original Greek using the acting skills he had acquired performing in productions around town with his wife Polly'.[9]

Pound and Fleming's shared interest in the *melopoeia* of Greek poetry comes to the fore in Pound's 1949 draft for a memorandum entitled 'Hellenists', which called for a revival of Greek culture, as a 'much greater diffusion of Greek studies is necessary to the conservation of decency' (Beinecke 106/4422). To this end, Pound wanted to set up a committee, with Rudd Fleming acting as secretary, and called for suggestions. He himself proposed, first, 'chearper and more informative bilingual editions of Homer and the Dramatists', and second, 'efforts to teach by the sound of choruses as (conjecturally) sung, that means sung loud enough to be heard in open air theatre, with the sense of the words carried clearly to auditors'. Musicians should study Greek prosody although Pound did not think 'the graph by accents, dating from Alexandria, is necessary complete or infallible. The musician must use his instinct in determining the melodic force, as he would in any other musical setting'. Yet 'there must be a definitive ictus on every marked syllable whether by acute, grave or circumflex, this implies syncopation, the life of verse' (ibid.). The second proposal is clearly a return to his ideas about *vers libre* and *melopoeia*, as formulated in the 1910s and 1920s.

In March 1949, Fleming sent a copy of Pound's memorandum to poet-novelist Osmond Beckwith in New York to see whether he would be interested in the project. Fleming explained that he and Pound had started reading Greek tragedies a few months before, and that they felt

> the need for a renewal of Greek studies. 'Obviously,' says Pound, 'singing Greek is the way to learn it.... After that comes the problem can it be sung on stage without boring intelligent people to death ... It has taken several centuries to evolve Noh; we don't expect to perfect Greek-plus-Noh criteria in three weeks, but a LOT of people must try, and start NOW.'
> Does this purpose interest you?
> It has at least three aspects which seem to me very important: to help strengthen a good tradition; to bring music and words closer together; and to move toward a more intelligent solution of the problems of poetic drama. I don't see how any of these things can be done if people remain insensitive to Greek.
> Mr. Pound cannot, in his circumstances, launch a 'movement' in his own name; but maybe something can be done even so: the Noh plays now being performed in Japan should be made available by photographs and sound-track; scholars should interest poets, dancers, actors, musicians in experimentation with Greek choral songs and dramatic movements in order to study the relation of voice to mask, of dramatic structure and value to rhythmic beat, etc.
>
> Lilly

Although this project of the 'committee' was never realized, it was part of the effort of translating *Elektra*.[10] Pound began doing so in early 1949 with the help of Fleming, who in 1972 recalled that he 'had been trying to work with [Pound] on just the sound of the Greek, when all at once he started translating it in a very vigorous sort of rough-talk English, shaking the Greek language, so to speak, almost angrily by the scruff of the neck' (Fleming 1972). Some of these phrases are very similar to a description of Pound's *Elektra* in a letter by Fleming of 15 October 1949 to Ernest Trova (1927–2009), painter and sculptor: 'It's hard to get into the play through available translations. Pound's version is very vigorous and rough – made for a drum-beat ... Pound's attack on the Greek play, though rough and sudden, is still the best yet' (Lilly). Pound would leave the final revision of the text to Fleming, and even allowed him to be named as the author of the translation, since Pound wanted to avoid the possibility that in being able to translate a Greek play, he would be deemed sane. Fleming, however, did not see it through, with the result that the play was neglected until 1987, when it was unearthed by Carey Perloff and presented by the Classic State Company in New York, and published later by New Directions in 1990.

Yet Pound and Fleming did plan a production of the *Elektra* in the early stages of the translation process. Supported by Pound's enthusiasm for Ernest Trova's mask drawings, Fleming in a letter of 15 October 1949 asked him to design masks for Elektra, Klytaimnestra, Orestes, and Aigisthos, as the production was 'not to be a vehicle for the character studies of individual actors.' In the letter, Fleming mentions that he has looked at pictures of Greek masks in an encyclopedia, and observes that 'it looks as if each character under the mask, whatever the dramatic moment may be asking of him in words and action, is concentrating (brooding) on the meaning of his role in the play – no, that's not exactly it – but something like that perhaps.' He suggested getting hold of an edition of the Pound-Fenollosa Noh plays, so as to get an idea of what they wanted. Perhaps the four masks of the 'two murderers and two murderees' could have four eyes wide open and four half shut, as it was Fleming's understanding that the Japanese Noh mask 'changes with light and movement' (Lilly). However, as we will see, Pound's version of *Elektra* ultimately makes far less reference to Noh than *Women of Trachis* does.

In his letter to Trova, Fleming mentions that Frank Ledlie Moore would compose music for the choruses (Lilly). Moore was a young musician who had visited Pound on 3 July 1949. He was attempting to set original Greek drama to music for voice and dance, and in the 1950s would work on the choral music for *Women of Trachis*. Pound supported Moore's idea of studying Native American dance in order to better understand 'the meaning and pattern of a Greek dance' (Cole 57), and also inspired him to study Byzantine tonalities, in an attempt to get at the 'original' music of Greek drama (Reck 107–108). Moore later recalled that he and Pound 'were both very excited about the possibility of creating not a

Greek drama, but an American drama as valid for the people as the Greek. Pound said "all dram is pussyfoot", and yet we talked in terms of making it new, making it that great.' Moore also remembered the day he first took the Greek-American sculptor Michael Lekakis to visit Pound: 'We left him and he went back to his room. Just as we were walking away from the little door at the foot of the stairs (Dorothy, Mike, and me), we heard a shout and saw Pound, up in his window, leaning out and singing Greek verse to us at the top of his lungs. Happy, full of happiness, and playing the part of Homer.'[11]

As the typescript of *Elektra* makes clear, Pound was interested in having the play performed with occasional musical accompaniment. He also indicated how the spoken lines should be delivered. Elektra's first line, for example, should be spoken with a 'crying suppressed voice' (*E* 7), while her speech beginning with the Greek words 'DEINOIS ENANKASTHEN' should start '*as if muttering*' (*E* 16). On occasion the directions use musical terminology, such as '*quasi sotto voce*' (*E* 10), and '*crescendo*' (*E* 60). Pound also suggested that the recognition scene should have 'kettle drum accompaniment' (*E* 71).

Although there was not to be a production of *Elektra* in Pound's lifetime, Fleming, together with his wife, directed a performance of his own version of Aeschylus' *Seven Against Thebes* in August 1951. The invitations for the performance called it a 'masque', and stated that it was 'adapted to five-seven drum beat', with music for choruses and choreography for 'war dances'.[12] Fleming's rendering, which is much freer than Pound's Greek versions, uses the same sort of plain and direct speech we will find in Pound's *Elektra*; for example, the opening line of Eteokles' speech reads: 'There's no use blinking the facts'. As in the *Elektra*, Fleming would, on occasion, use the original Greek. When Eteokles goes out to fight against his brother Polyneikes, the chorus in the Second Stasimon (*Seven Against Thebes* ll. 720–91) express their fear that both will die, thereby fulfilling Oedipus' curse that his sons will be destroyed by strife. Fleming first gives us a rendering in English, but then notes that in performance the chorus should also be in Greek, 'to mark the reversal'. When the bodies of both brothers are brought in, the chorus addresses Antigone and Ismene. Fleming inserted Greek phrases at this point, most likely to reinforce the emotional impact of the sisters' reaction (Lilly).

While *Elektra* was never finalized and would only appear posthumously, the fear of being found sane did not stop Pound from publishing *Women of Trachis* in full in the *Hudson Review* in the Winter issue of 1953–54, and later as a book published by Neville Spearman in London in 1956. Perhaps at this point Pound had begun to care less about his predicament, and could have published *Elektra* as well. Yet perhaps he was as dissatisfied with his translation as he had been with his *Agamemnon*. C. David Heymann in an interview of May 1971 asked Pound about the *Agamemnon*, and the poet answered that he gave it up because he 'couldn't find the appropriate language'. Olga Rudge then broke into the conversation by stating: 'And Electra ... You began work on the Euripides [*sic*] play during the "fifties".' Here Pound's reaction may be assessed as one of fatigue or of silent embarrassment:

> Pound looked up but did not speak. Instead, he returned to his hands, skin wrinkled at the wrists and the back of his hand, an invisible tremor causing a stir of motion in his fingertips. An earnest but impassive expression began to mould the contours of his face.
>
> Carpenter 905

Sophoclean masks

There are several reasons why Pound turned to *Elektra* and *Trachiniae*. As we have seen, the theme of betrayal and treacherous homecoming after the war inspired Pound to include references to the *Agamemnon* in *The Pisan Cantos*. In this light it is not surprising that Pound in his first years at St Elizabeths focused on the next step of the family saga by translating the *Elektra*, which emphasized notions of justice and revenge, as well as the possibility of the restoration of order. Wendell Flory argues that Pound at St Elizabeths saw 'in the desperation of Elektra and the agony of Herakles echoes of his own situation'. Elektra, 'humiliated, ill-treated, obsessively committed to righting a horrible injustice yet deprived of all power to act, speaks for him'. Elektra's situation is similar to Pound's own in that 'she herself has no freedom of action and must wait for someone from outside her own captivity to bring an end to her suffering and restore her to a position of honor' (Flory 174).[13] Although there is some truth in this, David Moody has rightly argued that more important for Pound 'would have been Elektra's having the courage of her convictions, her continuing to speak the truth to power in spite of being punished for it, and her refusing to compromise in calling for justice to be done' (Moody 298).

One may add that, given the emphasis on the depiction of Elektra's feelings in Pound's version, this sense of justice is very much tied to a restoration of order, both within herself and within her family. Only then can the state re-establish itself on a stable basis, a Confucian notion that permeates *The Pisan Cantos*, and is most forcefully expressed in the *Ta Hsio* or 'Great Digest', the translation of which Pound had been typing up in October-November 1945 just before he was flown from Rome to Washington, DC:

> The men of old wanting to clarify and diffuse throughout the empire that light which comes from looking straight into the heart and then acting, first set up good government in their own states; wanting good government in their states, they first established order in their own families; wanting order in the home, they first disciplined themselves; desiring self-discipline, they rectified their own hearts; and wanting to rectify their hearts, they sought precise verbal definitions of their inarticulate thoughts; wishing to attain precise verbal definitions, they set to extend their knowledge to the utmost.
>
> CON 29–31

In *The Great Digest*, Pound connected Confucius with the Greek concept of γνῶθι σεαυτόν [*gnōthi seauton*], 'know yourself', through *Tê*, usually translated as 'virtue', and glossed by Pound as

> the action resultant from [the] straight gaze into the heart. The 'know thyself' carried into action. Said action also serving to clarify the self-knowledge.
>
> CON 21

As such Elektra through a process of self-knowledge and insight displays for Pound the right *directio voluntatis* as she urges Orestes to bring the idea of justice into action by avenging the murder of Agamemnon by Klytaimnestra and her lover Aigisthos. Unlike her sister Chrysothemis, Elektra will not compromise and let the dire circumstances of being isolated get the better of her. She stands up for what she thinks is just and clings to her sense of civic duty and her moral responsibility to her family as well as to her belief in the necessity to combat evil and restore order. In this way Pound's version of the Sophoclean play becomes an expression of himself and his beliefs, and a vital link between the *Pisan Cantos*, his work on Confucius, and the later installments of *The Cantos*, *Rock-Drill* and *Thrones*, with their emphasis on the connection between love, justice, order, and good government.

Why did Pound favour the *Trachiniae*, for a long time the least admired of Sophocles' plays? It may be, as Irvin Ehrenpreis has pointed out, that the play 'reminded [Pound] of the occasion when he asked his own wife [Dorothy Shakespear] to share a home with his mistress [Olga Rudge]' in 1944–45 (Ehrenpreis 6). David Moody has quoted a remark by Dorothy Pound which shows that she at least saw the play as an allegory of this domestic situation, in which she was trying to win back her husband's love from Olga/Iole (Moody 302). This interpretation can be combined with Hugh Kenner's observation that

Pound, imprisoned at St Elizabeths, strongly identified with Herakles' sufferings (Kenner 523). Pound may have felt some sort of affinity with Herakles, who after a life of fighting and struggling met a fate that seemed to him to be out of all proportion in relation to the nature of his error. Be that as it may, Pound most certainly also had a literary interest in the play, which he regarded as 'the highest peak of Greek sensibility registered in any of the plays that have come down to us' (*WT* 23), and which he also connected to the Noh.

What about the other five surviving plays of Sophocles? We have seen that Pound did not think much of *Oedipus Rex*, and this may have kept him from its sequel *Oedipus at Colonus*. An additional reason may be that the plays had already been rendered by W. B. Yeats, with the aid of Jebb's translations, in two dramatic versions, produced in 1926 and 1927, and published in 1928 and 1934, respectively. As far as I can tell, Pound in his writings never referred to *Philoctetes* or to *Ajax*, although in his copy of the Loeb edition of Sophocles' plays, which he used as the basis for his *Elektra* and *Women of Trachis*, Pound put a mark next to line 131–32 of *Ajax*, where we find a maxim typical of Sophocles: ὡς ἡμέρα κλίνει τε κἀνάγει πάλιν / ἅπαντα τἀνθρώπεια [*hōs hēmera klinei te kanagei palin/ hapanta tanthrōpeia*], 'A day can prostrate and a day upraise/ All that is mortal' (Storr 19).[14]

Finally, we find only one reference to *Antigone* in Pound's creative work; in Canto 88, he quotes ll. 338–39 in the original Greek to describe the later years of Nathaniel Macon (1758–1837), an American statesman:

> In 1828 Macon retired.
> Used plough and hoe until he was sixty
> Γᾶν ἄφθιτον ἀκαμάταν ἀποτρύεται
> [*Gān aphthiton akamatan apotruetai*, 'he furrows the imperishable, inexhaustible earth']
>
> 88/604; my trl

As to translating *Antigone*, Pound apparently felt that the best possible modern version was already available. In his 'Paris Letter' in the *Dial* of March 1923, Pound praised Jean Cocteau's condensed version of *Antigone* (1922) in colloquial modern French, in which he 'has got a simple and direct speech, most of the time', although 'the glued, glass ornament phrasing of the official classic translation obtrudes at moments. The virtues are probably shared about equally between Sophocles and the adapter' (Pound 1923, 278). In 'Jean Cocteau Sociologist', published in the *New English Weekly* of 10 January 1935, Pound stated that nothing 'has been more use to Cocteau than domesticity with the

Greek language' (*SP* 405) as this enabled him to write his Greek dramas *Antigone* and *Oedipe Roi* (1925). Pound then referred to his own attempts at translating Greek drama by writing that

> before Cocteau published any, Eliot and I looked over the ground. This is no place to say what we thought of it. But it is, permissibly, a place to register the fact that we DID nothing about it, except possibly form a few critical opinions that we wouldn't have had, if we hadn't prodded and poked at father Aeschylus.
>
> ibid.

According to Pound, Cocteau 'has brought not a resuscitated old corpse, but an ephèbe out of the sepulchre, with a young step and a living language … [a] language full charged with meaning', and thereby has 'enlightened [the] darkness' (ibid. 405–406). Pound continued his praise in *Guide to Kulchur* by claiming that Cocteau 'by sheer genius has resurrected' Greek drama:

> Antigone 'T'as inventé la justice' rings out in the Paris play house with all the force any man ever imagined inherent in greek originals.
>
> There is neither anything past, nor anything less than the maximum charge, in the contest of Cocteau's Antigone with his Creon.
>
> *GK* 93

Pound concluded briefly but quite definitively: 'Done once, immortally, and not to be undone or followed' (ibid. 94).

Notes

1. For an analysis of the use of the dialect by Eliot and Pound, see North, 77–99.
2. See Flack 131–49.
3. Examples given by Flack 145.
4. See Moody 167–216.
5. Pound told Hugh Kenner in a letter of January 1954 that he was now 'focusing on Dante & Sophocles' (quoted in Moody 349).
6. On Pound and Earp, also see Ingber 135–36.
7. The Pound-Earp correspondence can be found in the Beinecke 14/646.
8. The Pound/Fleming correspondence can be found in the Lilly Library at Indiana University, Ezra Pound Manuscripts II, Box 5. Hereafter referred to as Lilly.
9. Fleming also gave memorable readings of W. B. Yeats's Noh plays, and could recite long passages from James Joyce's *Finnegans Wake* by heart 'with inflections that demonstrated a deep understanding of the text'. See www.flashpointmag.com/ruddfleming.htm.

10 According to David Moody, Pound 'sponsored but could not sign a statement issued in 1953 by ten professors, among them Hugh Kenner, Rudd Fleming, and H. M. McLuhan, expressing alarm at "the neglect of the Greek and Latin classics, milleniar source of light and guide in judgment of ideas and forms in the occident". They wanted them revived in order to maintain the life of the mind here and now and tomorrow and elsewhere' (349).
11 Quoted in Reck 107–8. On Pound and Lekakis, see Marsh 2015, 34.
12 The Lilly Library at Indiana University has Fleming's typescript of the play in Ezra Pound Manuscripts II 1900–1973, Box 5.
13 The programme note of the 1987 New York production of *Elektra* generally concurs with this in its claim that 'In the character of Elektra [Pound] had found a perfect mirror for himself: a woman locked up, treated as if insane, desperate to remind the world of her identity and her sanity, waiting – endlessly waiting – for a rescuer'; quoted in Gainor, 30.
14 In his companion to *The Cantos*, Terrell on p. 527 has wrongly identified the source of the phrase 'Τὴν τῶν ὅλων ἀρχήν' [*Tēn tōn holōn archēn*] in Canto 89/598 as *Ajax* ll. 1105–6, as it actually comes from Julian's *First Oration: Panegyric of Constantius* 7B.

4

Sophocles, Pound and *Elektra* I

Introduction: scholarly approaches to *Elektra*

In his introduction to the play in his edition of the *Elektra* (1907), R. C. Jebb describes how the story of Orestes and Elektra is presented by Homer and the three Greek tragedians (Jebb 1907, ix–lxvi). Homer in the *Odyssey* regards the vengeance of Orestes as 'a simple act of retributive justice' (ibid. xi), while he does not mention Elektra at all. As the title of his trilogy already indicates, Aeschylus' *Oresteia* focuses on the consequences for Orestes of having committed matricide. Haunted by the Erinyes or Furies, he is acquitted by a jury led by the goddess Athena. Aeschylus swerved from Homer's depiction of Orestes by making it clear that he 'could be saved from the Erinyes only by divine aid' (ibid. xxiv). In all this, Aeschylus gives Elektra a lesser role than Sophocles later would. In the *Choephoroi*, her main dramatic function is the recognition of Orestes at their father's tomb, and the help she gives him in carrying out the vengeance from inside the house. She only takes part in the first third of the *Choephoroi*, after which she disappears from sight. In contrast, in Euripides' *Elektra*, she is a much stronger character than Orestes, and even has the main part in the murder of their mother. After the killing, both Elektra and Orestes feel remorse and guilt, something not touched upon by Sophocles in his play.[1]

Where Aeschylus emphasizes the complex moral issues involved and the divine agencies at work in 'the working of an eternal law', to which the human characters are subordinate, and where Euripides denounces the matricide and implicitly criticizes Apollo for his oracle commanding it, Sophocles' primary interest is in 'the portraiture of human character' (Jebb 1907, xxxviii). In his *Elektra*, Sophocles offers us an insight into the mind and heart of Elektra before, during, and (briefly) after the revenge taken for Agamemnon's death. Elektra has been suffering for years in the hope that her brother will return to avenge their father's death. The dramatist also introduces a sister, Chrysothemis, who by comparison is weaker, thereby giving Elektra more depth and heroic stature.

In Sophocles' play, Elektra 'is present almost from the beginning to the end of the play, and the series of her emotions is the thread which gives unity to the whole' (ibid. xliii).

Sophocles avoids or evades a moral stance in his play by focusing on the *act* of vengeance of Orestes, who has no moral qualms and feels justified in killing his mother because of the oracle of Apollo who authorized (or appeared to authorize) the matricide. After the murder of Klytaimnestra and Aigisthos, there are no retributive Erinyes unlike those found in Aeschylus, nor are we shown what Orestes may feel or think about his actions – which is the very thing that Euripides shows us in his *Elektra*. Sophocles further 'minimizes' the matricidal stain by making Klytaimnestra more villainous than Aeschylus, and by making the death of Aigisthos the climax of his play (thereby reinforcing the version given in the *Odyssey*), whereas in Aeschylus' and Euripides' versions he is killed before Klytaimnestra, with the result that her murder gains more weight (and thereby raises more questions about the justness of the matricide).

Indeed, Sophocles wrote at a time in which the issue of justice as an objective notion and unchangeable moral standard versus a more flexible interpretation or application in varying circumstances was under debate, particularly since the Sophists introduced the concept of moral relativism. Sophocles, however, does not seem to be interested in this matter, only in the way in which Elektra deals emotionally with her situation. The murder of Klytaimnestra seems to be the only way she can be relieved from her misery, and Orestes in this respect is the one saving her from her distress. By offering no clear-cut perspective on the question of moral justification and justness of the act of matricide, Sophocles' *Elektra* has produced various and often opposing interpretations.

In his introduction to his modern edition of *Elektra*, Kells offers an overview of the three different general approaches to the play dominating twentieth-century scholarship (Kells 2–5). First, the 'amoralists' claim that Sophocles indeed was not 'interested in the ethical or legalistic aspects of the story' but merely wanted to present an exciting narrative about Orestes' home-coming. Sophocles, like Homer, sees Orestes' act of vengeance simply as one of merit. This is the theory endorsed by Jebb and, although Kells does not mention Earp, this also seems to be the stance taken in *The Style of Sophocles*, in which Earp noted the 'epic' colouring of the play. After considering the explanations offered by others to account for its archaizing tone, such as the possibility that Sophocles may have been 'vying with' Aeschylus' *Choephoroi*, or to give an old-fashioned 'counterblast' to Euripides' *Elektra*, Earp argues that it is most likely that Sophocles 'disapproved of the morals of the story, and took this way of dissociating himself from them by reminding us that the story belongs to a primitive age'. As such, the epic touches employed in the play make 'the required actions natural', and stop us from seeing Orestes as a criminal (Earp 158–59).

Secondly, there is the 'justificatory' theory claiming that Sophocles did not wholly avoid the moral issue, but by having Apollo command the matricide and by making Klytaimnestra so villainous, Orestes need feel no guilt, while there is also no need of the Furies, as their darkness is overcome by the brightness of Apollo.

Thirdly, there is an 'ironic' theory put forward by J. T. Sheppard in the *Classical Review* in 1927, a reading of the play 'almost universally dismissed or ignored by modern critics' (Kells 5). The crux of Sheppard's theory lies in Orestes' account of the Oracle, which is rather ambiguous. We never get to know with certainty whether there was an oracular mandate or how it was worded – the Oracle at Delphi was known for its deceptive statements – as we only have Orestes' report of it in his own words. This is also why, for example, Orestes after the killing of Klytaimnestra replies to Elektra's question whether all is well: *tan domoisi men/ kalōs, Apollōn ei kalōs ethespisen* (S ll. 1424–25), 'Things in the house are well, if Apollo oracled well.' Why would Orestes use 'if', and doubt the justness of his cause? Critics dismissed Sheppard's theory for being too subtle, and thus likely to be unclear to the audience in a performance.

Interestingly enough, however, Pound seemed to have adopted a similar approach as he appeared to have struggled with his rendering of Orestes' account of the Oracle, as we will see. In a set of general notes appended to his translation, we may read: 'EI eTHespisen/// beginning of O's doubt of the oracle foreboding later madness' (*E* 103). This also makes clear that Pound was familiar with Euripides' *Orestes* in which Orestes goes mad after the matricide. He added a handwritten note in Fleming's fair copy about Sophocles' *Elektra* ll. 1424–25: 'The *EI* beginning of worry & later madness. Contrast of O[restes]. & E[lektra]. from now on' (ibid.).

In his *Greek Tragedy*, first published in 1939 and revised in 1950, thus around the time Pound was working on his version, the classical scholar H. D. F. Kitto offered a careful analysis of the notion of justice in Sophokles' *Elektra*, 'a play which has troubled Sophoclean criticism more than any' (Kitto 128). He focuses on the notion of *dikē*, 'justice', and its application to the question of matricide. He rejects Jebb's reading of the play and notes how throughout the play, Elektra remains singularly driven to expose and avenge the injustice committed by her mother. Everything leads implacably to the killing, and Sophocles presents it as it is, 'a grim and bloody business', not as 'a deed of simple merit' (129). Kitto also rejects Sheppard's theory, which argues that Apollo did not approve of the vengeance, but wanted to punish the presumption of Orestes who asked the oracle not 'whether he should do it, but how' (130). For this impiety he was punished.

So how then to explain the shocking presentation of a violent action approved by Apollo, something that Sophocles as upholder of conventional morality and religious belief would not have dared to criticize but which he also apparently did not want to defend or explain explicitly? To account for this, Kitto elaborates on the meaning of the words *theos* and *dikē*. We should in the case of *theos* or 'god' not see this divine power in our terms as 'a personal, beneficent god', but simply as 'a power'. *Dikē* covers various shades of meaning, which may include 'retributive justice', but 'an early meaning of it was simply "the way" of something, hence "the right way".' Philosophers would regard it as representing 'the balance of forces in Nature' (132).

Kitto sees *dikē* in *Elektra* as '"the proper and natural order of things"' (133) in human affairs, social and moral. If the order has been disturbed by something, the balance must be restored, and this need not necessarily be achieved in an agreeable manner. By her murder of Agamemnon, Klytaimnestra has disturbed the order, and it was the concern of all involved, gods, divine powers, and humans to restore *dikē*. This is why Sophocles did not let Apollo himself voice the command, as the act of vengeance was already the natural thing for Orestes to do to counter the original crime. Sophocles therefore could still present the matricide as horrible, and not show the consequences. It may not be the beginning of a better order, but at least the order for the moment has been restored. At the same time, Sophocles does not dismiss the gods, as he shows what the effect of Klytaimnestra's impious prayer to Apollo is. In this light, the actions performed by Orestes and Elektra are part of a larger design, the working out of a natural law supported by the gods, who also on their plane of reality are willing to have *dikē* restored. There is no evidence that Pound was familiar with Kitto's book (although Earp refers to it in his book on Sophocles on pp. 168–69), yet, as we will see, the poet also saw the play as one about the restoration of order, and *dikē* for him also meant more than 'justice', but was part of a larger cosmic pattern. A note from the late 1920s sheds light on Pound's perspective on the ethical issues involved:

> The American or English or Xtian morality is dastardly because it is a lie; it is false. Greek mythology and science alike show us not a strife between a good and

a bad but a conflict of forces and inertias, a conflict of different necessities, modalities, each good in or in certain degree. The moral problem is not so simple; it is not merely bilateral.

Pound 1996, 112

Pound's *Elektra*

Princeton Library has a set of Pound's early ribbon typescript drafts, with many handwritten corrections, additions, and deletions. There is also a ribbon typescript of the translation, again with many handwritten revisions. Using the line numbering of the Greek text at the top of the pages, Pound would give his drafts in ribbon typescript with many handwritten corrections, deletions, additions, and questions, to Rudd Fleming, who would type a fair copy which incorporated the manuscript annotations. Pound then made handwritten revisions and comments on this fair copy, to which Fleming in turn responded. As a letter of 18 March 1949, shows, Fleming read Pound's version carefully alongside the original Greek and Jebb's version, and praised the poet: 'all the translations wobble away in different directions. Yours is the only one with ictus.' He recommended that Pound should use an etymological dictionary for 'cruxes of meaning', but noted with regard to the section on which he had been focusing (which seems to be ll. 169–208) that he could not find 'anything definitely off in the words of [Pound's] translation' (Lilly).

Richard Reid, the editor of the version published in 1990, has noted that Pound often forgot or ignored his later emendations when he went over his first efforts which Fleming had transcribed in his fair copy. As a consequence, Reid's text represents the best possible effort to arrive at an edition of a translation which at the stage when Pound stopped working on it, was still provisional, and would remain so, since both Pound and Fleming intended to make major revisions, especially of the choral lyrics, but never did (*E* xxi). This is why in the typescripts, Pound referred to some of his attempts as 'scaffold or draft' or 'provisional as scaffold', and noted about the passage entitled 'ELEKTRA'S LAMENT', 'possible ameliorations WHEN the music is actually written'. In my analysis of *Elektra*, I have relied on Reid's edition with its *apparatus criticus* and notes, but will supplement this with references to archival draft material.

While working on his translation, Pound used the 1939 Loeb edition by F. Storr, originally published in 1913, which he annotated throughout, and which is now in his library at Brunnenburg. In my analysis I have used some of these annotations. Pound also owned a copy of Jebb's *The Tragedies of Sophocles, Translated into English Prose* (Cambridge 1905), but this edition, also now at Brunnenburg, does not contain any notes. As the drafts make clear, Pound at some point started using Jebb's bilingual edition with commentary, *Sophocles: The Plays and Fragments, Part 6: Elektra* (Cambridge 1894, repr. 1907). All of the notes made by Pound in his Loeb demonstrate how carefully he read the Greek text and wanted to make sense of the original in terms of semantics and syntax (there is only one explicit reference in the drafts to W. W. Goodwin's *A Greek Grammar* [1894]). He jotted down in the margins of the Loeb a considerable number of meanings of the Greek words, making use of *A Lexicon to Sophocles, Principally Abridged and Translated from Ellendt*, Oxford: D. A. Talboys, 1841 (the original dictionary being Frid. Ellendt, *Lexicon Sophocleum*, 2 vols, Regimont, 1835). We know that he consulted Ellendt not only because of the references to it in his typescripts, but as his copy at Brunnenburg shows, he even at times corrected the line numbers of *Elektra* and *Trachiniae* in his dictionary to synchronize these with his Loeb text. Yet it is also clear that on occasion he consulted the famous Liddell-Scott Greek-English Dictionary, with which he was very familiar, as, for example, Canto 23 makes clear.

Pound wrote down many verbs in Greek in the indicative form in his Loeb edition, sometimes with their meaning next to them, while sometimes pondering which tense in the original he was dealing with. Thus we find, for example, for ἔφυ [*ephu*] in l. 235 the note '3rd. 2nd. Aor.?'. He also struggled with certain forms that were out of the ordinary, such as the contraction ἅγω (*hagō*, l. 259), even wondering whether it was a misprint in his Loeb (*E* 93).[2] It is understandable that Pound was confused by the use of the Doric instead of the Attic dialect in choral passages so that, for example, in his Loeb he jotted next to ἅτις (*hatis*, l. 187), the Doric form of the Attic indefinite pronoun ἥτις [*hētis*], 'who', the gloss 'ἄτη calam.[ity] ἄτε in as much as'. In a letter of 18 March 1949, Fleming helped him by pointing out that 'The breathing of the first word is rough according to Jebb's translation, at least, as well as my text; and means "who", "I, who"' (Lilly).

Most of the annotations in the Loeb are in English, but Pound at times used other languages, such as the Italian *senza*, which he wrote next to ἄνευ [*aneu*] in l. 186, and to χωρὶς [*chōris*] in l. 945. Occasionally he also commented on the text. Pound's set of annotations vary from light to medium to heavy, with some passages containing more than others. By 'light' I mean that a page contains only one (annotated) word or an underlining. 'Heavily marked' indicates that the Greek and its facing translation are covered fully with notes in the margins, with all sorts of annotations added between the lines of the Greek text as well. I adhere to Tim Redman's comment in his catalog of Pound's library that the 'medium' category is 'the most subjective and means only that large area in between' (Redman 213–14).

In my analysis of Pound's version, I have indicated at the beginning of each new section the number of lines in Sophocles (given as S + line numbers), followed by those of Pound's version (given as *E* + line number), and the total number of lines of each text. This then may show to what extent Pound condensed or amplified the original. Pound's version uses 1,802 lines to render the 1,510 lines of the original, but this number includes 263 lines of the passages and lines giving the Greek in transliteration (141 lines), after which in most cases Pound offers a translation. It also includes the stage descriptions (122 lines), indicating who is being addressed and in what manner, as well as what is happening on the stage. Noteworthy extensions of the original are the choral Odes (because of the transliterations), the Fourth Scene (S ll. 871–1057 = *E* ll. 958–1194) of the Second Episode in which we see the confrontation between Elektra and Chrysothemis (lengthy because of transliterations and stage directions), and the Third Episode giving us the 'recognition' scene between Elektra and Orestes (lengthy for the same reasons).

Prologue (S ll. 1–120; *E* ll. 1–140)

In his *Style of Sophocles*, F. R. Earp dates each of the plays as early or late on the basis of the analysis of Sophocles' style. In contrast to *Trachiniae*, which Earp sees as an early play, *Elektra* has less Aeschylean ὄγκος [*onkos*] or weight, and then mainly in the lyrical parts, so that the diction has become less elaborate and more simple, designating it as relatively later play. Earp points out that the dialogues in the later plays generally are 'tense and dramatic', with a greater emphasis on argument, and as such ὄγκος would be inappropriate (Earp 61). Still, in a few scenes of the *Elektra*, the language is more formal, which must have been intended to give the play a more epic colouring (49). The style of *Elektra*, then, is a mixture of Sophocles' early, more formal, style, and the later, more natural, one.

Earp singles out the opening speeches of the Paedagogus and Orestes as, at first sight, exemplary of the early style, as they contain heavy compounds, similes, periphrases, and some Aeschylean 'weight'. Yet the language is also 'simple and direct', typifying the second style (Earp 135–36). In the opening speech (S ll. 1–22 = *E* ll. 1–25), the Paedagogus addresses his former pupil Orestes and his friend Pylades, who have arrived at Mycenae from Phocis. The old tutor reminds Orestes that he took him from Mycenae after Agamemnon's death so that he could be reared to become 'the avenger of your father's murder' (S l. 14). He then urges the two young men to plan their revenge quickly.

Pound's rendering of the Paedagogus' words uses colloquial and conversational speech, while making clear that the old man is still a servant who shows the right amount of deference to those above him. As such, the reference to Io as *Inachou korēs* (S l. 5), 'daughter of Inachus', becomes 'Miss Inachus' (*E* l. 5). The 'Miss' is not used ironically, as the Paedagogus later refers respectfully to Orestes' companion as 'your dear friend Mr Pilades, stranger in these parts' (*E* l. 20). This is an extended translation of the Greek phrase *philtate xenōn* (S l. 15), 'dearest of friends'. Pound apparently knew that *xenos* means both 'guest-friend' and 'stranger'.

Pound's version puts more emphasis on the reason for Orestes' return, as he amplifies and renders more explicitly Sophocles' line *poluphthoron te dōma Pelopidōn tode* (S l. 10), 'and this is the palace of the Pelopidae which has suffered many deaths', as 'Pelop's place, the throne room / where the dirty murder was done' (*E* ll. 12–13). (Note how Pound is able to retain the dominance of the *p*s and *d*s of the original phrase, and so its sound.) The adjective 'dirty' also introduces what will be a main theme in Pound's version, that of defilement and purgation.

The sense of urgency displayed by the Paedagogus at the end of his speech is made clear by Pound through the staccato, paratactic build up of phrases (while employing the same sort of imagistic juxtaposition also used to great effect in the 'Seven Lakes' Canto 49 and the *Confucian Odes*), thereby gaining speed when compared to, say, Jebb's version:

> Our plans must be laid quickly; for lo, already the sun's bright ray is waking the songs of the birds into clearness, and the dark night of stars is spent. Before, then, anyone comes forth from the house, take counsel; seeing that the time allows not delay, but is full ripe for deeds.
>
> Jebb 1907, 9–11

> Get goin' quickly.
> Sun's risin', birds are a singin',
> stars going down, darkness broken,
> Get going before people start moving about
> and be clear in your own minds what you're up to.
>
> *E* ll. 21–25

In this passage Sophocles is presenting what will be a leitmotif throughout the play: the distinction between *ergon*, the deed, in this case the act of taking revenge, on the one hand, and *logoi*, the 'words, words, words' derided in *Hamlet*, on the other. Pound will retain this opposition in his version, but his last line, 'and be clear in your own minds what you're up to', is also a variation on the notion of *chêng-ming*, which plays a major part in *The Pisan Cantos*. In the pre-Pisan *Cantos*, Pound had used the Chinese character *cheng*[4] several times, meaning 'precise, correct' but also carrying the moral meaning of 'just, righteous', in combination with *ming*[2], 'name', to create the ideogram 'to define the correct term', that is, the 'precise verbal definition' (*CON* 31).[3] This notion is necessary for anyone who wants to establish good government or to create perfect art. In *The Pisan Cantos*, which deal with the restoration of order, Pound regarded 'sincerity' as the source of origin of *chêng-ming*, as seen in Canto 77: 'only the total sincerity, the precise definition' (77/488). Chapter 25 of *The Unwobbling Pivot* explains why Confucius/Pound emphasized 'sincerity, the perfect word, or the precise word' (*CON* 95):

> He who defines his words with precision will perfect himself and the process of this perfecting is in the process [that is, ... the total process of nature].
>
> Sincerity is the goal of things and their origin, without this sincerity nothing is ... He who possesses this sincerity ... has a further efficiency in perfecting something outside himself ... The inborn nature begets this activity naturally, this looking straight into oneself and thence acting. These two activities constitute the process which unites outer and inner, object and subject, and thence constitutes a harmony with the seasons of earth and heaven.
>
> CON 177–79

Here we find the Confucian emphasis on self-discipline and sincerity as a means to create order within oneself and thence within the world, resulting in harmonious order. Self-discipline, knowing exactly what one wants, the truth of the good, and just action are all connected: 'Sincerity, this precision of terms is heaven's process. What comes from the process is human ethics' (*CON* 167). In other words, human ethics is heaven-born sincerity taking a 'visible' shape, and the 'precise definition' reveals to a person their true nature, enabling them to create harmony with themselves, their community and the universe. Pound's adoption of the 'Chinese' tone in the Paedagogus' recommendation to be clear thus links his version of the *Elektra* to his appropriation of Confucian thinking about moral responsibility and order.

While Pound made no annotations to the Paedagogus' speech in his copy of the Loeb edition, Orestes' speech (S ll. 23–76) is marked by heavy annotations on the left and right, Greek and translated, pages. Orestes shows he is heeding his tutor's dismissal of long deliberations. Kells in his commentary on *Elektra* has rightly pointed out how his speech displays 'a tendency to military terminology and military thinking', portraying Orestes as an impatient soldier ready for action (Kells 81). Pound keeps the military tone, and presents Orestes as an energetic and eager youngster:

> Therefore I will unfold our plans, and thou
> Note well my words, and if in aught I seem
> To miss the mark, admonish and correct.
>
> S ll. 29–31; tr. Storr 129

> This is what we're agoin' to do,
> listen sharp and check up if
> I miss any bullseyes.
>
> E ll. 31–33

Orestes informs the old man what Apollo at the oracle at Delphi ('the Pythoness' per Pound) told him to do: 'That I alone [*auton*], unfurnished [*askeuon*] with shields [*aspidōn*] or army [*stratou*], by stealth [*doloisi*] should steal [*klepsai*] the righteous [*endikous*] killing [*sphagas*] of my hand [*cheiros*]' (S ll. 36–37). Pound renders this as:

> Don't start a war,
> take a chance, do it yourself:
> Kinky course, clean in the kill.
>
> E ll. 37–39

Here we have a clear example of the clarity and economy of Pound's translated speech, in which he retains the -a- assonance of the original as well as the alliterative quality of Sophocles' first line in his own concluding line. Although this last line is a free interpretation, Pound produced it on the basis of what was first a more literal rendering, as the original typescript shows: 'twisty, stealthy [sneaky], but a just [due] kill'; here Pound is translating the operative words of line 37: *doloisi . . . endikous sphagas*. In the next phase of his translation, he already swerves from the text with '[a sneak's trick, but the kill is due]' (*E* 6), before giving the final version in which 'clean' is used as synonym for 'righteous' (*endikos*), a choice of which Fleming approved (*E* 91). As noted in the preceding chapter, we do not know exactly what the oracle said, and as such we are not certain whether it was the oracle itself which deemed the proposed killing *endikos*, or whether the phrase *cheiros endikous sphagas* actually represents Orestes' own words and his own 'estimation of the killing (which he assumed the oracle would agree with)' (Kells 82). This is, of course, an important issue as Orestes apparently feels justified in committing matricide on account of the oracle. Pound's choice of 'clean in the kill' neatly retains this ambiguity.

On the basis of the oracle, Orestes now unfolds his plans (S ll. 39–76 = E ll. 40–80). Here Pound stays close to the original Greek, even to the extent that the English becomes awkward on occasion. When Orestes commands his tutor to go into the palace and act as spy, which will be possible because no one will recognize him after these years 'under all this herbage' (*E* l. 45), Pound is literally translating *hōd' ēnthismenon* (S l. 43). In his typescript he jotted down the verb 'anthidZo', and most likely consulted his Liddell-Scott dictionary which translates the verb *anthidzō* as 'to strew or deck with flowers' (*ēnthismenon* is the perfect participle singular of this verb). Liddell-Scott mentions later that Sophocles used the verb metaphorically as 'dyed, disguised' – hence Jebb's 'with that silvered hair' (13) or Storr's 'thy white locks, the blossom of old age' (129). The line 'Make yr cock-crow' (*E* l. 46) is not to be found in the original, and may be Pound's second rendering of *hopōs an eidōs hēmin angeilēis saphē* (S l. 41), 'so that you may report to us from clear knowledge', which Pound had already given as 'and keep us wise to the lot of it' (*E* l. 43).

As part of the plot to deceive Aigisthos and Klytaimnestra, Orestes tells the Paedagogus to inform them that he was killed in a chariot-race at the Pythian games. At first Pound seems to deviate from the Greek when he gives *hōd' ho muthos hestatō* (S l. 50), 'let your story be so constituted', as 'Put in the details' (*E* l. 50). However, as Jebb has noted in his commentary, the Greek line implies that 'the whole story is to rest upon this basis' (Jebb 1907, 14), that is, it can be worked out further from this information. Pound's version focused on the potential narrative of the basic 'fact' of (the manner of) Orestes' death, thereby emphasizing (more than the original) the deceitful nature of the story.

Meanwhile Orestes and Pylades will go to Agamemnon's tomb with libations and *karatomois chlidais* (S l. 52), a phrase explained by Jebb as '"ornaments" [luxuriant locks] "cut from the head"' (Jebb 1907, 14), and rendered by Pound as 'an' all my pretty curls' (*E* l. 52). He was not sure about the tone here, as he wrote in the typescript: 'ironic?'. Fleming wrote in his fair copy that there is no irony in the Greek here, just as there is not in the other ritual passages: 'here the tone clashes with the original; in the translation the statement of Orestes has got to be ironic and so, throughout, the clash will have to be *used*; the modern speech will struggle against the ritual and sometimes win and sometimes be overridden by the pressures of the dramatic situation itself towards ritualistic expression' (*E* 92). Pound heeded this advice, as we see a similar use of ironic language later in *E* ll. 470–71 in the context of Chrysothemis' libations for Agamemnon's grave. By contrast, he consistently used irony in his renderings of Orestes' speech, presenting him as a sort of 1950s 'rebel with a cause' who held a wry perspective on the activities of the older generation.

After the visit to the grave, Orestes and Pylades will go the palace with the urn containing Orestes' ashes. Orestes does not mind lying about his own death (traditionally regarded as a self-fulfilling omen), as the surprise will be much greater when it will turn out that he is still alive. This part of the speech ends as follows: 'Thus I trust [*hōs epauchō*] that from this rumour [*tēsde tēs phēmēs apo*] I too [*kam'*] as a living person [*dedorkot'*] will yet shine/ flash forth [*lampsein eti*] like a star [*astron hōs*] upon my enemies [*echthrois*]' (S ll. 65–66). Pound's rendering continues the military tone Orestes adopted from the beginning, by stating that he would not mind using a lie 'if it lets me bust out afterward/ and explode 'em.' (*E* ll. 65–66), a departure from the sedate tone of the original.

Orestes' description of himself as *dikēi kathartēs pros theōn hōrmēmenos* (S l. 70), 'sent by the gods in justice as your purifier', is given by Pound (who in his edition of Storr wrote in the margin of the Greek text the word 'expiator') as 'this clean up/ the gods are in me to do this/ clean the old home' (E ll. 69–71). Hereby he combines the notions of the divine mandate and of divine assistance in what he has to do. The image of the 'clean up' is directly linked to the murder of Agamemnon, referred to by the Paedagogus earlier as 'dirty', and the rendering of *endikos* ('righteous') as 'clean'. Later in Pound's version we find Elektra hoping that Orestes will 'come back and clean up the dirt' (*E* l. 691), and criticizing her mother's marriage to Aigisthos: 'a dirty job to marry an enemy' (l. 681); when Klytaimnestra scolds her for her lack of shame, Elektra retorts: 'dirty workers teach dirty work' (l. 707); and at the end of the play, Orestes triumphantly states, 'The house is cleaned up' (l. 1680).

Pound extended the depiction of the restoration of order, not surprising given how this forms a key theme in the Pisan and post-Pisan Cantos. In Sophocles's version, Orestes prays that he will attain *archeplouton kai katastatēn domōn* (S l. 72). The word *archeplouton* is rather complex; Jebb gives it in his commentary as 'master of my possessions', but notes how others would understand it to mean 'having ancient wealth'. However, as Jebb argues, if the first part of the compound (*archē*, which can mean both 'rule' and 'beginning') denotes 'beginning' rather than 'ruling', then *archeploutos* should mean '"a *founder* of wealth"'. In his Loeb edition, Pound wrote in the margin 'founder of fortune' (and again heavily marked the word ἀρχαιόπλουτα at l.1393). Jebb decided to translate the line as 'but grant that I may rule over my possessions, and restore my house!' (Jebb

1907, 17), while Storr in the Loeb translation attempted to do more justice to the web of connotations of *archē* by providing two lines in translation: 'But O! restore to me its ancient wealth, / May I refound its old prosperity!' (Storr 131). Pound does the same in his version:

> give back the heritage
> that I bring back the old rule of abundance
> and make it solid.
>
> *E* ll. 73–75

Like the Paedagogus, Orestes favours action over speech: 'Nuff talk' (*E* l. 76). The call for effective action, as opposed to talking, is a thread running through the play. Ideas have to be put into action, a notion also advocated throughout *The Cantos*. In Canto 13 Confucius admonishes his students to 'Get up and do something useful' (13/59). Orestes, Pylades and the Paedagogus now set about executing their plans, and Orestes' speech ends with a maxim: 'For this is the occasion [*kairos gar*, that is, this is the exact moment to do what we now should be doing], which [*hosper*] is for men [*andrasin . . . est'*] the greatest ruler [*megistos epistatēs*] of every enterprise [*ergou pantos*]' (S ll. 75–76). Storr gives this as: 'And watch the time, for opportunity / Is the best captain of all enterprise' (131). Pound adapts this rendering, although he tries to make the Greek statement even more pithy and universal:

> We'll be out here and watch for the moment,
> the time.
>   Best leader men have.
>
> *E* ll. 78–80

The opening of the last third of the Prologus (S ll. 77–120 = *E* ll. 81–140) begins with the lament of Elektra who is still inside the palace. Pound wrote at this point in the margin of his Loeb, 'sigh is suppressed'. The Paedagogus assumes it is the voice of a servant ('Some slavey howling', *E* l. 82), but Orestes thinks it may be Elektra and wants to stay. His old tutor, however, urges him to first go to Agamemnon's tomb and carry out the plan as agreed. What follows is a lyric lament (S ll. 86–120 = *E* ll. 89–140) or *thrēnos* by Elektra, whose speech in free anapests contrasts with the preceding passage, given in more prosaic and regular iambic trimeters. While the dialogue between Orestes and the Paedagogus was a rational discussion about their plan, Elektra's monologue is an emotional expression of her grief about her father. In Pound's Loeb, we find light annotations to this speech until l. 99, after which the markings become heavy.

At this point Pound's version provides the first transliteration of the original Greek text in capital letters, perhaps as a means to stress the great musicality as well as the emotional weight of Elektra's speech. As Stergiopoulou has rightly argued, the Greek lines given in transliteration throughout Pound's version often perform an 'expressionistic function: they declare or immediately follow the determination to continue speaking, crying, cursing, asking for justice' (Stergiopoulou 2015, 99). Most of the time Pound translates these transliterated lines, but on occasion he allows the original Greek phrases to 'speak' for themselves.

Pound begins Elektra's speech with a transliteration and its translation ('OO PHAOS HAGNON/ Holy light'), but he chooses not to translate the next Greek phrase:

Earth, air about us,
>   THRENOON OODAS POLLAS
>   D'ANTEREIS AESTHOU
tearing my heart out

E ll. 91–94

The (incorrect) Greek transliteration 'THRENOON OODAS/ POLLAS D'ANTEREIS AESTHOU' literally means, 'you have heard [*ēisthou*] the strains [*ōidas*] of my lament [*thrēnōn*], and the many straight [*pollas d'antēreis*]'.[4] In Pound's version the Greek phrase in transliteration is incomplete as the phrase *sternōn plēgas haimassomenōn*, 'blows upon my bleeding breast', of the line following should be supplied. Pound may have wanted to connect all the adjectives in his transliteration as qualifiers to the one noun *ōidas*, which then would have been translated as follows: 'you have heard the many straight strains of my lament'. Whereas in the original text Elektra states that the Chorus may have heard her beating her breast with her hands, Pound's line 'tearing my heart out' modernizes the expression of her grief and makes it almost literally heart-rending.

In his rendering of Elektra's speech, Pound has gone for emotional musicality, with impressive results. For example, the èta of the Greek word 'ANTEREIS' (ἀντήρεις) is evoked in Pound's 'air', 'tearing' and 'heart', while 'THRENOON' is sonically linked with 'Earth'. The result is that the 'soundscapes' of the Greek and the English are turned into a harmonious whole, where one is not given more weight than the other, but are made interdependent. The Greek gives rise to the English rendering, just as the rendering evokes the Greek, making both texts contemporaneous.[5]

In the following lines, Pound has managed to give a twist to the original by re-assembling some of the Greek words. The Greek reads:

τὰ δὲ παννυχίδων ἤδη στυγεραὶ
ξυνίσασ' εὐναὶ μογερῶν οἴκων,
ὅσα τὸν δύστηνον ἐμὸν θρηνῶ
πατέρ', ὃν κατὰ μὲν βάρβαρον αἶαν
φοίνιος Ἄρης οὐκ ἐξένισεν,
μήτηρ δ' ἡμὴ χὠ κοινολεχὴς
Αἴγισθος ὅπως δρῦν ὑλοτόμοι
σχίζουσι κάρα φονίῳ πελέκει,

ll. 92–99

And the wretched couch [*stugerai eunai*] of my woeful house [*mogerōn oikōn*] knows [*xunisas'*] by now [*ēdē*] my all-nighters [*ta pannuchidōn*], [knowing] how often [*hosa*] I weep [*thrēnō*] for my unhappy father [*ton dustēnon emon pater'*], to whom [*hon*] bloody Ares [*phoinios Arēs*] did not give his welcoming gift [*ouk exenisen*] in a foreign land [*kata barbaraon aian*, that is, Agamemnon did not get the honourable gift of being killed before Troy], but my mother [*mētēr hēmē*] and her bedsharing Aigisthos [*chō koinolechēs Aigisthos*] split open [*schidzousi*] his head [*kara*] with a murderous axe [*phoniōi pelekei*], just as [*hopōs*] woodmen [*hulotomoi*] <fell> an oak [*drun*].[6]

In his version Pound turned the Sophoclean passage into:

all night already horrible
been with me
my father weeping
there in that wretched house
weeping his doom
Not killed abroad in the war
but by mother and her bed boy Aegisthus.
Split his head with an axe as
a woodcutter splits a billet of oak,

E ll. 96–104

Here l. 96 is a literal rendering of the order of the Greek words in line 92 of the original, whereby the adjective 'horrible' qualifying the couch is now made to describe the night. 'Been with me' seems to be Pound's hasty translation of *xunisas'*, on the apparent assumption that here *xun-* or *sun-*, 'with', was combined with *isas'* as a form of the verb *einai*, 'being', instead of *oida*, 'to know'. However, it may well be that Pound wanted to give a more detailed depiction of how

Elektra keeps seeing the image of her father before her eyes every night. This would explain why he violated Greek grammar by turning the main verb *thrēnō*, 'I weep' (which is what Elektra is doing for her father), into a present participle. This presents Agamemnon himself in his lamentable state (as a haunting ghost): 'my father weeping'. Then Pound inserts a Greek phrase from an earlier line, *mogerōn oikōn*, 'wretched house', before turning the adjective *dustēnon*, 'unhappy', into a noun ('doom') as the object of Agamemnon's weeping. While the reference to Ares is periphrastically described in the original, Pound's version makes it explicit, replacing the more neutral 'bed-sharing' with the more explicit denunciatory alliterative compound 'bed-boy'. The gravity of the murder is given by Pound in a line of monosyllables (*E* l. 103), that could be seen as spondaic, while the ease of its execution is emphasized through a tripping rhythm (l. 104). Combined with the departures from the original grammatical construction, this produces a powerful evocation of Elektra's grief.

Pound takes this one step further in the lines following (*E* ll. 107–19), a very free rendering of Sophocles ll. 103–109:

> ἀλλ' οὐ μὲν δὴ
> λήξω θρήνων στυγερῶν τε γόων,
> ἔστ' ἂν παμφεγγεῖς ἄστρων
> ῥιπάς, λεύσσω δὲ τόδ' ἦμαρ,
> μὴ οὐ τεκνολέτειρ' ὥς τις ἀηδὼν
> ἐπὶ κωκυτῷ τῶνδε πατρῴων
> πρὸ θυρῶν ἠχὼ πᾶσι προφωνεῖν.

> Yet [*all'*] I will never stop [*ou men dē lēxō*] with my laments [*thrēnōn*] and wretched cries of sorrow [*stugerōn go-ōn*], as long as [*est'*] I see [*an leussō*] the all-shining [*pamphengeis*] vibrations [*ripas*] of the stars [*astrōn*], and this day [*tod' ēmar*], nor [*mē ou*] (will I stop) to proclaim [*prophōnein*] with wailing [*epi kōkutōi*] before these doors of my father [*tōnde patrōiōn pro thurōn*] my resounding cry [*echō*] to all [*pasi*], like the nightingale [*hōs tis aēdōn*] that killed her child [*teknoleteir'*, that is, Procne, mother of Itys, whom she fed to Tereus].

> Well I'm not going to forget it
> and the stars can shine on it, all of them
> tears of hate
> all flaming rips of the stars
> tide
> destiny
> and the day can look on it

I won't stand it and just keep quiet
>   ALL' OU MEN DE
>   LAEXOO THRENOON
You cant stop the nightingale crying, for her young, or me
on this house porch
let everyone hear it

E ll. 107–19

Line 107 is Pound's own addition, and at first it seems he has mistranslated *lēxō*, but it is clear that he knows its meaning, as he has transposed the verb to line 114: 'I won't ... keep quiet', followed it with the transliteration of the Greek words, emphasizing again the highly emotional state of Elektra who calls out for justice. Note how the last word of the transliteration, 'THRENOON', recalls its earlier use in line 92. Pound's rendering is an assemblage of words and phrases plucked from the Greek, where *pamphengeis astrōn* has produced both 'the stars can shine on it, all of them' (where the 'all' is taken from the *pam-*), as well 'all flaming rips of the stars'. In the latter phrase Pound has retained the melopoeic quality of the Greek *ripas* ('vibrations'), which (with possible interference from Pound's knowledge of Latin, in which *ripa* means 'bank of a river', 'shore of the sea') has produced 'tide', an appropriate apposition to 'tears of hate', Pound's rendering of *stugerōn go-ōn*. 'Destiny' may be the result of looking up the word ἦμαρ [*ēmar*] in Liddell-Scott, where the word for 'day' in combination with certain adjectives in Homer becomes 'the day of destiny', while Pound makes 'day' the subject instead of the object of the verb *leussō*, 'I see'. The result is an evocation of Elektra's state of mind, amplifying her grief in an almost paradoxical minimum of words. Stergiopoulou gives a metrical analysis of the opening song, and argues that Pound's rendering tries to produce quantitative equivalence by using spondees to mirror the long syllables of the Greek original provided in transliteration, employing words with long vowel sounds ('tears', 'hate', 'flaming', 'tide', 'destiny', 'day'), culminating in the line 'I wont stand it and just keep quiet'. However, she has to admit that 'in English prosody, unlike in Greek, one does not pronounce each syllable identically because stress or other pronunciation factors take over' (Stergiopoulou 2015, 102).

At the end of her lament (S ll. 110–20), Elektra prays to the powers associated with the Underworld to avenge her father's death. These are King Hades ('Hell'), Queen Persephone, and Hermes the *psychompompos* or guide of souls to the land of the dead. These powers also include Ara, here the personification of the curse or the prayer for vengeance uttered by the victim upon his murderer(s); and the Erinyes, called 'god seed' by Pound as he may have read the Latin word *semen* in *semnai theōn paides* (S l. 112), 'venerable children of the gods'. It is noteworthy that Pound again balances the Greek and the English, as the transliterations he gives from Sophocles ('OO DOOM' AIDOU/ OO CHTHONI'.../ ARA'; S ll. 110–11) find a counterpart in the capitalized English word 'CURSE' (*E* l. 127). Moreover, Pound now lets his rendering precede as well as follow the transliterated Greek of ll. 113–20, thereby moving freely between the two languages on an equal footing.[7] By dividing the translation of this emotional prayer and giving it before and after the transliteration, the latter part of Elektra's request is emphasized: 'and/ send me my brother/ I can do no more on my own/ this grief is too heavy' (*E* ll. 136–40).

Parodos (S ll. 121–250; *E* 141–305)

In the Parodos, heavily annotated in Pound's Loeb, the Chorus of older women enter. They point out to Elektra how she should overcome her grief, to keep hoping for Orestes' reappearance, and try to establish a more conciliatory relationship with her mother and Aigisthos. Elektra, however, feels that any change on her part would mean a certain disloyalty to her father. The form used here is that of a *kommos*, or dialogue, in an intricate rhythm between actor and chorus, consisting mainly of aeolics and dactyls. Pound made no attempt to reproduce these, or to come up with an internally consistent use of metre that would mark off the Parodos as a separate unit.

Pound gives the first strophe of the Chorus (S ll. 121–28) in a correct transliteration (apart from rendering OOD' without the aspiration), which indicates he was using Storr's Loeb edition for the Greek, as Jebb's text turns ll. 122–23 into one single line. The translation which follows is one of the best and most creative passages of his version. Giving first Pound's own transliteration (in capitals), I provide a literal translation, and then give Pound's rendering:

> O child [OO PAI], Elektra, child of a most wretched mother [PAI DUSTANOTATAS MATROS], why are you always pining [AEI TAKEIS] thus [{h}OOD'] in this insatiable lament [TIN' AKORESTON OIMOOGAN] for Agamemnon who long ago [TON PALAI AGAMEMNONA] was caught [HALONT'] in a most unholy manner [ATHEOOTATA] by the deceit [APATAIS] of your treacherous mother [EK DOLERAS MATROS], betrayed [PRODOTON] by an evil hand [KAKAI TE CHEIRI]? May the one who did this perish [HOOS HO TADE POROON OLOIT'], if it is allowed [EI THEMIS] for me [MOI] to say this [TAD'AUDAN].
>
> *E* ll. 141–47

> Poor Elektra
> you had a curse for a mother
> and are withered with weeping,
> Agamemnon was tricked and murdered.
> That was a long time ago,
> but a dirty hand did it, maternal,
> and to breed their destruction
> if my deem is heard in dooming.
>   EI MOI THEMIS TAD' AUDAN.
>
>   *E* ll. 148–56[8]

Sophocles' *dustanotatas*, 'most wretched', may either refer to Klytaimnestra's own pitiful state as the wife of Agamemnon, or to her wickedness, and Pound has been able to retain this ambiguity through 'you had a curse for your mother'. The phrase has Elektra blaming the deceit of her mother for the murder, while at the same time making her part of the larger fabric of the curse that has damned the family of the Atreids for generations. Pound's rendering has cut down the original to its essentials, while adding musicality by means of alliteration: 'withered with weeping', 'a dirty hand did it', 'my deem is heard in dooming' – with 'dirty' yet again evoking the theme of purgation. Moreover, the passage has a dental soundscape which culminates in the transliteration of the Greek line, with 'deem is' a sonic equivalent of 'THEMIS'. Although 'AUDAN' means 'to say', there may have been in Pound's ear an interference of the Latin *audire*, 'to listen', so he translates it as 'is heard'. Pound also puts poetic emphasis on Klytaimnestra's involvement in the murder by adding the word 'maternal' in paratactic apposition after 'a dirty hand', and implicitly includes Aigisthos in the Chorus' prayer for 'their destruction' without naming him – just as the Greek HO POROON makes clear that the Chorus is referring to a man without making explicit whom they mean. Pound emphasizes the respect of the Chorus at this stage by having the last line of the longer transliteration recur here, rounding off his rendering, by giving their modest prayer twice.

Pound then gives us Elektra's response (S ll. 129–36) in transliteration, again preceded and followed by a translation. He reduces the more periphrastic Greek to a few short phrases, while adding the word 'dead' twice (in the original, Agamemnon is called *athlios*, 'miserable'). In the following I have translated the response, using Pound's transliteration:

> O children of noble parents [OO GENETHLA GENNAIOON], you have come [HEKET'] in consolation [PARAMUTHION] for my sorrows [EMOON

KAMATOON]. I know [OIDA] and I understand [TE KAI XUNIEMI] this [TADE'], and it does not escape me [OU TI ME PHUNGANEI], but I do not want [OUD' ETHELOO] to give this up [PROLIPEIN TODE], and not lament [ME OU STENACHEIN] my miserable father [TON EMON PATER' ATHLION]. But [ALL'] oh you repaying [OO AMEIBOMENAI] kindness [CHARIN] in every sort of friendship [PANTOIAS PHILOTETOS], leave me [EATE M'] thus to wander [OOD' ALUEIN, that is, 'wander in distress', as Pound noted in his Loeb], alas [AIAI], I beg you [HIKNOUMAI]

E ll. 161–68

In his version of this passage, Pound retains the essence in his rendering of a few of the Greek words, and even repeats some of his phrases, thereby depicting an Elektra who cannot rest:

> Yes, you are come nobly to help me,
> I can feel that,
> But I must go on.
> DEAD, he is dead, I must go on
> ....
> (*to Chorus*) It's my job,
> I have never asked to neglect it
> Let me go alone
>
> *E* ll. 157–60, 169–71

Where Orestes sees it as his 'job' to avenge his father's murder, a task described by the Chorus as a 'big job' (*E* l. 370), Klytaimnestra will later justify Agamemnon's murder as a 'good job' (*E* l. 606), while Elektra regards the mourning of her father as her 'job' (*E* l. 169), a constant reminder of the injustice that needs to be put right.

In his translation of the Chorus' reply (*S* ll. 137–43) in the first Anti-strophe, Pound initially translates a few lines and then gives the transliteration while making clear in a stage direction what its purpose is: '*emphatic and explicit with meaning to ram it in*' (*E* l. 176). Pound hammers home the message by repeating the Greek word AMEXANON, 'without remedy, helpless', as 'nothing to be DONE' (*E* l. 184); that is, Elektra's grief serves no further purpose in the eyes of the Chorus. Elektra counters (*S* ll. 144–52) that a child must never forget parents who have died miserably, and she sympathizes with the nightingale (Procne) mourning for Itys, and with Niobe who never gave up lamenting the loss of her children. Pound supplies a full transliteration while showing that these mythological models of steadfast bereavement are at the core of her speech. The transliteration is preceded by a phrase taken from it ('a ITUN aien Itun', l. 188), and ends with a repetition of the last two transliterated lines (*E* ll. 203–04). Pound's version may be compared to a literal translation:

> Foolish [NEPIOS] is he who [HOS] forgets [EPILATHETAI] his parents [TOON GONEOON] who died pitiably [OIKTROOS OICHOMENOON]. But [ALL'] the mournful bird [HA STONOESS' ORNIS] fits [ARAREN] me, that is, my mind [EME ... PHRENAS], the distraught bird [ORNIS ATUDZOMENA], the messenger of Zeus [DIOS ANGELOS, that is, in announcing the new season of Spring], who always mourns for Itys, Itys [HA ITUN AIEN ITUN OLOPHURETAI]. Ah [IOO] all-suffering Niobe [PANTLAMOON NIOBA], I deem you a god [SE D' EGOOGE NEMOO THEON], you who [HAT'] are forever weeping [AIEI DAKRUEIS] in a rocky tomb [EN TAPHOOI PETRAIOOI].
>
> S ll. 144–52 = E ll. 189–96

In his version Pound emphasizes the first line by giving two different translations of it, while turning the general maxim into Elektra's personal observation by letting her internalize it, and substituting 'him' (=Agamemnon) for 'his parents'. The reference to Itys then immediately precedes and follows the transliteration, but Pound conflates the image of nightingale, the song it sings, and the cause of the song:

> I think my mind groans [transposing the adjective STONOESS' belonging to ORNIS to Elektra's PHRENAS] as the sound of Itys/ lamenting, terrified [combining the adjectives STONOESS' and ATUDZOMENA with the verb OLUPHURETAI] / bringing the news from Zeus
>
> E ll. 197–99

In Sophocles' play, this is the second reference to Procne and Itys (see S l. 107 = *E* l. 117), and it may have struck a particular chord in Pound who had used the myth in Canto 4 (13–14), and more recently in Pisan Cantos 78 (497) and 82 (545). He rounds off the speech by repeating in transliteration the depiction of Niobe. The phrase 'a better portion from heaven' (*E* l. 201), with which Elektra in his rendering is expressing her envy of Niobe's fate, is based on *nemō theon*, 'I think [you are] a god', as *nemō* can also mean 'distribute, to have as one's portion'.

The first half of the second Strophe of the *kommos* is sung again by the Chorus (S ll. 153–63), who implicitly criticize Elektra by pointing out that she is not the only one who lost a father, and that her sisters do not wallow in their grief. They also hope that Orestes will return. In the Greek his name gets full weight as it is withheld until the very end of their speech. Pound managed to retain this effect by alternating transliterated lines with his rendering, so that he at first refers to Orestes as Elektra's 'boy brother', and then gives the last four lines in Greek, ending in 'ORESTAN', preceded and followed by a translation in English:

> god send 'un back to Mycenae
> Happy [OLBIOS], whom [HON] the famous land of Mycenae [HA KLEINE GA MUKENAIOON] one day [POTE] will receive/welcome [DEXETAI] as a noble of the country [EUPATRIDAN], coming to this land [MOLONTA TANDE GAN] with the kindly guidance of Zeus [DIOS EUPHRONI BEMATI], Orestes [ORESTAN].
> Pound's transliteration; my trl
>
> (*English echo*)
>
> till Orestes come to the t h r o n e
> *E* ll. 216–22

The '*echo*' here signifies both a stage direction as well as a self-reflective indication that the line following is a translation, while the lengthening typography iconically reinforces this. Note how Pound has retained the -o- assonance of the original.

In her response Elektra expresses how much she is yearning for her brother to appear (S ll. 164–72). It is noteworthy that at this point Pound stays much closer to the Greek text than before, and does not include a transliteration, perhaps because he felt how successful his rendering was on its own. This includes spondaic (emotional) weight in the sequence 'childless, wretched/ unwed', which is followed by a semi-couplet, 'in a dither of fear/ muddly with tears' (*E* ll. 225–26), rhythmically effective in its sequence of two choriambs: 'in a **dith**er of **fear**/ **mud**dly with **tears**' (bold markings mine). Moreover, 'muddly with tears' is an attempt at homophonic equivalence of the Greek *dakrusi mudalea* (S l. 166) 'wet with tears'. There is also an iconic lengthening of the next line to stress Elektra's 'endless doom of woe' (Jebb 31): 'one thing after another, unending, and always worse;' (*E* l. 227).

In contrast, the Chorus' advice to Elektra in the Second Anti-strophe (S ll. 173–92) to take heart by pointing out that Zeus, Time, Orestes, and Hades have not forgotten about her, is not translated at all, but only given in transliteration (again the length and number of lines confirm that Pound employed Storr's Greek text instead of Jebb's). It may be that Pound assumed that the audience would think that this was yet another attempt by the Chorus to soothe Elektra, and decided simply to let the Greek speak for itself, and be sung for musical effect. The stage direction '*(chorus moving/ clear cut position: pause/ move)*' (*E* l. 233) here is ambiguous as it may indicate the physical movement of the Chorus, yet could also be regarded as a summary of what they are claiming. The repetitiveness of the Chorus' arguments is then reinforced by Pound who, after Elektra's reply, repeats the exact same passage ('*Chorus (chorus moving/ pause/ move)* THARSEI MOI etc . . . . ANASSOON.'; *E* 14, ll. 252–53). Fleming agreed with this repetition but only 'if sung' (*E* 13–14). This is, with one exception, the last of transliterations in this *kommos*.

While Pound gives the Chorus's Greek lines twice in transliteration, he also renders Elektra's response (S ll. 184–92) twice albeit with major variations in the second iteration. Here is the original passage:

ἀλλ' ἐμὲ μὲν ὁ πολὺς ἀπολέλοιπεν ἤδη
βίοτος ἀνέλπιστος, οὐδ' ἔτ' ἀρκῶ·
ἅτις ἄνευ τεκέων κατατάκομαι,
ἇς φίλος οὔτις ἀνηρ ὑπερίσταται,
ἀλλ' ἁπερεί τις ἔποικος ἀναξία
οἰκονομῶ θαλάμους πατρός,
ὧδε μὲν ἀεικεῖ σὺν στολᾷ,
κεναῖς δ' ἀμφίσταμαι τραπέζαις.

But [*all'*] with regard to me [*eme men*] the largest part of my life [*ho polus biotos*] has already gone [*ēdē apoleloipen*], without hope [*anelpistos*], and I no longer have strength [*oud' et' arkō*]: I who [*hatis*] am wasting away [*katatakomai*] without children [*aneu tekeōn*], whom [*has*] no loving man [*philos outis anēr*] protects [*huperistatai*], but [*all'*] like [*haperei*] some unworthy foreign resident [*tis epoikos anaxia*] I manage [*oikonomō*] the rooms [*thalamous*] of my father [*patros*], such as I am [*hōde*] with this shabby [*aeikei*] dress [*stolai*], and I stand [*amphistamai*, that is, have to eat standing instead of lying during meals like a mistress] at empty tables [*kenais trapezais*, that, empty because by the time she is allowed to eat, the food has gone.]

S ll. 184–92

Pound's first rendering (*E* ll. 244–51) is more succinct than the second one (*E* ll. 254–62). The latter one added the phrase 'fatherless' and deleted Elektra's reference to her lack of children. There may be two reasons for this: perhaps Pound wanted the combination 'fatherless/ loverless' (with the addition of 'without stand-bye' in the second rendering) to stand for her feeling of being deprived of a strong man who would help her overcome her current miserable state (an absence which would make the return of Orestes an even greater necessity). It is more likely, however, that he looked at the Loeb edition which, like Jebb's, in l. 187 has *tekeōn*, 'children', where the Greek manuscripts have *tokeōn*, 'parents'. But while Jebb translated the phrase *aneu tekeōn* correctly as 'without children' (Jebb 1907, 33), Storr, for whatever reason, went against his own Greek text and rendered *tekeōn* as 'Without a parent's love', reinforced a line later by 'An orphaned maid' (Storr 141). Perhaps misled by this, Pound in his edition wrongly wrote 'parent' as a gloss to τεκέων.

Pound's first rendering of Elektra's speech contains the rather awkward phrase 'housed beneath my father's bed', clearly based on *oikonomō thalamous patros*, 'I manage the rooms of my father'. Pound had used the Homeric word *thalamus* in the 'Odyssean' Canto 39 (194), where it indicated the bedroom. Then he improved upon this phrase in the second version: 'roofed where my father wed'. Pound does not give us *tis epoikos anaxia*, 'some unworthy foreign resident', the first time, but adds 'a worthless waif' in the repeated passage. Both times he understandably retains the alliterative 'shapeless sack' with the -a- assonance for *aekei stola*, but he has some difficulty with the last line, *kenais d' amphistamai trapezais*. The first time he produces a homophonic 'kenneled' for *kenais*, which then evokes Elektra's feeling that she is treated like a dog. He leaves this out in the second passage by giving a literal translation, and adding an extra line to clarify what the image means: 'to stand around the empty tables/ and to be fed on their trash' (*E* 14, ll. 261–62). It may well be that here again he consulted Storr who has Elektra waiting 'On fragments feeds' (Storr 141) – while the sound of the Greek word *trapezais* may have suggested the English 'trash'.

The Chorus opens the Third Strophe (S ll. 193–212) by depicting the murder of Agamemnon and its causes, and as such picks up on Elektra's reference to her father. Unlike Aeschylus who has Agamemnon murdered in his bath, Sophocles follows Homer by having him killed while lying on the couch at the dinner-table. Pound has retained the repetition of the word 'gloomy' (*oiktra*) to denote both Klytaimnestra's voice welcoming home her husband as well as Agamemnon's death-cry. Pound's ll. 266–70 constitute a powerful rendering of the original:

> Cunning was the planner, lust the killer,
> Both breeding terribly a terrible
> Shape, whether it was a god or one of the mortals
> Who did the deed.
>
> S ll. 197–200

> A twisty idea
> and a letch that killed him,

one vehemence led to another
procreating the form
whether god or man did it.

E 14

Elektra then recalls her father's murder (S ll. 201–12) at that *deipnōn arrētōn*, 'unspeakable dinner' ('beyond speakable language' in Pound), but where in the original she only imagines her father as seeing his own death at 'their twin hands', Pound turns the girl into an actual witness of the murder: 'I saw my father killed by the pair of 'em' (*E* l. 275) This is noteworthy as in his typescript he was still true to the perspective of the original: 'watched himself being killed impiously by the double hand', with Fleming adding: 'watched himself being killed' (*E* 15). Did Pound change this for dramatic effect, thereby making Elektra's trauma even more credible? She then prays to Zeus to avenge Agamemnon's death, and here Pound's version is more bitter and emotional in comparison to the original:

> May the great Olympian god [*theos ho megas Olumpios*] give [*poroi*] them [*hois*] avenging sufferings [*poinima pathea*] to suffer [*pathein*], and never [*mēde pot'*] may they benefit [*aponaiato*] from their splendour [*aglaias*], who have done such deeds [*toiad' anusantes erga*]

S ll. 209–12

> Zeus avenger, don't let 'em enjoy it unpunished,
> make it hurt. Them in their luxury! Agh!

E ll. 278–79

Aglaia can mean 'splendour, beauty, adornment', but also 'pomp, show, vanity'. Pound brilliantly retained its double sense with 'luxury', which plays on the Latin *lux*, 'light'.

In the Third Anti-strophe (S ll. 213–32), the Chorus again tries to calm Elektra down as they find her state of mind excessive, and only perpetuating her suffering. Instead, she should accept reality and try to come to terms with those in power now, advice which echoes throughout the play, as we will see: *ta de tois dunatois/ ouk erista plathein* (S ll. 219–20), 'but these matters cannot be disputed with the ones in power so as that one comes into conflict with them.' Pound renders this as: 'Don't take the discussable to the powerful / only give 'em a handle' (*E* ll. 283–84). In the typescript, Pound still had ll. 218–20 of the original in transliteration, but this was deleted from the printed version. However, he did transliterate the first line of Elektra's response, most likely to stress again the power of her emotions at this point: '*ELEKTRA (starts as if muttering)/*

DEINOIS ENANKASTHEN' (*E* ll. 285–86). The Greek phrase means 'I have been compelled by terrible things', that is, Elektra '*knows* that her conduct is abnormal. She has been *compelled* to it by her character and circumstances' (Kells 95–96). By cutting down Elektra's twelve lines (S ll. 221–32) to five, including the transliteration, Pound depicts the girl as both being tired of the Chorus' advice, however well-meant, as well as hardly able to express her grief and anguish. The last word in the Greek is *thrēnōn* (S l. 232), which is neatly captured in 'Let me have my cry out' (*E* l. 290).

We now come to the concluding Epode of this *kommos* (S ll. 233–50). The Chorus hastens to assure Elektra that they spoke to her out of motherly love, which harks back to the mother-image with which they began their advice (and which Pound retains, even adding 'dearie'). Elektra then reacts by universalizing her situation in a speech that makes clear the moral issues involved. Pound clearly struggled with the rendering of her words. The original reads:

καὶ τί μέτρον κακότατος ἔφυ; φέρε,
πῶς ἐπὶ τοῖς φθιμένοις ἀμελεῖν καλόν;
ἐν τίνι τοῦτ' ἔβλαστ' ἀνθρώπων;
μήτ' εἴην ἔντιμος τούτοις
μήτ', εἴ τῳ πρόσκειμαι χρηστῷ,
ξυνναίοιμ' εὔκηλος, γονέων
ἐκτίμους ἴσχουσα πτέρυγας
ὀξυτόνων γόων.
εἰ γὰρ ὁ μὲν θανὼν γᾶ τε καὶ οὐδὲν ὢν
κείσεται τάλας,
οἱ δὲ μὴ πάλιν
δώσουσ' ἀντιφόνους δίκας,
ἔρροι τ' ἂν αἰδὼς
ἁπάντων τ' εὐσέβεια θνατῶν.

S ll. 236–50

But what limit/proportion [*kai ti metron*] is there [*ephu*] to [my] suffering [*kakotatos*]? Tell me [*phere*], how can it be right [*pōs kalon*] to not care [*amelein*] about the dead [*epi tois phtimenois*]? In what human being [*en tini anthrōpōn*] was this [*touto*] inborn [*eblast'*]? May I never be held in honour among such [*mēt' eiēn entimos toutois*], never [*mēt'*], if I am involved [*proskeimai*] with something good [*tōi chrēstōi*], may I live with it [*xunnaioim'*] free from care [*eukēlos*], restraining [*ischousa*] the wings [*pterugas*] of sharp-toned lamentations [*oxutonōn go-ōn*] that dishonour [*ektimous*] my parents [*goneōn*]. For if [*ei gar*] he, the wretched dead [*ho thanōn talas*], is to lie [*keisetai*] in earth and nothingness [*ga te kai ouden ōn*], and *they* [*hoi*] will not give in return [*mē palin dōsous'*] the penalty for murder [*antiphonous*] of justice [*dikas*], then respect [*aidōs*] and reverence [*eusebeia*] must be gone [*erroi an*] from all mortals [*hapantōn thnatōn*].

This is one of the most linguistically complex passages in the play. In the following I will trace the process from typescript to printed version for some of the lines.[9]

For Sophocles' l. 236, Pound first produced a line constructed on the basis of what he apparently saw as the two key words: *metron*, 'limit', and *kakotatos* (which he took to be the superlative form of *kakos*, 'bad', instead of the genitive form of *kakotēs*, 'evil' or 'misery'). This resulted in 'But the worst goes beyond all limit', which distorts the Greek. He then realized that Elektra is talking about her *own* situation, so after several attempts he produced in typescript: 'Limit, is there any limit to what misery I have to endure'. However, he also realized that Elektra's words express both her situation as well as give a universalizing reflection, which in the final version became 'Is there any limit to the nature of misery?', which indeed strikes the balance sought between the personal and the general.

Pound's version of l. 237 of the original, 'Is there anything pretty about neglecting the dead?', is slightly awkward because of the poet's rendering of *kalon*. In an aesthetic context it can mean 'beautiful', but in this instance *kalon* is meant as 'morally beautiful', that is, 'good' or 'just'. Pound's 'pretty' is inappropriate here. In contrast, Pound's version of l. 238 is apt. Elektra asks whether the neglect of the dead is an inborn quality of human beings. As such she claims that 'her principles are an expression of *natural* law' or *phusis*, which was 'in the ideological conflict of the late fifth century, often contrasted with conventional law' or *nomos* (Kells 97). This inborn sense of decency was neatly covered by 'sprouted' in the typescript, based on Pound's notes to the passage in the margin of his Loeb: 'in what sprouts of men'. In the final version he settled for 'cropped up': 'Has that idea cropped up anywhere among men?'

Pound's rendering of Sophocles' ll. 239–43 is again fairly accurate, and his 'smothering my keening for the shame of this house' (with a strong choriambic pattern) is an apt poetical version of 'restraining the wings of sharp-toned lamentations that dishonour my parents'. For ll. 244–45, Pound came up with a rendering that stuck close to the Greek syntax: 'For if [*ei gar*] the dead [*ho thanōn*] lie down [*keisetai*] – earth [*ga*] and then [*te kai*] – nothing [*ouden*]/ wretched [*talas*]'.[10] Pound's 'death for a death' is an excellent translation of *antiphonous*, and he rightly decided to delete *dikas*, as it would have produced a rather tortuous sentence. Moreover, where Elektra in the original at the end of her speech becomes more personal, thinking of Klytaimnestra and Aigisthos through *hoi*, 'they', Pound continues to universalize her thoughts on murder, justice, and revenge. He ends with a maxim fit for a Greek tragedy. The consequence for *aidōs*, 'respect for opinions and feelings of mankind which condemns wrong-doing' (Jebb 1907, 41), and *eusebeia*, 'reverence for the gods' (Jebb 1907, 41; or, more broadly 'respect for law' (Kells 97)), if one would stop asking for justice is that: 'shame wd go wrack,/ all duty wd end & be nothing' (*E* ll. 304–05).

Here the *kommos* ends, with Pound having used 165 lines (*E* ll. 141–305) to render the 130 lines of Sophocles. This number is deceptive: Pound's *kommos* includes fifty-six lines of transliteration, including repeats (with eleven lines of the transliteration not translated), the repetition of part of Elektra's speech, while five of the six stage directions are also counted as lines. Taking these numbers into account, Pound actually condensed Sophocles' 130 lines to 106, mainly by removing most of the mythological references and by giving a terser rendering of the, at times periphrastically presented, information. While some parts of the *kommos* are transliterated and not translated to show the *melopoeia* of the original, Pound at times produced musical equivalents in English, and as the analysis above shows, he came up with some felicitously inventive renderings. By not translating some of the Greek passages and by adding some phrases of his own, Pound's version has broken down the conventional distinction between 'original' source text and translation, as well as the difference between foreignizing or domesticizing renderings. Here the Greek and English texts spark off from each other, with Pound taking away from Sophocles' play as much as he gives back to it.

Notes

1 Jebb rejects the theory that Sophocles' *Elektra* was written in response to Euripides' version (Jebb 1907, lvi). However, many scholars nowadays assume that Euripides' *Elektra*, written around 418 BCE, was indeed prior to Sophocles' play, composed around 413 BCE (Kells 1–2).
2 See Reid's notes at the end of his edition of *Elektra*, pp. 91–103 *passim*, for several instances of Pound's struggle with the Greek.
3 See Cantos 51/252; 60/333; 66/382; 68/400.
4 As the typescript makes clear, Pound did not always transliterate the Greek correctly, and it is noteworthy that even after the corrections from typescript to printed

version, there are occasional mistakes; it would be going too far to note all of them, but in this passage, for example, the second instance already wrongly gives 'OODAS' (*E* 8) instead of 'OOIDAS' for ᾠδάς (S l. 88). Furthermore, Pound does not distinguish between the epsilon (short e) and èta (long ē) as he transliterated both of them with an E, as in 'ANTEREIS' for ἀντήρεις (S l. 89); generally, he is inconsistent in transliterating the èta, as he also renders both èta with the iota subscriptum (ῃ) and the regular letter sometimes as AE.

5 For a fuller analysis of the 'sound' of both the Greek and the English in this opening speech, see Stergiopoulou 2015, 102–3.
6 Pound put a question mark in his Loeb edition beside Storr's rendering of ll. 91–93: 'By night for me is spread / No festal banquet in this haunted hall, / But my lone pallet bed' (133).
7 The transliteration of *E.* ll. 130–31 is rendered by Pound in ll. 125–26; the Greek of ll. 132–33 is already translated in l. 129; and the translation of the Greek transliteration of ll. 134–36 follows in ll. 137–40.
8 In her discussion of this passage, Stergiopoulou incorrectly translates the Greek words as 'if justice has told me so' (Stergiopoulou 2015, 100).
9 See *E* 16 for all the variants reflecting Pound's struggle.
10 Syros sees this English line as an exact equivalent in rhythm and accentuation of the Greek. Pound's rendering with its 'syncopated trochee . . . illustrates melancholic sadness mingled with anger'. Yet Syros also admits such equivalence is an exception (Syros 124–25).

5

Sophocles, Pound and *Elektra* II

First Episode (S ll. 251–471 = *E* 306–534)

The First Episode is rendered by Pound without any transliterations. The First Scene begins with a speech by Elektra (S ll. 254–309), which was heavily annotated by Pound in his Loeb, followed by a dialogue between the Chorus leader and Elektra, in which we find a repetition of the points raised in the choral lyric, but now in more 'calm' iambic trimeters.

Elektra's speech, which is meant as a justification of her behaviour, is in many ways similar in form to a speech before a court and makes use of several classical rhetorical techniques. First, she tries to gain sympathy from the audience (*captatio benevolentiae*) by apologizing for her behaviour, but then comes up with arguments to explain why she acts as she does. She uses rhetorical questions to get the audience involved in her situation – as retained by Pound in his ll. 314–15. She evokes her situation in detail, by using *prosopopoeia*, that is, by representing an absent person as speaking or acting. Here the depiction of Klytaimnestra and her speech as well as of Aigisthos through Elektra's focalization is very effective.

In the first part of her speech, Elektra apologizes for her laments but states that she has to vent herself, given what has happened and the fact that she still is in the hands of her father's murderers. This is mentioned in ll. 263–64, but in his version, Pound moved this to the opening of Elektra's speech, thus giving it more emphasis: 'I oughtn't to let 'em get me down' (*E* l. 309); 'They've got the power' (*E* l. 311). The lines in the original, 'and [*kak*] I am being ruled by them [*tōnd' archomai*], and [*kak*] from them [*tōnde*] comes [*pelei*] for me [*moi*] the receiving [*labein*, that is, of necessities] or the being deprived [of them] [*kai to tētasthai*] in equal measure [*homoiōs*]' (S ll. 264–65), were rendered by Storr as 'on whose will it rests/ To give or to withhold my daily bread' (145). Pound did not adapt this slightly Biblical phrase, and choose to show Elektra's harsh treatment in a far more forceful manner: 'and have 'em pushing me roud/ WHACK, take it, WHACK, leave it, / always the same, which ever way they've hexed it' (*E* ll. 320–22). The repeated 'WHACK' in capitals may be seen as a melopoeic attempt to reproduce the repeated *kak* (the contraction of *kai ek*) of the original.

Elektra continues to describe the daily behaviour of Aigisthos and Klytaimnestra (S ll. 266–281), rendered rather faithfully by Pound. He makes Sophocles' implication about Klytaimnestra acting as Aigisthos' lover more explicit: the phrase 'if she should be called a mother' in sharing his bed, becomes in Pound the more straightforward: 'a whore, a mother? Call it / a concubine' (*E* ll. 330–31). And where Aigisthos in Sophocles is called a *miastōr*, 'one who defiles by bloodshed' (Jebb 1907, 44), Pound turns him into 'the dirty slob' (*E* l. 332) – where the adjective once again reminds us of the theme of purgation. Pound struggled with the description of Klytaimnestra as *Erinun outin' ekphoboumenē* (l. 277) 'having no fear of any Erinys'. In the typescript we see how Pound turned to his Ellendt dictionary for 'Erinys'. While this gave it as 'vengeance', the poet preferred 'curse', and thus translated the phrase as 'no longer scared of the curse', to stress once again the larger Atreid background.

The use of more colloquial language is continued in Pound's rendering of Elektra's description of her treatment by her mother: 'Seeing this, I, wretched one, weep and pine away [*tetēka*] in the house [*kata stegas*], and bewail the most miserable banquet named after my father, all by myself' (S ll. 283–85). In his Loeb, Pound glossed *tetēka* as 'mouldy, melt', and *kata stegas* as 'roof-room', while in the draft he noted how *kata stegas* means 'my room … [wh is attic]' (*E* 17–18). This resulted in:

> Joke that is.
>   but it gets me down all the same.
> And I go moulder in an attic
> and blubber over "Agamemnon's bean-O," yes
> they call it by old pop's name.
>
>   *E* ll. 336–40

Klytaimnestra, depicted by Sophocles from Elektra's perspective as *hē logoisi gennaia gunē* (l. 287), 'the woman noble in her words' (that is, not in her deeds), becomes 'that old big-talk' (*E* l. 342), who addresses her daughter not as an 'Ungodly, hateful girl' (Storr 147), but simply as a 'slut' (*E* l. 346). Elektra ends her speech by describing how she keeps hoping that Orestes will return. Here, too, Pound is consistent in his more 'youthful' slangy speech although Elektra sounds at times dangerously close to being an American teenager. For example,

Sophocles's lines 'when [Klytaimnestra] hears anyone saying Orestes is coming, then she is mad with rage' (ll. 293–94), become 'when someone says Orestes is comin'/ then she gets scared and blows her top proper/ goes shoutin' frantic' (*E* ll. 347–49).

Aigisthos also receives his portion of scorn from Elektra: 'and present by her side [*pelas ... parōn*] her famous [*kleinos*] marriage-partner [*numphios*], alongside her [*sun*] spurs her on [*epotrunei ... autēi*] with regard to these things [*tauta*], that feeble man in all respects [*ho pant' analkos houtos*], that utter pest [*hē pasa blabē*], the man who fights his battles [*ho pas machas poioumenos*] together with women [*sun gunaixi*]'. (S ll. 299–302)

> ... and her ponce sicks her on,
> marvelous,
> of all the dastardly yellow pests,
> fightin' from under her skirts
>
> *E* ll. 354–57

Pound's last two lines neatly encapsulate Aigisthos' cowardice (he is 'yellow'), as well as the fact that he is Klytaimnestra's lover.

Elektra concludes her speech by stating that the Chorus now may understand why she is so emotional and bent on revenge. In short, *en kakois/ pollē 'st' anangkē kapitēdeuein kaka* (S ll. 308–09), 'in evil circumstances there is a big necessity also to practise evil'. As Kells notes, this 'reinforces the point, which is of great dramatic significance, that she does not claim that her conduct is *right*, but merely that it is forced upon her' (102). Pound renders this bluntly as 'and with all this rot I've gone rotten' (*E* l. 363), thereby retaining the alliterative pattern of the original. This final line makes the same point Elektra made in l. 211 of her lyric dialogue with the chorus, which Pound gave in transliteration without translation, 'DEINOIS ENANKASTHEN' (*E* 15), 'I have been compelled by terrible things'.

After the subsequent dialogue between Elektra and the Chorus leader, they see Chrysothemis approaching, who is carrying sepulchral gifts. In this Second Scene (S ll. 328–471 = *E* ll. 378–534) of the First Epeisodion (lightly annotated in the Loeb until l. 399, after which the annotations become medium to heavy), we have the first meeting between Elektra and her sister. Sophocles spends some time drawing her personality, making clear that in many ways she is the opposite of her sister. Although Chrysothemis also does not like the present circumstances, she has pragmatically accepted them in knowledge of her own weakness, something emphasized by Pound in his stage directions of the deliverance of her opening words as in a *'tone of thorough weariness, and discouragement'* (*E* l. 378).

The differences between the siblings come to the fore in their dialogue. Pound's rendering of Chrysothemis' opening words (S ll. 328–40) is fairly accurate. In his Loeb, Pound jotted down and underlined the word '<u>motto</u>' next to l. 330 of the Greek, where Chrysothemis wonders why Elektra has not learned to give up her anger over time. Compared to Elektra, her language and attitude is calmer and rational, evident in how she tells her sister that she is making things worse 'to let out every fool feeling you got in yr/ gizzard' (*E* 19, l. 381). Where 'fool feeling' for *thumōi mataiōi* (l. 331) grew out of 'useless fury' and 'vain rage' used in the typescript, Pound added 'gizzard' as he seemed to have known that *thumos* can be both 'anger, temper' as well as 'the seat of anger'. Chrysothemis ends with some advice most telling of her character: 'But if I am to live as a free woman, I must obey my rulers in all things' (S ll. 339–40), rendered by Pound as: 'but I've got to obey in order to keep my freedom of action' (*E* l. 389). In this she is echoing the Chorus' suggestion to Elektra that the best course of action (*E* ll. 283–84) is to not stand up against those in power.

Elektra gives a long response (S ll. 341–68 = *E* ll. 390–428), which was analyzed by Earp in his *Style of Sophocles* as concise and simple in diction, with only a few poetical words. The passage 'in fact could be turned into Attic prose without very drastic change' (Earp 116), and Pound's version reflects this. In her speech, Elektra stresses that she is not giving in on a matter of principle, and so criticizes her sister for not being willing to help her to overcome the situation. This culminates in what Pound considered to be the key phrase of the play in line 351, as indicated by the red markings in his Loeb edition, and which he gives full weight to by indicating a pause in the stage directions:

(*pause: very clearly enunciated: different tempo: pausing between each word*)

Need we add cowardice to all the rest of this filth?

E ll. 400–01

This is a translation of:

οὐ ταῦτα πρὸς κακοῖσι δειλίαν ἔχει;

S l. 351

do these things [*tauta*, that is, your conduct I have been sketching] not [*ou*] provide/give [*echei*] cowardice [*deilian*] to our miseries [*pros kakoisi*]?

Shall we to all our ills add cowardice?

Storr 151

> Does this not crown our miseries with cowardice?
>
> Jebb 1907, 55

In this denunciation of Chrysothemis' conduct as morally wrong, Storr is closer to Sophocles' plainness of speech than Jebb, and provided Pound with a solid basis for his rendering, also giving the line weight by indicating that in the delivery there should be a pause between each word, while in the text he left a blank space before and after the line.

Line 351 was such a vital sentiment for Pound that he even had stationery printed with this line, while it also became an epigraph for the short-lived magazine *Four Pages*, edited by Dallam Simpson. Pound also used (parts of) the line on three occasions in *Rock-Drill*, the segment of Cantos he began to compose in 1953, and which was published in 1955. *Rock-Drill* generally deals with standards of good government as part of the eternal struggle between economic justice and injustice, materialism versus spiritualism. Pound first quoted part of Elektra's line at the end of Canto 85, right after an Aeschylean reference to the idea of trial by a jury as depicted in his *Eumenides*:

> Jury trial was in Athens.
> Tyrants resisted
> οὐ ταῦτα . . . κακοῖσι δειλίαν
>
> 85/579

Pound quoted the phrase again with a variation in the next Canto, in a passage about trust which includes the Chinese ideogram *Hsin*, 'Fidelity to the given word. The man here standing by his word' (*CON* 22):

> All, that has been, is as it should have been,
>   but what will they trust in
>   信   now?
> "Alla non della", in the Verona statement
>   οὐ ταῦτα . . . κακοῖσι
>   Section Rock Drill.
>
> 86/584

Flory has related 'All, that has been, is as it should have been' to Mussolini's reputed comment '*Tutto quello che è accaduto, doveva accadere*' in a memoir attributed to him about the period after his downfall in July 1943 (Flory 174–75).[1] The phrase 'Alla non della' recurs in *The Cantos* as a reference to Mussolini's 'Verona Program' for the Republic of Salò, announced in November 1943, where the Italian leader talked about 'a right *to* property, not the right *of* property'

(Terrell 416). Alec Marsh has noted that in Pound's favourable response to this phrase, 'we see, if anywhere, a 'left-fascist' Pound responding to a Fascist-Socialist republic' (Marsh 2011, 155).

In Canto 87, Pound conflated phrases from *Elektra* and the *Trachiniae* to denounce modern civilization, and connected this to the notion of justice as depicted by Aeschylus in his *Eumenides*:

> The pusillanimous wanting all men cut down to worm size.
> Wops, maggots, crumbled from simple dishonesty.
> διάβορον . . . ἐδεστὸν ἐξ αὐτοῦ φτίνει πρὸς κακοῖσι . . .
>   quia impossibile est.
> ....
> Was not unanimous
>   'Αθάνα broke tie,
> That is 6 jurors against 6 jurors
>   needed 'Αθάνα.
>
>   87/590–91

In the phrase from the *Trachiniae* (676–77, *diaboron pros oudenos/ tōn endon, all' edeston ex autou phthinei*), Deianeira tells the Chorus what happened to the sheep's wool she had used to daub Herakles' shirt in the blood of Nessus: 'Destroyed by nothing within, but eaten by itself, it wastes away' (see the analysis of *Women of Trachis*). To these words Pound has added two words taken from *Elektra* l. 351, creating an ideogram expressing that one must stay sincere (as Confucius advocated), and not give in to unrighteous powers nor extend their dominance by internalizing their ideology of injustice.[2]

The remainder of Elektra's speech is rendered fairly accurately by Pound, with an occasional modernized phrase: 'you play ball with our father's assassins' (*E* l. 409); 'you swank about in' (l. 414). He adds a stage direction to show Elektra's contempt for Chrysosthemis having accepted gifts from Klytaimnestra and her lover, culminating in a summary line *soi de plousia/ trapeza keisthō kai perirreitō bios* (S ll. 361–62), 'for you let a sumptuous table be laid and let life be superabundant'. This, of course, refers us back to Elektra's 'empty table' of Sophocles l. 192 (= *E* l. 261). Pound extends this sentence to include a moral condemnation as a metonym of what Elektra considers to be her sister's cowardice:

> Have yr/ big dinners, comforts
> and everything easy,
>   your lie-down flow-about life.
>
>   *E* ll. 415–17

Pound enhances Elektra's personality here by working out this image: 'Because [*gar*] for me [*emoi*] let be [*estō*] my not vexing myself [*toume mē lupein*] my sole [*monon*] sustenance [*boskēma*]: I do not seek [*ouk erō*] to gain [*tuchein*] your honour [*tēs sēs timēs*, that is, the honour paid to you].' (S ll. 363–65)

> If I don't eat, I don't make myself spew with disgust.
> Keep my self-respect anyhow
> I wouldn't want to have a sense of honour like yours
>
> *E* ll. 418–20

Pound uses Elektra's speech to make the contrast between the sisters even more pronounced than in the original, and to flesh out Elektra's character in more detail, most likely to make clear how pivotal for him that key phrase of l. 351 actually is. He uses thirty-nine lines, including the stage direction, to render the twenty-eight lines of the original, in order to clarify the opposition between idealism and moral purity (Elektra) on the one hand, and the choice of material profit and self-centered common sense (Chrysothemis) on the other.

The ensuing dialogue between the two sisters once again demonstrates that Pound kept a close eye on Storr's translation. Chrysothemis states that she does not take offence at Elektra's words, but also *oud' an emnēsthēn pote* (S l. 373), 'I would not have mentioned this'. Pound swerves from the original with 'I wouldn't have come here now' (*E* l. 433), clearly based on Storr's 'Nor had I now approached her' (153). In Sophocles, we then have a quick succession of single lines exchanged between the sisters (S ll. 385–416), known as a *stichomythia*. Pound retains the tempo of this dialogue, sometimes by condensing the original, although he on occasion spreads the original single line out over two lines. Thus Chrysothemis' advice *tois kratousi d'eikathein* (S l. 396), 'yield to those who rule' (advice she gave earlier in S ll. 339–40 = *E*. l. 389), becomes 'I'm only telling you to bend and not break / when you come up against power' (*E* ll. 453–54). This underscores how Chrysothemis is pragmatic and sensible, while Elektra opts for what is just. Elektra's dismissal of her sister is neatly captured by Pound's 'Slobber over 'em. Not my way' (*E* l. 455).

The first part of the *stichomythia* ends with Chrysothemis realizing she will not be able to convince her sister, and she turns to go to their father's tomb. Pound marks off this transition by inserting a stage direction about Elektra '*noticing the offerings for the first time, having been up to now absorbed in her own fury*' (*E* ll. 466–67). Here some of Pound's phrases become awkward. The offerings are said to be *empura*, 'meant for burning' (S l. 405), not, as Pound would have it, 'all roasted' (*E* l. 470), although for some reason Fleming's fair copy shows he agreed with this: '"roasted" seems good for empura' (*E* 94). And Chrysothemis is sent by Klytaimnestra *tumbeusai chaos*, 'to offer libations at the tomb' (S l. 406), not 'to go water the grave' (*E* l. 471). Pound may have wished to associate the phrase with the Christian custom of family members visiting the graves of loved ones on All Souls, cleaning the site and laying fresh flowers. But for anyone without this knowledge, the phrase may have awkward connotations.[3] Interestingly enough, when Elektra later in l. 434 refers to *kterismata*, 'funeral gifts', and *loutra*, 'libations', Pound linked these words in the typescript to the Noh play *Nishikigi*, of which he had published a translation in 1916: 'KTERISMA, Eldt/fun/gifts OR rites. HISTEMI cause to stand cf/ Nishikigi loutron/ washing bath expiatory' (*E* 95). In *Nishikigi*, a young man puts up 'nishikigi' or 'wands used as a love-charm' (*T* 286) each night for his beloved: '[w]e make wands of mediation and deck them with symbols and set them before a gate when we are suitors'. Apparently, Pound saw a link between 'setting up' the charm in the Noh play and 'planting' the funeral gifts in *Elektra*.[4] This is one of only two instances where Pound related *Elektra* explicitly to the Noh (compare the stage direction in line 990), something he would do more extensively in *Woman of Trachis*.

The passage about Klytaimnestra's dream (S ll. 417–71) is rendered faithfully by Pound. According to Chrysothemis, Klytaimnestra was visited in her dream by Agamemnon, who took his former sceptre and planted it at the household altar, after which a branch grew out of it that overshadowed all of Mycenae – rendered iconically in Pound's text, as the line 'and spread all over Mycenae' (*E* l. 487) is separated and between blank spaces. Elektra tells her sister to hide the offerings so that one day Klytaimnestra may find them *katō* (l. 438), 'beneath the ground', when she dies – rendered by Pound as 'let her find 'em in hell, when she dies', turning *katō* into a specific location of punishment. After having described how Klytaimnestra murdered Agamemnon and wiped the bloodstains on her hands onto his head, Pound then adds a detail not worked out explicitly in Sophocles: she 'cut off his hands and feet to keep the/ ghost from walkin and grabbing her' (*E* ll. 509–10). These two lines are based on the Greek *emaschalisthē* (S l. 445), 'he was mutilated'. Pound's inventive amplification is clearly based on a note found in his Loeb edition which explains that the 'full meaning is: "to cut off the hands and feet and suspend them to the armpits." This was done to prevent the victim from taking vengeance' (Storr 161).

Elektra tells Chrysothemis to offer a lock of their hair and Elektra's belt, and to pray that Agamemnon's ghost may appear and that Orestes may return so that he may overcome her enemies. The Chorus supports Elektra's words: 'the girl [*hē korē*] speaks [*legei*] with proper piety [*pros eusebeian*]' (S l. 463), 'She's on the right track' (*E* l. 528). Chrysothemis promises to do this, but entreats her sister to keep quiet about it, lest their mother, presented by Pound as 'the old screw' (*E* l. 533), will hear about it. Interestingly enough, Pound originally had 'usuress', as he derived the Greek *hē tekousa* (l. 470), 'the female having giving birth', not from *tiktō*, 'to give birth', but from *tokos*, 'interest'. Of course, 'usury' is regarded by Pound as the greatest manifestation of moral evil throughout *The Cantos*, and seen as a force acting against (life-giving, nourishing and benevolent) nature. Fleming stated in his fair copy: 'I don't think the idea of usury is in the Greek, but the epithet fits the notion that the house of Atreus has fallen on vulgar days' (*E* 95). Although Pound in his reply insisted on the connection between *tekousa* and usury, he apparently decided that the specific word would take the play in another direction, so he dropped it in the final version. However, he did retain part of the economic vocabulary in his rendering of Chrysothemis' fear of her mother finding out that she had been disobedient: the original 'I think that then it will be a bitter enterprise which I will be attempting' (S ll. 470–71) becomes 'she'll make me pay for the risk' (*E* l. 534).

First Stasimon (S ll. 472–515; *E* ll. 535–88)

In the First Stasimon, heavily annotated by Pound in his Loeb, the Chorus addresses Elektra and explains Klytaimnestra's dream as a prediction of revenge. The tone of this choral ode is one of hope, as the chorus expects that Justice will be done. Dikē, the personification of Justice, is the force that restores the order of nature after the imbalance created by evil.

In the choral lyrics of Attic tragedy, the dramatists employ a metrical structure which is made up of one or more periods (=combinations of single metrical phrases), which recur in the same form either once or more often. Such a metrical unit is called a strophe, and when its same metrical structure is repeated, the second strophe is called the *antistrophe*. These two strophes may be followed by a third of different metrical form, known as the *epode*. Pound did not try to reproduce the complex metrical arrangement of Sophocles' original here with its choriambs, iambs, and dochmiacs, nor are we given a fully symmetrical rhymed translation as in Storr (163–65). Yet Pound throughout his ode employs an arrangement of three- and four-beat lines alongside alliteration, assonance, and rhyme ('right/ sight/ tight' [*E* ll. 535–37], 'axe/ smacks' [ll. 546–47]; 'out/ doubt' [549–50], 'tread/ bed/ unwed' [551–52, 554], 'mate/ fate'

[556–57], 'began/ man/ man' [559–51]) and half-rhyme ('once/ dunce' [539–40]). Apparently, Pound felt confident enough about the musical quality of his version of the strophe and anti-strophe to not transliterate the Greek, as he had done in the Parodos, until he comes to the Epode, or concluding stanza, of the Stasimon, where he wants the Greek in transliteration to be sung, and his translation to be spoken.

As the typescripts show (*E* 28), Pound struggled with his rendering, so it will be useful to look at this Ode in more detail. The first Strophe reads:

εἰ μὴ᾽ ᾽γὼ παράφρων μάντις ἔφυν καὶ γνώμας
λειπομένα σοφᾶς,
εἶσιν ἁ πρόμαντις
Δίκα, δίκαια φερομένα χεροῖν κράτη·
μέτεισιν, ὦ τέκνον, οὐ μακροῦ χρόνου.
ὕπεστί μοι θάρσος
ἁδυπνόων κλύουσαν
ἀρτίως ὀνειράτων.
οὐ γάρ ποτ᾽ ἀμναστεῖ γ᾽ ὁ φύσας σ᾽ Ἑλλάνων ἄναξ,
οὐδ᾽ ἁ παλαιὰ χαλκόπλακτος ἀμφάκης γένυς,
ἅ νιν κατέπεφνεν αἰσχίσταις ἐν αἰκίαις.

S ll. 472–88

If [*ei*] I was not born [*mē 'gō ephun*] as a demented seer [*paraphrōn mantis*] and lacking [*kai leipomena*] in judgements of wisdom [*gnōmas sophas*], Justice [*Dika*] the prophetess [*ha promantis*] will come [*eisin*], bringing [*pheromena*; yet this middle voice can also mean 'winning'] in her hands [*cheroin*] just triumphs [*dikaia kratē*]: she will go after them [*meteisin*, that is, the triumphs or the murderers], my child [*ō teknon*], very soon [*ou makrou chronou*]. I have courage [*hupesti moi tharsos*], just having heard [*kluousan artiōs*] of the sweet-breathing dream [*hadupno-ōn oneiratōn*, that is, Klytaimnestra's dream gives hope]. Because [*gar*] your father [*ho phusas*], the lord of the Greeks [*Hellanōn anax*] did never forget you [*ou pot'amnastei s'*], nor [*oud'*] did the old [*palaia*] bronze-striking [*chalkoplaktos*] two-edged axe [*amphakēs genus*], which [*ha*] killed him [*nin katepephnen*] in that most shameful assault [*aischistais en aikiais*].

Given the evidence of the typescript, Pound never doubted his rendering of his first three lines, in which he took his cue from *paraphrōn*, 'foolish', transposed *promantis*, 'prophetess', from Dikē to the Chorus, and most likely read *kratē*, 'victories', as a form of *kratos*, the genitive form of *kras*, 'head'. Pound had already struggled with *kratos* in l. 449. Fleming stated in his fair copy: '(kratos is gen. of kras meaning head, summit) tip' (*E* 95). The result is the following triplet:

> You can say that I never guess right
> a fool born without second sight,
> that my head was never screwed tight
>
> *E* ll. 535–37

Pound then encountered difficulties. The typescript has 'but if Justice don't once/ show the old swine for a dunce; win this case, I'm a dunce' (*E* 28). As this play appealed to Pound for its investigation into the nature of justice, the explicit mentioning of its divine personification at this point apparently made him tread very carefully so as to make the most out of this ode to Justice. In the typescript he explicitly added an object absent in the original, 'the old swine'. *Meteisin* means 'to come in pursuit (of)', but Sophocles left it open whom or what Dikē will be pursuing. In the final version, Pound decided to adopt this open-ended version.

Until now he had been employing rhyme. We see in the typescript that he at first continued to do so in his version, as the lines 'it's a long time indeed, to sprout up from its seed' illustrate, as the latter phrase was an invented addition presumably created to enable him to continue using rhyme. We may see a similar strategy in 'my spirits are now risin, / and in dreams most surprisin' (*E* 28). Yet Pound apparently felt that in retaining the rhyme he had departed too much from the original, and so deleted some of these phrases in the final version.

In the description of the dream, Pound took some liberties with the Greek, changing the presentation of the Chorus as having heard of Klytaimnestra's dream into that of the Chorus having had a dream themselves. He started in the typescript with 'Sure there music in me dream', perhaps inspired by Storr's 'That dream was music in my ears' (163), for *hadupno-ōn oneiratōn*. Ellendt's Dictionary has 'sweetly-breathing', jotted down by Pound in the margin of his Loeb. Liddell-Scott mentions that *hēdupnōs* means 'sweet-breathing' and is said of dreams in Sophocles, and of musical sound in Pindarus. Pound's final version settled on a more Shakespearean *Tempest*-like rendering: 'my dreams are breathing deep / with a free and airy sound' (*E* ll. 542–43). He retained the evocative personification of the axe calling for vengeance as well as the pattern of the -a- assonance of the original (*aischistais en aikiais*): 'and the double headed axe/ be payin back the smacks' (*E* ll. 546–47), before ending with a single line employing an assonance pattern of the -o-: 'and the bloody blood be flowin' once again' (l. 548). Although Pound remained dissatisfied with his version, as he told Fleming (*E* 96), the first strophe in its final version is one of the musical triumphs of the play.

In the second Strophe, the Chorus describes the avenging Fury:

ἥξει καὶ πολύπους καὶ πολύχειρ ἁ δεινοῖς
κρυπτομένα λόχοις
χαλκόπους Ἐρινύς.
ἄλεκτρ' ἄνυμφα γὰρ ἐπέβα μιαιφόνων
γάμων ἁμιλλήμαθ' οἷσιν οὐ θέμις.
πρὸ τῶνδέ τοί μ' ἔχει
μή ποτε μή ποθ' ἡμῖν
ἀψεγὲς πελᾶν τέρας
τοῖς δρῶσι καὶ συνδρῶσιν. ἤ τοι μαντεῖαι βροτῶν
οὐκ εἰσὶν ἐν δεινοῖς ὀνείροις οὐδ' ἐν θεσφάτοις,
εἰ μὴ τόδε φάσμα νυκτὸς εὖ κατασχήσει.

S ll. 489–502

She will come [*hēxei*], both many-footed and many-handed [*kai polupous kai polucheir*], the bronze-footed Fury [*ha chalkopous Erinus*] hiding in dire ambushes [*deinois kruptomena lochois*]. For [*gar*] an improperly-bedding [*alektr'*] and improperly-wedding [*anumpha*] striving [*hamillēmath'*] for a blood-stained [*miaiphonōn*] marriage [*gamōn*] set upon [*epeba*] those to whom [*hoisin*] it was not permitted [*ou themis*]. With regard to these things, then, [*pro tōnde*] I certainly [*toi*] have confidence [*m'echei*; very complex construction as the phrase literally means 'has me', with the subject constituted by all the words that follow] that we shall never ever have [*mē pote mē poth' hēmin*] a blameless [*apseges*] portent [*teras*] approaching [*pelan*] the doers of the deed [*tois drōsi*] and their accomplices [*kai sundrōsin*]. Surely [*ē toi*] prophetic powers [*manteiai*] of mortals [*brotōn*] do not exist [*ouk eisin*] in dreadful dreams [*en deinois oneirois*] or in oracles [*oud' en thesphatois*], if [*ei mē*] this vision of the night [*tode phasma nuktos*] shall end well [*eu kataschēsei*].

Here the Chorus is certain that murderers never get an 'innocent' vision of their future, implying that Klytaimnestra and Aigisthos should have every reason to fear the meaning and actual outcome of her dream. For if the dream would turn out to mean nothing and thus be ineffective, one may as well give up believing in the prophesying power of dreams and oracles altogether.

Pound managed to create a powerful equivalent of this exceedingly complex Greek passage in terms of syntax. His presentation of the avenging Fury retains her stealthiness ('hiding bush', *E* l. 550) and violent power ('brazen tread', l. 551). The second sentence of the Greek has been interpreted differently by scholars. Jebb takes as the subject of *epeba* the passion that drove Klytaimnestra and Aigisthos to their unlawful, adulterous bed (Jebb 1907, 72). Kells, however, takes the Fury as the subject of the verb, and thus has the Erinys set out against the desires of the lovers (Kells 119). This is also Pound's view, given his depiction of the Fury coming to the 'adulterous bed' in order to wipe out 'the stain' (*E* ll. 552–53), a rendering based on the 'blood-stained marriage' of the original. He is also explicit and less periphrastic in deleting and re-arranging some of the Greek words of ll. 492–93 [*alektr'. . . ou themis*] so as to produce the alliterative lines: 'to wipe out the stain/ as they wrestle there unwed' (note the -e- assonance) – with 'unwed' translating both *anumpha* as well as *ou themis*, that is, not being allowed to share the marriage-bed.

The original Greek of ll. 495–99 is extremely hard to translate, as indicated above, because of its condensation of thought. Pound's version 'unpacks' the Greek by making explicit all the implications of the original wording. First, he notes how any evildoer cannot escape their fate, and how this is foretold with certainty (*E* ll. 555–57). He then stresses twice that what goes around comes around, before repeating again that man is subject to fate (S ll. 558–60). Pound makes much of this given his interest in the play's dealing with justice, and creates Greek-like maxims (unified by assonance patterns of -a- and -o-, and by rhyme):

> ever with lock and sign
> ill doer and ill do's mate
> shall never dodge out of fate
> black ends that which black began
> fate shall out run any man
>
> *E* ll. 555–60

In rounding off the second strophe Pound at first stayed very close to the Greek. We find in the typescript: 'and the divinations of men / are not in awful dreamings nor in oracles / if that phantasm of the night / does not well / destroy / making a good smash' (*E* 28). He then created a more musical and more 'oracular' tone in the first two lines of the final version, as well as a more Anglo-Saxon compound equivalent for 'phantasm of the night' so as to have a more 'pounding' concluding line (what Earp would call ὄγκος):

> Nothing foretells tomorrow to man
> neither horrors in dreams nor in oracles
> ef thet night-sight don't damn well smash 'em.
>
> *E* ll. 561–63

After his careful rendering of the strophe and anti-strophe, Pound seemed less interested in the epode, in which the Chorus see the murder and adultery as yet another episode in the family history of Pelops' descendants. After the charioteer Myrtilus had helped Pelops to win the hand of Hippodameia, Myrtilus insulted her. Pelops then threw him into the sea where Myrtilus cursed him and his family. Pound first gives a transliteration of the Greek to be sung (with TADE GA instead of TAIDE GAI, and OIKOI instead of OIKOU), then added a translation. The original reads (using Pound's transliteration):

> O [OO] ancient [PROSTHEN] horsemanship [HA HIPPEIA] of Pelops [PELOPOS], full of sorrow [POLUPONOS], how [HOOS] you came [EMOLES] horrid [AIANES, that, as a horrid force] for this land [TADE GA]. For since [EUTE GAR] Myrtilus [HO MURTILOS], sunk into the sea [PONTHISTHEIS], was put to rest [EKOIMATHE], thrown [EKRIPHTHEIS] headlong [PRORRIDZOS] from the all-golden chariot [PANCHRUSEOON DIPHROON] by wretched outrage [DUSTANOIS AIKIAIS], an outrage full of sorrows [POLUPONOS AIKIA] never [OU TI POO] has left [ELEIPEN] this house [EK TOUD' OIKOU].
>
> S ll. 502–15

Pound decided to let the Greek 'sing' for itself, as his rendering (*E* ll. 583–88) is rather free. Although he retains the repetition of AIKIA, 'outrage', through his double use of 'curse', his 'rotting the earth' is his own addition, and results from the transposition of TADE GA. The result is a condensed rendering with greater emphasis on the impending doom: 'and the curse has continued/ on the house of Pelops/ rotting the earth' (*E* ll. 586–88).

Second Episode (S ll. 516–1057; *E* ll. 589–1194)

The First Scene (S ll. 516–659) of the Second Episode, heavily annotated by Pound in his Loeb, begins with the entrance of Klytaimnestra, who gives a speech of self-justification, followed by an *agon* or verbal contest between her and Elektra. Earp described Klytaimnestra's speech as straightforward and exemplary of Sophocles' later style. She is not giving a set speech: 'Her words come out in jerks, as the thoughts come into her mind', but this seemingly spontaneous speech is artfully constructed. Here Sophocles has learnt 'to make his characters argue logically, and yet seem to be speaking naturally ... The thoughts spring directly from the occasion, and the arguments are personal, not abstract.' Earp summarizes the tone of the speech as that of a 'bitter invective' (Earp 137), something which Pound in his version managed to retain.

The key word in the opening of Klytaimnestra's speech (S ll. 516–33) is *dikē* or Justice. Elektra thinks her mother is reigning *pera dikēs* (S l. 521), 'on the other side of justice', that is, unjustly, but Klytaimnestra counters that although she murdered Agamemnon, it was in fact Justice which killed him (l. 528) in retribution for the death of Iphigeneia. She therefore appeals to her daughter that Elektra 'should be supporting Justice, if you are sensible' (l. 529). Given his interest in the notion of Justice, Pound rendered Klytaimnestra's self-justification faithfully: 'with Justice on my side, I wasn't alone / as you'll have to admit if you think straight' (*E* ll. 608–09).

It is noteworthy that in Klytaimnestra's reference to the murder, Pound added the phrase 'a good job' (*E* l. 606), which is not in Sophocles, but a phrase Pound had used in his 1919 essay on Aeschylus, as part of Klytaimnestra's depiction of her murder of her husband in *Agamemnon* (ll. 1404–06). In that play Klytaimnestra claims the murder was justified, with the Greek words *dexias* and *dikaias* linking up the act with justice. As we saw in Chapter 2, Pound translated τῆσδε δεξιᾶς χερός,/ ἔργον, δικαίας τέκτονος (*tēsde dexiās cheros,/ ergon, dikaias tektonos*, *Ag.* ll. 1405–06) as 'Dead by this hand,/ And a good job' (*LE* 270). Pound inserted the phrase 'a good job' in his version of the *Elektra* to link it up to the *Agamemnon*, and to stress how Sophocles' play is about justice, self-justification, and the restoration of order. It may well be that the creation of this intertextual web was triggered by Storr's rendering of *hōs ex emou tethnēken. ex emou* (l. 526; 'because I killed him; I killed him') as 'Died by my hand, aye mine', as Pound heavily marked this Greek line in his Loeb edition.

The second part of Klytaimnestra's speech of self-justification (S ll. 534–45) deals with Agamemnon's motives for his sacrifice of Iphigeneia, and employs a large number of rhetorical questions, which Pound retained in his generally faithful version. On occasion, however, he is a bit crude in order to convey the terseness of the Greek. In ll. 532–33, Klytaimnestra refers to Agamemnon as 'not having shared an equal amount of pain, when he sowed [Elektra], as did I, when I gave birth to her'. In Pound, this becomes: 'he didn't have as much trouble in makin' her as I had / he put her in, I got her out' (*E* ll. 613–14). Pound is also somewhat careless: when Klytaimnestra wonders for whose pleasure her husband wanted to kill their daughter, she states *poteron Argeiōn ereis*; (S l. 535), 'for the Greeks, you will say?' – the word *poteron* merely indicates we are dealing with a question. Pound, however, read it as *poteros*, 'which of the two', and thus produced 'which of two greeks was it?' (*E* l. 618), thereby raising an awkward question. Yet the intense hatred Klytaimnestra feels for Agamemnon, *tōi panōlei patri* (S l. 544), 'the all-destructive father', is neatly captured in Pound's 'rotter' (*E* l. 626).

Then Elektra gives her views (S ll. 558–609). She rejects her mother's appeal to justice: Klytaimnestra's motive simply was 'your letch for that bounder you're living with' (*E* l. 646). Apart from this line, Pound's version is faithful, but his rendering of another phrase really stands out. Sophocles describes how Agamemnon boasted about having killed one of the stags of Artemis: 'with regard to the killing of it [*hou kata sphagas*] he chanced [*tunchanei*] while boasting [*ekkompasas*] to let fall/utter [*balōn*] a certain word [*epos ti*]' (S ll. 568–69). In his version, Pound intriguingly turned 'a certain word' into 'smutty jokes':

> but made smutty jokes about it, it was
> a kill
> not according to hunting rites.
>
> *E* ll. 653–55

More importantly, Pound seems to have misconstrued *hou kata sphagas* by reading οὗ (*hou*), the genitive of the relative pronoun of *hos* ('who'), referring to the stag, as οὔ (*ou*), 'not', and then connecting it with *kata sphagas*, 'with regard to the killing'. (In his Loeb edition, Pound underlined the phrase κατὰ σφαγάς.) The result is that in his version Agamemnon's kill of the stag was 'not according to hunting rites' (*E* l. 655) – a phrase he would also use twice in Canto 89 in the *Rock-Drill* section devoted to justice and good government: 'Judge Marshall, father of war. / Agamemnon killed that stag, against hunting rites' (622). One page later the Greek phrase is juxtaposed with a reference to Giuseppe Mazzini's *On the Duties of Man*: 'Mazzini: Doveri/ "κατὰ σφαγάς"' (623). Pound admired the Italian nationalist Giuseppe Mazzini (1805–72) for his economic ideas, and the way he wanted to bring about Italian unification by revolution but not at the cost of 'needless slaughter' (Terrell 536). In a letter of 11 May 1953, Earp explicitly expressed his puzzlement about Pound's rendering: 'As to Electra 568 I am not sure that I understand what you mean. You say that Agamemnon killed the stag "against the hunting rites." As it was the goddess's property, he had no right to kill it, but some versions of the legend, I think, say that he did not know it was hers. Sophocles says that he killed it in her sacred grove; so he must have known. And he makes him boast & thus offense by boasting, though does not say what the boast was. If you mean anything more recondite than this, I am afraid I cannot grasp it' (Beinecke 14/646). One may wonder whether Pound misread the Greek *(h)ou kata sphagas* or deliberately opted for his rendering, as his (mis)translation adds another element to the discussion about (un)just murder in the *Elektra*.

Having given the true reason for Iphigeneia's sacrifice, Elektra criticizes her mother for taking the law into her own hands, culminating in the following four lines:

> See that in having set up such a law for men, you do not establish suffering and remorse for yourself. For if we are to take a life for a life, you would be the first to die, you know that, if you were to receive justice.
>
> S ll. 580–83

> You'd better be careful setting up that sort of law
> for the rest of the world, you'll get into trouble
> and wish you hadn't.
> for if blood for blood makes justice,
> you'll be the first to go.
>
> E ll. 670–674

This statement goes to the very heart of the play: Elektra's warning that retributive justice is wrong and will have dire consequences for anyone committing it is at the same time, if unintentionally so, a condemnation of her and Orestes' plans to kill Klytaimnestra. As Kells rightly notes, here '*Elektra condemns herself out of her own mouth*' (128).

After this emotional outburst, Elektra becomes more legalistic again, denouncing her mother for her actions, including her bedding of Aigisthos: 'for it is not right [*kalon*] to marry an enemy for the sake of a daughter' (S ll. 593–94), where Pound gives for *kalon* 'a dirty job', most likely to counter Klytaimnestra's earlier use of 'a good job', and to return to the theme of purgation. Pound manages to find emotional equivalents for Elektra's phrases in the original. Her claim that she is not allowed to give advice to her mother *hē pasan hiēs glōssan hōs tēn mētera/ kakostomoumen* (S ll. 596–97), 'who keeps on saying [lit. 'lets loose her whole tongue'] that we slander our mother', becomes 'without your putting up a squawk about slandering mama' (*E* l. 684). And her reference to Aigisthos as *sunnomou* (l. 600), 'partner, associate', is turned into the alliterative 'your fellow-feeder'.

The Chorus responds to Elektra's speech with two lines, which may be taken either as a summary of Elektra's passionate delivery (seen as such by Jebb 1907, 89), or as describing Klytaimnestra's reaction (Kells 131): 'I see that she is breathing anger: but whether she is on the side of justice, I no longer see any care for this' (S ll. 610–11). This ambiguity is caused by the dissension between what just and righteous actions actually are in this context. Pound's rendering makes the Chorus use far more slangy speech than on earlier occasions: 'Gheez, she's a-goin' it fierce/ right or not she don't care a hang' (*E* ll. 697–98). Elektra states that despite her sense of shame and sense of what is appropriate, her words are the result of her mother's malignity and evil acts: *aischrois gar aischra pragmat' ekdidasketai* (S l. 621), 'Evil deeds are <the lessons> taught by evil deeds', given by Pound as: 'dirty workers teach dirty work' (*E* l. 707).

In Klytaimnestra's reaction to Elektra, Pound adds a puzzling negative. Sophocles has: 'O you shameless creature, surely I and my words and my actions make you say all too much' (S ll. 622–23). Pound's version reads:

> You beastly whelp, it's what I've said
> and NOT done, that makes you talk a great deal too much.
>
> *E* ll. 707–08

The addition of the 'NOT' is puzzling, as Elektra blames her mother that she 'did the job, not me' (*E* l. 711) – the 'good job' Klytaimnestra had been boasting about. Reid notes that 'Pound's otherwise incomprehensible turn upon the Greek of ll. 622–23 may have been influenced by his own line composed at Pisa: "Here error is all in the not done" (81/522)' (*E* 97). Indeed, that line of Canto 81 may be read as a denunciation of inaction, as opposed to an active direction of the will, where even a choice for an evil course of action is to be preferred to doing nothing at all. Pound had explored this theme already in Canto 5, where he also used quotations from the *Agamemnon* in connection to Alessandro di Medici and his 'abuleia' (5/19), that is, the inability to act.[5]

Still, that leaves open the extent to which any action is justified. This ties in with Sophocles' maxim in line 625, *ta d'erga tous logous heurisketai*, 'actions find for themselves the words', that is, Elektra is only putting into words what her mother has done. In his rendering, Pound does justice to this maxim by including a Latin phrase he attributed to Aquinas (*GB*, 92), a statement also used by Dante in his *Vita Nuova* XIII.4 (and based, in fact, on Justinian's *Institutiones* II.7.3): 'and things done get names/ *nomina sunt consequentia rerum*' (*E* ll. 712–13). The Latin reference is appropriate as the phrase encapsulates an important principle of Roman law. Moreover, in Pound's rendering of the Confucian *Analects* we find a similar phrase: 'the proper man's words must cohere to things, correspond to them (exactly)' (*CON* 249). This very much summarizes *Elektra*'s link between sincerity, words, and deeds, the theme already introduced at the beginning of the play.

After this dialogue between Elektra and Klytaimnestra, the latter makes a sacrifice to Apollo, requesting him to let her visionary dream have a positive outcome for her. Pound adds the stage direction '*sotto voce*' to indicate that she does not want to be overheard. Her 'you know all the rest I don't say' (*E* l. 749) is a silent prayer for the death of Orestes, but the very softly spoken words also allow Pound to add the phrase 'envious little bitch' (*E* l. 735) directed at Elektra, which is not derived from the original.

At this point the Paedagogus enters, pretending to be a messenger from Phocis. He claims to bring the good news of Orestes' death, of which he gives an account in a long 'Messenger' speech (S ll. 680–763), which Kells has termed 'one of the most splendid and effective in Sophocles' (137). Indeed, it is a brilliant evocation in full detail of the setting of the Pythian Games, of the excitement of the chariot-race for both participants and spectators, and of Orestes' fatal accident. Pound adopted a mock-Irish voice for the Messenger, by dropping the *h* in some of the *th*'s ('togedder', 't'rown', 'wid'), and the final *g*'s of the participles, while often adding an *a* ('a-rollin", 'a-lickin", 'a-snortin"), and some of the *i*'s into diphthongs ('He took all the foive prizes'). Fleming approved of Pound's transformation of the tutor into a comic character (*E* 97). Pound produced a vivid rendering, allowing himself the freedom to skip some of the details, but at times also staying very close to the Greek, although interestingly enough, there are no annotations to this speech in his Loeb.

After winning all the games, Orestes enters the chariot-race together with nine other charioteers. When the messenger starts describing the race, Pound gains speed in cutting some of the periphrastic details of the original, and gives excitement to the speech by the anaphoric and paratactic use of 'and', and the use of many present participles, up to the point where the race is between Orestes and the Athenian.

After the speech, we get the reactions of the Chorus, Klytaimnestra and Elektra. The Chorus is devastated as they think that with all the male members of the family gone, the house of Mycenae will cease to exist. Pound has emphasized their deeply emotional response by both translating and transliterating their two lines (omitting the word *genos*, as Fleming pointed out (*E* 38)):

> Alas, alas [*pheu pheu*]: the whole [TO PAN] stock [*genos*] of our ancient masters [DESPOTAISI TOIS PALAI], so it seems [HOOS EOIKEN], has perished [EPHARTHAI], root and branch [*prorrizon*].
>
> S ll. 764–65

> Ah, ah, that's the end of the dynasty
>   TO PAN DE DESPOTAISI TOIS PALAI
> They are blotted out root and branch.
>   HOOS EOIKEN, EPHTHARTAI.
>
> *E* ll. 835–38

In Sophocles, the vivid narrative about Orestes also has a powerful impact upon Klytaimnestra who, despite her earlier prayer for the death of her son, is moved to utter a heartrending cry of sorrow now that she is confronted by horrifying details of the manner in which he died. Her initial confusion on how to assess the news is rendered by Pound in staccato phrases. Indeed, is the news good, or terrible but still beneficial? Still, she now can rest assured that her life is no longer in danger, and that she only has to deal with Elektra, 'that worse plague living with me, while always draining the pure blood of my life' (S ll. 785–86), or in Pound's words, 'that worse little bloodsucker living here with me,/ the pest' (*E* ll. 857–58).

Elektra's reaction to the shocking news is rendered very freely by Pound:

Ah me, wretched one [*oimoi talaina*]! For now [*nun gar*] it is to me [*para = paresti*] to lament [*oimōxai*] your misfortune [*tēn sēn xumphoran*], Orestes [*Oresta*], when [*hoth'*] you in this state [*hōd' echōn*] are mocked [*hubrizei*] by your mother [*pros tēsd'... mētros*]. Is this not nice [*ar' echei kalōs*]?

S ll. 788–90

Ooooh, he's dead, and it fits the book
motherly excitement
very pretty

E 41, ll. 861–63

As he did earlier, Pound lets Elektra employ slangy expressions in her address to Klytaimnestra; thus the Sophoclean 'mock me: now you happen to be fortunate' (S l. 794), becomes 'Go on, keep it up. You're top dog, / you've hit the jack-pot' (*E* ll. 868–69).

After Klytaimnestra and the Paedagogus have left the stage, Elektra can fully vent her feelings (S ll. 804–822), a passage which in Pound's Loeb has light to medium annotations. Pound has emphasized her despair by transliterating the 'poor me / OO TALAIN' EGOO' of l. 807 of the original. He has greatly condensed her speech by deleting her address to Orestes and the expression of her crushed hopes of him coming for vengeance (S ll. 808–12), all summarized by Pound very effectively in the one line 'not ever' (*E* 42, l. 885). He also deleted ll. 813–17, and began translating again at l. 818.

In a *kommos* with Elektra (S ll. 823–72), consisting of short lines, in which she describes the loneliness of having lost both her father and her brother, the Chorus tries to comfort her. Pound retains the brevity of Elektra's utterances, and manages to convey the emotional speed of the original. A few points may be noted. In the original, Elektra utterly rejects any attempts to soften the blow of Orestes' death: 'If you suggest some hope regarding those who clearly have gone [*tōn phanerōs oichomenōn*] to Hades, you trample even more on me who is in tears' (S ll. 833–35). Apparently, as the typescript shows, Pound at first interpreted these lines as suggesting that even the dead may still influence life on earth, as he noted in the typescript that *phanerōs* does not mean 'manifestly dead' but should be connected to 'apparitions ... Hope for apparition of those in hell' (*E* 97). Later, however, Pound decided against the idea of an afterlife, and rendered the lines as: 'don't tell me about life after death/ that's only another kick when I'm down. / they're dead forever' (*E* ll. 902–04).

To comfort Elektra, the Chorus in Sophocles refers to Amphiaraus (ll. 838–39), who like Agamemnon was betrayed by his wife, but was later avenged by his son Alcmaeon who killed his mother. In his version Pound transliterated the Chorus's two lines before giving a spondaic-based translation, as he meant them to be sung, seeing that they are part of a *kommos* in lyrical metre. Their attempt at comfort is rejected at first by Elektra, who is '*disgusted and bored with the song*' (*E* l. 912). Yet the Chorus persists with another combination of translation and transliteration, in which Amphiaraus *pampsuchos anassei,* (S l. 841), 'reigns with full power of mind'. Jebb took the word *pampsuchos* to imply that he is still in full possession of his soul, and thus still able to act 'upon men through his oracles' (Jebb 1907, 120). Pound rendered the phrase as 'He reigns and lords his mind' (*E* l. 915). Then Elektra begins '*to cheer up, still dubious, but singing now and echoing the tone of the Chorus*' (*E* ll. 917–18). Pound indicates this by inserting transliterations into Elektra's speech, and cutting it down to its absolute essence, in the most lapidary style possible:

> I know, I know [*oid' oid'*]: for there appeared [*ephanē gar*] someone who cares for [*meletōr amphi*, that is, an avenger, Amphiaraus's son Alcmaeon] the one [*ton*] in sadness [*en penthei*]. But for me [*emoi d'*] there is no one anymore [*outis et' esth'*]; because he who was still there [*hos gar et' ēn*], has gone [*phroudos*], snatched away [*anarpastheis*, that is, by death].
>
> S ll. 846–48

known, over known
mid grief, an avenger.
OID' OID' EPHANE GAR MELETOOR
AMPHI TON EN PENTHEI.
I have none.
He was, and is not.
HOS GAR ET' EN

PHROUDOS ANARPASTHEIS
Vanished away, torn from me.

E ll. 924–32

In Sophocles, we get a repetition of words (which Earp saw as a hallmark of *Elektra*), initiated with *oid' oid'*, and continuing in the Chorus' response *deilaia deialiōn kureis*, 'unhappy one [*deilaia*], you confront [*kureis*] unhappy things/ circumstances [*deilaiōn*]' (S l. 849), to which Elektra reacts: *kagō toud' histōr, huperistōr*, 'and I know this, know this too well' (S l. 850). Pound has adapted this repetition or amplification of words, and extended it even further, while using -a- and -o- assonance:

CHORUS
sorrow attains thee, sorrow.

ELEKTRA
known, dont I know, over known,
day after day, moon over moon,
overfull, pain over pain
horrors of hate abate not
ever.

E ll. 934–38

Pound also emphasizes the bleakness of Elektra's emotional state of mind. When Elektra tells the Chorus to not lead her astray 'when there is [*pareisin*] no longer [*ou . . . eti*] the support [*arōgai*] from hope [*elpidōn*] {from someone} of a noble family [*eupatridan*] of the same parents [*koinotokōn*]' (S ll. 857–59), this becomes in Pound's version the request not to be led 'into emptiness / where there is no one at *all*' (*E* ll. 943–44). This last '*all*' is spoken in Pound's version simultaneously with the Chorus' '*all* men must die'. Where the Chorus in Sophocles states in reference to Orestes' death, *askopos ha lōba* (l. 865), 'the horror is unimaginable', Pound has the more cryptic 'unforeseen' (*E* l. 950), based on his reading of *askopos*, 'unimaginable', literally as *a + skopos*, 'un-seen', but in the sense of, as he noted in the typescript, 'the like as was never seen', that is, 'never seen before' (*E* 98).

While Elektra is lamenting the fact that her brother has been buried without her being present, her sister Chrysothemis appears, telling her that Orestes is still alive. Compared to the original, Elektra's speech in Pound's version contains many phrases denouncing her sister as mad: 'You're CRAZY . . . plumb crazy' (969), 'you're blotto delirious' (979), 'you always were soft in the head' (1019), 'you don't know whether you're on earth, or raving' (1021). When Elektra asks: 'from whom [*tinos brotōn*] have you heard [*eisakousas*'] this tale [*logon tond*'] which you believe [*pisteueis*] so much [*hōde agan*]' (S ll. 883–84), Pound renders it as: 'has anyone LIVING/ put that nonsense into your head?' (*E* ll. 974–75). This literal rendering of *tinos brotōn* as 'anyone LIVING', with an emphasis on the last word, may raise the question whether then there may have been an alternative (supernatural) source for the news. In his typescript, Pound explained his choice with regard to the Greek: 'i.e. EL/ thinks Cr/ has seen O's ghost/ position of the brotOn' (*E* 98). However, this assumption is only implied in the 'final' version.

Chrysothemis is unperturbed and asks Elektra first to listen and then judge whether she is 'batty' (*E* l. 981 = *mōran*, S l. 890). (Pound wrote '!gallina', the Italian for 'hen', at the top of his page of his Loeb.) In his rendering, Pound gives an explicit clue to his lifelong interest in the links between Greek tragedy and Japanese Noh, which he would pursue more thoroughly in *Women of Trachis*, as we will see. When Chrysothemis tells how she discovered rituals had been performed at Agamemnon's grave, Pound gives an elaborate stage direction to cue Elektra's response: '(*Elektra masked, at first not even looking at Chrysothemis but boredly into distance, gradually grows attentive. Slowness in turning of head, as per Noh*)' (*E* ll. 990–92). There is a hint of the epiphanic here, as an early foretelling of the later recognition scene between Elektra and Orestes. Chrysothemis is convinced that the lock of hair on the grave is Orestes', and she ends with a general observation and admonition:

> Come, my dear, have courage [*all', ō philē, tharsune*]! Surely [*toi*] not always [*ouch aei*] does the same of the daimones [*hautos daimonōn*] attend [*parastatei*] the same people [*tois autoisi*]. Ours [*nōin*] was [*ēn*] once [*ta prosthen*] gloomy [*stugnos*]; but this day [*hē de nun hēmera*] perhaps [*isōs*] will mark the beginning of [*huparxei*] the certainty [*kuros*] of many beautiful things [*pollōn kalōn*].
> S ll. 916–19

The term *daimon* represents a complex notion in classical thought as it can stand for a divine power guarding over us, or for our own inner genius, or for one's own fortune. In later antiquity, it attained the meaning of 'evil spirit, devil', and it was used as such in the New Testament. Jebb translated *daimonōn* as 'fortune' (131), Storr as 'destiny' (197). Pound, however, chose for 'devils', presumably because for him the word connoted Klytaimnestra and Aigisthos, although one could argue that such a reference would be out of character for Chrysothemis:

you buck up,
The same devils can't always run things,
ours have been pretty bad,
               But the luck's changing,
        happen a really good day might come in

E ll. 1014–18

Yet Elektra crushes her sister's hope by telling her about Orestes' death, after which she gives a longer speech (S ll. 946–89) to make clear what both sisters should be doing next, introduced by the statement 'You can't do a good job without work' (*E* l. 1044), another return to the theme of words versus action. In the typescript, Pound wrote that this was the 'Hardest speech in the play to manage.' He starts by rejecting Storr and Jebb's text, which in l. 947 has *akoue dē nun hēi bebouleumai poiein*, 'then listen how I have decided to act [*poiein*]'. Pound in his Loeb replaced ποιεῖν with τελεῖν, 'accomplish', writing next to the first verb, 'babble'. In the typescript he noted 'take variant from Ellendt. TELEIN stronger than poiein'. This is why he rendered the opening line as 'Well then listen, / I'm going to finish it up' (*E* ll. 1046–47). Pound's choice of *telein* shows how he saw Elektra as a very determined character.

Pound's version of Elektra's speech at first stays close to the original (S ll. 946–57 = *E* ll. 1046–58), but then he adds two lines to let Elektra stress their moral responsibility as well as the fact that no one else will help them: 'It's *our* father was murdered. / we've only got our own hands' (*E* ll. 1059–60). Elektra asks Chrysothemis:

> To what end [*poi*] will you wait [*meneis*] indifferent [*raithumos*], having fixed your look [*blepsas'*] upon [*eis*] some sort of hope [*tin' elpidōn*] still [*et'*] standing upright/ straight [*orthēn*]?

S ll. 958–59

As the typescript indicates, Pound struggled with this passage. In a crossed-out set of annotations, he wondered: '(syntax of blePsas d'orthen)??? / (You'll see it's the right thing to do)???/ orTHEN fem/ acc./ you'll be seen as a right (she) 'un/ will you etc' (*E* 51). Eventually, Pound renders it in three lines by using the word *orthēn* twice:

> might as well look at it straight. [= using *blepsas' orthēn*]
> wont get anywhere sittin still, [= using *poi meneis*]
> what hope is left standing [= using *tin' elpidōn et' orthēn*; here Pound uses Jebb's translation)]

E ll. 1061–63

Elektra thus advises action, not only out of piety for their father and brother, but also because then they will be free from Aigisthos' yoke, as otherwise they will not be allowed to marry or have children. As a free woman, Chrysothemis will have *gamōn epaxiōn*, 'a worthy marriage', *philei gar pros ta chrēsta pas horān* (S l. 972), 'because everyone loves to look at what is good' – or in Pound's version, 'People recognize quality, everybody does' (*E* l. 1077). They will also gain fame; here Elektra's speech becomes more modern again in a condensed rendering of the more periphrastic original (S ll. 975–83), depicting how people will praise how they 'threw out the crooks, settled the murderers' hash. / You just got to like 'em' (*E* ll. 1082–83). At this point Pound presents Elektra as going into a sort of trance; the passage he had been rendering in everyday speech (S ll. 977–983 = *E* 52 ll. 1080–88) is now repeated in transliteration, which emphasizes the emotion of her appeal to her sister. Elektra's last four lines (S ll. 986–89) summarize what she has been asking for, namely, to help the family to overcome their shameful existence.

Chrysothemis rejects her sister's appeal for help, and strongly advises her to not to pursue her plans (S ll. 993–1017). Her three arguments are that, first, it is not a woman's job; secondly, Elektra is not strong enough to overcome Aigisthos; and lastly, fortune seems to be against the sisters. Her speech, rendered fairly accurately by Pound (*E* ll. 1108–37), ends again with the by now familiar advice: *sthenousa mēden tois kratousin eikathein* (S l. 1013), 'when you are not strong, yield to those who have power', 'don't go up against the people in power' (*E* l. 1137).

The Chorus seems to side with Chrysothemis who is seen as having 'forethought, and a prudent mind' (*E* l. 1140 = Sophocles' *pronoias . . . nou sophou*, ll. 1015–16). This then evolves into another *stichomythia* between the two sisters (S ll. 1023–49), in which Elektra in an emotional manner keeps championing what is just (*dikē, dikaios*), and Chrysothemis, more calmly, what is sensible (*nous, phronein*). As such this dialogue repeats the discussion of the First Epeisodion. Pound captures the staccato effect of the *stichomythia* through his use of short phrasing, such as Elektra's 'Nice mind, no guts' (*E* l. 1151), for *dzēlō se tou nou, tēs de deilias stugō* (S l. 1027), 'I admire you for your good sense, but I hate you for your cowardice' (Pound marked this line in his Loeb edition). Elektra's repeated references to justice evokes Chrysothemis's strong response: *all' estin entha chē dikē blabēn pherei* (S l. 1042), 'but sometimes Justice brings harm' (also marked by Pound in his Loeb). It is perhaps Chrysothemis's most emotional criticism, and her statement 'might serve as a motto for the whole play' (Kells 177). Pound seemed to have recognized both its importance and its tone as he rendered the line in capitals: 'EVEN JUSTICE CAN BE A PEST' (*E* l. 1172). Yet in his Loeb he noted Elektra's constancy by writing next to line 1046, *kai mēn poēsō g' ouden ekplageisa se*, 'Surely I shall do it, in no way scared by you', the Spanish phrase *por mi vida*, 'upon my soul'.

The sisters then go their separate ways, not even agreeing to disagree. Pound amplifies the maxim at the end of Elektra's speech to make her even more aware of the hugeness of her undertaking, now that she finds herself on her own: 'For [*epei*] to chase [*to thērasthai*] vain things [*kena*] is of much folly [*pollēs anoias*]' (S ll. 1053–54).

It's useless to chase after shadows,

(mezzo voce, as if reflecting)

such a lot of them,

all of them void.

E ll. 1189–91

Notes

1 Pound also quoted the Italian phrase in a note to his *Women of Trachis* (*WT* 67).
2 Elektra's statement had a deep personal resonance for Pound. When, after his release from St Elizabeths in 1958, he went to live in Italy with his daughter Mary, she recalled near the end of her memoir that he was 'plagued by all kinds of remorse'. She did her best to take care of him, and one day her father

> summed up my frustrations in Greek: 'ou tauta pros kakoisi deilian echei.' 'What are you talking Greek for, I don't understand.' And he said: *Electra*. And I found:

Οὐ ταῦτα πρὸς κακοῖσι δειλίαν ἔχει;
Shall we to all our ills add cowardice?

Rachewiltz 306

3 See Fleming's discussion with Pound on this, *E* 95, s.v. 471.
4 See Mihalka 209.
5 On this matter, see Liebregts 2005, 150–51.

6

Sophocles, Pound and *Elektra* III

Second Stasimon (S ll. 1058–1097; *E* ll. 1195–1257)

In the Second Stasimon, heavily annotated in Pound's Loeb, the Chorus criticizes Chrysothemis and praises Elektra for her *eusebeia*, 'respect', shown to her father. Despite their attempts to reconcile the two sisters, they realize Elektra's claims are justified, and they express their admiration for her courage and perseverance. In the first Strophe (S ll. 1058–69), the Chorus holds up the behaviour of birds which support their parents as models for human children. Pound first gives the twelve lines of the original in transliteration, and the way he has cut off words makes clear he was using Jebb's Greek text here and not Storr's version in the Loeb. According to the typescript, he meant the transliteration to be sung, and to be followed by a 'brief summary sung in eng' (*E* 99). In his rendering, Pound did not translate the whole of the transliteration. At first he seems to have deleted the reference to the birds (S ll. 1058–62), most likely because this is a rather complex passage which has produced many conflicting interpretations.[1] However, he did transpose some of the words to the Anti-Strophe, so I will give a translation of the bird-passage here, using Pound's transliteration:

> Why [TI], when we see [ESOROOMENOI; Pound has an incorrect ESOPOOMENOI] the birds [TOUS OIOONOUS] above [ANOOTHEN] that are most wise [PHRONIMOUTATOUS] in taking care of the sustenance [TROPHAS KEDOMENOUS] of those from whom [APH' HOON] they came forth [BLASTOOSIN] and from whom [APH' HOON T'] they derive [HEUROOSI] pleasure [ONASIN; the α should be an η], do we not pay [OUK TELOUMEN] these things [TAD'] in equal measure [EP' ISAS]?
>
> *E* ll. 1195–99 = S ll. 1060–62

Having postponed for a moment the rendering of this passage, Pound then swerved away from the remainder of the original, which I translate here, using Pound's transliteration:

But by [ALL' OU] the lightning-bolt [TAN ASTRAPAN] of Zeus [DIOS] and the heavenly Themis [KAI TAN OURANIAN THEMIN], they are not untroubled [OUK APONETOI] for long [DARON]. Oh voice [OO PHAMA] on/ under the earth [CHTHONIA] for the mortals [BROTOISI], I ask you to cry out [KATA MOI BOASON] a piteous cry [OIKTRAN OPA] to the Atreidae below [TOIS ENERTH' ATREIDAIS], bearing [PHEROUS'] a joyless [AXOREUTA, literally: 'with no dancing {in celebration}'] message of dishonour [ONEIDE].

S ll. 1063–69 = E ll. 1200–06

Removing the depiction of the birds left Pound with a challenge. It is unclear in his version who exactly the 'they' are who will be experiencing trouble. In the larger context, they must be the ones who do not care properly for their parents, but in this particular context, it is not evident whether the Chorus is referring specifically to either Elektra or Chrysothemis. What in this case does 'properly caring' mean? Is it to continue to honour those who gave birth to you, no matter what they have done, which would refer to Chrysothemis, or to give them what is due, that is, to pay back parents who have failed in their loving duties, which would refer to Elektra? The Chorus has previously commended Chrysothemis, so they surely will not be stating that she will be punished with suffering. Another problem lies in the rendering of *phama chthonia*: is this the voice 'of the earth', that is, the rumour as spread among the living, or is it 'under the earth', thus the voice available to those already dead? Out of this hornets' nest of Greek phrases, Pound produced the following in which he reproduced the -o- and -ou- sounds of the original, while using many monosyllabic words to create spondaic weight and stress the solemn musicality of the Greek:

> Shall not justice be done
> by Zeus among men,
> Shall a sound be borne under earth
> to the sons of Atreus?
>   All
>   is not well in his hall.
>   His line dies out.

E ll. 1207–13

Pound does not retain the image of Themis, the goddess of law and order, but he transposes her into the abstract notion of justice dispensed by Zeus. Pound has picked a few words from Sophocles' lines 1063–66 (*ou, Dios, Themin, brotoisi*) to constitute a new sentence, while one may surmise that the 'be done' is based on *daron*, 'for long', which Pound mistakenly may have linked to the Latin *dare*, 'to give'. This rendering also reinforces the motif of doing versus talking. This condensed and free interpretation allowed Pound to avoid the obligation of having to solve the intricate complexity of what the original actually meant.

Contrary to the original, Pound put the references to justice and the message to be delivered to those in the underworld in the form of a question, perhaps to evoke the great sense of uncertainty of what will happen next. Pound's 'sons of Atreus' for *Atreidais* is grammatically correct, so that the twice used 'his' in *E* ll. 1212–13 refers to Atreus, not specifically to Agamemnon. However, here the ending of Pound's version of the Strophe has already rendered part of the Anti-Strophe, which he again transliterated on the basis of Jebb (S ll. 1070–81 = *E* ll. 1214–25). In the Anti-Strophe (S ll. 1070–81), we find the contents of the message, which is to inform Agamemnon of the situation in his palace, again provided here in translation alongside Pound's transliteration:

> <Tell> them [SPHIN] that [HOTI] their house [TA EK DOMOON] is now suffering from illness [EDE NOSEI], and that with regard to matters as to their children [TA DE PROS TEKNOON] the double/ mutual [DIPLE] battle/ strife [PHULOPIS, that is, between the children] is evened out [EXISOUTAI] no longer [OUKET'] in a loving [PHILOTASIOOI] way of life [DIATAI]. But [DE] Elektra, betrayed [PRODOTOS], alone tosses on the sea [MONA SALEUEI], always [AEI] bewailing [STENACHOUS'] the fate [TON; Jebb (147) here in his notes adapts the conjecture *oiton*] of her father [PATROS], unhappy girl [DEILAIA], like [HOPOOS] the always-grieving nightingale [HA PANDURTOS AEDOON], and not [OUTE] forethinking [PROMETHES] death [TI TOU THANEIN], but ready [HETOIMA] to no longer see [TO TE ME BLEPEIN, that is, the light of day], if she can bring down [HELOUS'] the two Furies [DIDUMAN ERINUN, that is, Klytaimnestra and Aigisthos]. Who [TIS] will ever be born [AN BLASTOI] so loyal to her father [EUPATRIS HOODE]?

Sophocles' Anti-Strophe compares Elektra to (the not explicitly named) Philomela, the nightingale singing from grief, to whom she had already compared herself in l. 107 (= *E* l. 117) and l. 148 (= *E* l. 198). This may be why Pound here transposed the bird imagery of the First Strophe, which he had not (yet) rendered, and used some of its Greek phrases in the first line of his Antistrophe: 'from above' = ANOOTHEN, while 'be wise birds of omen' is his rendering of PHRONIMOOTATOUS OIOONOUS ESOROOMENOI, where the present participle *esorōmenoi* is made to qualify the birds by interpreting the verb as meaning 'to foresee'.

Pound can fully focus on Elektra in his Antistrophe, and the typography becomes an iconic representation of her predicament of feeling emotionally lost and torn, not able to think clearly what to do next:

<pre>
from above   be wise birds of omen
Tossed and alone
              Elektra
                     mourns
constant aid hath she none
As Philomel in grief
                 her sire's shade
         so shamed of all the world
nor cares to live or die,
were he avenged.
</pre>

E ll. 1226–35

The arrangement of the words turns 'Elektra' into the lonely focal point of the Antistrophe, and gives full weight to her present state of mourning, while the indentations allow for various different combinations of the phrases in a sort of visual equivalent of Greek parataxis, such as 'mourns/ her sire's shade', and 'Elektra/ so shamed of all the world'.

In his rendering of the Second Strophe (S ll. 1082–89) and Anti-Strophe (S ll. 1090–97), in which the Chorus offer their praise of Elektra, Pound has his translation of the first three lines now precede the transliteration, meant as a 'Greek crescendo' (E 60). The Greek reads:

> For [YAR {sic} = GAR] no one [OUDEIS] of the noble [TOON AGATHOON] by living a bad life [DZOON KAKOOS] without glory [NOONUMOS] wants [THELEI] to shame [AISCHUNAI] a good reputation [EUKELIAN {sic} = EUKLEIAN], o my child, my child [OO PAI PAI]

It is clear that Pound's rendering of this in ll. 1236–38 rearranges some of the words, and again goes for a spondaic rhythm, while using repetition and -e-assonance to retain the double use of *pai* and have an equivalent of the assonance pattern of -a- of the original through his 'indeed/ . . . breed! heed, heed'.

After the transliteration, Pound then renders the rest of the Second Strophe and Anti-Strophe before ending again with a transliteration of only the Antistrophe (thereby deleting in his transliteration the last three lines of the Second Strophe). Lines 1085–97 of the original read:

> Thus so [hōs kai] you [su] have chosen [heilou] a life [aiōna] in common [koinon, that is, with the dead] full of tears [panklauton], and having spurned [kathoplisasa]

dishonour [*to mē kalon*], <you have chosen> to win [*pherein*] two prizes [*duo*] at once [*en heni logōi*], <namely,> to be called [*keklēsthai*] wise [*sopha*] and the best daughter [*arista pais*].

May you live [DZOOIS; should be DZOOIÈS], as far as I am concerned [MOI], superior [KATHUPERTHEN] in power [CHEIRI] and wealth [KAI PLOUTOOI] to your enemies [TEOON ECHTHROON] just as much as [HOSON] you now dwell [NUN NAIEIS] subject to them [HUPOCHEIR]. For I have found [EPEI EPHEUREKA] that you [S'] have been [BEBOOSAN] in not a happy state [MOIRAI MEN OUK EN ESTHLAI], but with regard to the greatest laws [HA DE MEGIST' NOMIMA] that ever came into existence [EBLASTE], <I have found that> you win [PHEROMENAN] the highest of them [TOONDE ARISTA] through your piety towards Zeus [TAI DZENOS EUSEBEIAI]

So fame's all-hovering   wing
shall bear her praise
for beauty of heart and mind
              for constant faith

    Nay, ere she die
    may power come
to lift her high,
    may yet her house be strong
as Zeus gave law.

E ll. 1243–51

In his version, Pound went his own way by adopting the *phama* which had been introduced in the First Strophe, and presenting it in its familiar image as having wings, used here to spread Elektra's name. The breadth of her reach is represented typographically through the use of indentations. The two 'prizes' of the original, to be called 'wise and the best daughter', are now turned into two periphrastic phrases, 'beauty of heart and mind' and 'constant faith'. *Aristos* can mean 'the best, noblest, most virtuous', and may have led to Pound's 'beauty of heart and mind' (*E* l. 1245), although his 'beauty of mind' may also cover *sopha*, 'wise'. The 'constant faith' (*E* l. 1246) seems to have been based on *en heni logōi*, literally 'by one argument'. The wish in ll. 1090–92 of the original is rendered by Pound in his ll. 1247–50, where *dzōiēs*, 'may you live', is turned into 'ere she die', while the complex construction in Sophocles' ll. 1093–97 is simply replaced by 'as Zeus gave law' (In his Loeb, Pound crossed out Storr's rendering of line 1096). It must be noted here that Pound made sense of the complex syntax, as we find this gloss in the typescript: 'we haven't found you in luck but observing highest piety in

Zeus' (*E* 99). Yet in his final, simplified version, Pound again stresses more explicitly the notion of retribution, justice and restoration of order. It is noteworthy that apart from the *melopoeia* of his version of this choral ode, Pound also produced a visually arresting translation.

Third Episode (S ll. 1098–1383; *E* ll. 158–1624)

Pound's Loeb has heavy annotations at the beginning of this Episode, but after Elektra's lament (S ll. 1126–70), there are only occasional medium-density annotations. In the Third Episode, we get the famous *anagnorisis* or recognition scene (S ll. 1098–1231). Orestes and Pylades enter with the urn, supposedly containing Orestes' ashes, after which Elektra and her brother engage in a long dialogue in which he slowly prepares her for the revelation of his identity. The beginning of Pound's rendering is marked by detailed stage directions, for all persons involved. Elektra at first is afraid that the 'Phocaeans' have brought the definitive proof of Orestes' death. When Orestes, still hiding his identity, points to the urn containing 'all that is left of him' (*E* l. 1291), Pound has Elektra burst out in a well-chosen pun: 'O. O it's all I can bear' (*E* l. 1293). And he puns again a few lines later with: 'It's the end of the line', that is, a confirmation of her sense of loss as well as the end of the family line. This is the beginning of a beautiful condensation of Elektra's speech. Sophocles' 'that I may weep and lament for myself and my whole family together with these ashes' (ll. 1121–22), becomes in Pound simply but powerfully: 'we're all there together:/ ashes' (*E* ll. 1300–01).

Elektra's long lament over the urn (S ll. 1126–70) is rendered by Pound under the title '*ELEKTRA'S KEENING*' (*E* ll. 1306–68). In his typescript he wrote down suggestions for performing the speech, which he wanted to be sung in antiphony, with Elektra's words in English echoed line by line in Greek by the Chorus, with a gradual crescendo. This lament was to one of 'Vocal orchestration'. In the published version, however, we do not see any sign of these Greek echoes, and Pound has Elektra herself both speak and sing to convey her alternation of strong emotions. Pound also noted in his typescript his different approach to lyrical passages in comparison to the dialogues: 'for the emotional passages translate the total emotion of the whole speech. for mental conflicts: the meaning, exact meaning word by word' (*E* 100). Pound thus cut down the original speech to its essentials while retaining the exact meaning of what, in his version, is a successful and powerful lament. This becomes clear if we compare the original opening, where Elektra addresses the urn, to his version:

> O remaining memorial of the life of Orestes, dearest of men to me, how far from the hopes with which I sent you away do I receive you back. For now I carry nothing in my hands, but my child, I sent you away from home when you were glorious. I wish I had given up my life before that moment when I sent you away to a strange land, stealing you away with these hands, and saved you from death, so that you could have died on that day, having got a share in your father's tomb.
>
> S ll. 1126–35

> All that is left me
> my hope was Orestes
> dust is returned me
> in my hands nothing, dust that is all of him,
> flower that went forth
>
> would I had died then
> ere stealing thee from slaughter
> died both together
> lain with our father
>
> E ll. 1307–15

Stergiopoulou has pointed out how the passage is translated in a version of Anglo-Saxon tetrameter to render Sophocles' iambic trimeters, with each line a hemistich having two beats, and the line end marking the caesura, while employing alliteration, assonance and archaic phrasing (Stergiopoulou 2015, 100–101). However, one may question her claim that each of 'Sophocles' lines begins with a spondee ... which Pound mirrors by beginning his lines with a stress' (101). While the spondee is a sign of demonstrable quantitative length, stress in this passage is more dependent on performance. One can argue, for example, over the stress in 'my hope is Orestes', 'would I had died then', or 'to soothe thy passing'. Still, I agree that underlying the pure stress-based metre is the possibility of accentual scanning, as most of Pound's lines can be read as adonics ($-\times\times-\wedge$, where the last syllable may be either short or long). This gives 'Elektra's Keening' a 'Greek feel' while simultaneously transposing the original text into clear English, making it 'new', alive and traditional, as Pound had done with Homer in Canto 1, and in line with his theoretical approaches to translation discussed in Chapter 1.

Elektra bitterly regrets that she was not able to perform the burial rites for Orestes. She recalls how in the past she was both a sister and nurse to him, and that she might as well be regarded as dead too. In his stage directions, Pound indicates that at this point her grief gives way to anger. This is made clear in the way the tone of the English, which up to this point was highly poetical and meant to be sung, now changes into a set of bitter lines intended to be spoken (and note the reference to the 'job'):

> And that bitch of a mother is laughing
> and they haven't sent back even the shape of him,
> but a ghost that cant do its job.
>
> E ll. 1340–42

These lines condense ll. 1153–59 of the original by combining four lines. First we have *mainetai d'uph' hēdonēs/ mētēr amētōr* (1153–54), 'the mother, who is no mother, is mad with joy'; and *hos s' hōde moi proupempsen anti philtatēs/ morphēs spodon te kai skian anōphelē* (1158–59), '<your fortune> which sent you thus to me as ashes and a useless shadow instead of your most beloved form'. Pound's l. 1342 is very effective in rendering the 'useless shadow'. In his re-arrangement of the lines of the original, Pound then repeats the spirit of this speech with variety, adding *ho dustuchēs/ daimōn* (1156–57), 'evil fortune', but now in a passage meant to be sung (as its poetic tone suggests):

> thou the avenger, no more avenging
> born to misfortune, ashes avail not
> shadows avail not
>
> ahi, ahi,
> bodiless
> brother that art not.
>
> E ll. 1345–50

The opening sound of 'avenger/ avenging' is repeated in 'avail not', stressing Elektra's hopelessness, with perhaps a hint of the Latin *ave* or 'farewell'. At l. 1160 in the original, Elektra is carried away by extreme emotion, as is evident by a few short outbursts (no longer in regular iambic trimeters), before she resumes 'regular speech':

> Ah me, ah me [*oimoi moi*]! O pitiable body, alas, alas! O dearest one, ah me ah me, sent on the most terrible road, how have you destroyed me! Yes, destroyed me, o my brother! Therefore receive me in this your room, me who am nothing, into this nothingness [l. 1166, *tēn mēden eis to mēden*], so that I may dwell with

you below forever. For even when you were on earth, I shared with you equally, and now I wish to die and not be separated from your grave. For I see that the dead do not suffer from pain.

S ll. 1160–70

Here Pound's rendering emphasizes Elektra's emotion by giving her a singing part while alternating translation and amplification of phrases from the original that repeatedly stress death, nothingness, and the desire to continue to be with Orestes forever (expressed in three variations):

thy death, my death
dred road thou goest
brother, my slayer
as ever above earth
let death divide not

(*singing to the urn*)

Oimoi Oimoi

take me in with you
I now am nothing, make place beside thee
naught into naught, zero to zero
to enter beside thee
our fortune equal
death ended pain.

E ll. 1356–68

Stergioupolou points out that the first two lines employ heavy syllables which can be seen as adding up to a spondaic line, although she admits that in speaking them we may tend to stress in different ways: 'Do we privilege the internal rhyme of *thy* and *my*, the assonance of *road* and *goest*, or the alliteration of *death*, *dying*, and *dred*?' (Stergiopoulou 2015, 101) But even if the English cannot transpose the quantitative regularity of vowel length of the Greek, Stergiopoulou is right in claiming that Pound attempted to mirror Sophocles' use of long vowels in this lament. As we have seen, this became his habit in this version whenever he wanted to stress the solemnity of tone, and give his version poetic ὄγκος.

Elektra's resolve to kill Aigisthos, even at the expense of her own life, now gives way to the desire to die herself. The Chorus tries to soothe her by pointing out how Agamemnon and Orestes were both mortals, and that she should accept the inevitable fact of human mortality and move on. Yet where the Chorus seems realistic, even clinical, Elektra's speech has moved Orestes so much that he feels he must reveal himself. This leads to another *stichomythia* (S ll. 1176–1231), in which Elektra gradually understands who the young stranger is. This process is represented partly through a repetition of each other's words. F. R. Earp pointed out in *The Style of Sophocles* that one sign of *Elektra* being a later play is the use of anaphora, which occurs when a word is repeated, generally for emphasis, or in dialogues when a second speaker repeats a word used by the previous speaker. Here we have in the Greek *horōn* (1187)/ *horāis* (1188); *monos* (1200)/ *monos* (1201); *eunoun* (1203)/ *eunoun* (1204); *pros dikēs ou steneis* (1211)/ *ou dikēi stenō* (1212); *atimos* (1214)/ *atimos* (1215); *Orestou* (1216)/ *Orestou* (1217); *taphos* (1217)/ *taphos* (1218); *philtaton* (1223)/ *philtaton* (1223). Marking this dialogue in his Loeb with the transliterated Greek word 'diagignosco', 'to discern, to distinguish', Pound has retained the form of the *stichomythia*, and on occasion also employed the device of repetition, as in 'assassins' (1396 and 1397), 'no one' (1403) – 'Nobody' (1404); 'fit' (1424 and 1426), while even on one occasion combining Greek and English with 'PHOS' (1437) – 'day' (1438).

Pound opted for more natural speech than the original. Thus, for example, Orestes' 'O body wasted ruthlessly and impiously' (S l. 1181) becomes 'what in hell have they done to you?' (*E* l. 1382). Pound also extended Elektra's words in line 1184, 'Why are you lamenting in looking at me this way?', to three lines, so as to give them full weight and insert a wry joke:

what are you lookin'at?
what you got to be sad about?
it isn't YOUR funeral

E ll. 1385–87

Pound stays close to the original Greek in this dialogue, which in one case produces an awkward statement. When Orestes decides to tell his sister who he really is, he wants Elektra to let go of the urn, which she at first refuses to do. He then claims *peithou legonti kouch' hamartēsei pote*, 'do as I say, and you will not ever make a mistake'. Pound, however, went for another meaning of *hamartaō* in his: 'Come on, you won't miss it' (*E* l. 1416), which does not fit the state of mind of Elektra here. Perhaps he was led astray by Jebb's 'Do as I say, and never fear to do amiss' (Jebb 1907, 163).

The moment of Elektra's insight is given by Pound in untranslated transliteration: 'O PHILTATON PHOS' (*E* l. 1437), 'O most happy light/day!' (S l. 1224). Pound apparently wanted to retain both the awareness that this day is the turning-point in Elektra's life, as well as the image of light as representing clarity and epiphanic insight. This moment in the play is what Aristotle in his *Poetics* XI (52a22) calls the *peripeteia*, the reversal or change of fortune 'to the opposite state of affairs ... in accordance with probability and necessity', that is, it is a surprising but still necessary outcome of the preceding actions. In the same chapter Aristotle also talks about *anagnorisis* or recognition (52a29), 'a change from ignorance to knowledge', as the 'most effective recognition is one that occurs together with reversal' (tr. Golden 118). Such a dramatic combination can be found here at this point, which is why Pound retained the Greek. (Incidentally, Storr assigned ll. 1230–31, the closing lines of the recognition scene, to Orestes, whereas Jebb has them spoken by the Chorus, as has Pound, another sign that he is relying here on Jebb's edition.)

The *stichomythia* in iambic trimeters is followed by a lyrical dialogue between the actors, a *melos apo skēnēs* divided into a strophe, anti-strophe, and epode (S ll. 1232–87), to release the strong feelings of Elektra now that she is reunited with her brother (who in 'rational' iambic trimeters tries to restrain her emotion and remind her of his mission). Pound noted in his typescript: 'gamut of emotion very great from 1232'. This is why Pound added the following stage direction at the beginning of Elektra's speech: '*ELEKTRA (singing starts sotto-voce, trembly; asides spoken rhythmically with kettle drum accompaniment*' (*E* l. 1448). Kells has rightly noted that Elektra reaches in these verses the 'greatest dramatic height' in her expression of her joy, uttered 'without consideration of consequences, or of the time, the place or the circumstances in which she and Orestes are placed' (198). This may well be why Pound after his relatively exact rendering of the stichomythia now took a freer approach to convey the emotional intensity of her speech. Elektra's initial outburst is condensed by Pound into an emotional equivalence:

 ἰὼ γοναί, [*iō gonai*, 'Oh child']
 γοναὶ σωμάτων ἐμοὶ φιλτάτων, [*gonai sōmatōn emoi philtatōn*, 'child of the
  body most dear to me']
 ἐμόλετ' ἀρτίως, [*emolet' artiōs*, 'you have arrived just now']
 ἐφηύρετ', ἤλθετ', εἴδεθ' οὓς ἐχρῄζετε. [*ephēuret', ēlthet', eideth' hous
  echrēidzete*, 'you have found, you have come, you have seen those whom you
  wanted']
                     S ll. 1232–35

The emotional weight of these four lines, ending in a rhetorical *tricolon*, is neatly captured in Pound's one-line 'heart, heart, heart thou art come' (*E* l. 1449). Elektra does not heed Orestes' plea to be silent, but her speech even increases in intensity, marked by another stage direction and a transliteration of the Greek:

ELEKTRA *(sings greek like Carmagnole. THIS song can be burst into. Like wild Sioux injun war dance with tommy hawks)*

ALL' OU MA TEN
ADMETON AIEN
ARTEMIN

E ll. 1455–59

'La Carmagnole' is a French song of victory originating from the French Revolution. The Greek transliterated words spread over three lines actually make up one line in the original, meaning 'But by the ever unmarried Artemis' (S l. 1239). Elektra in her joy shouts: 'I shall never think worthy of my fear this useless burden of women always staying indoors' (S ll. 1240–42), given by Pound as:

Oh to hell with all the hens
in the old hen house

I aint afraid of hens
cause they aint a bit of use.

E ll. 1460–63

This is connected to Pound's annotation in his Loeb when he described Chrysothemis as 'gallina'. But when Orestes notes that women can also have a fighting spirit, Elektra is reminded of Klytaimnestra and the cause of her misery (S ll. 1245–52). Pound struggled with this passage and Orestes' response, and wrote in his typescript: 'FIVE lines/ here, want Jebb/ and all possibilities of MEANING before I bother further.' He had similar problems with ll. 1253–56: 'also next speech, and ennepein dika (technical law jargon) free mouth'. To help him out, Fleming supplied Jebb's translation of ll. 1246–56. Let us first look at ll. 1245–50:

ὀτοτοτοτοῖ τοτοῖ,
ἀνέφελον ἐνέβαλες
οὔ ποτε καταλύσιμον,
οὐδέ ποτε λησόμενον
ἁμέτερον οἷον ἔφυ κακόν.

Alas! Alas! [*otototoi totoi*], you have called to mind [*enebales*] something not clouded-over [*anephelon*], never [*ou pote*] to be dispelled [*katalusimon*], and never [*oude pote*] to be forgotten [*lēsomenon*], <namely,> our misfortune [*hameteron kakon*] such as it is [*hoion ephu*, literally, such as it came to be born]

> Alas! Ah me! Thou hast reminded me of my sorrow, one which, from its nature, cannot be veiled, cannot be done away with, cannot forget!
>
> Jebb 1907:169

Despite this input from Jebb, via Fleming, Pound decided to give a literal rendering of ll. 1245–50 and keep to the Greek word order, a strategy he made explicit several times in the typescript by stating: 'gk/ word order more important than syntactic coherence' (*E* 98), and 'order of thought in gk more important than syntax' (*E* 99). In this instance, this did not result in communicative difficulty:

> OTOTOTOTOI
> clear again, not to be ended,
> not to be forgotten,
> how our ill started, trouble began.
>
> *E* ll. 1465–68

However, Orestes' answer is as puzzling in the Greek as it is in Pound:

> ἔξοιδα καὶ ταῦτ᾽· ἀλλ᾽ ὅταν παρουσία
> φράζῃ, τότ᾽ ἔργων τῶνδε μεμνῆσθαι χρεών.
>
> S ll. 1251–52

> I know these things as well [*exoida kai taut'*]: but when [*all' hotan*] opportunity/ their presence (?) [*parousia*] admonishes us [*phradzēi*], then [*tot'*] will be the moment [*chreōn*] to recall [*memnēsthai*] these deeds [*ergōn tōnde*].

The crux here is the word *parousia*. It can mean 'occasion' or 'presence'. Jebb takes it as referring to the presence of Aigisthos and Klytaimnestra as a reminder for action, so that 'these deeds' are their crimes (Jebb 1907, 169). Kells, however, chooses 'opportunity' (Kells 201–02), as does Storr in his Loeb translation by giving it as 'the hour' (227). In any case, by inverting the meaning in making the 'crime' the subject instead of the object of 'recalling', Pound created a semantic mystery:

> Don't I know it but
> to tell in its time
> when the DEED recalls it
>
> *E* ll. 1469–71

In the Anti-Strophe (S ll. 1253–72), Elektra continues to resist her brother's attempt to restrain her joy, or in Pound's depiction of Orestes's qualification, 'yr/ whoopee' (*E* l. 1480), to render the Sophoclean *chairousan* (l. 1271). It is a shame that Pound did not retain his earlier version given in the typescript as this would have been a great example of melopoeic equivalence: 'XAIrousan/carousin". As we have seen, Pound struggled with this passage, particularly with lines 1254–55, 'ennepein dika (technical law jargon) free mouth' (*E* 101). The Greek reads:

> ὁ πᾶς ἐμοί,
> ὁ πᾶς ἂν πρέποι παρὼν ἐννέπειν
> τάδε δίκᾳ χρόνος·
> μόλις γὰρ ἔσχον νῦν ἐλεύθερον στόμα.
>
> S ll. 1253–56

Any and every time [*ho pas chronos*], any and every [*ho pas*], when it comes [*parōn*], would suit [*an prepoi*] for me [*emoi*] to tell [*ennepein*] these things [*tade*] rightfully [*dikai*]: for [*gar*] with difficulty [*molis*] I obtained [*eschon*] a mouth [*stoma*] which is now free [*nun eleutheron*]

Each moment of all time, as it comes, would be meet occasion for these my just complaints; scarcely now have I had my lips set free.

Jebb 1907, 169

Pound created a puzzling statement here by having Elektra say: 'Any time's right, now, I've hardly got my mouth free' (*E* l. 1472), whereas the Greek text has her state that she only just now after a long time and with difficulty (*molis*) has gained the freedom to speak, and thus feels she has the right to discuss (*dikai ennepein*) her joy at the return of Orestes and the revenge of her father's murder. It is evident that ll. 1465–72 of Pound's version (his rendering of Sophocles' lines 1245–56), constitute a passage that is not readily understandable upon first hearing or seeing, and only makes sense by going back to the Greek. Here Pound may be said to have a 'Browningesque' moment.

In the epode, Elektra eventually starts to calm down but still has a favour to ask, namely, that she may touch her brother's face. Pound also seemed to have found the beginning of the epode challenging, which is understandable given the syntactical complexity of the Greek:

> ἰὼ χρόνῳ μακρῷ φιλτάταν ὁδὸν
> ἐπαξιώσας ὧδέ μοι φανῆναι,
> μή τί με, πολύπονον ὧδ' ἰδὼν.
>
> S ll. 1273–75

Ah [*iō*] after a long time [*chronōi makrōi*] you deigned [*epaxiōsas*] to appear [*phanēnai*] to me [*moi*] thus [*hōde*] on the dearest journey [*philtatan hodon*]

{OR after a long time you deigned to make the journey dearest to me [Jebb suggests to supply *elthein* with *hodon*]}, seeing me [*me idōn*] thus so full of suffering [*poluponon hōd'*], do not [*mē ti*] ....

In the typescript Pound gave an almost literal rendering of these lines, and noted with ironic surprise ('gosh') that he had used the verb 'deign', most likely with an eye on Jebb's version. He noted in the typescript that his translation in quotation marks was 'kidding the crib' (*E* 101), a joke he retained in the final version:

Oh a long long time to the right road/ you 'deign' (gosh) deign to show up here/ but not me, seeing me full of toil./ considering all my worries, troubles;

ts. *E* 73

It's been so long, long, but the road's right,
you 'deign' deign to show up here
now I can see you
& you see my troubles
but not me
      DON'T...

E ll. 1482–87

The problem in the Greek original is that Elektra does not complete her sentence 'do not...' until after the interjection of Orestes ('What shouldn't I do?'). The result is that the *me*, the accusative of *egō*, in l. 1275 is left hanging, but Pound connected it with the *mē ti*, and came up with 'but not me' in his typescript. Fleming's suggestions in his own typescript produced an initial version that made more sense with regard to the Greek:

It's been so long, long/ god bless the road,/ and then suddenly you come, and see all my troubles, Don't; find me LOOKING like this; [see what I've been thru]

F. 74–75

This, however, created confusion because of the ambiguity of 'LOOKING' as it can mean both 'seeing' and 'appearing'. Most likely without checking the Greek text, Pound came up with a version in the typescript that has both Orestes and Elektra looking at each other: '[Its been so long, long, but the road's right,/ now I can see you/ & you see my troubles]/' (*E* 74) This rendering may explain Pound's puzzling account in the final version given above, in which the phrase 'you see my troubles/ but not me' gives rise to an interesting psychological presentation of Orestes who in Elektra's view apparently only has an eye for the circumstances but not for his sister herself.

Elektra then ends the Epode on a lyrical note:

> Ah friends, I heard a voice I never could have hoped to hear, and yet I held back my emotion in silence and did not cry out when I heard it. Unhappy me! But now I have you: you have appeared with the dearest face, which I can never forget even in troubling times.
>
> S ll. 1281–87

Storr rendered this passage in couplets (231), perhaps to indicate that Elektra has composed herself again after her emotional outbursts. Pound also employed rhyme, albeit not consistently, despite his glossing of the epode in his Loeb as 'approaching excitement'. He took some liberties with the Greek in the middle section of the passage:

> Oh dearest friends
> if now's to ear
> a voice I ne'er
> had hoped to hear
>
> If joy shall not
> burst forth at this
> then ever dumb in wretchedness
> shd/ one live on in deep distress.
>
> Now thou art here
>   in full daylight
>   shall I not pour
>   forth my delight,
> who ne'er in deepest woe
>   had forgot thee.
>
> E ll. 1494–1507

In his typescript, Pound appended to this passage 'Yrs/ v.t. Thos/ Moore', and I agree with Reid's observation that Pound here was offering a parody here of the nineteenth-century Irish Romantic poet Thomas Moore (*E* 101).

In the remainder of the Third Epeisodion (S ll. 1288–1383), Elektra and Orestes discuss the plot of vengeance. This part of the Episode is faithfully rendered by Pound. It is Orestes who takes the initiative, and has enough of talk and reflection, as is evident from his speech, enhanced by Pound's stage directions (*E* ll. 1508–09). The self-presentation as a man of action in the original (S ll. 1288–1300 = *E* ll. 1510–25) is retained by Pound, who for Orestes' speech employs a great deal of imperatives in order to 'get on with the job ... to put an end to these bumptious bastids' (*E* ll. 1515 and 1519). Elektra who up to this point had taken the initiative and had been willing to do the job by herself, is happy now to let herself be guided by her brother.

Then the Paedagogus appears and informs Orestes about the situation in the palace: things are 'well' because Klytaimnestra is grief-stricken and therefore not on her guard, so this distraction, her actually 'not doing well', will make the revenge easier to execute. This is how one should read his complex statement in ll. 1344–45: 'as things are [*hōs de nun echei*], all is well with them [*kalōs ta keinōn panta*], even what is not well [*kai ta mē kalōs*].' Pound managed to render the cryptic words of the Paedagogus in his 'and the worse they do, the better …' (*E* l. 1576) There is a touch of humor in Pound's rendering of Orestes' address to his friend Pylades who has been there present all the time without saying anything: 'Pylades, this our task requires no further long speeches' (S ll. 1372–73). Pound turned this into: '*ORESTES (to Pylades who hasn't said a damn word.)*/ Come on, Pylades, cut the cackle' (*E* ll. 1613–14).

When both men enter the palace, Elektra prays to Apollo, a speech which Pound wanted to have performed as a '*sort of sing-song*' (l. 1616). The original has the prayer in ordinary iambic trimeters:

> Lord Apollo [*anax Apollon*], hear [*klue*] them [*autoin*, that is, Orestes and Pylades] favourably [*hileōs*], and me as well [*eme te pros toutoisin*], who so often [*hē polla dē*] stood before you [*se proustēn*] with a devout hand [*liparei cheri*; Ellendt's Lexicon has 'generous' for *liparei*] <making an offering> from what I had [*aph' hōn echoimi*]. And now [*nun d'*], O Lycean Apollo [*ō Lukei' Apollon*], with the things I have [*ex hoiōn echō*] I pray to you [*aitō*], I supplicate [*propiptō*], I implore [*lissomai*], be [*genou*] a willing helper [*prophrōn arōgos*] for us [*hēmin*] in these plans [*tōnde tōn bouleumatōn*], and show [*kai deixon*] men [*anthrōpoisi*] the wages [*tapitimia*] of impiety [*tēs dussebeias*] which [*hoia*] the gods [*theoi*] give [*dōrountai*].
>
> S ll. 1376–83

Pound condensed this prayer but retained the essential phrases, translating the Greek word *hileōs* twice immediately after the transliteration, and noting in the typescript that in the Greek, it is 'like the drone of a prayer, still in ritual, just as gabbled as still in Kat/ churches' (*E* 102):

> O King Apollo,
>   HILEOOS
> Favour us, favour us
> oft have I prayed thee

> my little I gave thee
> Phoibos, Lukeios
> aid the right now
> > let the gods show their godhead
>
> E ll. 1617–24

Third Stasimon (S ll. 1384–97; E ll. 1625–33)

Earp in *The Style of Sophocles* refers to this brief choral ode as an example of the playwright's occasional tendency to combine his early, rather archaic, and later, more natural, style. The ode at first seems rather Aeschylean, full of 'epic' colouring due to the use of periphrasis, amplification, and personification, yet the 'sentences move rapidly and … are easy to follow. And, what is more, they are closely related to the action and contain few general comments or descriptions.' Basically, all of the lines amount to this idea: '"The avengers are now in the house and we shall soon be relieved of suspense"' (Earp 157–58). Unlike the other Odes in Pound's Loeb, this one has only some medium annotations (in the Strophe), perhaps on account of its brevity and the relative simplicity of its Greek.

In this Stasimon, the Chorus describes the presence of Ares and the Erinyes in the palace, and how Orestes and Hermes are ready for the vengeful act:

> ἴδεθ' ὅπου προνέμεται
> τὸ δυσέριστον αἷμα φυσῶν Ἄρης.
> βεβᾶσιν ἄρτι δωμάτων ὑπόστεγοι
> μετάδρομοι κακῶν πανουργημάτων ἄφυκτοι κύνες,
> ὥστ' οὐ μακρὰν ἔτ' ἀμμενεῖ
> τοὐμὸν φρενῶν ὄνειρον αἰωρούμενον.
>
> παράγεται γὰρ ἐνέρων
> δολιόπους ἀρωγὸς εἴσω στέγας,
> ἀρχαιόπλουτα πατρὸς εἰς ἑδώλια,
> νεακόνητον αἷμα χειροῖν ἔχων· ὁ Μαίας δὲ παῖς
> Ἑρμῆς σφ' ἄγει δόλον σκότῳ
> κρύψας πρὸς αὐτὸ τέρμα κοὐκέτ' ἀμμένει.
>
> ll. 1384–97

See [*ideth'*] where [*hopou*] Ares moves forward [*pronemetai*], breathing [*phusōn*] the blood [*to haima*] of ugly strife [*duseriston*]. Already [*arti*] they have gone [*bebasin*] under the roof [*hupostegoi*] of the house [*dōmatōn*], the pursuers [*metadromoi*] of evil crimes [*kakōn panourgēmatōn*], the inescapable dogs [*aphuktoi kunes*], so that [*hōst'*] the vision of my mind [*toumon phrenōn oneiron*] does not have to wait long [*ou makran et' ammenei*] in suspense [*aiōroumenon*].

For [*gar*] the helper [*arōgos*] of the spirits [*enerōn*] with his stealthy tread [*doliopous*] is entering [*paragetai*] into the house [*eisō stegas*], into his father's seat [*patros eis hedōlia*] full of ancient wealth [*archaioplouta*], bearing [*echōn*] new-whetted [*neakonēton*] blood [*haima*, that is, the act of blood about to take place] in his hands [*cheiroin*]. And Hermes, the son of Maia, leads them [*ho Mias de pais Hermēs sph' agei*] to the goal itself [*pros auto terma*], hiding [*krupsas*] the guile [*dolon*] in darkness [*skotōi*], and he waits no more [*kouket' ammenei*].

Storr rendered the ode, which uses an iambic metre with dochmiacs ($\times - - \times -$), in couplets (239). Pound noted the musicality of the ode, but wrote in the typescript: 'DAMN/ rhythm a twister' (*E* 102). He chose to find an equivalent through a (chor)iambic rhythm (with lines 1628 and 1633 ending in spondaics), and through repetition of words and phrases. Furthermore, in order to evoke the sensation of the Chorus as eyewitnesses, not knowing where to look first as the action is very fast, Pound employed irregular lines visually spread across the page. To gain speed, he confined himself to rendering only the first half of the ode, and adapted from the second half the phrase *dolon skotōi*, 'the guile in darkness'. Stergiopoulou has rightly noted how the consonants of 'prey' split into 'palace roof', and then reunite in 'proof' and 'presage' (Stergiopoulou 2015, 104). In the following I have appended the Greek phrases to Pound's translation, and have given the repeated phrases in bold:

    Mars breathing blood [*Arēs phusōn haima*]
    hounds that never miss their prey [*aphuktoi kunes*]
miss never their spring, under the roof [*hupostegoi*],
seeking the doers of ill [*metadromoi kakōn panourgēmatōn*], all ill, by stealth, by guile, [*dolon skotōi*]
    Mars, breatheth blood,
    dogs that never miss their prey,
    the palace roof,
nor yet under-long to wait for the proof [*ou makran et' ammenei aiōroumenon*],
of my presage [*toumon phrenōn oneiron*]
    will, heart, and all.
              E ll. 1625–33

The last line is Pound's invention to stress how emotion and resolve go hand in hand here, and its dimeter mirrors the opening one. Apparently, he was so pleased with his own melopoeic result that he dispensed with giving the Greek in transliteration.

Exodos (S ll. 1398–1510; *E* ll. 1634–1802)

The First Scene (S ll. 1398–1441 = *E* ll. 1634–97) of the Exodos deals with the death of Klytaimnestra, and consists of a *kommos* with an alternation of spoken iambic trimeters and sung lyrical metres, divided into two metrically corresponding Strophes (1398–1421 and 1422–41). In the Strophe, Elektra enters and informs the Chorus that the two young men are about to commit the revengeful deed, after which we hear the shriek of Klytaimnestra. In the Antistrophe, Orestes and Pylades come out of the palace, but go back in again when they see Aigisthos approaching.

In his rendering of the first half of the scene (*E* ll. 1634–76), Pound did not retain the alternation of spoken and sung verse, but indicated the 'lyrical emotion' involved by transliterating Elektra's command to the Chorus 'to wait in silence': 'SIGA PROSMENE' (*E* l. 1639). As Reid rightly notes (*E* 102), this is 'a deliberate echo' of the phrase used in the '*Agamemnon*' Canto 5/19 (see below). The agitation of the Chorus is represented by deleting the spacing between the words of their anxious question: 'whataretheydoing?' (*E* l. 1642). The only part sung in Pound's version, comprising a '*cry of misery*', is his rendering of ll. 1413–14 in the original: 'O city [*ō polis*], o unhappy family [*ō genea talaina*], now [*nun*] your [*soi*] day by day [*kathameria*] fate [*moira*] is dying, is dying [*phthinei phthinei*].'

> O city, o WRETCHED house
> and the curse's tooth gnaws
>   day after day
>
>   *E* ll. 1660–62

Pound was at first confused by the Greek of ll. 1413–14: '"(crib and Loeb diametric opposite meanings. OUT, eroding/ ELLENDT reads PHTHinein. phTHinein"' (*E* 102). The Greek *phthinein* means 'to decay, dwindle, perish, pass away', but can also have a more causal meaning, 'to make to pine away', and thus 'to consume, to destroy'. Jebb translated the passage as: 'Ill-fated realm and race, now the fate that hath pursued thee day by day is dying – is dying!' (Jebb 1907, 189); Storr gives: 'Unhappy realm and house,/ The curse that dogged thee day by day/ Is dying, dying fast' (241). Pound's translation in the typescript originally stayed closer to the more general meaning of *phthinein* by rendering 'the curse is thinning out', thus using *moira* and *phthinei*. He then chose to bring out the agency of *moira* more by using the causal meaning of the verb: 'and the curse gnaws, with the day', and 'and the curse's tooth, gnaws by the day', before he reached the final version given above. Perhaps he wanted to continue the image of the relentless dogs of the preceding Stasimon here, and may have been led to do so by Storr's translation, 'The curse that dogged thee day by day' (241).

Pound then connected the murder of Agamemnon with that of Klytaimnestra, which is understandable as Sophocles in ll. 1415–16 gave to Klytaimnestra the very same phrases Aeschylus had given to her husband in his *Agamemnon* 1343, ὤμοι πέπληγμαι, 'Ah I am struck', and 1345, ὤμοι μάλ' αὖθις, 'Ah me once again'. Yet Pound wanted to emphasize this Aeschylean link even more:

> Klytaimnestra: 'Ah, I am struck!'. Elektra: 'strike again, if you can!'
> Klytaimnestra: 'Ah me, once again.'
>
> S ll. 1415–16

> KLYTAIMNESTRA
> That's done it.
>
> ELEKTRA
> Hit her again.
>
> KLYTAIMNESTRA
> Twice, twice.
> always twice.
>
> E ll. 1663–66

Pound in his Loeb edition wrote down 'echo Aeschylus' next to l. 1416, and in the typescript 'echo of Aeschylus when Ag/ is killed' (*E* 102). In his rendering of *Elektra*, then, Pound presented Klytaimnestra as being fully aware of what she has done to Agamemnon. Indeed, Klytaimnestra's 'That's done it' refers to her claim in ll. 1405–06 of the *Agamemnon*, τῆσδε δεξιᾶς χερὸς,/ ἔργον, δικαίας τέκτονος, which Pound rendered in his 1934 footnote in 'Translators of Greek' as: 'I did it. That's how it is' (*LE* 270). Yet Pound's repetition of 'twice' can also be read as a meta-literary reflection on the c(o)urse of history in the manner he had used it in Canto 5, as well as on the intertextual links between Aeschylus, Sophocles and Pound himself who, never the 'invisible' translator, makes his own presence known.

After the murder, the Chorus comments:

The curses are at work [*telous' arai*]; those who lie [*hoi keimenoi*] beneath the earth [*gas hupai*] live [*dzōsin*]. For [*gar*] those who died long ago [*hoi palai thanontes*] drain [*hupexairousi*] the blood [*haim'*] of the killers [*tōn ktanontōn*], which flows in turn [*palirruton*]

S ll. 1419–21

Pound struggled with these lines at the end of this Strophe, as is clear from some of his comments. The typescript shows he disagreed with Storr's version of l. 1419: 'The curses work; the buried live again' (243). Pound noted: 'neither THE curses, nor live AGAIN in the text' (*E* 102). However, Pound must have known that Greek occasionally dispenses with articles, as seen here in the case of *arai*, while the sentence *dzōsin hoi gas hupai keimenoi* (S l. 1419), 'those lying under the earth live', may imply that the dead have come back to life. Pound's rendering of the opening words *telous' arai* indicates that he remembered the verb *telein* which he had substituted earlier for *poiein* in Jebb's text. The verb can mean 'to complete' or 'to accomplish', but also 'to pay one's dues', while the word *telos* means 'end', 'result', and in its adverbial usage 'at last'. *Ara* means 'prayer' or 'curse', or can stand for 'the effect of the curse'; it cannot, however, mean 'fate', unless one would interpret a certain fate as the outcome of a prayer. Be that as it may, Pound extended his rendering of the two Greek words *telous' arai* over two lines 'In the end, weight unto weight/ fate works out to its end' (*E* ll. 1669–70), which makes triple use of *telous'* to indicate that ultimately there will always be a restoration of order because of the workings of (the scales of) justice. He then translated the following lines, and emphasized in his version that although the dead do not come back to life *again*, they still may act upon the living: 'They live who lie under ground/ the blood of the dead, long dead/ overfloods their slayers' (*E* ll. 1671–73), or as he stated in the typescript: 'living the living, tho they lie low under ground' (*E* 83). As we will see, this rendering is linked to Pound's ideas about staging this final scene.

The Chorus continues to sing in the Anti-strophe:

Ah now [*kai mēn*], they are here [*pareisin hoide*]! And a bloody hand [*phoinia de cheir*] drips [*stadzei*] with the sacrifice to Ares [*thuēlēs Areos*], and I cannot [*oud' echō*] blame it [*psegein*].

S ll. 1422–23

The dead hand drips Mars
And the slain,
        I can't blame 'em.

E ll. 1674–76

This is a rather curious rendering. Pound here uses a zeugma, 'drips', to have the murderous hand drip blood (Mars as a metaphor) on Klytaimnestra (the slain), and although the hand is singular, the "em' must be Orestes and Pylades. But why a 'dead hand'? If we are not dealing with an enallage here, where the adjective 'dead' should (superfluously) go with 'slain' but is linked to 'hand' instead, there must be another explanation. Although Pound did not translate the verb *pareisin*, 'they are here', which refers to Orestes and Pylades, he assumed in the typescript that the word perhaps referred to 'the presence of the ghost of Ag/? Can we make 'em see the DEAD WITH Orestes?' (*E* 102). On the basis of this possibility he then appended the following general note to his revised translation in the typescript: 'Perfectly easy to throw (magic-lantern) ghost of Agamemnon on white surface (flat white marble beside door or opening behind Orestes. ITS hands dripping RED blood' (*E* 102). This makes clear that Pound thus envisaged the ghost of Agamemnon instead of Orestes to have been responsible for the killing of Klytaimnestra (which is also why Pound deleted the reference to Orestes as the agent of murder in the Third Stasimon). Sophocles used the lines 'for those who died long ago drain the blood of the killers, which flows in turn' (1429-21) to denote the inevitable workings of justice, as Orestes has now avenged the murder of his father. Pound took these lines literally and had Agamemnon himself take revenge upon his wife for his death – hence the 'dead hand'.

After Orestes has told Elektra their mother is dead, they see Aigisthos approaching the palace. In Pound's version, the Chorus ironically commends Orestes by employing Klytaimnestra's phrase about her murder of Agamemnon: 'Good job so far. Now the next one' (*E* l. 1689). They think it is best to address Aigisthos amicably, *lathraion hōs orousēi pros dikas agōna* (S ll. 1440-41), 'so that [*hōs*] he may rush [*orousēi*] upon [*pros*] a stealthy [*lathraion*] trial [*agōna*] of justice [*dikas*].' Both Jebb and Storr have Aigisthos rush into 'doom', but given the importance of the notion of Justice in this play, it is essential that Aigisthos' impending fate is also presented as being just. In his version, Pound gets this nuance right: 'so he wont guess he's rushin'/ plumb bang into ruin,/ an' he damn well deserves it' (*E* ll. 1694-96).

In the Second scene of the Exodos (S ll. 1442-1507), Aigisthos is happy to hear the news of Orestes' death, and Elektra tells him her brother's body is now in the palace. Pound presents Aigisthos in an offensive manner as an effeminate character with a '*rather sissy voice, even a slight lisp*' (*E* l. 1698). Pound's version of his dialogue with Elektra stays close to the original, perhaps because of the short *stichomythia* (S ll. 1450-57). However, Pound lost his patience with Aigisthos' subsequent speech (S ll. 1458-63), as he wrote in the typescript: 'SYNTAX gorDAMMMit' (*E* 103). This is why ll. 1462–63, in which Aigisthos states that at the sight of Orestes' body everyone will now do as they are told, 'and not wait for my violent chastisement to become wise', becomes in Pound: 'and not wait till they're dead to find out' (*E* l. 1729). Elektra agrees with him, and her reply must be seen as ironic, since her 'No use goin' up against people in power' (*E* l. 1731) recalls Chrysothemis' earlier advice *tois kratousi d'eikathein*, 'yield to those who rule'.

Aigisthos orders the doors of the palace to be opened wide so that all may see Orestes' body, but when he lifts the veil, he discovers it is Klytaimnestra's corpse. Pound does not waste too many words on the climax, and his short phrases produce an emotionally charged exchange between Orestes and Aigisthos. In his Loeb, Pound marked Orestes' slightly cryptic Greek lines 1478–79, *ou gar aisthanei palai/ dzōntas thanousin hounek' antaudais isa;*, 'why [*gar*], do you not notice [*ou aisthanei*] that [*hounek'*] for some time [*palai*] you have been answering [*antaudais*] the living [*dzōntas*] equally [*isa*] to the dead [*thanousin*]?', that is, you have been talking to someone whom you thought to be dead. Pound rendered this more straightforwardly and with visual and auditory (alliterative) emphasis in his final version:

> Haven't
>   you
>   ever learned
> That the
>   DEAD
>   don't
>   DIE?
>
>   *E* ll. 1750–56

Orestes orders Aigisthos to go inside so that he will die in the same place as Agamemnon. In the original, Aigisthos suggests that his murder will lead to yet another act of retributive killing: 'Is it necessary that this house should see the present and future evils of the Pelopids?' (S ll. 1497–98). Pound renders this as: 'Fate. fate, under this damned roof of Pelops/ everything happens here' (*E* ll. 1776–77). This removes the idea of the killing as one in a series that can go on endlessly, perhaps because Pound had in mind the ending of Aeschylus' *Eumenides* where Orestes' vengeance is considered just by the jury headed by Athena, ending the family curse. For Pound, then, order is restored in *Elektra*. In his typescript, Pound implicitly praised Sophocles for his poetic gifts, which made it possible 'NOT including Aeg's death in actual play. One murder enough in action. One implied, with no doubt about it, but not visibly demonstrated. one doesn't at first realize that it is not actually in the text.' For him, this was a sign of true art: 'poetry = see/ stage/ = & hear' (*E* 103).

After Orestes has taken Aigisthos into the palace, the Chorus concludes the play with three short lines, in which they rejoice that finally the house of Atreus is restored again.

ὦ σπέρμ' Ἀτρέως, ὡς πολλὰ παθὸν
δι' ἐλευθερίας μόλις ἐξῆλθες
τῇ νῦν ὁρμῇ τελεωθέν.

S ll. 1508–10

O seed of Atreus [*ō sperm' Atreōs*], how [*hōs*], having suffered much [*polla pathon*], you have come [*exēlthes*] at last [*molis*] into freedom [*di' eleutherias*], made perfect [*teleōthen*] by today's enterprise [*tēi nun hormēi*].

This becomes in Pound's hands:

CHORUS (*sings*)

O SPERM' ATREOOS
                Atreides, Atreides
come thru the dark.

(*speaks*)

My god, it's come with a rush

(*sings*)

Delivered, Delivered.
            TEI NUN HORMEI TELEOOTHEN
swift end
      so soon.

F. ll. 1792–1802

Pound offers the beginning and ending of the song in transliteration. He emphasizes a new beginning for the Atreids, partly through an implicit reference to Elektra's earlier epiphanic phrase 'PHILTATON PHOS' (*E* l. 1437), 'beloved light', by rendering *polla pathon* as 'come thru the dark'. He reads *hormē* more literally as 'violent movement, rage, stir, impulse' – in his Loeb he glossed it as 'impetus'. Pound seems to have used it twice in 'it's come with a rush' and 'swift end', where 'end' is based on the noun *telos* he detected in *teleōthen*, 'finished, completed', but also given by Pound twice as 'delivered'. There is also a sort of sexually charged sense of release which is linked up to the 'SPERM'', while the use of 'rush' may have been suggested by W. B. Yeats's 'Leda and the Swan', in which Leda's body, 'laid in that white rush', experiences 'A shudder in the loins [which] engenders there/ The broken wall, the burning roof and tower/ And Agamemnon dead' (Yeats 260). Yet at the same time this passage is also a meta-poetic comment on the swiftness of (Pound's version of) the dramatic action now having found fulfillment. It may also be a proud statement by Pound that, after his failure to translate the *Agamemnon*, he now has managed to produce a complete rendering of a Greek play, doing justice to 'the whole rush of the action' he had detected in the *Agamemnon* but could not put into English beyond its opening lines. The result is a conclusion that is more powerful in venting emotions than the detached observations offered in the original.

Conclusion: the style of Pound's *Elektra*

The Princeton holdings include a few pages of Pound's general notes on Sophocles in typescript, one of which is about his intentions and translational strategy for his *Elektra*:

LEX

1. There must be real person speaking possible speech NOT goddam book-talk.
2. Must be the stage SEEN, the position of the person speaking and their movements.
3. Modification of speech MINIMUM or NONE for the sung parts. They shd/ be as straight as Drink to me only with thine eyes. BUT cantabile.
4. When danced, the foot-beat must be indicated BY the words, from them to the tune.
5. for the sung part the translation need NOT adhere to literal sense (intellectual) of the original but must be singable IN THE EMOTION of the original.

Princeton 1/2

Pound did not want to use the stilted diction that in his view marred so many translations of ancient texts. The texts should be made alive and new and relevant.[2] Perhaps inspired by F. R. Earp's analysis, Pound generally uses colloquial and conversational speech, so that he could appeal directly to a modern audience in the same way as Sophocles' original must have resonated with his Athenian audience. And just as every Greek tragedy combines contemporary speech with a variety of dialects, such as Doric in the choral odes, and archaic and Homeric words, resulting in what must have been an artificial and literary yet still immediately understandable style, Pound's version employs a great variety of registers to create an equivalence of expression. Thus we find slang and colloquial speech, as in the Chorus commenting on Elektra criticizing her mother: 'Gheez, she's a-goin' it fierce, / right or not she don't care a hang' (*E* ll. 697–98); Elektra addressing Klytaimnestra: 'You're top dog, / you've hit the jack-pot' (868–69); Elektra talking to her sister Chrysothemis: 'you're blotto delirious' (979); and the Chorus hearing Klytaimnestra being murdered: 'Gimme the creeps' (1652). Syros has rightly claimed that the 'strong colloquial undertone or even slang character' of Pound's language may be accounted for if we consider that people under extreme pressure may 'resort to the informal and brute expression of the moment' (Syros 136). We also have the 'snappy' speech of Orestes, the man of action: 'keep us wise to the lot of it. Snap' (*E* l. 43); 'Nuff talk' (76). There is the modernity of expression in phrases like: 'you play ball with our father's assassins' (409); 'this stuff .... / that you swank about in' (411–14), 'always so full of lip' (1703), and words like 'ponce' (354), 'dastardly' (356) There is the occasional cliché Hibernicism in the Messenger's speech delivered by the Tutor: 'He went up for the big Delphic proize' (773); 'and he got the proize uv the first race' (778); 'He took all the foive proizes' (782), 'the droivers in front of 'em' (803). Yet there is also the archaic formality when Pound feels there is need for it, as in Elektra's lament for Orestes whom she presumes is dead: 'I am dead also, the great wind in passing/ bears us together. / Mirth for our foemen' (1336–38). In all this variety of diction, Pound goes for speed, the 'sense' of the emotions involved, and communicability, but then also on occasion lets us listen to the soundscape of the Greek language itself through the transliterations so that his audience might have some sense of the *melopoeia* of the original.

Pound made no attempt to retain any of the metres of the original, such as the iambic trimeters conventionally used in the majority of the dialogue, let alone the complex rhythms employed in the choral odes. As we have seen in Chapter 1, Pound recognized the extreme difficulty of exactly transposing the Greek rhythm determined by syllabic length into English which works with stress patterns. Moreover, Pound also did not try to create his own regular metrical equivalents in *Elektra*, but, as we have seen, he employed other means to make his renderings of the choral odes distinguishable from the regular dialogue scenes.

Pound's version of *Elektra* steers a middle way between a word-for-word equivalence and a paraphrase, and between domestication and foreignization in its mixture of different speeches and transliterated Greek. It is both a creative translation in which Pound as translator is not really 'invisible', as well as a means to adopt a *persona*.

Coda: Elektra in Canto 90

As we have seen, Pound referred to *Elektra*'s sense of justice (and self-justification) in Cantos 85, 86, and 87 of *Rock-Drill*, where we find three adaptations of line 351, which the poet considered the key phrase of the play. The final tribute to Elektra's constant devotion to order and justice is found in Canto 90, which Pound began to draft in July 1954 as a poem about illumination, love and paradise. Near the end the poet has a vision:

> out of Erebus, the delivered,
>   Tyro, Alcmene, free now, ascending,
> e i cavalieri,
>   ascending,
> no shades more,
>   lights among them, enkindled,
> and the dark shade of courage
>   Ἠλέκτρα
> bowed still with the wrongs of Aegisthus.
>
> 90/628–29

Leon Surette has argued that this passage raises uncertainty about 'the purely paradisal nature of the world into which one is emerging'. He admits that the shades 'out of Erebus' like Tyro and Alcmene are now delivered through an ascent '*from* death', but he then reads the lines about Elektra 'bowed still with the wrongs of Aegisthus' as a description of the non-paradisal world to which they ascend (Surette 237–38).[3] However, it seems to me that these lines should be regarded as describing the way Odysseus had seen the ghosts in the Underworld in Book 11 of the *Odyssey*, presented to him by Persephone. Both Tyro (*Od.* 11.235–59) and Alcmene (266–68) had had intercourse with gods (Poseidon and Zeus, respectively), and thus in the Neoplatonic framework of *The Cantos*, had a vision of the divine.

Homer never mentions Elektra in the *Odyssey*, but Pound pictures her here as still trapped in a (mental) state which does not yet allow an 'ascent' as a reward for her courageous actions for the cause of justice. Given that Pound admired Elektra for having spoken her mind and for having incited others to action, we may see his use of her in this Canto as a statement of self-justification. In his view, he himself also had had the courage to stand up for justice and defy the authorities he deemed morally unjust, and as a result was punished. At the moment of drafting the Canto he still was locked up in St Elizabeths, with no control over his own life. The fact that he refers to 'the wrongs of Aegisthus' rather than to those of Klytaimnestra shows that he wanted to avoid the complexity of being right versus being just, one of the bones of contention in *Elektra*. After all, one may see Klytaimnestra's point in having murdered Agamemnon for his sacrifice of their daughter, but for Aigisthos, the weak collaborator without a will of his own, there is no excuse whatsoever. We see Elektra/Pound, then, still at the point where (s)he in isolation is waiting for someone to put the situation right and restore order, as they too have deserved their ascent.

Notes

1 See Kells 179–81.
2 For a good general account of Pound's language and use of melopoeia in *Elektra*, see Syros.
3 Cp. Tryphonopoulos 168.

7

Women of Trachis – Introduction

Scholarly approaches to the *Trachiniae*

Of Sophocles' seven extant tragedies, the *Trachiniae* was the least studied until its reputation was rehabilitated in the course of the twentieth century. For a long time scholars had difficulties in appreciating its structure and plot, and in reconciling its characterization – with Herakles as an atypical hero – and style with the other plays by Sophocles. This disillusionment with the play often resulted in either seeing it as an early tragedy, or on the contrary, as a late 'experimental' one. Nowadays the consensus seems to be that *Trachiniae*, *Ajax* and *Antigone* constitute the earliest group of Sophocles' extant plays.[1]

Where Jebb placed the date of the *Trachiniae* between 420 and 410 BC, so turning it into a relatively late play, F. R. Earp in *The Style of Sophocles* pointed out that Sophocles has used a large number of Homeric, epic-like and Aeschylean words here, the latter especially in dialogue. This is one of the marks of Sophocles' early style, which is still elevated (Earp 40–41), while metaphors and similes also tend to be more frequent in the earlier plays, which in terms of style have more affinity with epic (94–96). In terms of figures of speech, the *Trachiniae* has the lowest number of uses of antithesis, which is natural, as in this play 'argument is less prominent' (95), as opposed to the quantity found in a later play like *Elektra*. Moreover, in the early plays, the dialogues are less dramatic and less natural, as they 'develop a thesis or describe scenes and actions with little reference to the audience, and are often literally or virtually soliloquies' (165). As 'a rule, the characters take longer to express themselves'. Earp exemplified this by pointing out that Hyllus's speech in answer to Deianeira's agitated questions takes up sixty lines (S ll. 749–812), which is 'in the circumstances hardly natural' (Earp 165). Some of the speeches are undramatic, as they do not advance the action greatly, and 'are rather poetry than drama', maybe also because Sophocles is dealing with actions more remote from 'real' life and using 'still half legendary figures' (165). In fact, Earp claimed, the character of Herakles 'would be repulsive, if we did not accept him as a somewhat remote and legendary figure' (166).

Apart from the style, Earp saw the division into two halves as another argument for an early date for the play. His analysis is worth quoting in full, because Pound would not have fully agreed with it, as we will see:

> Sophocles, as critics point out, has used various devices in the earlier part of his play to bring Heracles before our minds and prepare us for his entry, but when at last he appears, he somehow fails to interest us as much as we expected. It is not that he is uninteresting in himself, but that we seem somehow to have wandered into a different story. That story is casually connected, no doubt, with the earlier scenes, but it seems to belong to another and more primitive realm of legend … Sophocles himself appears to have felt this, for in Deianira's first speech and in his later chorus about the combat with Achelous he is at pains to remind us that we are in a world where strange things happen, and one inhabited by strange monsters. But even so our imaginations are a little strained and find this Heracles hard to accept.
>
> 170

Indeed, for most commentators, the main difficulty of the *Trachiniae* resides in the fact that the play seems to fall into two halves, with Deianeira as the central figure of the first half, and Herakles of the second, a division which scholars found difficult to reconcile with the unity they perceived in Sophocles' other plays, which revolved around the fortunes of one central character, such as Oedipus, Elektra or Philoktetes. Yet if one does away with the notion of one leading figure and looks for a unity of theme instead, one can then regard the play as a description of the events leading up to the death of Herakles, and of all those involved. The play's unity seems to lie in the fact that the driving force behind the entire chain of events is the all-powerful *eros* or force of violent passion, personified in Aphrodite, who claims both Deianeira and Herakles as victims. Herakles sacked Oechalia out of lust for Iole. In turn Deianeira, afraid of losing Herakles, is prompted to send him the robe smeared with the poison given to her by Nessus when Herakles prevented him from satisfying his feelings of lust for her. At the end of the play, Herakles suffers the consequences of all these different manifestations of *eros*.

The notion of Love, *eros*, as a force that overrides all reason very much appealed to Pound, as *The Cantos* may be said to be dominated by the theme of the struggle between egotistical, self-interested Lust and selfless, altruistic Love. This struggle affects all human beings who throughout history in their confrontation with Love must, by a conscious *directio voluntatis* or effort of will, choose between Good and Evil, or at least a lesser Evil. Moreover, the contrast between divine knowledge and mortal ignorance, which is such a central issue in Sophocles' works, is also a major key to *The Cantos*.

Pound's methodology for translating the *Trachiniae*

As in the case of *Elektra*, Pound used the Loeb edition by Storr as the base for his *Women of Trachis*. He annotated the copy, now in his library in Brunnenburg, throughout, and seems to have relied more on it than in the case of *Elektra*. All of the notes made by Pound in his copy demonstrate how he made a careful study of the Greek text, writing in the margins a considerable number of meanings of the Greek words, again using his edition of Ellendt's *Lexicon to Sophocles*, although he also seems to have used the dictionary of Liddell-Scott. Pound's jottings include many Greek verbs in the indicative form, sometimes with their meaning next to them, while occasional question marks express his struggle with the modality of the verb. Occasionally he also commented on the text.

Sophocles' original has a total of 1,278 lines, whereas Pound's translation contains 1,242 lines, so the works are almost the same length. Pound shortened the beginning of the play, namely in the Prologue (minus nineteen lines), the Parodos (minus thirteen lines) and the First Episode (minus eleven lines), producing 453 lines against the first 496 of the original. After the First Stasimon, which he extends by seven lines, Pound generally stays fairly close to the number of lines of the original, although it must be noted that in the Exodos, he compensates his deletion of twenty-two lines at the beginning of this final part (971–92) with short extensions of each of the speeches of Herakles.

The contemporary reception of Pound's version

When *Women of Trachis* was published in the *Hudson Review* in 1954, many critics objected to Pound's style, finding it an uneven mixture of the extremely colloquial and the formal, or archaic. In the Fifth Issue of the *Pound Newsletter* (1955), some leading classicists and translators discussed Pound's style. The British classical scholar Sir Maurice Bowra described it as 'colloquial American', F. R. Earp called it 'slang', while Richmond Lattimore, translator of Homer, objected to the way Pound had made Deianeira sound 'like a brassy, cocksure guttersnipe ... And all the other characters talk the same way.' He noted that Pound had used 'a special dialect, part hillbilly, part city-tough, part purely Pound colloquialism' (Bowra 3–8).

In 1957, Thomas H. Carter noted in the *Kenyon Review* that Pound had made '(for him) a straight translation' in view of his belief that a translation must not render the letter but the spirit of a classic work. He praised Pound's choral passages as 'magnificent, probably better than those by Yeats in *Oedipus Rex*', but considered the variety of languages of the dialogue to be unsuitable (Carter 458–61). In 1961 Bernard F. Dick described Pound's version in *The Classical World* as 'a burlesque of Greek tragic poetry – caustic, pedestrian, and often in dubious taste', with the Sophoclean diction turned into 'subway-circuit dialogue' (Dick 236). H. A. Mason in *Arion* (1963) saw in Pound's rendering a mixture of the banal and non-creative on the one hand, and on the other some very felicitous renderings which made the Greek play come alive for modern times. Yet he objected that Pound had not done Deianeira justice. As regards the contents, Dick blamed Pound for having failed to give his version some intrinsic value, such as using myth to reflect a contemporary situation, or to advance an ideology. By not 'throwing new light on traditional material', Pound merely 'contaminate[d]' Sophocles' original (Dick 237). Carter, in turn, regarded the version as a flawed criticism of the play, refuting Pound's attempt at finding the play's whole meaning in Herakles' death.

One champion for its defence, albeit in private, was Edith Hamilton (1867–1963), the classical scholar who published several popular books about classical culture, such as *The Greek Way to Western Civilization* (1930), and who was a regular visitor to St Elizabeths. She wrote to Pound on 9 December 1954, that she liked *Women of Trachis*, and 'pray[ed] it may be a beginning only. If you would but do the Oresteia?' (Beinecke 20/896). Two years later, in a letter of 14 December 1956, she stated that she liked the play's 'frankness and strength ... When will you do us others? We could do today with a bit more Greek spirit, I think' (Beinecke 20/903). We do not know what Pound's response to Hamilton's praise was, but ironically enough, this was the same person who, according to Mary Barnard, came to consult Pound on one occasion regarding a translation of a Greek play by an unnamed young man, and had complained that the translation had no dignity, unlike those of Gilbert Murray. She lectured Pound 'for a good quarter of an hour on the beauties of Gilbert Murray's translations from the Greek', and Barnard expected Pound to stand up in rage, but he kept silent, smiled and just listened to Hamilton, looking 'more delighted every minute' (Barnard 267)

Stanislaw Viktor Jankowski, a Polish scholar with whom Pound shared an interest in the writings of the Latin Neoplatonist Richard of St Victor, defended Pound in his introduction to the 1956 edition of the play, pointing out that the Greek dialogue consisted of 'plain conversation' (*WT* 13), and that Pound in his version 'calls up a distinct mental picture of the people of 2,000 years ago and makes them speak their idioms and slogans, utter their screams and ejaculations' (*WT* 14). In the end, however, as Jankowski claimed, it is not the style that 'determines the nature of [Pound's] translation. It is the atmosphere of the play and the truth it conveys... It is the firm belief of the translator that the force of the Greek classic lies in its truth alone' (*WT* 19). All of this leaves the student of Pound to either challenge or confirm the statement made by the classicist D. S. Carne-Ross in his 1979 discussion of Sophocles' play: 'The vagaries of Pound's *Women of Trachis* are for the most part unilluminating, since they are not governed by any clear grasp of the statement the play is making. As a workshop study of the formal and stylistic problems Greek tragedy poses for translation... his version is of the greatest interest' (Carne-Ross 253 n. 6).

Given Pound's admiration for F. R. Earp, it is of interest to see what advice he offered the poet in their unpublished correspondence from 1953–54. Unfortunately, a recurrent topic of Earp's letters is that he is often not in a position to help Pound with detailed questions which arose during the process of composition on account of his bad eyesight. The correspondence makes clear, however, that Earp made some penciled notes in the typescript, hoping, as he states in a letter of 9 August 1953, that they

> will be of some use. If I could have compared your version with the Greek, I could have been of use, for I should have spotted cases in which your translation misrepresented the Greek. You say you know little Greek, & as I have been studying it for over 70 years I ought to know what Sophocles means. But when it comes to style, the only effective way to help would be to get into the other man's head & that's impossible. Things look so differently to different minds that whatever I say can't mean exactly the same to you.
>
> Beinecke 14/646

By the time Earp received the published version of *Women of Trachis*, his eyesight had greatly improved, and he expressed his regret in a letter of 28 February 1954, that had his eyes 'behaved as well, when I went over your Trachiniae, I should have been able to compare with the Greek throughout, & so would have really been of use' (ibid.). However, as we will see in the analysis of Pound's version in the following chapters, Earp still gave some detailed criticism in his letters.

Another recurrent topic in the correspondence is Pound's style. In a letter to Pound of 26 June 1953, in which he acknowledged the receipt of the typescript of *Women of Trachis*, Earp noted, that while his bad eyesight had impeded him from comparing Pound's version with the Greek original, he

> can't criticize its accuracy, but so far as I have read, I like your translation. It is clear & vigorous. I have not read the Loeb translation, which you say is dull. Yours is certainly not dull, but I notice you indulge in colloquialisms & slang, or what seems so to an English ear. It may strike an American differently & probably does in some cases.
>
> ibid.

He repeated this criticism of the style in another letter three days later, in which he also discussed in some detail the use of language and choice of diction in ancient Greek poetry:

> All the great Greek poets from Homer onwards pay great attention to the sound of their verse, & what is more striking, write in an artificial dialect combining many archaic forms derived from more than one dialect. It is always a convenience to a poet to have more than one form of a word available. And they chose forms that sounded well.
>
> ibid.

After some digressions about the archaeologist Heinrich Schliemann and his own classical education, Earp then writes:

> I have read three quarters of your translation now, & I like the latter last quarter very much, but I feel I should be happier, if it were a translation from Euripides. But that is not your fault: no one has produced a translation of Sophocles to please me ... I feel that you have sometimes resorted to colloquialisms or slang where I could find an ordinary [*sic*] which would have been as effective. Where I felt that, I put a query, or underlined a word in pencil. I hope you won't mind my saying this, & doing this. You paid me the compliment of consulting me, & this is the only way of making my impression clear.

Earp ended his letter by warning Pound that the words of the chorus in Greek plays were intended to be heard,

> & if you set them to elaborate music with plenty of instruments, they are not heard. I saw a performance of the <u>Agamemnon</u> at Cambridge & the choruses were set to elaborate Wagnerian music, & though I know the choruses nearly by heart I could not catch the sense. That in Aeschylus is quite fatal. It is not quite so fatal in Sophocles, but still the odes are made to be heard, & as I see that you have

suggested the instruments for each ode, it is worth mentioning. Instruct your producer not to drown the words ...

If your play were by Euripides, the music would not matter. In a few of his plays the odes are important, but in many they have little to do with the play.

ibid.

Pound responded to this criticism on 30 July:

Renewed thanks. Problem your eyes and my physical exhaustion.
   Theatre vs / library
Period english or the horrible american language of 1953?
Dialect forms in greek wd/ indicate authors attending greatly to sound, and
   what they cd/ hear in imagination their characters saying.
Stage vs/ the actual subject.
My problem Herakles, 'one tough guy' who is also a god.
   the 'one' here not a numeral, not exactly an 'un' or 'uno' of french or italian but
   equivalent to 'a very'.
i.e. the article PLUS an intensive.

ibid.

In a letter of 24 August, Earp reacted by noting how difficult it is to render Sophocles in modern day English:

I am afraid the problem of translating Sophocles into English now is nearly insoluble. Your translation has the virtue of vigour, & would probably go well on the stage. But obviously it has not the beauty of Sophocles, & in the present state of the language it can't have that. As you say, the use of various dialects show that they were sensitive to the sound of words. Nearly all the language of classical Greek verse is an artificial compound of dialects.

ibid.

For Earp, Pound's use of slang became a sore point, as a letter of 18 November attests: 'Your translation is vigorous, & I don't urge you to diminish the vigour, but you may find ways to keep the vigour without the use of slang' (ibid.). He repeated this point in a letter of 15 February 1954, in which he noted 'that T. S. Eliot thinks your slang not up to date & your answer to that seems sufficient'. Still, there 'was plenty of dialect in antiquity, but little slang, & we don't meet much slang in general in use till the 19th century. It must be something in our civilization, which produces it' (ibid.). However, after Earp heard the BBC broadcast of the play in April 1954, he modified his criticism, as a letter of 2 May shows:

I heard your version on the wireless last night. A friend of mine, who was once one of my assistants in town & is a good Greek scholar, wrote last week to say he had heard it & found it quite exciting & interesting, & added that it was to be repeated last night. So of course I listened in for once, though I usually turn it off at the end of the news. My friend thought the Herakles particularly good, but I could hardly hear him – my wireless is very old & at 83 I should renew it. Deianira I heard well & she must have a more penetrating voice, but I rather disliked her. But I liked the Messenger best, probably because he could understand his part better. Most of the others struck me as being a little out of their depth. But the thing I really want to tell you is that I hardly noticed the slang. On the stage it is less startling than in the study. So in a way I feel you were right. Your play is certainly alive & if the only way to get the play over is to use the kind of language with which the audience is familiar, you are justified in using it.

ibid.

Earp's criticism, despite the assurance of this letter, may have touched a nerve in Pound, as evidenced by a long letter, dated 17 May 1954, in which he has a favour to ask:

To become combative, I shd/ prob/ y throw out the term slang altogether. Going back nearly ½ a century, and adding autobiography, I started using archaisms/ much puzzled when I got to London by term 'Wardour St' (strada ignota in Wyncote, Pa.) Wardour St vocabulary. Poet but can't write English.
by which they meant Lionel Johnson oxfordese of the 1890s

By the time I had been prodden into interest in spoken tongue of the era, I had an embarrassing luncheon with Robt. Bridges in Oxford. NOT having then read his works. RB pulled the original 'Personae' from one pocket and 'Exultations' from the other, picked up the word 'forloyn', and said enthusiasticly 'We'll get 'em ALL back.' Having had a few rudimentary instructions in civility I was embarrassed.

* * *

decades later I want a fly-swat for people who are, in TOTAL ignorance of even greek first declension, talking about 'adaptation'. My 'Homage' to Propertius is a 'persona'/ not a translation. What I want now is a certificate that in Women of Trachis I have invented nothing, that there is not a shred of meaning in my 'slang' that is not there in Sophokles greek. If Gib. Murray is accurately quoted by the mutt in yr/ national sewage sheet, and if that scavenger hasn't taken a phrase of G.M&/ out of context. He wd/ apper to exist at a lower level than even I had suspected. But knowing the allergy of the licensed victualers, I hesitate to attribute this squalor even to a britisch official. As the notice stands Murray cannot be speaking of the translation but of the original, but the daily press does NOT like to transmit accurate information, and this may be just another typical distortion.

ibid.

In his reply of 29 May, Earp writes:

> I see that you want a certificate that there is nothing in your version which is not in Sophocles himself. When my <u>Hudson</u> comes back [which he has lent out to a friend], I will look & see, but don't expect my account soon, for it again will be a long job, for I shall have to compare every line with the Greek.

ibid.

On 7 August, he sent Pound a reassuring letter:

> I have now compared your translation with the Greek, not throughout, but in about half the play, in passages taken at random. I think I can give you the required guarantee that you have added nothing to Sophocles. In fact you have rather taken away, for you often omit: e.g. in l. 49–61, the Nurse's first speech, you have six lines for 12 in the Greek. Here and elsewhere you seem to omit what would be unintelligible or uninteresting to a modern audience; & as only a fraction in these days study Greek or Latin, or know anything about Greek mythology, that leaves many omissions.

ibid.

The style of Pound's *Women of Trachis*

So what can one generally say about Pound's rendering of Sophocles' speeches and dialogues in his translation of the *Trachiniae*? First of all, Pound has remained true to his life-long ideal of bringing poetry close to everyday speech. In his version of the *Trachiniae*, as in the *Elektra*, he has rejected the classicizing English which we find, for example, in Storr's Loeb edition. Pound's version is far more modern, and employs slang and colloquial expressions, derived from both American and British English, like 'We been outlawed'; 'What's she say? Lemme hear' (*WT* 26); 'No credit to you'; 'we're done for' (27); 'get going' (28); 'a local bloke' (30; for *tou astōn* [l.188], 'one of the citizens'); 'some damn foreign desert' (32); 'to get back at the man/ who'd double-crossed him' (33); 'I dunno' (35); 'What's this screw-ball?' (38); 'don't weasel to me' (39); 'nope' (45); 'damn it' (49); 'God's bitch' (62; for *akoitis Dios* [1048], 'Zeus' wife'). Pound also employs old-fashioned informal expressions like 'she might be top drawer' (35) and poeticisms like 'Bitter ache of separation brought on me' and 'Black trouble' (26). On occasion he accords the Greek names a certain familiarity: he calls Iphitus 'Iphytz' (26), and styles Deianeira, *teknon Oineōs* (l.598), 'child of Oineus', as 'Madame d'Oineus' (45). He refers to *Eurutou polin* (l. 74), 'the city of Eurytos', as 'Eurytusville' (27), and to *to Thēbēs astu* (1154), 'the town of Thebes', as 'Thebes-burg' (66). However, unlike the language in Pound's rendering of the speeches, the language of his choral lyrics is far more poetical and archaic, as it generally is in the original.

Secondly, the speeches in Greek tragedy usually have a rhetorical structure which allows us to divide longer speeches into smaller parts. In his version, Pound often depicts these divisions graphically by turning such sections into separate paragraphs, divided from each other by spaced lines. Moreover, he has the tendency to further subdivide the original sections so that smaller parts become paragraphs in their own right, enabling Pound to fully convey the emotional and dramatic impact of certain phrases and thoughts. My analysis of Deianeira's prologue in the next chapter will give examples of this feature.

Thirdly, Pound's free rendering of Sophocles' iambic trimeters is more than mere prose chopped into separate lines, as he employs many poetic techniques as a substitute for the Greek playwright's verse pattern. In Deianeira's prologue, for example, we may read how the river god Achelous appeared *en trisin morphaisin* (l. 10), 'in three shapes'. Pound renders this with the alliterative, kenning-like description 'a three-twisted river' (*WT* 25). Where Sophocles describes how the second shape Achelous adopted was that of an *aiolos/ drakōn heliktos* (ll. 11–12), 'a gleaming rolling snake', Pound extends the image by using a 'hissy' alliteration: 'a licky snake with scales on it/ shining'. Finally, Sophocles states that Achelous' third shape is that of a man with the head of an ox, *ek de daskiou geneiados/ krounoi dierrainonto krēnaiou potou* (ll. 13–14), 'while from his shaggy beard/ there poured streams from a spring of water'. Here the Greek *krounoi*, 'streams', and *krēnaiou*, 'spring', alliterate. Pound tries to retain this poetical description by matching it with another alliteration, by changing the 'beard' into 'whiskers': 'with water dripping out of his whiskers, black ones'. As a final example, one could refer to Pound's rendering of lines 34–35, which Storr translated accurately as: 'Such life was his [=Herakles]/ That kept him roaming to and fro from home,/ To drudge for some taskmaster' (Storr 261). Pound has translated these lines extremely freely, using repetition and assonance to create a powerful rhythmic paragraph:

> Always away on one assignment or another,
> one terror after another,
> always for someone else.
>
> *WT* 26

Pound made no attempt to transpose the iambic trimeters into a regular English equivalent. The number of stresses in each line of his version depends on its length as well as on its emotional weight, since Pound varies neutral phrasing with emphatic speech. The opening lines by Deianeira, which constitute the first paragraph of Pound's version (*WT* 25), are a good example. I have marked the primary stress in bold, and the secondary in italics:

> '**No man knows** his **luck** 'til he's **dead**.'
> They've been **say**ing **that** for a **long time**
> but **it's not true** in **my** *case*. **Mine's** *soggy*.
> **Don't** *have* to *go* to **hell** to *find* **that** out.

The first octosyllabic line has five primary stresses, that is, on the content words, while the monosyllabic and spondaic weight emphasizes the gnomic truth of the maxim. In the second line, we have five primary stresses, where the stress on 'saying' highlights the difference between theoretical maxim and lived experience, the opposition that dominates lines 2–3. The last two words 'long time' each receive a stress to underscore once again the supposedly universal validity of the maxim. As a result, Deianeira's denial of its truth in the third line becomes all the more powerful, and Pound gives it added weight by employing five primary stresses and one secondary one in this decasyllabic line. The monosyllabic weight of the last decasyllabic line balances that of the first, and underscores the strong connection between the proverb and its rejection through personal experience.

Themes of Pound's translation

In his list of *dramatis personae* (*WT* 24), Pound has transliterated Δηάνειρα ('Dēianeira'), commonly given as 'Deianeira' (and as 'Deianira' by both Storr and Earp), as 'DAIANEIRA', which he explains punningly as 'The Day's Air'; Pound refers to Deianeira as 'DAYSAIR'.[2] In contrast, he describes Iole as 'Tomorrow, daughter of Eurytus'. Both descriptions demonstrate that Pound approached the play as a play about the power of Love and its hold over the passions of Herakles, whose love for Deianeira turns out to be short-lived.

Pound's reference to Herakles as 'the Solar vitality' (*WT* 24), and as such linked to the permanence of eternal light, suggests that he may have studied the introduction of Jebb's edition of the *Trachiniae*, which refers to a 'natural' interpretation of the poisoned robe:

> The garment of Heracles ... has naturally been claimed for the wardrobe of the solar myth. It is the glow which enwraps the dawn or the sunset. Then Iolè is 'the violet cloud' who is to marry the rising sun (Hyllus), when his precursor (Heracles) has sunk to rest upon a flaming couch. The servitude to Omphalè is the apparent descent of the sun (Heracles) from the zenith to the horizon. Deianeira is the darkness which awaits him in the west.

Jebb, however, rejects this explanation, because it turns the characters into mere symbols of natural phenomena: 'Even the more limited theory, that Heracles was evolved from some older solar divinity, ill agrees with the central point of the fable, – promotion, painfully won, from earth to heaven' (Jebb 1908, xli).

Given the fact that light is a dominant motif in the play leading up to its finale, Pound also added many references to light and dark. In this respect, Carne-Ross has observed that 'both imagery and action do a good deal to associate Herakles with light, Deianeira with aspects of night. Like night and day they directly or indirectly destroy each other, and Deianeira's device for winning back Herakles' love will literally put him to bed in flame' (Carne-Ross 64). Although I agree with the association of Herakles with light, I fail to see the same strong connection between Deianeira and night. Even Carne-Ross has to admit that 'there is [not] any neat equivalence; Deianeira's reflective intelligence suggests light rather than darkness' (ibid.). In contrast to Carne-Ross, I suggest that the opposition between light and darkness in the play is attributable to Herakles and the non-human forces (Akheloos, Nessus), respectively, which merely use the unwitting Deianeira as their instrument. This is most likely also Pound's interpretation, given the fact that he defines Achelous in his list of *Dramatis personae* as 'symbol of the power of damp and darkness' (*WT* 24) – as opposed to the light and (later) the fire associated with Herakles (and the air with Deianeira). This is also why Pound added the word 'cloud' to his rendering of the depiction of the river-god, because later in the play it is a cloud, that is, a symbol of darkness and death, that will envelop Herakles in his hours of agony.

Pound's use of light and darkness as states of enlightenment and ignorance also came to the fore when he jotted midway through the Greek text of the play at the bottom of page 308 of his Loeb on which the Chorus express their eagerness to welcome back Herakles: '? Noche di S. Juan' – a reference to St John's illumination after his 'dark night of the soul'. On the next page (310) Pound wrote 'Deianeira daughter of Darkness' and 'plura diafana'. The later phrase comes from the medieval philosopher Robert Grosseteste, one of Pound's Neoplatonic 'heroes'. In his essay 'Cavalcanti', published in *Make it New* (1934), Pound had first quoted his phrase *per plura diafana* (*LE* 161), 'through many things diaphanous', to explain that light only reaches us through or becomes visible in translucent bodies (*diafana*). In the Pisan and later Cantos, Pound used this concept to link vision and knowledge of the intelligible. In *Rock-Drill* and *Thrones*, the phrase *per plura diafana* becomes a shorthand for a sudden insight into the intelligible through transformation of sense knowledge.[3] On pp. 322–23 of the Loeb, where the Chorus depicts the effect of the poisoned robe on Herakles, we find the annotations 'black-coated mind' and 'dred cloud of nothingness'. These annotations highlight how one potential reading of *Women of Trachis* is a Neoplatonic one.

Influence of Noh

David Moody has argued that Pound began thinking about the *Trachiniae* in 1950 or 1951 (301). However, when the version of *Elektra* was still in process, Fleming was 'working on pronunciation of Trachinae', as he wrote to Pound on 6 June 1949. This may have been to get a better sense of Greek melopoeia in order to improve their joint work on *Elektra*. Yet, as another letter of 6 August 1949 makes clear, Pound had also been reading the *Trachiniae*, as Fleming wrote: 'After looking over the parts of the Trachiniae you gave me Wednesday, I see ... I was only trying to use a few trick devices to exploit the play without half looking at it – fatuously imagining that any such weasel-work can take on the shape of a genuine dramatic encounter' (Lilly). Pound's enthusiasm for the *Trachiniae* is already evident in a letter of April 1951 to Otto Bird, in which he called the play the 'highest point of greek consciousness/ antithesis to Electra'. He repeated the sentiment to Huntington Cairns, when he contrasted 'Elektra (Soph)/ blood and savagery' to 'Trachiniae / infinitely higher state of consciousness / unsurpassed in Xtn/ licherchoor, the HIGH for all gk/ consciousness' (quoted in Moody, 301). Pound, then, regarded the *Elektra* as a play about hate resulting in revenge as a means to restore order, whereas in the *Trachiniae*, the hatred and passions ultimately lead to insight and deliverance.

Pound's high estimation of the play is also reflected in the description of the *Trachiniae* found in the 1956 edition as '*the highest peak of Greek sensibility registered in any of the plays that have come down to us, and [it] is, at the same time, nearest the original form of the God-Dance*' (*WT* 23). This is a clear reference to an earlier discussion in '*Noh' or Accomplishment: A Study of the Classical Stage of Japan* (1916) about 'the god dance' being 'the central feature' of a Noh play (*T* 279). In the early 1950s Pound was rereading Fenollosa's notes and versions of the Noh, and decided to translate the *Trachiniae* to see 'how the Greek would measure up' to it (*Confucius to Cummings* xi). As he stated in his interview with Donald Hall in March 1960 for the *Paris Review*: 'The *Trachiniae* came from reading the Fenollosa Noh plays for the new edition, and from wanting to see what would happen to a Greek play, given that same medium and the hope of its being performed by the Minorou company [an ancient family of Noh actors]' (Hall 40).

When Pound studied Fenollosa's notes on the Noh, he embraced his recurrent references to Greek drama as a means to ease the understanding of what he believed to be its Asian counterpart. Following Fenollosa, Pound described a Noh play as an embodiment of 'some primary human relation or emotion' which is always fixed 'upon idea, not upon personality' (*T* 279). Pound believed that the unity of Noh plays 'lies in the image', and that 'they are built up about it as the Greek plays are built up about a single moral conviction' (ibid. 247). This single image or single mood is enforced by the refined speech, the music and the stylized gestures. In this way the Noh as a still existing form of drama is 'as primitive, as intense, and almost as beautiful as the ancient Greek drama at Athens' (ibid. 269). Both forms had arisen out of religious rites, the Greek drama in the fifth century BCE out of 'the religious rites practised in the festivals of the God of Wine', the Japanese twenty centuries later out of the rites practised in the festivals of the Shinto gods. Both dramas

> began by a sacred dance, and both added a sacred chorus sung by priests. The transition from a dance chorus to drama proper consisted, in both cases, in the evolving of a solo part, the words of which alternate in dialogue with the chorus. In both the final form of drama consists of a few short scenes, wherein two or three soloists enact a main theme, whose deeper meaning is interpreted by the poetical comment of the chorus. In both the speech was metrical, and involved a clear organic structure of separate lyrical units. In both music played an important part. In both action was a modification of the dance. In both rich costumes were worn; in both, masks.
>
> ibid. 269–70

Pound notes how it has been said that Greek drama has influenced all later drama, and just 'as the Greek conquest gave rise to a Greco-Buddhist form of sculpture on the borders of India and China, Greek dramatic influence entered also into the Hindoo and Chinese drama, and eventually into the Noh of Japan' (ibid. 270).

The passages quoted above exemplify Pound's method of removing any reserve a Western audience may have with regard to the unfamiliarity of Noh drama. As such he also notes that the individual Noh plays deal with 'for the most part known situations, in a manner analogous to that of the Greek plays, in which we find, for instance, a known Oedipus in a known predicament' (ibid. 222). Yet Pound also noted some differences between Greek tragedy and the Noh, such as the fact that in Japanese drama the dance was by a god dancing alone, whereas in Greek drama it was the chorus that danced (ibid. 273); and where in Greece 'the chorus not only sang but danced; in Japan the chorus did not dance or act, but was merely contemplative, sitting at the side' (ibid. 276).

Fenollosa noted that 'a human being, the hero of a dramatic crisis' may be substituted for the traditional deity, but still

> the god dance remains the central feature. All the slow and beautiful postures of the early dramatic portion invariably lead up to the climax of the hero's dance (just as the Greek had planned for the choric dances) ... During the closing dance the chorus sings its finest passages ... Its function is poetical comment, and it carries the mind beyond what the action exhibits to the core of the spiritual meaning ... The audience sits spellbound before the tragedy, bathed in tears; but the effect is never one of realistic horror, rather of a purified and elevated passion, which sees divine purpose under all violence.
>
> ibid. 279.

The last statement may be seen as combining Aristotelean *katharsis* with the epiphanic.

Pound's claim in *Gaudier-Brzeska* (1916) that any Japanese Noh play 'is gathered about one image' (*GB* 94) is linked to his definition of the image in 'A Few Don'ts By An Imagiste' (1913) as 'that which presents an intellectual and emotional complex in an instant of time ... It is the presentation of such a "complex" instantaneously which gives that sense of sudden liberation; that sense of freedom from time limits and space limits; that sense of sudden growth, which we experience in the presence of the greatest works of art' (*LE* 4). I have argued elsewhere that Pound's definition of the 'Image' continued his earlier adaptation of the Neoplatonic and mystic notions that underlie *A Lume Spento* and *Canzoni*, in which a poem can be a record of a 'delightful psychic experience' that lifts its speaker for a moment out of the phenomenal world into a higher reality. However, the difference between the earlier Pound and Pound the Imagist-Vorticist lies in the fact that the earlier emphasis on the epiphanee, the subjective *persona* having the experience, is now replaced by an emphasis upon the objective presentation of the Image that may represent the event itself.

The primary function of the image, then, is the objectification of a subjective experience without comment. Imagism-Vorticism thus offers the poet the possibility to use the image as 'the word beyond formulated language' (*GB* 88), that is, as an embodiment of the transcendental.[4]

In *Women of Trachis*, Pound connected his Neoplatonic approach to the Image with his notion of what a Noh play is by turning Herakles' pyre into the dominant and representative image. The whole play is framed by the image of fire, from the pyre in the opening chorus to Herakles' death at the end. As Pound stated in Canto 87, the play is 'shaped from φλογιζόμενον' (591), 'blazing with fire'. On his pyre Herakles gains his insight into the universe *sub specie aeternitatis*, as expressed through what Pound regarded as the play's key phrase 'What splendour it all coheres'. As Herakles is a god, his escape into eternity and recovery of his true Self on the level of Being is not a temporary but a permanent state, and we may see this transformation taking place before our very eyes. This is Pound's Greek variation of the god dancing in the Noh play.

Soon after publication, there were plans to perform *Women of Trachis* as a Noh play. Michael Reck asked Pound in a letter of 5 March 1954, to send copies of *Women of Trachis* to Michio Ito:

> Ito will take them to the No people, with an eye to production. We are not sure how they would do it though, whether in adaptation or translation – or, in fact, whether they would undertake it at all. But the way to find out, of course, is to give them copies.

Reck also informed Pound that he and Fujitomi Yasuo had begun

> a rough translation into Japanese. We've met three times & only done 1/10th, so you can see it will take us a while.
> (Sophocles's? I've ordered the original)
>
> Beinecke 44/1852

Reck even boasted in a letter four days later that they were 'doing a good translation of your play. I fancy it is better than the original' (ibid.). However, the translation was never completed.

In a long letter to Reck on 12 March 1954, Pound gave instructions as to how the translation of Sophocles could fit it into the Noh form.[5] He stated that Reck could disregard the Greek, 'unless the jap chorus could get closer to the greek rhythm', and not to imitate either the Greek or the English texts, but to go for 'the equivalent feeling'. He emphasized how his version was a mixture of styles, as was the original, and that they should aim for natural speech:

> dont bother about the WORDS, translate the meaning.
>
> in the spoken parts/dialog, this should be CLEAR, and be what the speaker would SAY if getting over the meaning in japanese. NOW in the XOROI, go for the FEELING. The two KINDS of language are quite different / in the first real people are speaking/ saying what carries forward the action / in the XOROI they are singing (except the few lines marked 'spoken'/ . . .
>
> . . ..
>
> In the sung parts, be as classic as you like / drag in phrases from Noh itself if they fit and intensify the situation.

Pound also pointed out in detail what they could do in terms of performance. 'Ito cd/ do some fine chorography for the Analolu/ xorus', and as to the Chorus in general, there was no need for more than one voice most of the time as 'a lot of voices might blurr the words'.[6]

Pound was aware that the appearance of Aphrodite as a *dea ex machina* might cause some problem on a Japanese stage:

> The Venus is practically naked behind the gauze curtain/ I dont know quite how naked a jap goddess can be in apparition/ at any rate from the crutch up. She aint eggzakly a Kuanon / but the willow bough cd/ be brought in definitely. she cd/ hold one.

Pound also made clear what he thought about Sophocles' original:

> The form of the play is magnif/ everythin fits / Daysair goes INTO the tragic mask. Herak emerges from it.
>
> TRAX in antithesis to Antig/ and other Soph/ lays in that NO ONE has any evil intentions, NO bad feeling, vendetta or whatso. All of 'em trying to be nice/ BUT the tragedy moves on just the same.
>
> Daysair, Queen and woman/ top of all greek descriptive writing in the Nurse's description of her before the suicide. HERAK/ tough guy who is also a God.
>
> Reck 82

In Pound's stage directions, Daysair or Deianeira is said to enter '*in the tragic mask*' (*WT* 48) at the moment when she realizes what may happen to Herakles after she has seen the effect of the poison on a piece of wool.

All of the above explains why Pound dedicated his *Women of Trachis* to Kitasono Katue, one of the leaders of Japanese avant-garde poetry and a correspondent with Pound since the 1930s, in the hope that 'he will use it on my dear old friend Miscio Ito, or take it to the Minoru if they can be persuaded to add to their repertoire' (*WT* 23). In his letter to Reck of 12 March, Pound was looking forward to the BBC production on the Third Programme of 25 April 1954, and again noted the importance of the Noh for his version:

> Goacher [=actor-poet Denis Goacher] who is doing the Hyllos for BBC/ has sent on some prize bestialities in other translations. They dont even understand that LAMPRA. after that phrase Hera who has been cursing D/ for a bitch never utters a reproach. THAT is like the transformation in Noh.
>
> ....
>
>   even "grammar dont matter if the speech is alive/ it can be ungrammatical IF it is the way people speak/ the way a Queen, or a hobo, speaks NOW in Japan. Day/ is an aristo/
>
> and also sensitive, very delicately. The Hyllos the next role in so far as it requires understanding presentation. That is why I am so glad to have got Goacher for it. They say their BBC Herak/ is a colossus who can roar. The nurse narrates so that is less difficult /
>
>   but Ito might do a choric dance, combine a choric movement to occur silently while she is describing the suicide. IN fact, all the intelligence they have got can be turned on / and let 'em ENjoy themselves.
>
> ….
>
>   ALZO/ p. 511, enter Nurse. Better she also enter in a tragic mask (small mask, quite different from Daysair's) The Minoru will understand difference.
>
> Reck 82

The following day, Pound wrote to Wyndham Lewis: 'B.B.C. says it is projectin some Sophokles Ezd/on the 25 Ap. prox. I suppose the chit shd/read' (Pound 1985, 279). And a few months later, in another letter to Lewis of 2 August 1956, Pound wrote: 'At last the bloody TRAX is in roofs in London/three years lag' (ibid. 294).

Yet the BBC production may not have been the first one. Alec Marsh has a report by Pound's right-wing disciple John Kasper about a reading of *Women of Trachis* with musical accompaniment he attended early in 1954, with the then still unknown James Dean as Hyllus. On the day it was preceded by Gilbert Murray's translation of Euripides' *Electra*, and Kasper noted how the audience was nearly asleep until Pound's play shook them up. Kasper was not impressed by the actor doing Herakles, but generally the 'whole meaning was there from start to finish thru and thru … The choruses were the utmost melopoeia, particularly when different persons said a single line at the same time. Very like a fugue' (quoted in Marsh 2015, 58–59).

Pound noted proudly in a letter of 15 June 1959 to James Laughlin that he got requests from Denmark and Turkey for the play, and expressed his hope that 'someone might bribe Stravinsky to set the XOROI PROPERLY' (Pound 1994, 269). This wish most likely came forth out of the fact that Stravinsky's opera-oratorio *Oedipus Rex* (1927) used a libretto, based on Sophocles' tragedy, by Jean Cocteau written in French and then translated by Abbé Jean Daniélou into Latin. *Women of Trachis* was translated into German by Eva Hesse, and Pound was invited by the Mayor of Darmstadt to be the guest of honour at the première on 10 December 1959. Pound immensely enjoyed the production, and even appeared on stage after the performance to receive several ovations (Moody 467). In a letter to H. D., Pound stated that his play 'evidently git across in the Kraut version, and I think it will get on the Hun air. Gawd knows what happened in deh teeyater. But I seem to have got the thing out of moth balls' (Beinecke 20/896). Unfortunately, the first full performance on a stage of *Women in Trachis* in English was not very successful, according to Michael Reck. He wrote to Pound on 12 August 1960, that the production in New York by the Living Theatre was 'a rather soggy affair. After a hard struggle, Sophocles defeated the actors' (Beinecke 44/1854).

Notes

1 See Easterling 1982, 23.
2 On Pound's annoyance when he noted that in the proofs of Canto 87, the name was spelled as Δηάνειρα (and actually would remain so), see Kindellan, 117–19.
3 See Liebregts 2004, 286–87. On the phrase in the Cantos, see Canto 83/550, 93/653, 95/664, 96/671, 100/742.
4 See Liebregts 2004, 80–96.
5 Quoted in Reck; letter in photo reproduction following p. 82.
6 Cp. Pound's remark to Ronald Duncan in 1960 about a performance of *Women of Trachis* that the Chorus 'ought to be declaimed by one good voice – with the chorus moving to the thud of the words'. He also noted: 'sometimes a lot of syllables start same level of pitch & may relapse into speech for particularly emphatic statement'; quoted in Moody, 470.

8

Sophocles, Pound and *Women of Trachis* I

Prologue (S ll. 1–93; *WT* 25–28: ll. 1–74)

Unlike Sophocles' other tragedies, which open with a dialogue (or, in the case of *Elektra* with two speeches), to convey to the audience the essential information needed to understand the action, the prologue of the *Trachiniae* opens with a long *rhēsis* or set speech by Deianeira, the principal female character. In her monologue she expresses her feelings with regard to the long absence of her husband Herakles, and the high degree of her dependency upon him. This speech is charged with emotion, and Pound has attempted to retain and even enhance this. He has not only done so by his choice of words, but also by giving the subdivisions of the speech separate paragraphs, giving full weight to Deianeira's expression of her feelings. In his Loeb edition of the play, this speech is heavily annotated.

As Davies has noted, Deianeira's speech 'opens with a rhetorical mode of emphasis whereby the speaker's rejection of a traditional viewpoint focuses attention on the speaker's own divergent opinion' (55), a device known in the later rhetorical tradition as the *refutatio sententiae*. The 'traditional viewpoint' to which Deianeira refers is one of the great Greek commonplaces: 'call no man happy until he is dead' – of which perhaps the most famous expression can be found at the end of *Oedipus Rex* where the Chorus summarizes the fall of the once mighty king. This saying, which is introduced in lines 1–3, is contrasted in lines 4–5 with Deianeira's personal experiences, given here in Storr's faithful rendering:

> There is an old-world saying current still,
> 'Of no man canst thou judge the destiny
> To call it good or evil, till he die.'
> But I, before I pass into the world
> Of shadows, know *my* lot is hard and sad.
>
> S ll. 1–5; tr. Storr

Because, ironically enough, the maxim will be justified at the end of the play, it gains special dramatic force by already being introduced here. To emphasize this, Pound decided to turn it into the very first line of his version:

> 'No man knows his luck 'til he's dead.'
> They've been saying that for a long time
> but it's not true in my case. Mine's soggy.
> Don't have to go to hell to find that out.
>
> WT 25

We already saw in a letter to Iris Barry of August 1916 that one of the reasons Pound disliked Greek drama was because of its use of 'Statements to the effect that Prudence is always more discreet than rashness, and other such brilliant propositions' (SL 94). He therefore omitted some of the Greek phrasing of the maxim, but more importantly, he also emphasizes how Deianeira rejects it from *personal* experience. Where the original indicates that the value of a man's life in the end can only be judged by others, Pound emphasizes the notion of subjective self-evaluation, although he still maintains that a human being is not able to judge their life until they are dead. This not only gives Pound's version a more cynical twist, but also enables him to emphasize his more personal approach to Deianeira's character. This approach may also be seen in the way in which Pound modifies the 'objective phrases' of Sophocles as expressions of subjective moods. Where Deianeira in the original describes her life as 'sad and hard' (*dustuchē te kai barun*; l. 5), Pound's version evaluates it as 'soggy', thereby emphasizing how her life is truly a 'vale of tears' (and a good example of Pound's long-time practice of transforming what he regarded as verbosity into concise, everyday speech). And where Sophocles uses the neutral phrasing *kai prin eis Haidou molein* (l. 4) for Deianeira's claim that she already knows that her life is hard 'even before she will go into Hades', Pound stays true to his subjective approach by having Deianeira suggest that her present life is already a living hell.

In the second part of her speech, Deianeira describes her history in a long account which emphasizes her fear and loneliness throughout its three sections: her courtship as a young girl; the fight between the rival suitors; and her married life up to this point. In the first section (ll. 6–17), Deianeira informs us how afraid she was when the river god Acheloös courted her. Pound reduced this passage to its essence, exemplified in his condensation of the three-line lament 'Expecting such a suitor I, miserable one, constantly prayed that I would die before I would approach such a marriage-bed' (ll. 15–17) into the one line: 'Bed with that! I ask you!' (*WT* 25). Pound stresses its emotional weight by turning it into an isolated line spaced away from the text preceding and following it.

In this first section Pound made one addition to the description of Acheloös by rendering Sophocles' *enargēs tauros* (l. 11), 'a bull in visible form', as 'bullheaded cloud'. Pound's 'bullheaded' neatly captures Sophocles' *bouprōiros* (l. 13), a compound peculiar to the playwright, according to Earp (84). The word *enargēs* is a standard word to express how gods may manifest themselves to mortals. Many deities of water, symbol of instability, had the power of self-transformation, as, for example, Proteus in Book 4 of the *Odyssey*. In the *Trachiniae*, the river god is said to have appeared as a bull, as a snake, and as a man with the head of an ox, but there is no mention of any cloud. Pound's choice for this word can be related to his description of Acheloös in the list of *dramatis personae* as 'a river, symbol of the power of damp and darkness, triform as water, cloud and rain' (*WT* 24).[1]

Herakles comes to the rescue in the second section (S ll.18–27.5), condensed to 4.5 lines by Pound, in which he emphasizes both the fear of Deianeira of the river-god himself ('wet horror') as well as her terror in watching the fight between him and Herakles:

> And Herakles Zeuson got me out of it somehow,
> I don't know how he managed with that wet horror,
> you might find out from some impartial witness
> who could watch without being terrorized.
>
> Looks are my trouble. And that
> Wasn't the end of trouble.
>
> *WT* 25

Pound has emphasized l. 25 of the original describing Deianeira's fear *mē moi to kallos algos exeuroi pote*, 'that my beauty would one day bring me pain', by giving his rendering 'Looks are my trouble' a paragraph of its own, together with a line pointing forward to the third section of the original (ll. 27–35), in which Deianeira discusses her married life up to this point. 'Trouble' is a keyword used in her description of her past and present, and Pound in this respect is far more concise than Sophocles, who uses four lines to let Deianeira describe her plight:

> For since, his chosen bride, I shared the home
> Of Heracles, my cares have never ceased;
> Terror on terror follows, dread on dread,
> And one night's trouble drives the last night's out.
>
> S ll. 27–30; tr. Storr

Pound used Storr's translation 'terror on terror' for *tin' ek phobou phobon* (l. 28; 'one fear after another'), and transposed it to his rendering of ll. 34–35, which rounds off Deianeira's lament about her husband's absence: 'Such [*toioutos*] is the life [*aiōn*] that was always sending [*epempe*] my husband [*ton andr'*] home [*eis domous*] or away from home [*te kak domōn*] in servitude [*latreuonta*] to somebody [*tōi*]' (S ll. 34–35).

> Always away on one assignment or another
> one terror after another,
> always for someone else.
>
> *WT* 26

Pound has turned Sophocles' wording *tin' ek phobou phobon* into a description of both Deianeira's fear of the outcome of her husband's exploits, as well as of the nature of these exploits themselves. This is a good example of Pound's translation being both free and economical, as he reserves the right to employ good poetic material in different positions for greater effect.

Deianeira rounds off her speech by describing her present exile at Trachis, where she is anxiously waiting for news of Herakles (S ll. 36–48). Pound has used eleven lines in his version, dividing the section into three separate parts, namely, the reason for their exile, Deianeira's present fears, and the reference to the writing-tablet or 'memo' Herakles left behind with a message on it. It is noteworthy that in his rendering of ll. 41–42, Pound is more faithful to the Greek than Storr. Deianeira says she feels 'bitter/painful (*pikras*) anxiety (*ōdinas*) for him (*autou*)'. The Greek word *ōdinas* literally means 'the pangs of childbirth', but it is also used of other kinds of pain, as in this case, where it is used to circumscribe Deianeira's fear for Herakles' welfare which is so intense that it gives her physical distress. Storr translated these lines as follows: 'He has gone and left me here to yearn and pine'. Pound is more literal: 'bitter childbirth in separation' (*WT* 26). However, this rendering makes his version rather awkward, because it suggests that Deianeira has given birth to a child during Herakles' absence, yet he has been away 'ten months then five'. Pound's faithfulness to the Greek, then, has produced a rather odd line in this context – although 'childbirth' fits the alliterative b-pattern of this paragraph where we find words like 'bitter' (twice) and 'black'.

At the end of her speech, Deianeira refers to the tablet (*deltos*) which, as we will learn later, contains the oracle given to Herakles at Dodona that he should have rest at the end of twelve years, a period which now has passed. A comparison with Storr's dated translation shows how much Pound's rendering uses everyday speech without wasting any words:

Surely some mischief has befallen him,
....
Some dread calamity, as signifies
This tablet that he left me. Oh! how oft
I've prayed it prove no harbinger of woe.

S ll. 43, 46–48; tr. Storr

worried for some awful calamity.
Black trouble may be connected with
    this memo he left me.

I keep praying it doesn't
    mean something horrible.

WT 26

This combination of the archaic 'calamity' with the poetic 'black trouble' and the modern 'memo' (for *deltos*) makes Pound's version rather timeless.

The aged nurse suggests to Deianeira that one of her sons, perhaps Hyllus, should go in search of his father. Pound condensed Sophocles' twelve lines to six, and then added two lines not to be found in the Greek ('If you felt like to tell him, / if....'), which betray something of the nurse's knowledge of Deianeira's frame of mind and her attitude towards Hyllus.

The Prologue ends with a dialogue between Deianeira and her son Hyllus, who has just arrived (S ll. 61–93; WT 44–74), a passage heavily annotated in Pound's Loeb. Pound has remained very faithful in this part while rendering it in life-like speech. One nice detail, perhaps unintended, may be found in his translation of lines 88–89 where Hyllus explains that until now, he had never felt the urge to seek his father: 'But, as it was [*nun d'*], my father's [*patros*] customary fortune [*ho xunēthēs potmos*] prevented [*ouk eia*] me [*hēmas*] from having too much fear and anxiety [*protarbein oude deimainein agan*].' Pound gives this as: 'I've never worried very much about him/ one way or the other. Luck being with him' (WT 27). Because *xunēthēs potmos*, 'customary fortune', is kept out of the first sentence, Hyllus' words seem to imply that he is a callous son, perhaps in reaction to his father's habit of being away all the time. Pound, however, does render the *xunēthēs potmos* in the next sentence, but because it is delayed, Hyllus seems to utter it as an afterthought in order not to appear as an unloving son. In this subtle shift Pound may have wanted to give his view on the relationship between father and son.

The dialogue ends with Deianeira sending Hyllus off to find his father: 'Go then [*chōrei nun*], my son [*ō pai*]. Because even [*kai gar*] to one who is late [*usterōi*], good fortune [*to g'eu prassein*], if he should hear of it [*epei puthoito*], brings in gain [*kerdos empolai*].' This is a periphrastic variation on the idea of 'better late than never'. The verb *empolai* has the optative form which gives the particular statement a general validity. This may be the reason why Pound rounded off his version of the prologue in a similar manner:

> 'Well, get going. A bit late, / but a good job's worth a bonus'.
>
> WT 28

Parodos (S ll. 94–140; *WT* 28–29: ll. 75–108)

In the Parodos, heavily annotated in Pound's Loeb, we have the entrance of the Chorus of young women of Trachis which gives the play its title. The original has different metrical (largely dactylic) agreements between the 1st Strophe and Antistrophe, and the 2nd Strophe and Antistrophe, while the iambic epode stands alone. As the predominantly iambic pattern of his own choral lyrics and the uneven length of his verse paragraphs demonstrate, Pound made no attempt to recreate the intricate Greek verse pattern, nor did he create responding Antistrophes. Instead, he used assonance and internal rhyme to create a unifying musical effect.

Pound's 1st Strophe, in which the Chorus asks the Sun to reveal where Herakles is, has after its trochaic opening a predominantly iambic pattern (I have marked the stresses in bold, and the secondary stresses in italics here and throughout):

> **PHOEBUS, Phoe**bus, **ere** thou **slay**
> and **lay** flaked **Night** up**on** her **bla**zing **pyre,**
> **Say,** ere the **last** star-**shim**mer is **run:**
> **Where** lies Alkmene's **son,** a**part** from **me?**
> Aye, **thou** art **keen,** as **is** the **light**ning **blaze,**
> **Land** *way,* **sea** *ways,*
> in **these** some **slit** hath **he**
> **found** to es**cape** thy **scru**tiny?
>
> WT 28

Pound's rendering of the 1st Strophe opens with a heptasyllabic – a four-beat metre that regularly begins and ends on a beat – followed by a line of blank verse. The third line has an initial inversion of the iamb, producing a choriamb ($- \times \times -$), which is mirrored at the end; the entire third line thus becomes an adonic ($- \times \times -$)

extended with a choriamb. The fourth and fifth lines (with initial inversion) are lines of blank verse; the sixth line is heavy because its four syllables have two primary and two secondary stresses. The seventh and eighth lines with their iambic pattern are connected through enjambment. The iambic pattern with its rising rhythm, creating a sense of expectation, fits the stanzaic structure with its double questions. It is also noteworthy that the first question has a caesura after 'Alkmene's son', making the isolated rhythmic phrase 'apart from me' decidedly iconic.

If we compare Pound's version to the original (with my crib) and to Storr's translation, the superiority of the former is clear.

ὅν αἰόλα νὺξ ἐναριζομένα
τίκτει κατευνάζει τε, φλογιζόμενον
Ἅλιον Ἅλιον αἰτῶ
τοῦτο καρῦξαι, τὸν Ἀλκμήνας πόθι μοι πόθι παῖς
ναιει ποτ', ὦ λαμπρᾷ στεροπᾷ φλεγέθων,
ἢ ποντίας αὐλῶνας ἢ δισσαῖσιν ἀπείροις κλιθείς,
εἴπ', ὦ κρατιστεύων κατ' ὄμμα.

S ll. 94–101

You, whom [hon] the gleaming night [aiola nux, i.e. 'gleaming with stars'], when she is slaughtered [enaridzomena], brings forth [tiktei], and lays to rest [kateunadzei] as you blaze with fire [phlogidzomenon], you, Helios, Helios [Halion, Halion], I ask [aitō] to tell me this [touto karuxai moi]: where, where ever the child of Alkmena is [Alkmēnas pothi pothi pais naiei pot']; oh, you who blaze [phlegethōn] with brilliant flashing light [ō lamprai steropai], tell me [eip'] whether [ē] [he dwells] in the sea-straits [pontias aulōnas] or [ē] is leaning [klitheis] on the two continents [dissaisin apeirois], oh you with the best sight [ō kratisteuōn kat'omma, lit. 'mightiest in respect of the eye']

Child of star-bespangled Night,
    Born as she dies,
Laid to rest in a blaze of light,
Tell me, Sun, O tell me, where
Tarries the child of Alcmena fair;
    Thou from whose eyes,
Keen as lightning, naught can hide.
Doth he on either mainland bide?
Roams he over the sea straits driven?
Thou, omniscient eye of heaven,
    Declare, declare!

tr. Storr

The Greek contains many examples of assonance with the vowel -a-; indeed, the alpha is the dominant sound of this strophe, appropriate in this prayer-like hymn to the Sun, the 'First' power which determines the rhythm of the universe. Furthermore, there is the pairing of *-idzomena* and *-idzomenon*, and a double invocation (*Halion*), while Sophocles has also employed a double interrogative *pothi* ('where') in connection with *pot'* ('ever') to add some emotional weight to the question.

Storr has tried to retain the dominant alpha in his rendering ('star-bespangled', 'laid', 'blaze', 'tarries', 'fair'), as well as the repetition ('tell me', 'declare'). In Pound's version, however, we not only find a more convincing pattern of assonance, but in addition we have internal rhyme to connect the words involved ('slay', 'lay', 'say', 'way'); furthermore, Pound has been more successful in retaining the repetition of phrases (the double invocation of 'Phoebus'; 'blazing'/'blaze'; 'way'/'ways').

The Parodos shows that the Chorus has not yet heard that Herakles is in Euboea. They try to comfort Deianeira (1st Antistrophe), by arguing that despite his varying fortunes, Herakles has always come through because of divine favour (2nd Strophe); because everyone is subject to a mixture of joy and sorrow, as given by Zeus, Herakles too will find joy again after sorrow (2nd Antistrophe). Sophocles has depicted this universal rhythm of alternating fortunes by employing the imagery of night and day, birth and death, and the movement of the sea and the stars.

In the 1st Strophe, we find the metaphor of day and night, and the pattern of *tiktei*, 'brings forth', and *kateunadzei*, 'lays to rest'. The night is the parent of the day, which in turn destroys the night, which again lays the day to rest, in a perpetual cycle. Pound, however, has not retained this image, but assigned the Sun a wholly active part, and the night a purely passive role, something which may have to do with his view of Herakles as 'the Solar vitality' and Deianeira as the passively waiting wife. By focusing on the day (Herakles) as the slayer of night (Deianeira), Pound turns the paratactically used *tiktei kateunadzei te* into two separate temporal clauses which retain most of the words of the Greek, but in a re-arranged form. In the first clause, it is the Sun instead of the night which becomes the subject; the medio-passive present participle *enaridzomena*, belonging to *nux*, is given as an active main verb to the Sun, while the second participle *phlogidzomenon*, which belongs to the Sun, is transferred to the night. The main verb *kateunadzei* is also given to the Sun instead of the night, while *tiktei* has been deleted:

PHOEBUS, Phoebus, ere thou slay [*enaridzomena*]
and lay [*kateunadzei*] flaked [*aiola*] night [*nux*] upon her blazing pyre
   [*phlogidzomenon*],
Say, ere the last star-shimmer is run:

WT 28

'Say' condenses the *aitō touto karusai* ('I ask you to tell me this'), while 'the last star-shimmer is run' is Pound's own invention, which more or less repeats the idea of the *aiola nux* ('the night gleaming with stars'). Pound may have wanted to re-arrange the relation between subject and object of the original to emphasize what in his view is the dominant image of the play, that of light. Light connotes 'splendour' and 'insight', and is evoked by Pound at the beginning of the Parodos to do away with darkness, which is associated with fear and ignorance. This may also be the reason why Deianeira refers to Herakles' tablet in her prologue as connected with 'Black trouble' (*WT* 26). In the invocation to the Sun, Sophocles has used two apostrophes, *ō lamprai steropai phlegethōn* ('oh you blazing with a brilliant lightning flash'), and *ō kratisteuōn kat' omma* ('oh you being the mightiest in respect of the eye'). Pound has toned down these heavily poetical phrases by giving the second simply as 'thou art keen', and by turning the first into a simile, 'as is the lightning blaze'. This reinforces his depiction of light as an instrument of sharp vision and insight.

Line 100, *ē pontias aulōnas ē dissaisin apeirois klitheis*, '[tell me] whether [he dwells] in the sea-straits or is leaning on the two continents', is a notoriously difficult problem. Several solutions have been offered, including the most plausible one by Lloyd-Jones who has suggested that the *pontias aulōnas* are to be identified with the Black Sea in the east, and the two continents with the Pillars of Herakles in the west (Lloyd-Jones 141). Pound may not have been aware of the problem or simply has avoided all difficulties in his rendering of the essence of the periphrastic question ('is Herakles on land or on sea?') by giving it as 'Land way, sea ways'. The last three lines of Pound's version of the First Strophe contain a question which is not in the original Greek; it is likely that he adapted Storr's translation, which also added a thought to the original (indicated in italics here):

> Thou *from whose eyes*,
> Keen as lightning, *naught can hide*.

tr. Storr

Land way, sea ways,
in these some slit hath he
found to escape thy scrutiny?

WT 28

Here Pound creates a Greek-like grammatical construction by the use of prolepsis – that is, placing an element in a syntactical unit before that to which it corresponds – and the inversion of the normal word order of a question.

The First Antistrophe (ll. 103–111), depicting Deianeira's sorrow, reads:

ποθουμένᾳ γὰρ φρενὶ πυνθάνομαι
τὰν ἀμφινεικῆ Δηιάνειραν ἀεί,
οἷά τιν᾽ ἄθλιον ὄρνιν,
οὔποτ᾽ εὐνάζειν ἀδακρύτων βλεφάρων πόθον, ἀλλ᾽
εὔμναστον ἀνδρὸς δεῖμα τρέφουσαν ὁδοῦ
ἐνθυμίοις εὐναῖς ἀνανδρώτοισι τρύχεσθαι, κακὰν
δύστανον ἐλπίζουσαν αἶσαν.

For I hear [*gar punthanomai*] that Deianeira, disputed by many lovers [*tan amphineikē Dēianeiran*], with an ever aching heart [*pothoumenai phreni aei*], like some sorrowful bird [*hoia tin' athlion ornin*], can never [*oupot'*] put the longing of her eyes [*blepharōn pothon*] to rest [*eunadzein*], so as to make them without tears [*adakrutōn* is proleptic]; but [*all'*] cherishing [*trephousan*, lit. 'feeding'] a mindful fear [*eumnaston deima*] for the journey [*hodou*] of her husband [*andros*], she is consumed [*truchesthai*] by/on her husbandless bed [*eunais anandrōtoisi*] in her mind [*enthumiois*], expecting [*elpidzousan*] a disastrous and wretched destiny [*kakan dustanon aisan*].

Storr has allowed himself considerable freedom in his translation in order to compose a rhyming stanza (abaccddb):

For like bird bereft of her mate
   (Sad my tale)
Deianira, desolate,
She the maiden of many wooed,
Pines by fears for her lord pursued;
Ever she bodes some instant harm
Ever she starts at a new alarm,
With vigils pale.

tr. Storr

It is likely that Pound used Storr in creating his own version, as his First Antistrophe – which is, metrically speaking, far more regular than his First Strophe – opens with:

> DAYSAIR is left alone,
>   so sorry a bird,
> For whom, afore, so many suitors tried.
>
> WT 28

The first line is not in the original Greek, but it, in combination with the following line, suggests that Pound has followed Storr rather than Sophocles. Pound's 'afore' is simply a mistranslation of *aei*, 'ever, always', used here to refer to Deianeira's ever-aching heart. He may have picked up 'afore' from a casual glance in Liddell-Scott, which gives the combination δεῦϱ' ἀεί, 'until now', as the first of several more specific translations of *aei*.

Pound's next four lines, all in blank verse, employ some of the Greek phrases in a free rendering:

> And shall I ask what thing is heart's desire,
> Or how love fall to sleep with tearless eye,
> So worn by fear away, of dangerous road,
> A manless bride to mourn in a vacant room,
>
> WT 28

The only words of the first line which are actually in the Greek is the Yeatsian-sounding phrase 'heart's desire', a rendering of *pothoumenai phreni*, 'with aching heart'. Where in Sophocles the Chorus strictly confines itself to a description of the fear and loneliness of Deianeira, the 'Khoros' in Pound first generalizes her emotions into abstract questions ('And shall ... tearless eye'), and then more specifically deals with the case of Deianeira ('So worn ... vacant room'). Pound turns *pothon*, 'longing, desire', the object of *eunadzein*, 'put to rest', into the subject 'love' of that same verb, while retaining *adakrutōn blepharōn* as a single phrase in his rendering of its proleptic force. 'So worn by fear away' is a condensed phrase based on *deima trephousan truchesthai*, while Pound adds 'dangerous' to his 'road' (*hodou*). By sticking to the translation of *eunais* as 'marriage-bed', Pound first transposes the 'husbandless bed' of Deianeira into a description of Herakles' wife herself as 'a manless bride', and then produces another variation of the Greek phrase as 'vacant room', a variation which may have been suggested by a consultation of Liddell-Scott which gives *eunē* also as 'abode'. The last two lines of Pound's First Antistrophe are fairly accurate. All in all, his version stays far closer to the Greek than Storr's, although Pound in his First Antistrophe has continued, unlike the original, the questioning mood of the First Strophe.

This feeling of uncertainty, expressed through question marks, also dominates his rendering of the second half of the Parodos. This is in strong contrast to the self-confident and reassuring tone with which the Chorus at this point tries to comfort Deianeira in Sophocles' original. The Second Strophe reads:

πολλὰ γὰρ ὥστ' ἀκάμαντος ἢ νότου ἢ βορέα τις
κύματ' ἂν εὐρέι πόντῳ βάντ' ἐπιόντα τ' ἴδοι,
οὕτω δὲ τὸν Καδμογενῆ στρέφει, τὸ δ' αὔξει,
    βιότου πολύπονον ὥσπερ πέλαγος
Κρήσιον. ἀλλά τις θεῶν αἰὲν ἀναμπλάκητον Ἅιδα
    σφε δόμων ἐρύκει.

ll. 112–20

For just as [*gar hōst'*] one may see [*tis an idoi*] many waves [*polla kumat'*] of the unwearying south or north wind [*akamantos ē notou ē borea*, i.e. waves raised by these winds] having passed by and coming on [*bant' epionta*] in the wide sea [*eurei pontōi*], so [*houtō*] as it were [*hōsper*] a Cretan sea [*pelagos Krēsion*] full of life's troubles [*biotou poluponon*] at one time whirls back [*strephei*] the son of Cadmus [*ton Kadmogenē*] and at another time [*to d'*] exalts him [*auxei*]. But some one of the gods [*alla tis theōn*] ever keeps him free [*aien sphe erukei*] of error [*anamplakēton*] and from the house of Hades [*Haida domōn*].

For as the tireless South or Northern blast
    Billow on billow rolls o'er ocean wide,
So on the son of Cadmus follows fast
    Sea upon sea of troubles, tide on tide;
And now he sinks, now rises; still some god
Is nigh to save him from Death's whelming flood.

tr. Storr

NORTH WIND or South, so bloweth tireless
wave over wave to flood.
Cretan of Cadmus' blood, Orcus' shafts err not.
What home hast 'ou now,
    an some God stir not?

WT 28

This stanza compares the vicissitudes of Herakles to the periodical succession of *polla kumat'*, 'many waves', on the sea, *bant' epionta*, 'going past and coming on', a rhythmic movement of assonance rendered by Storr as 'Billow on billow' and by Pound as 'wave over wave'. Unlike Storr ('For as … So'), Pound does not make the comparison explicit, but makes an ideogrammic transition to 'Cretan of Cadmus' blood, Orcus' shafts err not'. 'Cadmus' blood' is a fair translation of *Kadmogenē*, but in the context of the play it means no more than 'Theban' or 'born in Thebes', since Herakles was not one of Cadmus' descendants. In this respect, Pound's 'Cretan' is equally misleading. Here it appears that Pound condensed Sophocles' comparison of Herakles' 'trouble-filled life' (*biotou poluponon*) to a *pelagos Krēsion*, 'a Cretan sea', into the phrase 'Cretan of Cadmus' blood', not only because he had already used 'flood' in the previous line, but also because he wanted to create an ideogrammic connection through rhyme and rhythm, as both phrases have the pattern of a dodrans $(-\times\times-\times-)$:

> **wave** over **wave** to **flood**.
> **Cre**tan of **Cad**mus' **blood**,

Furthermore, had Pound wanted to retain the phrase 'Cretan sea', the simile would not have been clear to a modern audience which would not know that this sea was notoriously rough.

Pound's last three lines of his Second Strophe are based on the last two of Sophocles: 'But some one of the gods [*alla tis theōn*] ever keeps him free [*aien sphe erukei*] of error [*anamplakēton*] and from the house of Hades [*Haida domōn*]'. Pound's rendering is rather awkward:

> …, Orcus' shafts err not.
> What home hast 'ou now,
>   an some God stir not?

The Latin word 'Orcus' may refer to Hades, the Underworld itself, or to Death, although Hades does not carry shafts as his attribute. By changing the adjective *anamplakēton*, 'unerring', said of Herakles, into an active verb, 'to err not', and linking it to Orcus, Pound may have wanted to express man's inability to elude or escape death, unless some god intervenes on his behalf. We find this thought also in Sophocles, but Pound has rephrased the Greek, using the *domōn*, 'house', no longer in connection with Hades, but as a term to denote a place of refuge for Herakles under the protection of a god. Because Pound has taken the entire Parodos as an expression of doubt, fear and uncertainty, he also ends the Second Strophe with a question.

Pound's rendering of the Second strophe is unified through its rhythm:

> **NORTH** *WIND* or **South**, so **blow**eth **tireless**
> **wave** over **wave** to **flood**.
> **Cre**tan of **Cad**mus' **blood**, **Orcus'** **shafts err not**.
>
> *What* **home** *hast 'ou* **now**,
>   **an** some **God stir not**?

The Second Strophe begins with an iambic pentameter with initial inversion, and continues with an iambic trimeter, also with initial inversion, producing a dodrans. This metrical colon is repeated at the beginning of the third line, a repetition strengthened by the use of rhyme ('flood', 'blood'), which in turn is picked up with a half-rhyme at the end of the line ('not'). Moreover, this second half of the third line is in metrical agreement with the fifth line, with which it also rhymes, while the intervening fourth line has the same number of syllables, which adds to the feeling of the second half as another semi-separate unit. This turns the words 'Orcus' shafts err not' into a key phrase. As in the First Strophe, the Second Strophe ends on a note of ambiguity: the reader again must decide whether to give the last 'not' a primary or a secondary stress.

In the Second Antistrophe, the Chorus offers advice to Deianeira:

> ὧν ἐπιμεμφομένα σ᾽ αἰδοῖα μέν, ἀντία δ᾽ οἴσω
> φαμὶ γὰρ οὐκ ἀποτρύειν ἐλπίδα τὰν ἀγαθὰν
> χρῆναί σ᾽· ἀνάλγητα γὰρ οὐδ᾽ ὁ πάντα κραίνων
>   βασιλεὺς ἐπέβαλε θνατοῖς Κρονίδας·
> ἀλλ᾽ ἐπὶ πῆμα καὶ χαρὰ πᾶσι κυκλοῦσιν, οἷον
> ἄρκτου στροφάδες κέλευθοι.
>
>   ll. 121–30

Because I reprove [*epimemphomena*] you [*s'*] for these things [*hōn*], I shall speak [*oisō*] with respect [*aidoia men*] but in opposition [*antia d'*]. For I say [*phami gar*] that you [*s'*] must not wear out [*ouk apotruein chrēnai*] good hope [*elpida tan agathan*]: for [*gar*] Kronos' son [*Kronidas*], the all-disposing king [*ho panta krainōn basileus*], has not given [*oud' epebale*] mortals [*thnatois*] a lot free from pain [*analgēta*], but [*all'*] sorrow and joy [*pēma kai chara*] come round to all [*pasi kuklousin*], just as [*hoion*] the revolving paths [*strophades keleuthoi*] of the Great Bear [*arktou*].

The Second Antistrophe is the first stanza in Pound's version which does not end with a question, but with an optimistic statement, albeit only to soften a harsh rhetorical question. Here Pound has reduced the lyric to its essence. He renders *aidoia*, 'respect', as 'PARDON' and gives it as the opening word to express the Chorus' deference. The second line is Pound's own invention and presents the Chorus as the very opposite of Sophocles': where the women in the original are counseling Deianeira in a spirit of diplomatic and empathic optimism, Pound's women have become direct and almost cruelly realistic in their attempt to 'save thee false hopes delayed' (*WT* 29). The poet goes even further in the last four lines:

> Thinkst thou that man who dies,
> Shall from King Chronos take
>   unvaried happiness?
> Nor yet's all pain.
>
> WT 29

The infinitive *apotruein*, 'wear out', which forms part of the advice to Deianeira to keep up her hopes, now becomes 'dies', probably under the influence of Storr's 'Why by fair despondency is fair hope *slain*?' (my italics), his rendering of φαμὶ γὰρ οὐκ ἀποτρύειν ἐλπίδα τὰν ἀγαθὰν χρῆναί σ᾿. Pound has condensed the general statement of the second half of the Antistrophe by turning 'the son of Kronos [=Zeus], the all-disposing king' into 'King Chronos' himself, that is, Time as the ruler of all, while the *analgēta*, 'a lot free from pain', has become 'unvaried happiness'. Pound's last line is meant to comfort Deianeira and to balance the bleak view expressed in the preceding lines. Here Pound stays closer to the thought in the original that sorrow and joy come to each in turn.

The Epode concludes the Parodos with a word of encouragement based on a realistic acceptance of the ways of the world:

> μένει γὰρ οὔτ᾿ αἰόλα
> νὺξ βροτοῖσιν οὔτε κῆρες
> οὔτε πλοῦτος, ἀλλ᾿ ἄφαρ
> βέβακε, τῷ δ᾿ ἐπέρχεται
> χαίρειν τε καὶ στέρεσθαι.
> ἃ καὶ σὲ τὰν ἄνασσαν ἐλπίσιν λέγω
> τάδ᾿ αἰὲν ἴσχειν· ἐπεὶ τίς ὧδε
> τέκνοισι Ζῆν᾿ ἄβουλον εἶδεν;
>
> ll. 131–40

For [*gar*] neither the gleaming night [*out' aiola nux*] nor calamities [*oute kēres*] nor good fortune [*oute ploutos*] abide [*menei*] for mortals [*brotoisin*], but each is gone [*bebake*] in a moment [*aphar*], and the rejoicing [*chairein*] and the loss [*steresthai*] goes to someone else in turn [*tōi d' eperchetai*]. Wherefore [*ha*, lit. 'with respect to these things'] I command [*legō*] you [*se*], my Queen [*se tan anassan*], to ever hold to [*aien ischein*] these things [*tad'*] in hope [*elpisin*]: for who has seen [*epei tis eiden*] Zeus [*Zēn'*] so unmindful [*hōde aboulon*] for his children [*teknoisi*]?

The 'gleaming night' (*aiola nux*) echoes l. 94, which 'reinforces the sense of unity conveyed by the imagery of this ode: the heavenly bodies, the sea, the fortunes of men are all part of the same pattern of unending mutability' (Easterling 1982, 92). Having given an exposé on the constant succession of pain and sorrow, the Chorus tells Deianeira to regard the fact that both she and Herakles are part of this universal rhythm as a certainty that all will be well again (In his Loeb, Pound glossed the Epode with 'calm neutral air'). Pound has expressed this inescapable law which man and all of nature must obey beautifully through the lines: 'The shifty Night delays not, / Nor fates of men, nor yet rich goods and spoil' (*WT* 29). His third line, 'Be swift to enjoy, what thou art swift to lose' (ibid.) makes more explicit what in the original is only implied in the Chorus' description of the alternation of gain and loss. Pound's last three lines then conclude with a fairly accurate rendering of the Greek, although he transposes the 'seeing' by someone [*tis eiden*] into the all-seeing 'eye' of Zeus:

> Let not the Queen choose despair.
> Hath not Zeus no eye (who saith it?)
>   watching his progeny?
>
> *WT* 29

Pound's Epode retains the rhetorical question of the original. Of all the questions posed in his rendering of the Parodos, this is by far the most 'positive' one.

First Episode (Sophocles ll. 141–496; *WT* 29–41: ll. 109–453)

The First Episode, heavily annotated by Pound up to l. 225, begins with Deianeira's speech to the Chorus (S ll. 141–77), in which she responds to the women's counseling by describing the general course of a young woman's life and the predicament of the married state. By presenting herself as an older and experienced woman, she dismisses the Chorus' optimism by implying that they are still too young to imagine her anxieties (ll. 141–52). Pound's version of this part of the speech is fairly accurate, although he has transformed part of the general description of young people growing up in some sheltered spot, unafflicted by extreme weather ('neither by the sun god's heat not by rain, nor any winds'), into phrases which parody parental advice:

One grows up, gets fed. 'Don't get sun-burnt.'
'Don't get wet in the rain. Keep out of draughts.'
That's a girl's life till she's married.

WT 29

In her speech, Deianeira first describes a general reason for her anxiety: after all, married life makes a woman live in fear for the welfare of her husband and her children. She then adds a more specific reason, referring to the tablet Herakles left behind when he departed fifteen months ago (S ll. 153–77). It is the same tablet ('old slab of wood', *WT* 29) to which Deianeira had already referred in l.47, but we now learn that it contains the text of a prophecy concerning her husband.

Again, Pound stays fairly close to the original, but makes a mistranslation at a crucial point. Sophocles describes how the oracle predicts that when Herakles will be absent for fifteen months, he will either die or continue to live a life free from pain. The period of fifteen months is given in the Greek as *trimēnon kaniausion* (ll. 164–65), 'three months and a year', but for some strange reason Pound missed out the last word in his rendering and translated the line as 'Time to work out in three months', which completely contradicts his correct rendering of Deianeira's earlier reference to Herakles' absence: 'Bitter ache of separation brought on me,/ ten months then five, and no news' (*WT* 26). This mistake is even more remarkable as Pound marked Storr's Loeb translation ('Saying that when a year and three full moons') with a purple line.

At the end of her speech, Deianeira justifies her feeling of anxiety, because the moment for the fulfilment of the prophecy has come:

καὶ τῶνδε ναμέρτεια συμβαίνει χρόνου
τοῦ νῦν παρόντος, ὡς τελεσθῆναι χρεών·

S ll. 173-74

And [*kai*] the exact moment [*namerteia*] for these predictions [*tōnde*], when [*hōs*] it is destined [*chreon*] that they should be fulfilled [*telesthēnai*], is coming to pass [*sumbainei*] at the time [*chronou*] now present [*tou nun parontos*]

Storr has translated this as: 'And now, this very day, the hour has struck/ For confirmation of the prophecy.' Storr's notion of 'confirmation' is echoed in Pound's simple yet powerful: 'Time up, / see how much truth was in it' (*WT* 30). As we will see, the verb *sumbainei*, 'coming to pass', will appear again at a crucial point towards the end of the play.

The Chorus interrupts Deianeira by saying that they see a man approaching. This messenger brings good news: he has heard from Lichas the herald that

Herakles is still alive. When Deianeira asks why Lichas has not come himself to deliver the news, the messenger tells her that the herald is being detained by many people who want to hear the news. More importantly, the messenger reports that Herakles is 'looking splendid' (Pound's invention), thereby foreshadowing the 'splendour' of the climax of the play. In his criticism of the play, Earp missed Pound's intention when he pointed out to the poet in a letter of 7 August 1954: 'I think you sometimes mistake the sense. E.g. l. 186 you say "he's looking splendid", where the Greek says "appearing with victorious might".'

Deianeira cries out in joy, thanking Zeus and commanding the women to rejoice:

> O Zeus, to whom belongs the unshorn meadow of Oeta, you have given us joy at long last. Raise your voices, women within the house and outside the courtyard, for we now enjoy the unexpected [*aelpton*] dawning [*anaschon*] of this radiant news [*omm'... phēmēs ... tēsde*]
>
> S ll. 200–204

This is the first mention of the mountain Oeta, which will form the setting for Herakles' funeral pyre (the grass of the meadow is not mown in honour of Zeus). Pound typographically depicts the natural division of the speech into the prayer and the command, while he emphasizes Deianeira's joy, by extending the single Greek word *aelpton* into two full lines ('I had ... see it'):

> Zeus in the long grass of Oeta,
> joy hast Thou given me with its season.
>
> Tune up, you there, you women, inside
> and out here.
>   I had given up hope.
> Never thought I would see it.
> Let's sing and be happy.
>
> WT 31

One would at this point expect the First Stasimon or Choral Ode, but instead Sophocles gives us a so-called *hyporchēma* or dance-song, to express the Chorus's delight in hearing the good news. Jebb (1908, 34) regards it as a paean to Artemis and Apollo, but Easterling (1982, 104) has rightly pointed out that the song is not easy to define as Sophocles seems to have amalgamated different lyrical elements, namely, an *ololugmos* or cry to the gods as an expression of joy or hope (ll. 205–7), a paean or hymn of thanksgiving to Apollo (208–10) and Artemis (211–15), and a dithyramb or hymn addressed to Dionysus (216–21). There is also a metrical difficulty as the song is astrophic, that is, it does not have metrically responding units, but it is dominated throughout by a fast iambic rhythm to underscore the expression of joy and excitement. The *hyporchēma* (ll. 205-24) reads:

> ἀνολολυξάτω δόμοις ἐφεστίοις
> ἀλαλαγαῖς ἁ μελλόνυμφος, ἐν δὲ
> κοινὸς ἀρσένων ἴτω
> κλαγγὰ τὸν εὐφαρέτραν
> Ἀπόλλω προστάταν· ὁμοῦ δὲ
> παιᾶνα παιᾶν᾽ ἀνάγετ᾽, ὦ παρθένοι,
> βοᾶτε τὰν ὁμόσπορον
> Ἄρτεμιν Ὀρτυγίαν
> ἐλαφαβόλον ἀμφίπυρον,
> γείτονάς τε Νύμφας.
> ἀείρομαι οὐδ᾽ ἀπώσομαι
> τὸν αὐλόν, ὦ τύραννε τᾶς ἐμᾶς φρενός.
> ἰδού μ᾽ ἀναταράσσει,
> εὐοῖ μ᾽,
> ὁ κισσὸς ἄρτι βακχίαν
> ὑποστρέφων ἅμιλλαν. ἰὼ ἰὼ Παιάν.
> ἴδ᾽, ὦ φίλα γύναι,
> τάδ᾽ ἀντίπρῳρα δή σοι
> βλέπειν πάρεστ᾽ ἐναργῆ.

Let those about to be married [*ha mellonumphos*, i.e., 'maidens'] raise a shout of joy [*anololuxatō*] for the house [*domois*], with shouts of triumph [*alalagais*] at the hearth [*ephestiois*]; and let a song [*klanga*] of the men [*arsenōn*] go up [*itō*] in one accord [*koinos*] for Apollo of the fine quiver [*ton eupharetran Apollō*], the defender [*prostatan*]; and at the same time [*homou de*], maidens [*ō parthenoi*], raise up [*anaget'*] the paean, the paean [*paiana paian'*], call upon [*boate*] his sister Artemis of Ortygia [*tan homosporon Artemin Ortugian*; Ortygia=Delos, her birthplace], the shooter of deer [*elaphabolon*], with a torch in either hand [*amphipuron*], and upon her neighbouring Nymphs [*geitonas te Numphas*]!

I rise up [*aeiromai*] and I shall not reject [*oud apōsomai*] the flute [*ton aulon*], o ruler of my mind [*ō turanne tas emas phrenos* = Dionysos]! See me [*idou m'*], Euoi [*euoi*]!, the ivy [*ho kissos*] excites [*anatarassei*] me, whirling me round [*hupostrephōn*] at this moment [*arti*] in the swift Bacchic dance [*bakchian hamillan*]. Ioo, ioo, Paian [*iō iō Paian* = Apollo]! See, dear lady [*id' ō phila gunai*], this [*tad'* = news of Herakles' triumph] is clear [*parest'enargē*] for you to see [*soi blepein*] before your eyes [*antiprōira*].

my trl.

A typescript draft now among the Pound papers at Princeton has an earlier version of this song, much shorter (eleven lines) than the published version, and also inferior to it, as a comparison of the two illustrates. In the typescript draft Pound seemed to have wanted to condense the song to its bare essentials:

>   Sing on the heart stone
>   Not men alone for Apollo
> high voices with low
>   let the song show
>   Praise for Apollo
> Praises to Artemis,
>   in all Ortigia, deer for the hunting
>   dance with torches
>   Let the woodnymph call
>   with fife screaming,
>   Maenad, sing Paean/
>
>   Princeton 1/13

The final, published, version reads:

> APOLLO
>   and Artemis, analolu
>   Artemis,
> Analolu,
> Sun-bright Apollo, Saviour Apollo
>   analolu,   .
> Artemis,
> Sylvan Artemis,
> Swift-arrowed Artemis, analolu
> By the hearth-stone
>   brides to be
> Shout in male company:
>   APOLLO EUPHARETRON.
> Sylvan Artemis,
>   torch-lit Artemis
> With thy Ortygian girls,
>   Analolu
> Artemis,
>   Io Zagreus,
> Join now, join with us
>   when the great stag is slain,

> Lord of hearts, Artemis,
> Ivied Zagreus,
>   Analolu,
> Dancing maid and man,
> Lady or Bacchanal
>   dancing toe to toe
> By night,
> By light shall show
>   analolu
>   Paian.
>
> WT 31–32

In the published version, Pound focuses far more on the melopoeia of both Sophocles and his own rendering. He now uses seventy-eight words (including four compounds) to translate the sixty-eight words of the original, and employs thirty-one lines in comparison with the nineteen lines as printed in Storr's Loeb-edition. This comparatively large number of lines is due to Pound's habit of typographically representing, and thereby emphasizing, the individual rhythmic units of the passage. These are extremely short to match the ecstatic, frenzied iambic rhythm of Sophocles' *hyporchēma*, which moves very fast – indeed, Pound in his Loeb jotted down the remark 'voila que je suis excitee'. Moreover, Pound's version relies heavily on repetition: of the seventy-eight words, 'Apollo' occurs four times, 'Artemis' nine times, 'analolu' seven times. This means that more than a quarter of the number of words consists of two invocations and a ritual cry, which gives his rendering a very hymn-like and ecstatic feel. This is in line with Sophocles' own repetitive use of *paiana paian*' and *iō iō Paian*, a repetition which is 'idiomatic in the context of ritual cries or the expression of religious excitement' (Davies 103). Pound has used short lines and repetition to convey the essence of the rhythm and character of the original in a far more effective way than he did in his draft.

Where Sophocles' Choral Song seems to consist of three distinct lyric elements (the *ololugmos*, the paean and the dithyramb), Pound has made his version of the *ololugmos* or cry of joy in prayer or sacrifice (*analolu*) part of the invocation and worship of the three deities. The Poundian phrase 'analolu' is, of course, based on the first word in the Greek, *anololuxatō*, from *anololudzō*, meaning 'to shout aloud', 'to raise the *ololugmos*'. Pound's 'analolu' instead of the more exact transliteration 'anololu' is probably due to the fact that the poet associated the idea of 'raising' with the preposition *ana*, 'up, upwards'.

This invocation is then repeated with the addition of Homer-like epithets for the gods: three of these four epithets are not in the original Greek, but they denote the conventional assocations of Apollo as Phoebus Apollo, the 'Sun-bright', and his sister Artemis as living in the woods ('Sylvan') and as a huntress ('Swift-arrowed'). Only the fourth epithet, 'Saviour', for Apollo, is based on the Greek *prostatan*, 'defender'. This first part of Pound's published version displays repetition at its most dense.

This invocation is temporarily interrupted by an 'objective' depiction of those who are performing the religious worship. Here Pound has adapted some of the Greek phrases at the beginning of the *hyporchēma* where the Chorus command the *mellonumphos* or marriagable maidens of the household to raise the religious cry:

By the hearth-stone
        brides to be
Shout in male company:
                APOLLO EUPHARETRON

WT 31

Here Pound has connected the adjective *koinos*, 'in one accord, common', which belongs to *klanga*, 'song', with the genitive plural *arsenōn*, 'of men'. Since *koinos* is often used in connection with social and political relations, as in federations, associations or guilds, the rendering 'in male company' is defensible, since Pound uses it to depict how both men and women alike invoke the gods. He retains, not entirely correctly, the original Greek epithet *eupharetran* ('of the fine quiver') as *eupharetron*, as he most likely thought the *-on* ending would be the fitting masculine declension; the *-an* ending, however, is a Doric declension, as Attic drama used the Doric dialect for its choral parts.

This third address to Apollo, now in capital letters, leads to a concomitant invocation to Artemis, again as 'Sylvan', and then as 'torch-lit' – a rather peculiar rendering of *amphipuron* – and finally as 'With thy Ortygian girls', which combines *Ortugian* (l. 212) with the *geitonas te Numphas* (l. 214).

In the original Greek we find in ll. 216-21 a description of the Chorus's excited dance; the references to the ivy, aulos and the cry *euoi* evoke the worship of Dionysus. Although Sophocles does not mention his name, Pound explicitly names him in his 'Io Zagreus'. He also suggests a far closer connection between the paean to Artemis, and the dithyramb to the god of ecstasy. Pound's version now becomes very free and associative: 'when the great stag is slain' may have been suggested by *elaphobolon* ('shooter of deer'), while 'Lord of hearts' is based on the address to Dionysus (or the flute) as *turanne tas emas phrenas*, 'ruler of my mind/heart'. The epithet 'Ivied' is derived from the substantive *kissos*, while the last three lines depict a dancing scene based on the line *bakchian/ hupostrephōn hamillan*, 'the swift Bacchic dance'.

In l. 221 the cry *iō iō paian* brings us back to the worship of Apollo, as Pound also does in his invocation:

> By night
> By light shall show
>   analolu
>   Paian.
>
>   WT 32

Pound's addition of the phrases 'By night/ By light', is significant as it emphasizes again how the poet regarded the play as being dominated by the interplay between the forces of darkness and light. Pound's version ends here and thus ignores the last three lines of the *hyporchēma*. These lines address Deianeira, telling her how the victory of Herakles is clear for her to see. Yet Pound wanted to present her as staying in the dark, and thus the next lines introduce a new scene, in which Lichas comes on the stage with a group of female captives, including Iole.

This so-called 'deception scene' (ll. 225–334), which Pound did not annotate in his Loeb edition, begins with a dialogue between Deianeira and Lichas, who is followed by a train of captive Euboean women. I will focus on the beginning of the scene to illustrate the manner in which Pound gives his version additional dramatic force, and how he has carefully tried to convey the emphasis given to certain words in the Greek. Lines 225–28, spoken by Deianeira, read in a literal translation: 'I see, dear women, nor does the sight of this procession escape my watchful eye; and I bid the herald welcome [*chairein*], who has now at last [*chronōi pollōi*] appeared, if indeed you bring something welcome [*charton*].' Pound has deleted the unnecessary Greek idiomatic phrasing of the first two lines, and, as my italics show, has extended the phrase *chronōi pollōi* into a polysyndetic sentence to stress Deianeira's long and anxious wait for news:

> Yes, my dear girls, I make out the crowd
> *and finally and at last and at leisure*
> the herald, to be received,
>   and,
> if his news is good,
>   welcomed.
>
>   WT 32

In the Greek, the idea of joy and welcome is present in the word-play of *chairein* and *charton*. Pound has retained this emphasis by giving 'welcomed' as a distinct last word of Deianeira's speech after the conditional clause.

The messenger graciously thanks Deianeira for her kind words: 'for when a man is doing well, he must gain [*kerdainein*] favourable words' (ll. 230–31). Storr translated the latter part as 'He who speeds well a welcome fair deserves'. Pound, however, took the Greek word *kerdainein*, 'to make a profit', far more literally in order to stress the traditional depiction in tragedy of the messenger's eagerness for a reward. This also occurs in ll. 190–91 where the messenger, who had heard the news from Lichas, had wanted to be the first to deliver the news to Deianeira ('I came on ahead, thought I might get/ a tip for the news' [*kerdanaimi*], *WT* 31). Although Lichas uses the verb metaphorically in line 231, Pound still presents him as more concerned with receiving a reward than as honestly wanting to relieve his lady's burden:

> That is is, Milady,
>   and worth hearing,
> and paying for.
>
>   *WT* 32

The following four lines give a good example of Pound's ideal of economic speech in combination with retaining the poetical quality of the original:

> Deianeira: O dearest of men [*ō philtat' andrōn*], first [*prōth'*] tell me [*didaxon*] what [*ha*] I wish for [*boulomai*] first [*prōta*], whether [*ei*] I shall receive [*prosdexomai*] Herakles [*Heraklē*] alive [*dzōnth'*].
>
>   Lichas: I [*egōge toi*, with emphasis] left him [*sph' eleipon*] strong [*ischuonta*] and alive [*te kai dzōnta*] and flourishing [*thallonta*] and not heavy with sickness [*kou nosōi barun*].
>
>   S ll. 232–35

Pound condenses Deianeira's speech, and gives an equivalent for Lichas' polysyndetic inner rhyme (*-onta*) in *ischuonta te / kai dzōnta kai thallonta*:

> DAYSAIR: Is Herakles alive?
> LIKHAS: Sound in wind and limb, mind and body.

Lichas then explains to Deianeira in a long speech (S ll. 248–90), not annotated in Pound's Loeb, why Herakles has been away so long. Easterling has given a careful analysis of the circular structure of this speech:

> Narrative of past events occupies most of this long speech: the time sequence is b-c-a-b-c: Heracles a slave in Lydia (248–53); his sack of Oechalia in revenge

(254–60); the history of his quarrel with Eurytus, culminating in the murder of Iphitus (260–9, 269–73); Zeus's punishment: enslavement in Lydia (274–80); the outcome of the sack of Oechalia (281–85)

Easterling 1982, 110

Pound's rendering of ll. 248–60 is fairly accurate up to the point where Herakles goes to the palace of Eurytus, king of Oechalia, who is presented as the initial cause of all of the demi-god's misfortunes and hence his long absence. The crucial part of Lichas' account is the murder of Iphytus, the son of Eurytus, by Herakles, because Eurytus offended Herakles. Zeus punished Herakles by having him sold into slavery, after which Herakles returned to Oechalia, sacked the city, and took Iole, daughter of Eurytus, with him.

In Pound's version, we have a double account of the quarrel with Eurytus and the killing of Iphitus (S ll. 260–73). Pound first has Lichas state that Herakles 'blamed it all on Eurytus'. He then (temporarily) skips ll. 263–68, that is, the details of the history of his quarrel with Eurytus, and goes on to deal with the murder of Iphitus in such a condensed manner that *prima facie* Herakles seems to have acted like a total madman who was rightly punished by Zeus:

> Swore in foreign troops and went to Eurytus' palace
>   as he blamed it all on Eurytus. [= S ll. 259–61]
> Well, he was drunk [= l. 268], and he killed a man [extension],
> threw him off a cliff [= l. 273], and was punished [= l. 276].
> Zeus wouldn't stand it [= ll. 274–76],

WT 33

It is not clear why Pound rendered this passage in this particular way. It may be that he wanted to show Lichas' eagerness to explain the reason for Herakles' absence in the briefest number of words possible so as to mislead Deinaneira as best as he can by not mentioning Iole. But Pound then has Lichas, as if the messenger himself understands that his report has produced a rather unfavourable and unjust picture of Herakles, give another, extended, version of the same report:

> and Herakles blamed it on 'Rytus [= S ll. 260]
>   who had insulted him [= ll. 263–268, condensed]
>   and had him thrown out of the dining hall [= ll. 268–9],
> which was how he came to be on the cliff
>   up at Tirunth [= ll. 270–71]
> when Iphytz was there hunting lost horses [= l. 271],
> and he killed him, and so on, [repetition]

and Zeus wouldn't stand it. [= ll. 274–76]
[deletion of 278–80]

WT 33

In this second report, Pound now has Lichas give the reason for Herakles' quarrel with Eurytus (ll. 263–68), to account for what initially seemed Iphytus' senseless murder. Pound then continues his version with a summary of what happened after Herakles' punishment by Zeus:

So when he'd done his time, he got a gang together
and sacked 'Rytus' city. [= S ll. 258–59 + ll. 281–83]
    These are the captives. [= ll. 283–85]

WT 34

Interestingly enough, Pound's version after this point stresses more than the original does, Herakles' justification for his actions by again referring to Eurytus before rounding off with a maxim based on ll. 281–82:

That's what comes of big talk. [= S l. 281]
Said Herakles couldn't shoot as well as his kids, 'Rytus's. [= ll. 265–66]
Hell's full of big talkers. [= ll. 281–82]

WT 34

Pound then ends Lichas' speech, as Sophocles does, with a reference to Herakles' imminent arrival:

He'll be along as soon as he's finished
    the celebration. [=S ll. 287–89]. All very fine —
Sacrifice captives.
    C'est très beau.

WT 34

'All very fine' and 'C'est très beau' constitute Pound's rendering of ll. 289–90, 'for of this long story [*gar logou pollou*] happily told [*kalōs lechthentos*], this [*touto*] is the sweetest to hear [*hēdiston kluein*]'. Pound's 'Sacrifice captives' neatly summarizes Herakles' present activities as well as what now is present before Deianeira's eyes. It appears that the latter phrase is based on the typical choral couplet which rounds off Lichas' long speech (S ll. 291–92): 'Queen, now your delight is manifest [that is, assured beyond all doubt], partly because of the present circumstances, partly because of what you have heard described [namely, Herakles' return]'. Having already used part of it, Pound therefore was forced to give a different rendering of the couplet as 'Yes, isn't it, Your Majesty. / Everything will now be all right' (*WT* 34).

In a long speech (S ll. 293–310), Deianeira expresses her joy with some reservations, a passage condensed by Pound to just two lines:

> If it lasts, yes. Looks all right, why can't I feel easy about it?
> My luck runs with his. I wonder.
>
> *WT* 34

'My luck runs with his' is clearly based on Storr's translation of l. 295, 'our two fortunes run in parallels'. The Greek would read in a literal translation, 'Of course it [=Deianeira's rejoicing] must match [lit. 'run to meet'] this [=Herakles' success]'.

Deianeira then looks at the captives and at Iole (298–313), a passage which Pound has accurately reduced to its essence. He marked the beginning of the passage by writing the word 'pity' next to l. 298 in the Greek in his Loeb edition. Pound also carefully condensed the dialogue between Deianeira and Lichas (311–34), in which the Queen unsuccessfully tries to find out who Iole is, as Lichas is constantly being evasive. When he and the captives have left the stage, the Messenger blocks Deianeira's path, and in a long speech enlightens her about the identity and status of the young girl (351–74). Pound has attempted to individualize the Messenger as a character through his highly colloquial speech, which contains phrases as ''Arf a mo', Ma'am!', 'Jus' lis'en a bit', 'one heck of a messenger', 'he had a letch for the girl', 'on the Q.T.', and 'Too het up', while he lets the speaker 'trip' at his one attempt to use a word not normally part of his vocabulary, 'pro-eh-Genitor' (*WT* 35–36).

In his typescript draft, in which the Messenger uses the phrase 'crime ov passion', Pound still used twenty-two lines to render the twenty-four lines of the speech. This version shows how much he relied on Storr's translation (Princeton 1/13). The published version only takes ten lines, and constitutes a successful piece of economical translation while retaining the individual flavour of his style. Pound plunges *in medias res* of the speech which stresses that Herakles' real reason for his long absence was love/lust for Iole:

> All started when he had a letch for the girl,
> [=S ll. 354–5, 'it was Eros alone among the gods that bewitched him']
> and when her pro-eh-Genitor 'Rytus wouldn't
>   let him put her to bed on the Q.T.
> [=S ll. 359–60, 'when he could not persuade her father to give him his daughter,
>   to have as his secret [*kruphion*] love']
>
> *WT* 36

Pound's rendering of Deianeira's reaction to the news is far more emotional and direct than that of the original:

> Ah me, unhappy one! what is my situation?
> What disaster have I received in my house,
> unknowingly? Ah me, miserable one. Is she nameless,
> just as he who brought her swore?
>
> S ll. 375–78

> What have I done, what have I done!
> Just a nobody, and he took oath that she was.
>   What a mess.
>
> WT 36

Pound has replaced Deianeira's three rhetorical questions by a repetitive rhetorical exclamation, and then uses the word 'nobody', which in the original is applied to Iole, as the Queen's expression of her awareness of her predicament. In this manner, Pound already makes explicit what is more implicit in the original, namely, that as a ruler over Herakles' heart Deianeira has had to give way to Iole. The Greek text at this point suggests a link between Iole and Herakles by having the messenger describe her as 'certainly dazzling [*lampra*] in name and appearance' (l. 379). The word *lampra* is for Pound part of the key phrase attached to Herakles later, which may be a reason he toned it down in his rendering: 'She's somebody, all right, all right' (*WT* 36). The translation continues to present Deianeira in a state of shock, and in fact renders the original iconically through the use of the rhetorical device known as *aposiopesis*:

> 'What must I do, women? I am struck dumb by the words we just heard.'
>
> S ll. 385–86

> What shall . . . what shall . . . my dear girls,
>   what, what . . .
>
> WT 36

In a three-cornered dialogue between Lichas, Deianeira and the Messenger, the first is challenged in an interrogation by the latter (393–435). Pound rendered this passage in short sentences of modern everyday speech. He may have been guided by Jebb, who claims that Sophocles uses a style here 'which is "expressive of character" ':

> Take . . . the scene where the Messenger, in Deianeira's presence, taxes Lichas with deceit (vv. 393–435). The shades of language most skilfully characterise the

three persons, – the gentle but resolute lady; the herald, nervously deferential to her, but angrily assertive of his dignity against his humble cross-examiner, the Messenger; and lastly the Messenger himself, with his traits of blunt and familiar speech

Jebb 1908, xlvii

Earp concurs with this, as is evident from a letter to Pound of 29 May 1954, in which he berates the poet, once again, for his use of slang, but thinks it is justified at this point: 'you make the herald Lichas use it of the messenger. That would fit, for Lichas is trying to disparage his evidence.'

Pound remains faithful to the Greek text here, with an occasional modern idiomatic quip, as in his rendering of ll. 398–99:

> DAYSAIR: Have you any respect for the truth?
> LIKHAS: So help me God. Nothing but ...

WT 37

We find a similar modernization when Pound renders *poikilias* (l. 412), 'dark sayings', and *andros ouchi sōphronos* (l. 435), 'of an unwise man', twice as 'screwball' (*WT* 38; 39).

The Messenger exposes Lichas by repeating to him (and Deianeira) the story told by Lichas on the agora of Trachis, namely, that Herakles had sacked the city of Eurytus out of love for Iole. Although Lichas still tries to evade the issue, Deianeira in a long speech (S ll. 436–69) appeals to him to finally reveal the truth to her by stating that she does not blame Herakles because she knows how powerful Love can be. Therefore, Deianeira claims, Lichas no longer has any reason to hide the truth, nor does he have to fear for the fate of Iole: the Queen, having had experience with Herakles' amorous adventures before, pities her. Pound has rendered this speech, heavily annotated in his Loeb, fairly accurately.

Lichas recognizes how reasonably Deianeira behaves in this awkward situation, and he decides to reveal the whole truth (S ll. 472–89). He claims that it was not Herakles who asked him to lie but that he himself did not want hurting her. Pound has made an accurate rendering of this speech (also heavily annotated in his edition), but at the end he has made one of the gravest mistranslations of his entire version. Lichas concludes by stating:

> Because [*hōs*] he who [*ekeinos*] in all other matters [*tall'... pant'*] excells [*aristeuōn*] in might [*cheroin*, lit. 'with his two arms'], has been altogether vanquished [*eis hapanth' hēssōn ephu*] by his passion [*tou erōtos*] for this girl [*tēsde*].

S ll. 488–89

Pound gives these lines as

> He beat all the champions into subjection
> and now Eros throws him down with all his inferiors.
>
> WT 41

Pound here retains the strong contrast between Herakles' invincible physical strength and his helplessness against the power of Love. However, his phrase 'with all his inferiors' is quite incomprehensible in context: to whom would Lichas be referring? Pound here has mistranslated the Greek phrase *eis hapanth' hēssōn ephu*, which literally means 'at all/altogether – weaker/inferior – he is'. Pound has taken *hēssōn*, a nominative singular (M/F), as a plural genitive, 'of inferiors' (which would have been *hēssonōn*), and added it to *hapanth'*, 'all'. The mistake is understandable, yet the result is not, unless Pound consciously wanted to emphasize the contrast expressed by the two lines even more by making Herakles superior to all men but equal to them in their helplessness against the power of Love. This power of Eros is again implied in Deianeira's request to Lichas to bring Herakles some gifts, one of which is the robe which Deianeira hopes will return his love to her.

First Stasimon (Sophocles ll. 497–530; WT 41–43: ll. 454–94)

The First Stasimon, heavily annotated in Pound's Loeb, celebrates the power of Love, personified by Aphrodite, and includes the story of the fight between the rivergod Acheloös and Herakles, which was already told by Deianeira at the beginning of the play. This song has a very elevated style, reinforced by the use of Homeric language, while the ode is given a close unity by a pattern of repeated words (*sthenos, Kupris, akoitin/akoitan, es meson/ en mesōi, prosmenous'/ ammenei*). The First Strophe reads (ll. 497–506):

> μέγα τι σθένος ἁ Κύπρις ἐκφέρεται νίκας ἀεί.
> καὶ τὰ μὲν θεῶν
> παρέβαν, καὶ ὅπως Κρονίδαν ἀπάτασεν οὐ λέγω,
> οὐδὲ τὸν ἔννυχον Ἅιδαν
> ἢ Ποσειδάωνα τινάκτορα γαίας·
> ἀλλ' ἐπὶ τάνδ' ἄρ' ἄκοιτιν
> τίνες ἀμφίγυοι κατέβαν πρὸ γάμων,
> τίνες πάμπληκτα παγκόνιτά τ' ἐξῆλθον ἄεθλ'
>   ἀγώνων;

Great [*mega*] is the strength of victory [*ti sthenos nikas*] which the Cyprian [*ha Kupris* = Aphrodite] always carries off [*ekpheretai aei*]. I pass over [*pareban*] the stories of the gods [*ta theōn*], and I do not relate [*kai ou legō*] how [*hopōs*] she deceived [*apatasen*] the son of Kronos [*Kronidan* = Zeus], and Hades, the lord of darkness [*ton ennuchon Haidan*], or Poseidon, the shaker of earth [*ē Poseidaōna tinaktora gaias*]. But for this bride [*all' epi tand' ar' akoitin*], which antagonists (*tines amphiguoi*) went into contest (*kateban*) for the marriage [*pro gamōn*], who set out (*tines exēlthon*) for the ordeal of battle [*aethl' agōnōn*], full of blows [*pamplēkta*] and much dust (*pankonita*)?

The opening gnomic line on the power of love is reinforced by the following lines which refer to the three mightiest gods in the universe, depicted as all subject to Aphrodite's might. Storr rendered the first line as 'Many a trophy of war the Cyprian bears away', which probably supplied Pound with the word 'trophy' in his (failed) attempt to turn the line in the most succinct generalization possible: 'KUPRIS bears trophies away' (*WT* 41). Pound's version is more convincing in emphasizing the omnipotence of the power of Love by turning Poseidon's epithet into one which universally applies to all mighty beings:

> Kronos' son, Dis and Poseidon,
> There is no one
>   shaker unshaken.
> Into dust they go all.
> Neath Her they must
>   give way.
>
>   *WT* 41

To reinforce the universality of this description, Pound not only used heavy monosyllables, but he also took from the end of Sophocles' strophe the words *pankonita t' exēlthon*, turned the prefix *pan-* ('all') of the adjective *pankonita* into the subject of the verb *exēlthon* ('they went out'), and made *pankonita* into an accusative of direction in order to give 'Into dust they go all.' He then added two lines of his own in an iconically intended graphic arrangement. Here Pound's Strophe ends, as he used the last three lines of the original Strophe to begin his own Antistrophe: 'TWO gods fought for a girl, / Battle and dust!' This line seems to have been taken from Storr's 'dust of battle' (299). The Homeric *amphiguoi*, which Pound renders as 'TWO gods', is difficult to translate. Liddell-Scott's Greek Lexicon notes:

> ἀμφίγυος, ov, in Hom. always epith. of ἔγχος [=spear, lance], either ... *with a limb at each end, double-pointed,* or ... *bending both ways, elastic* ...; prob. *stout rivals*, S. *Tr.* [=Sophocles' *Trachiniae*] 504.

Pound here seemed to have relied on the dictionary but also wanted to retain the *amphi-* ('on both sides'; 'double'), and thus came up with 'two gods', which in the context of this choric song about the fight between the two superhuman beings, Herakles and Achelous, for Deianeira is a fitting rendering.

Sophocles' Antistrophe (ll. 507–16) describes the two contestants with Aphrodite as the umpire:

> ὁ μὲν ἦν ποταμοῦ σθένος, ὑψίκερω τετραόρου
> φάσμα ταύρου,
> Ἀχελῷος ἀπ' Οἰνιαδᾶν, ὁ δὲ Βακχίας ἀπὸ
> ἦλθε παλίντονα Θήβας
> τόξα καὶ λόγχας 'ρόπαλόν τε τινάσσων,
> παῖς Διός· οἳ τότ' ἀολλεῖς
> ἴσαν ἐς μέσον ἱέμενοι λεχέων·
> μόνα δ' εὔλεκτρος ἐν μέσῳ Κύπρις 'ραβδονόμει
>   ξυνοῦσα.

One [*ho men*] was [*ēn*] a mighty river [*potamou sthenos*], [in] the shape of a bull [*phasma taurou*], long-horned [*hupsikerō*], four-legged [*tetraorou*], Achelous from Oeniadae [*Achelōios ap' Oiniadan*]; and the other [*ho de*] came [*ēlthe*] from Bacchic Thebes [*Bakchias apo Thēbas*], brandishing [*tinassōn*] his springing bow [*palintona toxa*], spears and club [*lonchas rhopalon*], the son of Zeus [*pais Dios*]. They then met together in the middle [*hoi tot' aolleis isan es meson*], longing for her bed [*hiemenoi lecheōn*]; and Cypris, who brings wedded happiness [*eulektros Kupris*], was there alone in their midst [*mona en mesōi xunousa*], to act as umpire [*rhabdonomei*].

This passage is one of the most freely rendered parts of Pound's entire version, in which we may detect a predominant iambic/choriambic pattern:

> Might of a River with horns
>   crashing.
> Four bulls together
>   Shall no man tether,
> Akheloös neither,
>   lashing through Oneudai
> As bow is bent
>   The Theban Cub,
> Bacchus' own, spiked is his club,
> HE is God's son.
>   Hurled to one bed,
> Might of waters like a charge of bulls crashing.

> Get a dowsing rod.
> Kupris decides
> To whom brides
>   fall.
>
> WT 42

'Might of a River' is a literal translation of *potamou sthenos*, but 'crashing' is Pound's own invention, and given in iconic typography. Although *tetraorou* in this stasimon must clearly mean 'four-legged', 'standing on four legs', it is almost always used as an epithet of four horses yoked together, or of the chariot drawn by them. Pound's 'Four bulls together/ Shall no man tether' simply becomes his own rhyming generalization, while the next two lines ('Akheloös … Oneudai') also constitute a swerve from the Greek text. Although the syntax of these four lines is clear enough in its description of the inability of any mortal to overcome the river-god, there is no logical connection with 'As bow is bent' (*palintona toxa*?), so that Pound's translation becomes somewhat obscure. This also applies to the next lines: the phrase 'The Theban Cub' succinctly evokes the well-known image of Herakles wearing a lion's skin (although it is again Pound's own invention), but the phrases 'Bacchus' own' and 'HE is God's son' here confuses the issue of Herakles being the son of Zeus. Pound also adds new elements to his text, based either on a misunderstanding of the Greek or on Storr's version. Thus 'Hurled to one bed' is Pound's translation of *hiemenoi lecheōn*, probably because Liddell-Scott give '*speed oneself, hasten*' as a first meaning of *hiemai*, the medium form of *hiēmi*. If Pound had bothered to read on, he would have found that *hiemai* followed by a genitive means 'to be set upon, to long for a thing' (the Lexicon even refers to this instance in the *Trachiniae* l.514 as an example!). Pound's 'Get a dowsing rod' is most likely based on Storr's 'with her umpire wand', which is not in the Greek original.

    This passage, then, could well be used in evidence of Pound's impatience and/or weak command of Greek: he seems to have rushed through the text, let himself be (mis)guided by Storr, picked up a few familiar words, and then connected them along some general lines he thought to discern in the Greek syntax. This led to a confusing version which may not be understood without recourse to the original text – one of Pound's 'Browningesque' moments. However, from a poetical viewpoint, the passage is rather musical, with its alliteration of 'bow' and 'bent', and very effective in its use of rhyme ('together'-'tether'; 'cub'- 'club'; 'decides'- 'brides'), while the last word 'fall' is a good instance of Pound's tendency to use typography for iconic purposes.

Sophocles ends his First Stasimon with an Epode (ll. 517–30):

τότ᾽ ἦν χερός, ἦν δὲ τόξων πάταγος,
ταυρείων τ᾽ ἀνάμιγδα κεράτων·
ἦν δ᾽ ἀμφίπλεκτοι κλίμακες,
ἦν δὲ μετώπων ὀλόεντα
πλήγματα, καὶ στόνος ἀμφοῖν.
ἁ δ᾽ εὐῶπις ἁβρὰ
τηλαυγεῖ παρ᾽ ὄχθῳ
ἧστο, τὸν ὃν προσμένουσ᾽ ἀκοίταν.
ἀγὼν δὲ μαργᾷ μὲν οἷα φράζω·
τὸ δ᾽ ἀμφινείκητον ὄμμα νύμφας
ἐλεινὸν ἀμμένει·
κἀπὸ ματρὸς ἄφαρ βέβακεν,
ὥστε πόρτις ἐρήμα.

Then [*tot'*] there [*ēn*] was a clatter [*patagos*] of fists [*cheros*] and of the bow [*de toxōn*], and of the bull's horns [*taureiōn keratōn*], all together [*anamigda*]; and there were [*ēn*] legs wound around waists [*amphiplektoi klimakes*], and there were [*ēn*] deadly blows [*oloenta plēgmata*] on foreheads [*metōpōn*], and a groan [*stonos*] from both [*amphoin*]. But she [*ha d'* = Deianeira] in her delicate beauty [*euōpis habra*] sat [*hēsto*] by a distant hill [*tēlaugei par' ochthōi*], awaiting her bridegroom [*ton hon prosmenous' akoitan*]. And the fight [*agōn de*] went on raging [*margai*], as I describe [*hoia phradzō*]; but the face [*to d' omma*] of the bride [*numphas*] who is the object of their strife [*amphineikēton*], waits there [*ammenei*] piteously [*eleinon*]. And suddenly [*aphar*] she is gone [*bebaken*] from her mother [*apo matros*], like a calf [*hōste portis*] that has wandered [*erēma*].

Sophocles' epode conveys how the fight was violent, energetic and full of noise, as well as how the object of the passion of the two rivals, Deianeira, was silently awaiting the outcome. Davies (146) has rightly noted how the description of the fight, given in dactylic metre and employing harsh consonants and onomatopoeic adjectives and nouns like the 'guttural' *plēgmata* ('blows'), is contrasted to the depiction of Deineira's resignation, given in iambic metre and through more ornamental epithets and 'soft' vowels. Pound's version greatly emphasizes Sophocles' *melopoeia*:

ROCK and wrack,
Horns into back,
Slug, grunt and groan,
     Grip through to bone.
Crash and thud
Bows against blood

>   Grip and grind
>   Bull's head and horn.
> BUT the wide-eyed girl on the hill,
> Out of it all,
>   frail,
> Who shall have her?
> To stave her and prove her,
> Cowless calf lost,
> Hurtled away,
>   prized for a day?
>
>   WT 42–43

The first part ('ROCK ... horn'), using cretics ($-\times-$) and choriambs ($-\times\times-$), is almost perfectly monosyllabic, and full of harsh sounds and 'guttural alliteration'. Here the consonants seem to repress the vowels, whereas in the second part the language softens, and expresses the girl's passivity and frailty through the uncertainty of its two questions. Note how the outcome of the fight of which she is the prize is expressed in a rhythm wavering between an iambic and trochaic pattern, while the last two choriambic lines clearly connect the girl with the battle. Pound's rendering of this passage is one of the most memorable of his version:

Second Episode (S ll. 531–632; WT 43–46: ll. 495–598)

The Second Episode, heavily annotated in Pound's Loeb, continues where the First Episode left us. Deianeira returns with her gift for Herakles, to be taken to him by Lichas, and tells the Chorus the story of Nessus and how his blood may work as a love charm. Pound's version of this Episode is distinguished by some noteworthy elements, such as his playful approach to the Greek. For example, when Lichas says *Hermou tēnde pompeuō technōn/ bebaion* (ll. 620–21), 'I exercise reliably this art that belongs to Hermes', Pound renders it as 'Properly trained in Hermes' messenger-service' (*WT* 46). He sometimes uses renderings that extend the meaning of the Greek; for example, *ou ... orgainein kalon/ gunaika noun echousan* (S ll. 552–53), 'it is not honourable for a woman of sense to be angry'. This becomes in Pound's version: 'it's not nice for a woman to be too crotchety,/ the ones with nice minds are not peevish' (*WT* 44). On occasion Pound uses free renderings which alter the original; for example, in ll. 534–35 Deianeira approaches the Chorus, 'Partly [*ta men*] to tell you [*phrasousa*] what I have made with my hands [*chersin hatechnēsamēn*], and partly [*ta d'*] to get comfort from you [*sungkatoiktioumenē*] for my suffering [*hoia paschō*].' Pound has translated this as: 'Let's figure out how we are to manage this cohabitation' (*WT* 43). Here Pound has transformed Deianeira's *hatechnēsamēn* ('what my hands have wrought'), combining the relative *ha* with *etechnēsamēn*, the first-person singular aorist of *technadzō*, 'employ art, contrive', into a verb which more directly involves the Chorus in her scheme: 'Let's figure out'. He has also mistakenly stemmed *sungkatoiktioumenē*, a future medium participle (nominative singular feminine) of *sungkatoiktizomai*, 'to lament with, to lament together', from the verb that is one lemma above it in Liddell-Scott, namely, *sungkatoikeō*, 'dwell with one' or 'live together'; hence his awkward translation 'this cohabitation'.

Some of Pound's translations are clearly based on Storr; a good example can be found in ll. 537–38 of the original, in which Deianeira informs the Chorus how she has received Iole 'as a captain takes on a cargo, a merchandise that is destructive of my wits'. The simile describes a trader who takes one piece of cargo too many on board, so that his ship sinks. Storr's tendency to sometimes make the implications of the Greek text more explicit, is evident here as he extends the simile to a metaphor of the seatrade: 'I have harboured (as some merchant takes on board/ An over-freight) to wreck my peace of mind' (301). Pound's rendering uses the metaphor but gives a twist to it in order not only to show Deianeira's mind in a new light but also her rejection of Herakles' new mistress: 'Too much cargo, contraband, / but keep my mind afloat somehow' (*WT* 43).

In the description of Deianeira's plan, the opposition of light-darkness, that will dominate the second half of the play, comes to the fore. Deianeira gives Lichas the robe, and tells him that Herakles is not to leave it lying in the sun, nor near the fires of his altar, since Nessus had told her to keep his blood 'in a secret place always removed from fire and from the sun's warm ray' (S ll. 685–86). This, of course, associates the blood with darkness. Deianeira also admits to the Chorus that her plan may be shameful, but as long as such acts are done *skotōi*, 'in the dark', they will bring no shame (S ll. 596–97). Pound gives this as 'You can get away with a good deal in the dark' (*WT* 45), and adds to the Greek by rendering the rather neutral depiction of Deianeira having hidden Nesus' blood *domois*, 'in the house', as 'in a cool dark place' (*WT* 44).

Notes

1 Pound uses the name of the river god in Canto 101 to evoke a Greek landscape: 'The hills here are blue-green with juniper, / the stream, as Achiloös there below us' (745).

9

Sophocles, Pound and *Women of Trachis* II

Second Stasimon (S ll. 633–62; *WT* 46–48: ll. 599–629)

At the end of the Second Episode, Lichas departs to bring the anointed robe to Herakles. In the Second Stasimon, heavily annotated in Pound's Loeb, the Chorus sing both of the expected return of Herakles and of Deianeira's waiting. In the last stanza they depict what they hope will be the effect of Nessus' love charm on Herakles. In each of his stanzas of this section Pound has employed a different vowel assonance pattern.

The First Strophe (633–39) addresses the inhabitants of the whole region:

ὦ ναύλοχα καὶ πετραῖα
θερμὰ λουτρὰ καὶ πάγους
Οἴτας παραναιετάοντες, οἵ τε μέσσαν Μηλίδα πὰρ
    λίμναν
χρυσαλακάτου τ' ἀκτὰν κόρας,
ἔνθ' Ἑλλάνων ἀγοραὶ
Πυλάτιδες κλέονται·

O [ō] dwellers [*paranaietaontes*] by the ship-harbouring [*naulocha*] hot springs [*therma loutra*] amid the rocks [*petraia*] and by the hills of Oeta [*pagous Oitas*], and you [*hoi te*] beside the Malian sea in the middle [*messan Mēlida limnan*; i.e. 'landlocked'], and on the coast [*aktan*] sacred to the goddess of the golden shafts [*chrusalakatou koras* = Artemis], where [*henth'*] at the Gates [*Pulatides*] the gatherings of the Greeks [*Hellanōn agorai*] are renowned [*kleontai*; i.e. 'where the renowned gatherings are held']

In his version, Pound has tried to stay as closely as possible to the Greek word order in his evocation of the landscape, while unifying the passage through the employment of an -a- assonance pattern:

    SAFE the port, rocky the narrows,
    Streams warm to a glaze on Oeta's hill,

> Malis' pool and Dian's beach
> Neath her golden-shafted arrows
> > Ye who live here and disdeign
> > All greek towns less than the Pelean,
>
> WT 46–47

Pound's last two lines have swerved greatly from the Greek by depicting the inhabitants of the region as 'nationalistic': apparently, 'the Pelean' to him meant the area of Thermopylae, which in the original is only celebrated in the first two lines, but which Pound regarded as including the entire landscape described in the stanza. In a letter of 7 August 1954, F. R. Earp noted: '633ff. mistake. The warm springs at Thermopylae, which is close to the area.'

In the First Antistrophe (640–46), the Chorus looks forward to Herakles' return:

> ὁ καλλιβόας τάχ᾽ ὑμῖν
> αὐλὸς οὐκ ἀναρσίαν
> ἀχῶν καναχὰν ἐπάνεισιν, ἀλλὰ θείας ἀντίλυρον
> > μούσας.
> ὁ γὰρ Διὸς Ἀλκμήνας κόρος
> σοῦται πάσας ἀρετᾶς
> λάφυρ᾽ ἔχων ἐπ᾽ οἴκους·

soon [*tach'*] shall the beautiful sound of the flute [*kalliboas aulos*] go up again [*epaneisin*] for you [*humin*], sounding [*achōn kanachan*] not harsh [*ouk anarsian*], but like that of the lyre of the divine Muse [*theias antiluron mousas*]. For Zeus's Alkmena-son [*ho gar Dios Alkmēnas koros*] is hastening home [*soutai ep' oikous*] with the trophies [*laphur' echōn*] of all/supreme valour [*pasas aretas*]

In his rendering Pound inverted Sophocles' description of the beautiful sound of the flute, and stressed emphatically that on this occasion the music is noisy and shrill, as conveyed by the use of -i- assonance. This makes his third and fourth lines rather ironic:

> SOON shall hear the skirl and din
> Of flutes' loud cackle shrill return,
> Dear to Holy Muses as
> Phoebus' lyre ever was.
> > From the valours of his wars
> Comes now the God, Alkmene's son
> Bearing battle booty home.
>
> WT 47

Pound suggested the militant return of Herakles through the spondaic last line, with its -b- alliteration.

In the Second Strophe (ll. 647–54), the Chorus recalls Deianeira's miserable wait for news of her husband:

ὃν ἀπόπτολιν εἴχομεν παντᾷ,
δυοκαιδεκάμηνον ἀμμένουσαι
χρόνον, πελάγιον, ἴδριες, οὐδέν·
ἁ δέ οἱ φίλα δάμαρ
τάλαιναν δυστάλαινα καρδίαν
πάγκλαυτος αἰὲν ὤλλυτο·
νῦν δ' Ἄρης οἰστρηθεὶς
ἐξέλυσ' ἐπίπονον ἁμέραν.

[Herakles] whom [*hon*] we had [*eichomen*] utterly [*pantai*] absent from our town [*apoptolin*], across the sea [*pelagion*], while we were waiting [*ammenousai*] for twelve months [*duokaidekamēnon chronon*], knowing nothing [*idries ouden*]; and his dear wife [*ha de hoi phila damar*], most miserable [*dustalaina*], ever all-tearful [*panklautos aien*], was pining in her sad heart [*talainan kardian ōlluto*]. But now Ares, stung to madness [*oistrētheis*, i.e. Herakles' passionate activity at Oechalia], has put an end [*exelus'*] to the day of toil [*epiponōn hameran*].

Using -e- assonance throughout, Pound's rendering reads:

TWELVE moons passing,
    night long, and day.
Exile, exile
Knowing never, to come? to stay?
Tears, tears, till grief
Hath wrecked her heart away,
Ere mad Mars should end him
    his working days.

WT 47

The first four lines show a great difference between Sophocles' tendency towards 'objectivity' or neutral description, and the 'subjective' rendering by Pound. While Sophocles simply mentions the period of time of Herakles' absence, Pound evokes its experience, its *réelle durée*: 'TWELVE moons passing,/ night long, and day' – note the spondaic 'heavy' ending. The state of Herakles' absence, described in the Greek in the rather neutral terms *apoptolin* and *pelagios*, is intensified by Pound through his repeated use of the word 'exile'. In the Greek we find wordplay in the combination of *talainan dustalaina*, describing Deianeira's heart and the woman herself, respectively. Pound has more or less retained this emphasis on Deianeira's grief through the repetition of 'tears'. As a note in his Loeb on p. 309 indicates ('vid Ajax l. 131'), Pound saw in the Chorus's words of comfort a link with line 131 of Sophocles' *Ajax*, an evocation of the vicissitudes of fortune. Pound put a mark next to line 131–32 of *Ajax*, which is a maxim typical of Sophocles: 'A day can prostrate and a day upraise/ All that is mortal' (Storr 19).

In the Second Antistrophe, the Chorus prays for Herakles to return:

ἀφίκοιτ᾽ ἀφίκοιτο· μὴ σταίη
πολύκωπον ὄχημα ναὸς αὐτῷ,
πρὶν τάνδε πρὸς πόλιν ἀνύσειε,
νασιῶτιν ἑστίαν
ἀμείψας, ἔνθα κλήζεται θυτήρ·
ὅθεν μόλοι πανίμερος,
τᾶς πειθοῦς παγχρίστῳ
συγκραθεὶς ἐπὶ προφάσει φάρους.

ll. 655–62

May he come, may he come [*aphikoito*]! May the many-oared ship [*polukōpon naos*] that bears him [*ochēma autōi*] not halt [*mē staiē*], before [*prin*] he shall have reached [*anuseie*] this town [*tande pros polin*], having left [*ameipsas*] the altar on the island [*nasiōtin hestian*], where he is said to be sacrificing [*entha kleidzetai thutēr*]. May he come [*moloi*] from there [*hothen*] filled with desire [*panimeros*], steeped in love [*sunkratheis*] through the precept [*epi prophasei*] of the robe [*pharous*], the well-anointed [precept] of persuasion [*tas peithous panchristōi*, i.e. the love charm].

Pound swerves from the meaning of the original to evoke the feelings of eagerness, anxiety and impatience of the Chorus, in a passage much dominated by an -o- assonance and monosyllabic words, features which emphasize the open-endedness and tempo of the anxious statements:

TO PORT, to port.
Boat is still now;
The many oars move not.
      By island shrine ere he come to the town
Day long, day long
If the charm of the gown proves not?
'Tis dipped, aye in the unguent

drenched through it, in every fold.
Told, told,
in all as she had been told.

WT 47–48

Pound has more or less retained the optative mood of the double *aphikoito* by the Chorus' repeated cry 'to port'. However, he has turned the same mood of the prayer into a statement of fact to enhance the Chorus' impatience in hearing that Herakles is making a sacrifice before his final return. The phrase 'Day long, day long' indicates that Pound read *panameros*, 'all day long', instead of *panimeros*, 'filled with desire', a reading which is supported by some manuscripts, and which is mentioned by Jebb in his edition (Jebb 1908, 102). The third optative of Sophocles' stanza (*moloi*), expressing the hope for a successful outcome of Deianeira's application of the love charm, has been replaced by a question which expresses the Chorus's anxiety over the efficacy of the robe. The repeated use of 'told' at the end, while probably based on the words *peithous* and *prophasei*, seems an attempt at comfort: since Deianeira has done everything exactly as Nessus prescribed, how could anything possibly go wrong? It is clear that, while Sophocles gives us a far more confident Chorus, Pound has underlined their anxiety, and his version of the stasimon is permeated with a greater sense of foreboding.

Third Episode (S ll. 663–820; *WT* 48–53: ll. 630–878)

In the Third Episode, very heavily annotated in Pound's Loeb, Deianeira returns distressed as she has discovered that the piece of wool she had used to put the love charm on the robe, is destroyed. She now fears that her gift to Herakles may be dangerous. In his rendering of this passage (ll. 663–749), Pound stays fairly close to the original, although some details are of note.

Deianeira's first words on entering the stage are somewhat euphemistic: 'I am afraid that [*dedoika mē*] in all I did lately I went too far'. Pound transports the main verb *dedoika* to the end of Deianeira's lines as a powerful summary of her state of mind: 'I'm scared' (*WT* 48). Pound then simplifies ll. 666–67, which in a literal translation read: 'I do not know [*ouk oid*'], but I am disheartened [*athumō*] at the thought that soon I may be shown to have done great harm [*kakon meg*'] arising from the expectation [*elpidos*] of good'. In his version, Pound seemed to have simply taken the Greek words which I have given in italics, and put them in a logical order: 'I don't know, I dunno, I hoped/ and I don't hope./ Something awful will come of it' (*WT* 48).

Deianeira tells the Chorus in ll. 676–77 what happened to the sheep's wool she used to daub her husband's shirt in the blood of Nessus: *diaboron pros oudenos/ tōn endon, all' edeston ex autou phthinei*, destroyed by nothing within, but eaten by itself, it wastes away'. Pound rendered this as:

> ... just disappeared.
> Nobody touched it.
>   Seemed to corrode of itself.
> Ate itself up,
>
>   *WT* 48[1]

The translation of Hyllus' speech (S ll. 749–812) shows us at times a sloppy Pound, impatient with philological meticulousness. Although the speech is correct in broad outline, Pound here demonstrates his occasional tendency to translate words at a glance. Line 754 is a good example of this. It reads βωμοὺς ὁρίζει τεμενίαν τε φυλλάδα, 'he marked the bounds of altars and a sacred grove [*temenian phullada*]'. Pound, however, takes *temenian*, 'sacred', as a form of the verb *temnein*, 'to cut', and renders *temenian phullada* as 'cutting the leaves' (*WT* 50). In a letter of 7 August 1954, Earp reprimanded Pound for this: '754 There is nothing about anything grass here. The Greek means: 'to mark out altars & the leafage of a temenos'. Some Greek temples had a temenos attached to them. The meaning of τέμενος varies, & often it had trees in it, & φυλλάδα implies that Herakles' τέμενος had them.' A similar inappropriate rendering may be seen in Pound's translation of the phrase σεμνῶν ὀργίων (765), 'sacred offerings', as 'Holy Orgy' (*WT* 51), perhaps an echo of the opening passage of *Homage to Sextus Propertius*, in which Pound in his rendering of Propertius III.1.4, gives *orgia*, the 'holy objects carried by worshippers in some ritual procedure' (Camps 53), as 'orgies' (*P* 205).

Yet at times Pound's choices are felicitous. In line 758, Lichas is bringing the *thanasimon peplon*, 'the deadly robe'. It seems Pound has confused *thanasimon* with a word like *thaumastos*, 'wonderful', so he translates the phrase as 'the marvellous peplon' (*WT* 51), which gives Hyllus' words an irony or sarcasm not present in the original. However, in the context of Herakles' future splendour, and the marvel of his transformation on the pyre, Pound's version makes clear that putting on the robe is the first step of his apotheosis, however deadly it may be. This is part of a series of implied Christian overtones: the man-god first has to die before he can be resurrected unto eternal life (and perhaps Pound was thinking of the robing of Christ prior to his walk with the cross).

Pound also tries to do justice to Hyllus' agitated state of mind by chopping up the longer Greek periods of his speech into more clear-cut emotional outbursts. In his version of ll. 772–74, for example, Pound clarifies far better than Storr does in his translation, Deianeira's involvement in Herakles' death:

Next [*entautha dē*] he shouted at [*'boēse*] the unhappy Lichas [*ton dusdaimona Lichan*], who was in no way guilty [*ton ouden aition*] of your crime [*tou sou kakou*], by which [*poiais*] devices [*mēchanais*] he had brought [*enengkoi*] the robe [*tonde peplon*].

> Thereupon
> He [= Herakles] called for Lichas, who, poor witless wretch,
> Had in thy guilt no part or lot, demanding
> Who hatched the plot and why he had brought the robe.
>
> Storr 319

Pound singles out the sentence *ton ouden aition tou sou kakou* (l. 773) about Lichas, 'in no way guilty of your crime', and turns the latter phrase into a separate unit of information as 'You were', thereby giving it more weight:

> And he [=Herakles] howled for the miserable Likhas
>   who wasn't guilty. You were.
> To know who'd hatched the shirt trick.
>
> WT 51

Pound effectively brings out the emotions at the end of Hyllus' speech when he bitterly attacks his mother:

You have been found guilty [*elēphthēs*], mother [*mēter*], for having planned [*bouleusas'*] and putting into action [*kai drōs'*] these things [*toiaut'*] for my father [*patri emōi*], for which [*hōn*] avenging Justice [*poinimos Dikē*] and the Fury [*Erinys*] may punish you [*se . . . tisait'*]. And if it is right/just [*ei themis d'*], I pray for this [*epeuchomai*], and it is right [*themis d'*], since you made this right for me [*epei moi tēn themin su proubales*], for killing [*kteinas'*] the noblest man of all [*pantōn ariston andra tōn*] on earth [*epi chthoni*], one such other [*hopoion allon*] you shall never see again [*ouk opsei pote*].

ll. 807–12

Pound has rendered this legal language with heavy emphasis on the thrice-used word *themis*, 'just(ice)', in straightforward words, setting them in a context that highlights Hyllus' emotions:

> That, my dear mother is what you have thought up
>   to do to my father.

> Hell take you, and the Furies, and do you right.
> Justice, eh, Justice, if...
> > lot of justice you had for me!
> You spewed it out when you killed
> > the best man on earth
> what you see henceforth will be of a different kind.
>
> WT 52–53

However, despite occasional felicities, Pound has attained in the last 300 lines, from the First Stasimon to the Third (S ll. 497–821), the heights and depths of his abilities as a translator of Greek poetry. His version of the First Stasimon combined the meticulous, melopoeic and outstanding, with the careless, incomprehensible, and confusing. Having demonstrated his craftsmanship in the Second Stasimon (S ll. 633–62), he showed hurried impatience in Hyllus' speech (S ll. 749–812). This alternation between care and carelessness will continue to dominate his translation as we shall see in the Third Stasimon.

Third Stasimon (S ll. 821–62; *WT* 53–55: ll. 788–832)

In the Third Stasimon, very heavily annotated in Pound's Loeb, we find a sort of time-sequence: the Chorus first looks back to the prediction of the oracle, then pictures the present agony of Herakles and the anguish of Deianeira as its fulfilment, before foreseeing some great disaster in the near future.

In the First Strophe (821–30), the Chorus suddenly realizes that the oracle's prediction about Herakles' 'rest from toil' was not an allusion to his final release from his labours but a reference to his death. Unlike the tone of the stanzas following it, this strophe is still rather 'matter of fact':

> ἴδ᾽ οἷον, ὦ παῖδες, προσέμιξεν ἄφαρ
> τοὔπος τὸ θεοπρόπον ἡμῖν
> τᾶς παλαιφάτου προνοίας,
> ὅ τ᾽ ἔλακεν, ὁπότε τελεόμηνος ἐκφέροι
> δωδέκατος ἄροτος, ἀναδοχὰν τελεῖν πόνων
> τῷ Διὸς αὐτόπαιδι· καὶ τάδ᾽ ὀρθῶς
> ἔμπεδα κατουρίζει. πῶς γὰρ ἂν ὁ μὴ λεύσσων
> ἔτι ποτ᾽ ἔτ᾽ ἐπίπονον πόνων ἔχοι θανὼν λατρείαν;

See, maidens [*id' ō paides*], how [*hoion*] swiftly [*aphar*] has come upon us [*prosemixen*] the oracular word [*toupos to theopropon*] of the foreknowledge declared long ago [*tas palaiphatou pronoias*], which shouted [*ho t' elaken*] that when [*hopote*] the twelfth year [*dōdekatos arotos*] with its full complement of months [*teleomēnos*] should come to an end [*ekpheroi*], it would put an end [*telein*] to the undertaking of labours [*anadochan ponōn*] for the true son of Zeus [*tōi Dios autopaidi*].[2] And these things [*kai tad'*] are truly [*orthōs*] coming to fulfilment without fail [*empeda katouridzei*]. For how [*pōs gar*] could one who no longer sees [*ho mē leussōn*, i.e., is dead], still [*eti pot' et'*] maintain [*an echoi*] his toilsome servitude [*epiponon ponōn . . . latreian*] when he is dead [*thanōn*]?

In his rendering of this Strophe (*WT* 53), Pound does not follow the narrative pattern of the original, but switches back and forth between lines, restructuring the song. Pound opens his version with 'OYEZ', a shout used by law officials to catch people's attention, emphasizing the importance he attached to this particular Stasimon.

This First Strophe and the First Antistrophe are the most metrically complex of all the lyrics in the play, and Pound makes no attempt to reproduce the Greek metre, but unifies his rendering through a predominantly (chor)iambic rhythm (provided we regard the secondary stress in English as a weak stress in classical-metrical terms). In his second line, Pound combines the two adjectives *palaiphatou* and *theopropon*, used to describe the oracle, in a phrase with a rising rhythm: 'Things foretold and forecast'. The expectation created by the rhythm is fulfilled in the *creticus* ($-\times-$) 'Toil and moil', here given to render Sophocles' double use of the word *ponōn*, 'labours', in *epiponōn ponōn*. Pound then continues this half-rhyme through the addition of 'turmoil' in his (iambic-choriambic) translation of the prediction of the oracle (S ll. 824–26):

God's **Son** from **tur**moil **shall**
– when **twelve seed**-*crops* be **past** –
be **loosed** with the **last**,
        his own.

WT 53; bold/italics mine

Pound then returns to the beginning of the Strophe, and again renders the adjectives *palaiphatou* and *theopropon*, but now in a new context. Here the version is extremely free as Pound combines translations of Greek words with phrases of his own in a passage which has a predominantly choriambic rhythm and a pattern of -o- assonance:

Twining to**get**her, **god**word [*toupos to theopropon*] found **good**,
Spoken of **old** [*palaiphatou*],
    as the wind **blew**, **truth's** in the **flood**.

WT 53

The last line is most likely based on *katouridzei*, which Jebb (1908, 124) glosses as 'coming into haven before a fair wind'; here Storr's translation, ' 'Tis wafted on the gale' (323), may have guided Pound.

After this Pound goes back to the very beginning of the strophe for a second time, only now translating the first line of the original (l. 821), which he then combines with a free version of the conclusion of the Greek Strophe (ll. 829–30) in order to place the phrases expressing the Chorus's realization of the fulfilment of the oracle and those underlining the fact that this fulfilment consists in Herakles' death side by side:

> We and his brood [*paides*] see [*id'*] in swift [*aphar*] combine [?*prosemixen*],
> here and at last that:
> Amid the dead is no servitude
> nor do they labour.
>
> WT 53

The verb *prosemixen* is the aorist form of *prosmeignumi*, and here means 'approach, come upon'. Pound's translation 'combine' suggests, apart from the fact that he (deliberately?) mistook a third-person singular for a first-person plural, that he did not bother to look up the word and focused on *meignumi* only, which indeed means 'mix, bring together'. The first two lines with their rising rhythm culminate in a falling rhythm in the last two. Although 'that/Amid' must be read with enjambment, Pound has put a colon after 'that' because he wanted to end with a sententious statement, as Sophocles had done.

In the First Antistrophe (ll. 831–40), the Chorus becomes more emotional, and describes with horror the suffering of Herakles due to the poisoned robe:

> εἰ γάρ σφε Κενταύρου φονίᾳ νεφέλᾳ
> χρίει δολοποιὸς ἀνάγκα
> πλευρά, προστακέντος ἰοῦ,
> ὃν τέκετο θάνατος, ἔτρεφε δ' αἰόλος δράκων,
> πῶς ὅδ' ἂν ἀέλιον ἕτερον ἢ τανῦν ἴδοι,
> δεινοτάτῳ μὲν ὕδρας προστετακὼς
> φάσματι; μελαγχαίτα δ' ἄμμιγά νιν αἰκίζει
> Νέσσου ὑποφόνια δολιόμυθα κέντρ' ἐπιζέσαντα.

> For if [*ei gar*] the deceptive compulsion [*dolopoios anagka*] of the Centaur [*Kentaurou*] with its bloody cloud {of death} [*phoniai nephelai*][3] stings [*chriei*] his sides [*pleura*; lit. *sphe . . . pleura*, 'stings him, his sides'], as the poison soaks in [*prostakentos iou*], which Death begat [*hon teketo thanatos*] and the gleaming

serpent [*d' aiolos drakōn* = Hydra] nurtured [*etrehe*], how could he look [*pōs hod' an idoi*] upon tomorrow's sun [*aelion heteron ē tanun*, lit. 'upon another sun than the one this moment'], stuck fast as he is [*prostetakōs*] to the most terrible shape of the Hydra [*deinotatōi hudras phasmati*]? And the black-haired [*melanchaita*] Nessus' murderous guileful stings [*Nessou hupophonia doliomutha kentr'*], boiling over [*epidzesanta*], torture [*aikidzei*] him [*nin*] confusedly [*ammiga*].

Herakles' struggle with the robe is metaphorically represented as an encounter with Nessus and the Hydra, while the stanza is chiastically arranged: Nessus/ Hydra/ Hydra/ Nessus. In his version, which is metrically more regular than his First Strophe, Pound has retained this structure. Note how the regular rhythm of Pound's rendering is again (chor)iambic, while the combination of iambs and choriambs has produced four times a dodrans ($- \times \times - \times -$):

> **LO**, beneath **deadly cloud**
> **Fate** and the **Cen**taur's **curse**, **black** venom **spread**.
> **Dank** Hydra's **blood**
> **Boils** now through **every vein**, **goad** after **goad**
> from **spot**ted **snake** to **pierce** the **holy side**,
> nor **shall** he **last** to **see** a **new** day's **light**,
> **Black** shaggy **night** descends
>   as Nessus **bade**.
>
>   *WT* 54; bold mine

In this stanza, Pound has remained more faithful to the text of the original than in the previous one, although he has made certain re-arrangements. He sticks to the more common translation of *ananka* as 'Fate', and has connected its corresponding *dolopoios* ('treacherous') with *Kentaurou* in his 'the Centaur's curse'. His 'black venom spread' retains the genitive absolute construction of the original, after which Pound glosses the venom as 'Dank Hydra's blood', and 'spread' as 'Boils now through every vein'. His 'goad after goad' is a powerful translation of *kentra* as it evokes the continuous pain of Herakles. Pound calling Herakles' side 'holy' evokes the sufferings of Christ, whose side was pierced by a lance during the crucifixion. The last two lines, employing *melanchaita*, 'black-haired', constitute Pound's summary of events more than reflecting the Greek text to this point. One may also notice how Pound has extended the imagery of blackness/night/death to underscore how one element of the power of darkness, that is, the 'cloud' of Akheloös referred to at the beginning of the play, is to be connected with another evil elemental power (Nessus). In turn, it may be seen as connected to the image of Herakles, who in agony is shrouded in the smoke of the fire of the altar (S l. 794).

In the Second Strophe (S ll. 841–50), the Chorus express their pity in describing Deianeira's unwitting guilt and despair, and utter a sense of coming doom:

ὧν ἅδ' ἁ τλάμων ἄοκνος μεγάλαν προσορῶσα
    δόμοισι βλάβαν νέων
ἀίσσουσαν γάμων τὰ μὲν αὐτὰ προσέβαλε, τὰ
    δ' ἀπ' ἀλλόθρου
γνώμας μολόντ' ὀλεθρίαισι συναλλαγαῖς
ἦ που ὀλοὰ στένει,
ἦ που ἀδινῶν χλωρὰν
τέγγει δακρύων ἄχναν.
ἁ δ' ἐρχομένα μοῖρα προφαίνει δολίαν
καὶ μεγάλαν ἄταν.

Of this [*hōn*] the poor lady [*had' ha tlamōn*] was unaware [*aoknos*] when she saw [*prosorōsa*] the great disaster [*megalan blaban*] of the new marriage [*neōn gamōn*] rushing [*aissousan*] towards the house [*domoisi*]; part of the mischief [*ta men*] she applied herself [*auta prosebale*], but another part [*ta d'*] came from another's counsel [*ap' allothrou gnōmas molont'*] during a fatal meeting [*olethriaisi sunallagais*]; assuredly [*ē pou*], she laments [*stenei*] <being> lost [*oloa*], assuredly [*ē pou*] she sheds [*tengei*] fresh dew [*chlōran achnan*] of thickly falling tears [*adinōn dakruōn*]. And the approaching fate [*ha d' erchomena moira*] reveals [*prophainei*] a treacherous and great misfortune [*dolian kai megalan atan*].

The Chorus defends Deianeira by stating that she was unaware of the consequences when she applied the charm to prevent Herakles from taking Iole as his new wife. Pound's version reads:

WHAT MOURNFUL case
    who feared great ills to come,
New haste in mating threatening her home,
Who hark'd to reason in a foreign voice
Entangling her in ravage out of choice.
Tears green the cheek with bright dews
                            pouring down;
Who mourns apart, alone
Oncoming swiftness in o'erlowering fate
To show what wreck is nested in deceit.
                                                      WT 54

The third line, an evocation of Herakles' state of mind from Deianeira's point of view, is based on the linking of the adjective *neōn*, the genitive plural of *neos* ('young, fresh', 'new'), not with the noun *gamōn*, 'marriage', as in the Greek, but with *aissousan*, a present participle (meaning 'rushing') which Pound has turned into a noun ('haste'). *Gamōn* is rendered as 'in mating'. Pound gives this line as the reason why Deianeira listened to 'reason in a foreign voice'. Sophocles has used the word *allothrou* to contrast Deianeira's own action with the agency of another person (Nessus); therefore most commentators and translators render the word as a synonym of *allotrias*, 'another's'. Strictly speaking, however, *allothrou* does indeed mean 'speaking in a foreign language', and Pound may have wanted to stick to this original meaning because it would stress how the counsel given by Nessus is one Deianeira would not have listened to in normal circumstances, and actually also would not have fully understood (as now becomes clear).

The Chorus's observation that Herakles' suffering is partly Deianeira's own fault (because she applied the poison, however ignorant of its real nature), and partly the Centaur's, is changed by Pound to suggest that Deianeira's decision was in a sense made for her by being overcome with emotion: 'Who hark'd to reason in a foreign voice/ Entangling her in ravage out of choice.' Pound's last two lines of this stanza constitute one of his most beautiful and successful attempts to transpose the spirit of the Greek into English. Pound's rendering evokes the inevitable and fast approach of fate, and makes the implication of *dolian kai megalan atan*, 'a treacherous and great misfortune', more specific, that is, that the deceit of Nessus, and betrayal of Herakles with Iole, has resulted in a great disaster, namely, Deianeira's suicide and Herakles' death.

Pound in the First Strophe and Antistrophe, and the Second Strophe, generally used a (chor)iambic rhythm, which suggests that he saw them as closely connected in their descriptions of events and reactions. The Second Antistrophe is very different: Pound seems to have wanted to draw attention to what, in his view, was one of the key statements of the entire play. In this Second Antistrophe (ll. 851–61), the Chorus links the agony of Herakles and Deianeira to its causes, namely, the sacking of Oechalia and the carrying off of Iole. They end by seeing in all this the hand of Aphrodite:

ἔρρωγεν παγὰ δακρύων· κέχυται νόσος, ὦ πόποι,
    οἷον ἀναρσίων
οὔπω Ἡρακλέους ἀγακλειτὸν ἐπέμολε πάθος
    οἰκτίσαι.

ἰὼ κελαινὰ λόγχα προμάχου δορός,
ἃ τότε θοὰν νύμφαν
ἄγαγες ἀπ' αἰπεινᾶς
τάνδ' Οἰχαλίας αἰχμᾷ·
ἁ δ' ἀμφίπολος Κύπρις ἄναυδος φανερὰ
τῶνδ' ἐφήνη πράκτωρ.

The flood of tears [*paga dakruōn*] has burst forth [*errōgen*]; a disease is diffused [*kechutai nosos*], alas [*ō popoi*]!; never [*oupō*] was such a suffering [*hoion pathos*] to be pitied [*oiktisai*] brought by his enemies [*anarsiōn epemole*] upon the glorious Herakles [*Herakleous agakleiton*]. Alas [*iō*], you black point [*kelaina lonchā*] of the spear [*doros*] in the forefront of the battle [*promachou*], which [*ha*] with its might [*aichmai*] lately [*tote*] brought this swift bride [*tande thoan numphan*; i.e. 'brought this bride swiftly'] from lofty Oechalia [*ap' aipeinas Oichalias*]; but Kupris, the silent attendant [*ha amphipolos anaudos*], has been clearly revealed [*phanera ephēnē*] as the doer [*praktōr*] of these deeds [*tōnd'*].

Aphrodite is called *anaudos* because until now we did not know that she was more or less responsible: Herakles kept silent about his real motive for his sacking of Oechalia (while Iole herself has not revealed it because she has not spoken a single word when on stage). All of this led to Deianeira's anxious suspicions and their fatal consequences. Since the passion of Herakles is now disclosed as the supreme motive for his actions, the last insightful remark by the Chorus shows that the key theme of the play consists of the power of Love as a force that overrides all reason.

This may explain why Pound emphasized the role of the goddess in his version, not only by giving his rendering of the stanza a form very distinct from the other three in this Stasimon, but also by adding a stage direction or description in which he used the term *dea ex machina* to underline how it was the machinery of Aphrodite that determined the course of events:

LET the tears flow.
 Ne'er had bright Herakles in his shining
Need of pity till now
 whom fell disease burns out.
How swift on Oechal's height
 to take a bride.
Black pointed shaft that shielded her in flight,
Attest

That
Kupris stood by and never said a word,
Who now flares here the contriver
manifest ...
and indifferent.

[*The dea ex machina, hidden behind a grey gauze in her niche, is lit up strongly so that the gauze is transparent. The apparition is fairly sudden, the fade-out slightly slower: the audience is almost in doubt that she has appeared.*]

WT 54–55

The first six lines stay fairly closely to the Greek, although Pound once again emphasizes Herakles' association with light by rendering *agakleiton Hērakleous*, 'the glorious Herakles', as 'bright Herakles in his shining'. The apostrophe to the spear in the original is an implicit address to the might of Herakles (as well as a phallic symbol), seen as being the overt instrument that carried Iole to the palace. In his version, Pound makes a more explicit connection between this instrument and the agency of Aphrodite. In this he may have been influenced by Storr's translation:

> O bloodstained spear that bore
> From proud Oechalia's height
> Stormed by the hero's might,
> A vanished bride, how clear
> The Cyprian's wiles appear!
> Unseen, thy spear she steeled
> And now she stands revealed.

Storr 325

The graphic arrangement of Pound's version underscores the importance of the revelation, while the typescript at the Beinecke has the stage direction 'is with l. 861 lit up' (Beinecke 140/6184), that is, the line of the original containing the phrase *phanera/ tōn d'ephēnē praktōr*, 'revealed as the doer of these deeds'. Pound's stage direction enhances the significance of the Chorus's epiphanic insight, while emphasizing its suddenness and its brevity. Furthermore, the labial consonance in 'flares', 'contriver', 'manifest', and 'indifferent' are Pound's musical renderings of the Greek *amphipolos, phanera,* and *ephēnē*, with the English words also alluding forward to the force of fire which at the end will deliver Herakles on Mount Oeta. His death on the pyre is thus also seen as a result of Aphrodite's action.

Fourth Episode (S ll. 863–946; *WT* 55–58: ll. 833–915)

The first part (S ll. 863–95) of the Fourth Episode consists of a dialogue between members of the Chorus among themselves, and between the Chorus and the Nurse, about the cry they heard. This passage not only prepares us for the account of Deianeira's suicide by the Nurse (896–946), but also confirms the sense of foreboding the Chorus had expressed in their song. (Pound's Loeb has very heavy annotations to l. 931, and then no more until the end of the Episode, while on the top of p. 326, where the Nurse enters to talk with the Chorus, he wrote 'Make new'.) In his version, Pound has stayed fairly close to the Greek, and sometimes even retained the original syntax: the following lines spoken by the Nurse (874–75), for example, almost constitute a crib:

βέβηκε Δηάνειρα τὴν πανυστάτην
ὁδῶν ἁπασῶν ἐξ ἀκινήτου ποδός.

She's gone [*bebēke*] .... Daysair [*Dēianeira*],
The last [*tēn panustatēn*] road of all roads [*hodōn hapasōn*]
   ...without walking [*ex akinētou podos*, lit. 'without stirring a foot']

WT 55

And the Nurse's words πάντ' ἀκήκοας (*pant' akēkoas*, 'You have heard it all') become 'That's all. You heard me.' This literal-mindedness of Pound also explains why he made the Chorus address the Nurse rather cruelly here as 'you fool': according to Jebb (1908, 132), the words ὦ ματαία (*ō mataia*, l. 888) are said 'with a mixture of pity and impatience', and to be translated as 'poor helpless one'. Pound, however, stuck to one of the standard meanings of the word.

On the other hand, the dialogue between the Nurse and Chorus also contains a passage where Pound goes very wide off the mark:

ἔτεκεν ἔτεκε δὴ μεγάλαν
ἁ νέορτος ἅδε νύμφα
δόμοισι τοῖσδ' ἐρινύν.

ll. 893–95

This new bride [*ha noertos hade numpha*, i.e. Iole] has given birth, has given birth [*eteken eteke*] to a mighty Fury [*megalan Erinun*] for this house [*domoisi toisd'*].

That new girl's doin' it.
I'll say she's effective.
Bride is she, and a fury. Holy Erinyes!

WT 56

There are some strange lines in Pound's rendering of the Nurse's speech. Sophocles describes how Deianeira, 'falling upon the altars, cried out that they [=the altars] would become desolate' (ll. 904–905). Pound gives this wrongly as 'sank down there groaning because her brood had deserted her', possibly wishing to connect this line with the preceding ones, in which Deianeira sees Hyllus preparing a litter to fetch his father. Another example is when Deianeira is depicted as weeping 'whenever [*hotou*] she touched [*psauseien*] any of the things [*organōn*] she, poor woman [*deilaia*], had used in the past [*hois echrēto paros*]. She moved [*strōphōmenē*] this way and that [*allēi de kallēi*] in the house [*dōmatōn*]' (ll. 905–07). Pound's version gives the following:

Then pitifully stroking the thing she had used before,
went wandering through the best rooms
didn't know I could see her, from a sort of kink
in the wall –
drawing her hands over the things she used to.

WT 57

Organōn are Deineira's familiar household objects, but in his version Pound rendered the word twice at the beginning and end of this passage, with the first instance clearly meant in an erotic sense (perhaps to emphasize again the power of *eros* which in the past had bonded Herakles to Deianeira). Pound also inserted a line describing the Nurse as witness of what is happening, which is l. 914 in the original, *kagō lathraion homm' epeskiasmenē/ phrouroun*, literally 'and I watched her shadowed with regard to my eye so that it would be secret'. Thus the nurse watched Deianeira while making sure she herself was not seen. In a letter of 7 August, 1954, Earp objected to Pound's translation: 'There is no "kink in the wall" in the Greek. The Greek means literally "shading a stealthy eye". In this case & some others the change may be deliberate. Many of your changes evidently are, but in several cases I am not sure.'

Having described Deianeira's suicide, and Hyllus' reaction to it, the Nurse's speech ends with a maxim which was common in Greek thought, about the foolishness of trying to plan one's life too far ahead: 'if anyone reckons on two days or more, he is a fool, because there is no tomorrow until one has got safely through today in happiness' (S ll. 943–46). In Pound's version this becomes, 'You can't count on anything for tomorrow,/ got to wait till today is over' (*WT* 58). The fact that these words echo Deianeira's opening statement ironically show 'how wrong she was when she claimed to know already the full extent of her misfortunes. The action of the play has demonstrated that there was indeed worse to come' (Easterling 1982, 193).

Fourth Stasimon (S ll. 947–70; *WT* 58–59: ll. 916–38)

In the Fourth Stasimon, very heavily annotated in Pound's Loeb, the Chorus mourns the death of Deianeira, and looks anxiously forward to the procession that will bring Herakles home: is he dead or merely sleeping when they see him lying immobile on the litter? According to Easterling (1982, 193–94), the First Strophe and Antistrophe of the Stasimon (ll. 947–52) have 'all the features of a *threnos*' or lament, that is, 'initial hesitation expressed in terms of questions', as well as 'antithetical style, effects of assonance and repetition':

πότερα πρότερον ἐπιστένω,
πότερα μέλεα περαιτέρω,
δύσκριτ' ἔμοιγε δυστάνῳ.

τάδε μὲν ἔχομεν ὁρᾶν δόμοις,
τάδε δὲ μένομεν ἐπ' ἐλπίσιν·
κοινὰ δ' ἔχειν τε καὶ μέλλειν.

Which woes [*potera melea*] shall I bewail [*epistenō*] first [*proteron*], which woes [*potera*] further [*peraiterō*]? <These things are> hard to judge [*duskrit'*] for me, unhappy one [*emoige dustanōi*]. We can see [*echomen horan*] one sorrow in the house [*tade men domois*], and another [*tade de*] we await in expectation [*menomen ep' elpisin*]: having [*echein*] and being about to (have) [*te kai mellein*] are just the same [*koina*].

In his version of the First Strophe, Pound maintained the antithesis and repetition of the original, while replacing the assonance with rhyme. The third line was rendered more freely, in order to enhance its emotional range:

> TORN between griefs, which grief shall I lament,
> which first? Which last, in heavy argument?
> One wretchedness to me in double load.
>
> *WT* 58

Here Pound played with the connotations of the prefix *dus-* with its notions of 'bad', 'hard', 'unlucky', as in *duskritos*, 'hard to judge'. The prefix is used in Greek to increase the bad sense of a word, hence Pound's 'double load'.

Pound's First Antistrophe is more explicit than the original, and maintains its link to the preceding Strophe through rhyme ('load ... road'): 'DEATH'S in the house,/ and death comes by the road.' It is also noteworthy that, for once, Pound has established a close metrical parallel between the original and his own text: in the Greek, lines 947–48 and 950–51 are iambic dimeters, while lines 949 and 952 are choriambic dimeters. In Pound, we also have a regular iambic pattern which includes two choriambs: '**TORN** between **griefs**' and '**DEATH'S** in the **house**'.

In the Second Strophe (ll. 953–61), the Chorus expresses its longing to escape from all this:

εἴθ' ἀνεμόεσσά τις
γένοιτ' ἔπουρος ἑστιῶτις αὔρα,
ἥτις μ' ἀποικίσειεν ἐκ τόπων, ὅπως
τὸν Δῖον ἄλκιμον γόνον
μὴ ταρβαλέα θάνοιμι
μοῦνον εἰσιδοῦσ' ἄφαρ·
ἐπεὶ ἐν δυσαπαλλάκτοις ὀδύναις
χωρεῖν πρὸ δόμων λέγουσιν
ἄσπετόν τι θαῦμα.

Oh that [*eith'*] a favourable gusty wind [*tis anemoessa epouros aura*] might come [*genoit'*] to the hearth [*hestiōtis*, i.e. 'to our house'], that [*hētis*] might bear me [*m' apoikiseien*] from this place [*ek topōn*], so that [*hopōs*] I would not die of fear [*mē tarbalea thanoimi*] straight away [*aphar*] from the mere sight [*mounon eisidous'*] of the mighty son of Zeus [*ton Dion alkimon gonon*], for [*epei*] they say [*legousin*] that he is approaching the house [*chōrein pro domōn*] in pains that cannot be got rid of [*en dusapallaktois odunais*], an unspeakable wonder [*aspeton ti thauma*].

Pound's version has freely adapted the Greek phrases, as the following annotated passage illustrates:

THAT WIND might bear away [*eith' aura apoikiseien*] my grief and me,
Sprung from the hearth-stone [*hestiōtis*; 'sprung' may have been derived from Storr's "that a gale might suddenly upspring" (Storr 333)], let it bear me away [repetition of *eith' apoikiseien*].
God's Son is dead [=the accusative *ton Dion gonon* turned into a subject, and the 1st. person sg. optative *thanoimi* into a 3rd person sg. indicative],
    that was so brave and strong [*alkimon*],
And I am craven [periphrastic *tarbalea*] to behold [*eisidous'*] such death [the verb *thanoimi* turned into a noun]
    Swift on the eye [*eisidous' aphar*],
Pain hard to uproot [*dusapallaktais odunais*],
    and this so vast [?*aspeton*]
A splendour [*thauma*] of ruin.

WT 58–59

The Chorus in witnessing what they assume to be the dead body of Herakles is struck dumb. Pound turns the 'unspeakable' (*aspeton*) into a qualification of the magnitude of their grief ('so vast'), which cannot be expressed. By using capitals in the phrase 'God's Son', Pound continues the implied link between Herakles' suffering and the Christian Passion, while the 'splendour of ruin' prepares for the more glorious use of the word later on.

In the Second Antistrophe (ll. 962–70), the Chorus witnesses how Herakles is brought silently towards the house:

ἀγχοῦ δ᾽ ἄρα κοὐ μακρὰν
προύκλαιον, ὀξύφωνος ὡς ἀηδών.
ξένων γὰρ ἐξόμιλος ἥδε τις βάσις.
πᾷ δ᾽ αὖ φορεῖ νιν; ὡς φίλου
προκηδομένα βαρεῖαν
ἄψοφον φέρει βάσιν.
αἰαῖ, ὅδ᾽ ἀναύδατος φέρεται.
τί χρὴ θανόντα νιν ἢ καθ᾽
ὕπνον ὄντα κρῖναι;

So [*ara*] it was for something near [*anchou*] and not far off [*kou makran*] when I lamented in advance [*prouklaion*], like a shrill-voiced nightingale [*oxuphōnos hōs aēdōn*]. For [*gar*] here is a procession [*ēde tis basis*] of strangers [*xenōn*], from abroad [*exomilos*]. In what manner then [*pai d' au*] are they carrying him [*phorei nin*, i.e. 'What sort of (silent) procession is this?']? As caring [*hōs prokēdomena*] for a loved one [*philou*], the procession moves on its way [*pherei*, lit. 'carries', 'bears'] with a heavy silent step [*bareian apsophon basin*]. Alas [*aiai*], he [*hod'*] is borne along [*pheretai*] speechless [*anaudatos*]. What must we think [*ti chrē krinai*]: that he is dead [*thanonta nin*] or sleeping [*ē kath' hupnon onta*]?

Pound's Second Antistrophe reads:

> THAT NOW is here.
> As Progne shrill upon the weeping air,
> 'tis no great sound.
>   These strangers lift him home,
> with shuffling feet, and love that keeps them still.
> The great weight silent
>   for no man can say
> If sleep but feign
>   or Death reign instantly.

WT 59

The relative pronoun 'THAT' refers to 'A splendour of ruin' of the preceding line, and in this way Pound makes a definite choice for 'a lament for something near'. Apart from their mistranslation, Pound's second and third lines ('As Progne ... sound', a reference to the myth of Procne also used in Canto 4) make no sense without recourse to the original text, as we here only have the vehicle of the simile itself, not its tenor (the lament of the Chorus). The fourth and fifth lines are closer to the Greek, even though Pound has changed the simile 'as if mourning for a loved one' into a statement of fact. His sixth and seventh line play with the Greek word *anaudos*, 'without speech', which first occurs in the phrase 'The great weight silent', referring to Herakles, and then in 'for no man can say' in which *anaudos* is used to make a generalization, namely, that no one really knows whether Herakles is already dead ('Death reign instantly') or merely pretending to be asleep ('If sleep but feign').

Exodos (S ll. 971–1278; *WT* 59–71: ll. 939–1242)

This final part of the play was very heavily annotated by Pound in his Loeb until the final dialogue between Herakles and Hyllus starting at l. 1114. The first part of the Exodos is devoted to the entrance of the procession (971–92). Curiously enough, Pound has deleted this entire passage, perhaps, as Stergiopoulou (2014, 384) has rightly suggested, 'for dramatic effect'. The deleted passage describes how Hyllus is expressing his grief, while an old man is trying to restrain him for fear of disturbing Herakles (971–82). When the hero awakes, he first does not know where he is, but his confusion soon gives way to a feeling of overwhelming pain (983–87). Then the old man reproaches Hyllus for having woken his father, while the son is looking helplessly at Herakles (988–92), who starts making his second speech. It is at this point that Pound's version continues the play, thus immediately after his rendering of the Fourth Stasimon.

The opening of Herakles' first speech (993–1003) reads:

ὦ Κηναία κρηπὶς βωμῶν,
ἱερῶν οἵαν οἵων ἐπί μοι
μελέῳ χάριν ἠνύσω· ὦ Ζεῦ,
οἵαν μ' ἄρ' ἔθου λώβαν, οἵαν·
ἣν μή ποτ' ἐγὼ προσιδεῖν ὁ τάλας
ὤφελον ὄσσοις, τόδ' ἀκήλητον
μανίας ἄνθος καταδερχθῆναι.
τίς γὰρ ἀοιδός, τίς ὁ χειροτέχνης

ἱατορίας, ὃς τήνδ' ἄτην
χωρὶς Ζηνὸς κατακηλήσει;
θαῦμ' ἂν πόρρωθεν ἰδοίμην.

O Kenaean base of altars [*ō Kēnaia krēpis bōmōn*], what thanks [*hoian charin*] you have rendered me [*epi moi ēnusō*], unhappy one [*meleōi*], for such offerings [*hierōn hoiōn*], o Zeus [*ō Zeu*]! What ruin [*hoian lōban*] have you brought upon me [*m' ar' ethou*], what ruin [*hoian*]! Would that I [*hēn egō ophelon*], wretched one [*ho talas*], had never set eyes on you [*mē pot' prosidein ossois*], and had looked upon [*kataderchthēnai*] this incurable [*tod' akēlēton*] flower of madness [*manias anthos*]. Who is the singer [*tis aoidos*], who the practitioner of medicine [*tis ho heirotechnēs iatorias*] who [*ho*] shall lull to rest [*katakēlēsei*] this plague [*tēnd' atēn*], other than Zeus [*chōris Zēnos*]? I would see [*an idoimēn*] <this> as a wonder [*thaum'*] from afar [*porrōthen*; i.e., both 'it would be a miracle if such a skilled doctor existed' and 'I will never see such a person near at hand' (Easterling 1982, 200).]

On p. 336 of his Loeb, Pound glossed this speech as 'unappeasable vehemence of madness'. His rendering of the first words spoken by Herakles is a good example of how he characterizes the speaker through style:

Holy Kanea, where they build holy altars,
done yourself proud, you have,
nice return for a sacrifice:
   messing me up.
I could have done without these advantages
And the spectacle of madness in flower,
   incurable, oh yes.
Get someone to make a song for it,
Or some chiropractor to cure it.
A dirty pest,
   take God a'mighty to cure it and
I'd be surprised to see Him
     coming this far ...

WT 59

Pound has stayed fairly closely to the Greek text, but his choice of words at times as well as the use of irony and sarcasm gives a more complex psychological portrait. His Herakles is a defiant, self-assured, cynical, egocentric and assertive man, with an occasional sense of wry humour ('advantages', 'I'd be surprised ... far'; or, as the mouthpiece of Pound creating a Greek joke: 'chiropractor'). Also note that Herakles appears per the stage directions '*in the mask of divine agony*' (*WT* 59), which in the context of a Noh play would immediately mark him as a god.

Lines 1004–43 are given to several actors, but mainly to Herakles. Here Herakles lashes out at the people surrounding (ll. 1010–11), *pothen est', ō/ pantōn Hellanōn adikōtatoi aneres*, 'Of what descent are you, o you most unjust men of all Greeks', that is, you are no Greeks if you do not help me (after all I have done for you). Pound's version is clearly based on Storr's 'O Greeks, if ye be Greeks indeed, most faithless of your race!' (337):

> You greeks are the dirtiest,
> > damn you, if you are Greeks at all,
> where do you come from?
>
> > > > > > > > > > > > > > > > > > > *WT* 60

The phrase 'where do you come from' is a literal translation of the Greek *pothen est'*. Because Pound also adapted Storr's 'if you are Greek at all', which is a rather free rendering of the same phrase, he has translated *pothen est'* twice. Another example of the influence of Storr's translation is found at ll. 1016–17, where Storr's Greek text has *oud' aparaxai krata biai thelei/ molōn tou stugerou*, 'and will no one come [*oud' thelei molōn*] and sever [*aparaxai*] the head [*krata*], at one fierce stroke [*biai*], from this wretched (man) [*tou stugerou*]'. In a note, Storr remarks that the manuscripts have *biou* ('life, existence') for *biai* (Storr 338), and Pound's version demonstrates that he adopted this reading, because his rendering 'of this loathsome existence' (*WT* 60) combines *biou* with *tou stugerou*, 'of this wretched life'.

We have seen in our discussion of *Elektra* that Pound struggled with the word *daimon*, 'god' or 'destiny'. Here in l. 1026 he renders it as 'What rotten luck' (*WT* 61), whereas on a previous occasion in l. 910 where Deianeira was 'lamenting her fate' [*ton autēs daimon' anakaloumenē*], Pound gave it as '[she] cried to her daemon' (*WT* 57). This passage also demonstrates how Pound sometimes struggled with literal meanings. When Herakles refers to his *nosos* ('sickness', 'pain') as *apotibatos* (1030), 'unapproachable', Pound gives it as: 'I can't get at it' (*WT* 61). And Pound retained both meanings of the word *agrios*, 'wild', 'savage' (of animals) or 'fierce', 'wild' (of temper), in his rendering of the phrase *agria nosos* (1030) as 'beastly pain' (*WT* 61). However, this is actually an improvement on Jebb's 'cruel pest' and 'fierce plague' (Jebb 1908, 151). Indeed, Davies has rightly noted that in the Exodos, the poison or disease (*nosos*) attacking Herakles 'is characterized by expressions which treat it as a wild beast or an Erinys' (225). Yet

Pound's literal-mindedness sometimes also leads to extreme interpretations. For example, when Herakles in his address to Hyllus refers to Deianeira as *sa matēr atheos*, 'your godless mother', the adjective *atheos* is intended to connote 'impious' or 'wicked', but Pound stuck to its literal meaning, and rendered *sa matēr atheos* as 'Damn'd atheist, that is what she is' (*WT* 61).

The choral couplet (ll. 1044–45), in which the Chorus expresses its horror and pity for Herakles and his sufferings, marks 'the change of pace and tone between the agitated lyric passage and Heracles' *rhesis*' (Easterling 1982, 204). This long speech by Herakles in normal iambic trimeters (S ll. 1046–1111) combines his cries of pain and desire to take revenge on Deianeira, with his sense of helplessness and his longing for death. The trimeters are interrupted twice (1081 and 1085–86) by lyric outbursts to convey the intensity of his suffering. Pound's rendering of the speech is fairly accurate, although confusing or awkward at times on account of his literal translations. These tendencies are clearly illustrated by his rendering of ll. 1050–52:

> ... τόδ' ἡ δολῶπις Οἰνέως κόρη
> καθῆψεν ὤμοις τοῖς ἐμοῖς Ἐρινύων
> ὑφαντὸν ἀμφίβληστρον, ᾧ διόλλυμαι.
>
> ... the daughter of Oineus [*ē Oineōs korē*] with treachery in her looks [*dolōpis*] has put upon my shoulders [*kathēpsen ōmois tois emois*] this woven net [*tod' huphanton amphiblēstron* = the poisoned robe] of the Furies [*Erinuōn*, i.e. 'deadly'], by which I am perishing [*ōi diollumai*].

In his version Pound uses the verb *kathēpsen*, 'has put upon', twice, once in (wrongly) depicting Deianeira outdoing the Furies, and once rightly to describe her actions:

> And now Miss Oineus
> with her pretty little shifty eyes
> > *m'la calata*,
> has done me to beat all the furies,
> got me into a snarl, clamped this net on to me
> > and she wove it.
>
> > > > *WT* 62

This blunder sits alongside a far more successful rendering, namely that of the adjective *dolōpis*, used to describe Deianeira. Here Pound outdoes Jebb and Storr, who both have given it as 'fair and false' (Jebb 1908, 153; Storr 341). *Dolōpis*, however, means something like 'with treachery in her [beautiful] looks', and

Pound has retained this sense with his 'with her pretty little shifty eyes'. Meanwhile, the Italian phrase *m'la calata* is connected to '*m'l'ha calata*', 'he's tricked me', which occurs in Canto 9/37, where it forms part of a phrase spoken by Sigismundo Malatesta at a point where he is brought to his end by treachery. Peter Davidson has rightly claimed that the use of the phrase in *The Women of Trachis* establishes Herakles 'more firmly in the sequence of Poundian heroes' (Davidson 414).

Pound has emphasized the sarcasm and self-pity of his Herakles by giving him strongly worded and gendered language: when Herakles states *hōste parthenos bebrucha klaiōn* (1071–72), 'I am crying out, weeping like a young girl', Pound has him say 'Me blubbering like a flapper'; and the hero's description of himself as a *thēlus*, 'a womanish creature', becomes 'I'm a sissy' (*WT* 63). And where Sophocles' Herakles denounces the Centaurs as *diphuē t' amikton . . . stratōn thērōn* (1095–96), 'an army of animals of a double nature, not mingling with others', Pound's rendering turns them into 'those unsociable bardots' (*WT* 63).

In lines 1114–78, Hyllus tells his father the truth about Deianeira. This passage again shows how much Pound relied on Storr, who, for example, translated *tēn talainan Alkmēnēn Dios matēn akoitin* (ll. 1148–49), 'the unhappy Alkmene, in vain [*matēn*] the bedfellow of Zeus', as: 'Alcmena, bride of Zeus – an empty name –' (349). Pound adapted this in his 'Alkmene, ill-starred for the empty name/ of the Godhead' (*WT* 66). Hyllus' words give Herakles a flash of insight in a momentary 'dark night of the soul'. Sophocles has in ll. 1143–45:

> Alas, alas [*iou iou*], miserable one [*dustēnos*], I am undone [*oichomai talas*]. I am dead, I am dead [*olōl' olōla*], there no longer [*ouket'*] is [*esti*] light [*phengos*] for me [*moi*]. Ah me [*oimoi*], I know now [*phronō dē*] in what misery [*xumphoras*] I stand [*hestamen*].

Pound made this crossroads in Herakles' destiny even more explicit by resorting to the light/ dark imagery we find throughout his translation:

> Misery. I'm going out
> And my light's gone.
>   The black out!
> I understand perfectly well
> Where things have got to . . .
>
>   *WT* 65

Herakles expounds in ll. 1157–78 how he suddenly sees at this moment that the oracle at Dodona, which had foretold the time of his release, coincides with another, earlier oracle, which had foretold that he would be slain by the dead. Herakles realizes how these oracles have been fulfilled in his being 'released' through the love charm of (the dead) Nessus:

> φανῶ δ' ἐγὼ τούτοισι συμβαίνοντ' ἴσα
> μαντεῖα καινά, τοῖς πάλαι ξυνήγορα,
> ἃ τῶν ὀρείων καὶ χαμαικοιτῶν ἐγὼ
> Σελλῶν ἐσελθὼν ἄλσος εἰσεγραψάμην
> πρὸς τῆς πατρῴας καὶ πολυγλώσσου δρυός,
> ἥ μοι χρόνῳ τῷ ζῶντι καὶ παρόντι νῦν
> ἔφασκε μόχθων τῶν ἐφεστώτων ἐμοὶ
> λύσιν τελεῖσθαι
>
> ll. 1164–71

And I shall reveal [*phanō d'egō*] new prophecies [*manteia kaina*] coming out in agreement [*sumbainont' isa*] with these [*toutoisi*], corroborating [*xunēgora*] the one of the past [*tois palai*], the ones [*ha*] I wrote down [*eisegrapsamēn*] from the ancestral oak with many voices [*pros tēs patrōias kai poluglōssou druos*] when I entered [*eselthōn*] the grove of the Selli [*Sellōn halsos*; that is, the priests of the oracle of Zeus at Dodona], who live in the mountains [*tōn oreiōn*] and sleep upon the ground [*chamaikoitōn*]. [The oak at Dodona] said to me [*moi ephaske*] that at the time that is alive [*chronōi tōi dzōnti*] and now present [*kai paronti nun*], my release [*moi lusin*] from the labours [*mochthōn*] laid upon me [*tōn ephestōtōn emoi*] should be accomplished [*teleisthai*].

Pound has:

> and that fits another forecast
> breathed out at the Selloi's oak –
> Those fellows rough it,
>   sleep on the ground, up in the hills there.
> I heard it and wrote it down
>   under my Father's tree.
> Time lives, and it's going on now.
> I am released from trouble.
>
> WT 66[4]

The importance of the Selloi for Pound is evident from Canto 87, in which he referred to the *Trachiniae*:

> "We have", said Mencius, "but phenomena."
>   monumenta. In nature are signatures
>   needing no verbal tradition,

oak leaf never plane leaf. John Heydon.
        Σελλοί sleep there on the ground

87/593

Natural phenomena are an expression of the divine reality manifesting itself in this material world, and should be approached in the spirit of Plotinus, who regarded material reality as a means to give access to the attainment of the divine. This is why the Selloi are mentioned here: they guarded the sacred oak of Zeus at Dodona through which the supreme god gave his oracles, and so refer to the oracle as an image of understanding the divine through nature.

Pound did not render the adjective *poluglōssou*, 'with many voices', which qualifies Zeus' oak, although he had done so in an earlier typescript (as 'with many toungues'; Beinecke 140/6184), and he would also use it in Canto 95: 'πολύγλωσσος/ There were many sounds in that oak-wood' (95/663–64). Stergiopoulou (2014, 395) has rightly argued that in his version of the *Trachiniae*, Pound left out the word intentionally, because after all the false prophecies, rumours and speculations about Herakles' whereabouts and fate, the actual truth is about to be revealed in full and unmistakable coherence, as we come to what Pound regarded as the key to the play. Herakles suddenly realizes the full truth about the oracle:

                κἀδόκουν πράξειν καλῶς.
τὸ δ᾽ ἦν ἄρ᾽ οὐδὲν ἄλλο πλὴν θανεῖν ἐμέ.
τοῖς γὰρ θανοῦσι μόχθος οὐ προσγίγνεται.
ταῦτ᾽ οὖν ἐπειδὴ λαμπρὰ συμβαίνει, τέκνον,
δεῖ σ᾽ αὖ γενέσθαι τῷδε τἀνδρὶ σύμμαχον
καὶ μὴ 'πιμεῖναι τοὐμὸν ὀξῦναι στόμα,
ἀλλ᾽ αὐτὸν εἰκαθόντα συμπράσσειν, νόμον
κάλλιστον ἐξευρόντα, πειθαρχεῖν πατρί.

                                                    S ll. 1171–78

and I thought [*kadokoun*] that I would be happy [*praxein kalōs*], but it [*to d'*, that is, the promise of release] was nothing else [*ēn ouden allo*] than that I should die [*plēn thanein eme*]. After all [*gar*], toil [*mochthos*] comes no more [*ou prosgignetai*] to the dead [*tois thanousi*, that is, the dead do not have to labour]. Since then [*oun epeidē*], my son [*teknon*], these things [*taut'*] are clearly [*lampra*] being fulfilled [*sumbainei*], you must in turn be [*dei s' au genesthai*] my ally [*tōide andri summachon*], and do not wait [*kai mē 'pimeinai*] so as to sharpen my tongue [*toumon oxunai stoma*, that is, make me angry by delaying], but consent and help me [*auton eikathonta sumprassein*], finding [*exeuronta*] that the most beautiful of laws [*nomon kalliston*] is to obey your father [*peitharchein patri*].

Pound has translated ll. 1171–74 as follows:

> I thought it meant life in comfort. [=1171]
> It doesn't. It means that I die. [=1172]
> For amid the dead there is no work in service. [=1173]
> Come at it that way, my boy, what
>
> SPLENDOUR,
>   IT ALL COHERES [=1174]
>
> WT 66

In his Loeb, Pound marked l. 1174 with a big line and cross in red. Indeed, as he stated in a note in the published version of *Women of Trachis*, 'SPLENDOUR, / IT ALL COHERES' is 'the key phrase, for which the play exists' (*WT* 66), expressing Herakles' insight into the mysteries of life and death. That this constitutes the touchstone of the play is also clear from the margin of a typescript draft in which Pound had rendered Deianeira's speech about the poisonous love charm meant to win back her husband's love (*WT* 45–46), where he wrote 'What splendour! See how it all works out/ λαμπρα συμβαιναι [sic]' (Princeton 1/13).[5]

In his note to l. 1174 to the published version, Pound stated that 'At least one sensitive hellenist who has shown great care for Sophocles' works, has failed to grasp the main form of the play, either here or in the first chorus, and how snugly each segment of the work fits into its box' (*WT* 66–67). Pound's references to Herakles' insight and to the first chorus, which celebrates the irresistible power of Love, make clear that the poet saw 'the main form of the play' as a unity, not as a tragedy in two halves. The 'sensitive hellenist' to whom Pound refers is probably Jebb who, like many others, saw 'one serious defect' in the play, namely its disunity:

> However effective the Heracles scene might be on the stage, I cannot help suspecting that an attentive spectator, in full sympathy with the spirit of the best Greek work, would be apt to feel, *at the end*, that he had seen two tragedies; one, which closed with the death of Deianeira, and was of consummate excellence; then a second a shorter one, most pathetic, most powerful in its own way, but produced at a moral disadvantage.
>
> Jebb 1908, xxxviii–xxxix

For Pound, on the contrary, all the characters and events of the *Trachiniae* were linked by the all-powerful force of *eros*. This is what Herakles recognized when he realized in that moment of lucidity in agony that all the oracles about his life were now being fulfilled, and that Nessus and Deianeira were only instruments in the hands of Zeus.

In this respect, Pound related Herakles' *taut' oun . . . lampra sumbainei* (1174), 'these things are now clearly being fulfilled', to Deianeira's words spoken after the period of fifteen months which would bring either prosperity or death for Herakles: *kai tōnde namerteia sumbainei chronou/ tou nun parontos, hōs telesthēnai chreōn* (174–75), 'and the exact moment when these things [i.e. prosperity or death] should be fulfilled falls at the time now present'. *Sumbainei* is the third person singular present indicative active voice of the verb *sumbainō*, which means 'to come together', 'to come to an agreement', 'to agree', 'to come to pass', 'to happen'. It occurs here for the first time, when all options still seem open – although in practice Herakles has already been doomed to die because of his *eros* for Iole. The second occurrence of *sumbainei* in l. 1174 marks Herakles' insight that the oracles are coming true, a result of all the different manifestations of *eros* (as violent passion in himself, in Deianeira and in Nessus). Thus the word *sumbainei* connects Deianeira and Herakles as principals in the play, although they never meet on stage, and the exact moment of the fulfilment of the oracles. While Pound's translation of *taut' oun . . . lampra sumbainei* as 'SPLENDOUR, IT ALL COHERES' accords the Greek words a semantic weight they cannot sustain, Pound clearly regarded the phrase not only as an expression of Herakles' insight, but also as an evaluation of the play's unity. His rendering here thus epitomizes his creative translation of the *Trachiniae* as a form of literary criticism.[6]

Pound had already used the word 'splendour' earlier to translate the Greek word *thauma* (l. 961), 'sight, spectacle, wonder', in order to describe Herakles 'objectively' from the outside by the Chorus as 'A splendour of ruin' (*WT* 59). In translating l. 1174, he uses 'splendour' again but now to render *lampra* ('clearly', 'splendidly', 'brightly') as an expression of Herakles' 'subjective' state of mind. This also fully explains why Pound in his list of *dramatis personae* described Herakles as 'the solar vitality', the eternal force behind the alternation of human fortune.

After the moment of Herakles' insight, the play focuses on the way in which the hero must now face his predestined goal, and how Herakles does this willingly, thereby gaining in divine stature. Sophocles did not include the hero's apotheosis on Mount Oeta, where he died in the clarity of fire, but lets the play end with Hyllus' comment on the cruelty of the gods. As such, as Easterling (1982, 10) has rightly noted, the play is not about the apotheosis, but 'the emphasis of the action is on suffering and mortality'. This is why Pound, with his insight into the unified structure of the play, emphasized line 1174. He believed that the tragedy at this point had more or less concluded by contrasting Herakles' (divine) insight with Hyllus' (human) failure to understand the full significance of the course of events. Although Easterling (1982, 10) points out that in the *Trachiniae* Herakles is shown as not really understanding whether the fulfilment of the will of Zeus will lead to a good or bad end, for Pound there was no question about this: in his eyes, Herakles at line 1174 overcomes the gulf between human and divine knowledge. This also accounts for a difference in the stage directions. When first appearing on stage, Herakles is said to enter '*in the mask of divine agony*' (*WT* 59). Yet after the moment of the hero's insight, Pound inserts the following description which emphasizes his conception of both Herakles and the plot of the play:

> [[Herakles] *turns his face from the audience, then sits erect, facing them without the mask of agony; the revealed make-up is that of solar serenity. The hair golden and as electrified as possible.*]
>
> *WT* 67

In ll. 1179–1258, heavily annotated by Pound in his Loeb, Herakles commands Hyllus to build a pyre on which he is to be burned alive, after which Hyllus must marry Iole. There will be no discussion of the matter, as the *nomon kalliston* is *peitharchein patri* (ll. 1177–78), 'the noblest law' is 'to obey your father'. Pound renders this as: 'This is the great rule: Filial Obedience' (*WT* 67) – a phrase that sounds Confucian. Indeed, in *The Unwobbling Pivot* we may read: 'Filial piety is shown in the rectitude and precision wherewith one executes the will and completes the work of one's forebears' (*CON* 141).

In his generally accurate rendering of this section, Pound's main goal seems to have been concision, intended to sustain the dramatic tension, which would have been lost if he had stuck to a too literal translation of the text.[7] Compare a literal translation of Sophocles' ll. 1179–90 with Pound's version:

HYL. Father, I am afraid at coming to such a point in our conversation, but I will obey whatever you decide
[=*WT*: "I will obey."]
HER. First of all, place your right hand in mine.
[=*WT*: "(*extending his hand*). Put her there."; the 'her' refers to the Greek word for 'hand', *cheira*, which is female.]
HYL. With what in mind do you press this pledge on me, more strongly than you need to?
[=*WT*: "I'll do it. I don't need to swear."]
HER. Will you not give your hand quickly and not disobey me?
[=*WT*: "Put it there."]

HYL. See, I stretch it out, and you will not be spoken to in opposition.
[=*WT*: "(*complying*) What am I swearing to?"]
HER. Now swear by the head of Zeus who fathered me.
HYL. What must I swear to do? You must tell me that also.
HER. You must swear to perform the action that I speak of.
[=*WT*: "Repeat: 'By the head of Zeus',/ You will do what I tell you to."]
HYL. I swear, with Zeus as my witness.
[=*WT*: "I swear, so help me God."]
HER. Pray that when you break this oath, you may incur penalties.
[=*WT*: "'And God damn all perjurers.'"]
HYL. I shall not incur them, for I shall do it. Nevertheless, I pray for this.
[=*WT*: "I'll keep it anyhow."/ (*adds after almost imperceptible pause*)/ And God DAMN all perjurers."]

WT 67

In his Loeb, Pound glossed l. 1191, translated by Storr as 'Thou know'st the peak of Oeta, shrine of Zeus?' (351), with a line from *Elektra*: 'εφορᾶ πάντα και κρατόνει E. 170'. The Greek is taken from *Elektra* l. 175, which describes Zeus as someone who ἐφορᾶ πάντα καὶ κρατύνει [*ephorai panta kai kratunei*], 'foresees and controls everything'. Pound regarded Herakles' instructions to his son as a way to help him prepare for his death, fulfilling the oracle of Zeus.

In his Loeb, Pound glossed the 'deep-rooted oak' (l. 1195) which Hyllus has to chop down for his pyre as 'Hygdrassil'. This is the World Tree of Norse mythology, the Tree of Life as well as of Knowledge, which connects all the known worlds, reaching from beneath the earth to the world of the gods. Although Pound did not use the word in his version, his gloss indicates that he saw Herakles' death as an act bridging the material and the divine realms. Hyllus hesitates to set fire to his father's pyre: 'Alas once more [*oimoi mal' authis*], what things [*hoia*] you ask of me [*m' ekkalei*], father [*pater*], to become your murderer [*phonea genesthai*] and polluted with your blood [*kai palamnaion sethen*]' (S ll. 1206–7). In his Loeb, Pound glossed this line with 'Aesc. Agam.', as indeed the first three words recall Agamemnon's cry during his murder, ὤμοι μάλ' αὖθις δευτέραν πεπληγμένος, 'Aaagh, me again, I have been struck a second blow' (*Agamemnon* 1145). Yet in the *Trachiniae*, Herakles reassures his son that he will not be a murderer, but a 'healer of my sufferings' (l. 1209).

Herakles' second command is that his son will marry Iole (S ll. 1216–58). Pound deletes ll.1230–32, and thereafter exhibits a tendency in his translation to become more literal-minded, perhaps influenced by Storr's version. A good example of this tendency can be seen in the rendering of ll. 1238–40 which read in a literal translation: 'This man, it seems, will not render due respect to me who am dying; but be assured that the curse of the gods awaits you if you disobey my words.' Storr's translation seems to have guided Pound's rendering:

> The boy, it seems, is not inclined to heed
> A father's dying prayer; but heaven's curse
> Awaits full sure a disobedient son.
>
> Storr 357

> The fellow doesn't seem to want to carry out
> his dad's last request.
> God's worst curse falls on a disobedient son.
>
> WT 69

Storr's generalization of Herakles' prediction of Hyllus' predicament has been adapted by Pound, perhaps to underscore the repetition of the Confucian theme of filial obedience, which Pound, as seen, regarded as a universal law.

Pound's literal-mindedness comes to the fore in his version of l. 1247, which reads in the original: 'Then you order [*anōgas oun*] me to do this [*prassein me tade*] with full justification [*pandikōs*]?', that is, his father's command turns it into a solemn duty. In his line, Pound used the word *pandikōs*, 'most justly', twice, first in a rendering which attempts to retain the word order of the original, and then in a repetition of the meaning of the word in order to convey Hyllus' doubts: 'If you order me to, is that legal? /Perfectly all right?' (*WT* 70). Another good example of Pound staying close to the word order of the Greek, and thereby producing a translation that makes even more sense than the original, is the beginning of l. 1252, *kalōs teleutais*, 'you end well' (that is, after your initial tendency to disobey me), as said by Herakles to Hyllus. In Pound we read, 'Fine. At last' (*WT* 70).

In ll. 1259–78, Herakles is carried to Mount Oeta. With his last words the hero 'steels' himself to display courage in his final hours: 'Come now, my stubborn soul, before you stir up again this plague, give me a curb of steel set with stones [i.e. to endure the pain without a sound], suppress your cry, accomplishing this involuntary task as if it were a joyous one.' Pound changes this self-address into words of advice to Hyllus in a rendering which in its use of modern speech and industrial imagery detracts somewhat from the solemnity and emotional pitch of this passage:

> Come ere the pain awake,
> O stubborn mind.

(catches sight of HYLLOS' face and breaks off with)

And put some cement in your face,
reinforced concrete, make a cheerful finish
even if you don't want to.

WT 70

In his final speech (1264-78), Hyllus addresses his companions to carry Herakles. Pound's rendering of ll. 1264-70 is not fully comprehensible without taking recourse to the original which reads:

αἴρετ᾽, ὀπαδοί, μεγάλην μὲν ἐμοὶ
τούτων θέμενοι συγγνωμοσύνην,
μεγάλην δὲ θεῶν ἀγνωμοσύνην
εἰδότες ἔργων τῶν πρασσομένων,
οἳ φύσαντες καὶ κλῃζόμενοι
πατέρες τοιαῦτ᾽ ἐφορῶσι πάθη.
τὰ μὲν οὖν μέλλοντ᾽ οὐδεὶς ἐφορᾷ,

Lift him [*airet'*], companions, [*opadoi*], having [*themenoi*] great sympathy [*megalēn sungnōmosunēn*] for me in this [*moi toutōn*], and recognizing [*eidotes*] the great cruelty [*megalēn agnōmosunēn*] of the gods [*theōn*] in the deeds that are being done [*ergōn tōn prassomenōn*], [the gods who [*hoi*], although they beget us [*phusantes*] and are called [*klēidzomenoi*] our fathers [*pateres*], look from a distance [*ephorōsi*] at such sufferings as these [*toiauta pathē*]. The future [*ta mellont'*] none [*oudeis*] can see [*ephorai*]...

Hoist him up, fellows.
    And for me a great tolerance,
matching the gods' great unreason.
They see the things being done,
calamities looked at,
sons to honour their fathers,
and what is to come, nothing is seen. Gods!

WT 70

In l. 1267 Pound has transferred the participle *eidotes*, 'recognizing', which belongs to the *opadoi*, the companions who are carrying Herakles, to the gods. Thus the original meaning of ll. 1266-67, 'recognizing the great cruelty of the gods in the deeds that are being done', becomes in Pound's version: 'They [=the gods] see the things being done'. After this line, his version becomes a muddle, and the last two lines ('sons ... nothing is seen') are incomprehensible without looking again at the original text.

The last line of Sophocles' play, spoken by Hyllus, honours the great power behind the death of his father and all his sufferings: *kouden toutōn ho ti mē Zeus* (1278), 'and none of these things is not Zeus', rendered by Pound as 'And all of this is from Zeus' (*WT* 71). Zeus is present in everything that has happened. Here Pound's interpretation of the play goes against traditional readings of the text, as exemplified by Jebb who argued that Hyllus's last line 'gives utterance to the deepest and bitterest of the feelings inspired by his father's cruel fate. Heracles dies forsaken by Zeus ... [and] there is no presage of his reception among the gods' (Jebb 1908, xxxi). For Pound, on the contrary, the play ends on a glorious note, as Herakles' death is a triumph over any physical limitations, a perfect image of a transformation into a god, or of an ascent into the divine, or at least to a mindset that goes beyond our limited human understanding.

Coda: l. 1174, Neoplatonism, and Pound's *Cantos*

As noted, 'SPLENDOUR / IT ALL COHERES' is regarded by Pound as the key phrase of the play. As I have shown in my *Ezra Pound and Neoplatonism* (2004), Pound used and adapted Neoplatonic notions throughout his work to express his own religio-philosophical worldview. At the time Pound was translating the *Trachiniae*, he was also drafting the *Rock-Drill* Cantos, and was reading up on Plotinus.[8] In the 'founding text' of Neoplatonism, the *Enneads*, Plotinus uses the word *aglaia*, rendered by Stephen MacKenna as 'splendour', to describe the Intelligible when it is attained in the mystic vision, that is, when one attains a sudden and full insight into the workings of the divine. The final *Ennead* VI.9.4 describes the difficulty of attaining a vision of the beauty of the Intelligible:

> The main source of the difficulty is that awareness of this Principle comes neither by knowing nor by the Intellection that discovers the Intellectual beings but by a presence overpassing all knowledge ...
>
> Our way then takes us beyond knowing ... knowing and knowable must all be left aside; every object of thought, even the highest, we must pass by, for all that is good is later than This and derives from This as from the sun all the light of the day ...
>
> There are those that have not attained to see. The soul has not come to know the splendour [*aglaias*] There; it has not felt and clutched to itself that love-passion of vision known to the lover come to rest where he loves.
>
> tr. MacKenna 539–40

The use of the word 'splendour' gives *Women of Trachis* a strong Neoplatonic colouring. This is why Pound regards the 'splendour' of line 1174 as the focal point of the entire play, as from here, looking both forward and backward in time, all events and actions become meaningful.

Although, then, Herakles suffered severe physical pain through the inflammation of the poison on his clothes, from which only the fire of the pyre could relieve him, Pound saw Herakles' insight as the moment in the play when the 'body of light' took over from the 'body of fire', to use phrases found in Canto 91.[9] Indeed, 'fire' in MacKenna's translation of *The Enneads* is also linked to 'splendour'. In *Ennead* I.6.3, Plotinus tries to give a sense of the Intelligible by stating that 'Fire itself is splendid beyond all material bodies ... as very near to the unembodied ... hence the splendour of its light, the splendour that belongs to the Idea' (tr. MacKenna 48). This is why Pound referred in Canto 87 to the *Trachiniae* through the lines

> The play shaped from φλογιζόμενον
>   gospoda Δηάνειρα, λαμπρὰ συμβαίνει
> From the dawn blaze to sunset
> "What has been should have
>
> 87/591–92

Phlogidzomenon (φλογιζόμενον), 'blazing with fire' is taken from the First Strophe of the Parodos of the *Trachiniae*, which is, as we have seen, both an invocation and celebration of the sun, whom the night 'brings forth [*tiktei*], and lays to rest [*kateunadzei*] as you blaze with fire [*phlogidzomenon*]' (l. 95) – rendered here by Pound as 'From the dawn blaze to sunset'. The Parodos does much to associate Herakles (the 'solar vitality') with light and to present Deianeira as a sort of essential link in Herakles' awareness of his own destiny and position in the Chain of Being. Deianeira in Canto 87 is referred to as 'gospoda'; in his Loeb edition, Pound had glossed the Greek phrase *despoinan Artemin*, 'lady Artemis', in *Elektra* l. 626 with 'yugoslav gospodin'. In Canto 87, then, Pound also accords Deianeira a sort of divine stature.

In Canto 87, Pound connects λαμπρὰ συμβαίνει with the phrase 'What has been should have', which, as we have seen in our analysis of *Elektra*, is a rendering of Mussolini's reputed comment '*Tutto quello che è accaduto, doveva accadere*', given in a memoir attributed to the *Duce* about the period after his downfall in July 1943. These words of Mussolini are also quoted in Pound's notes to his phrase 'SPLENDOUR / IT ALL COHERES' in his *Women of Trachis* (*WT* 66–67). Flory convincingly states that Pound links Herakles' tragic fate of feeling betrayed, but also his stoic acceptance of his destiny, to Mussolini's life and death. She rightly states that Pound here evades the question of the *Duce's* own guilt, as he himself, unlike Herakles, had to suffer consequences arising from his own political choices (Flory 174–75).

After *Women of Trachis*, Pound in the late Cantos would continue to use the Plotinian word 'splendour' (his rendering of *lampra*) as a shorthand for visionary insight.[10] This is consistent with his earlier uses of the word to connote an epiphany. It first occurs as such in Canto 17, which includes a reference to Odysseus' stay on the island Scheria where the Phaeacians are enjoying a paradisal existence. After three days, Odysseus is brought home to his rocky island Ithaca:

> And for three days, none after,
> Splendour, as the splendour of Hermes,
> And shipped thence
>   to the stone place
>
> 17/79

Here 'the splendour of Hermes' is a periphrastic reference to the herb *moly* which the messenger of the gods gave to Odysseus so that Circe would be unable to transform him into a swine. 'Splendour' is thus linked to the force of *eros* (denoting Odysseus' later relationship with the semi-divine Circe) enabling man to have visions of a higher level of reality. We see a similar use in Canto 47, in which *eros* is presented as a life force leading to a mystical experience in which one sees nature *sub specie aeternitatis*:

> The light has entered the cave. Io! Io!
> The light has gone down into the cave,
> Splendour on splendour!
> By prong have I entered these hills:
> That the grass grow from my body,
> That I hear the roots speaking together,
>
> 47/238

However, it must be admitted that these positive connotations of the word 'splendour' became tainted by its use in Pound's Italian Canto 73, written at the end of 1944. Here the spirit of the poet Guido Cavalcanti tells the story of a peasant girl whose spirit he had met at Rimini. She had been raped by Canadian soldiers, after which she was told to give them directions to the Via Emilia. The girl answered she would lead them there herself, but she deliberately guided them into a minefield. Cavalcanti praises her courage and self-sacrifice: 'Conquistò la sorte / peregrina .... / raggiunse lo scopo. / Che splendore!' (73/440), 'She conquered her exceptional fate .... / she reached her aim. / What splendour!' (my translation). In this blatant piece of Fascist propaganda in support of Mussolini's war against the Allied forces, 'splendour' is used to promote Pound's political agenda.

The other key word of l. 1174, *sumbainei*, occurs three times in the late Cantos. In addition to Canto 87, Pound uses it in Canto 100, part of a group of five Cantos (100–104), which are 'altogether concerned with the struggle to achieve any kind of civilized order in public affairs' (Moody 403). Such a struggle sometimes involves personal suffering in pursuit of public welfare, however defined. Here Pound uses the example of John Law (1671–1729), who set up the Royal Bank with the power to issue paper currency, and who believed that the state should have credit in the same way as a bank. When he got into financial difficulties, Law fled to Venice where he died in poverty and was buried in San Moise. In *The Cantos*, this Poundian hero receives his apotheosis, albeit through a wrongly transliterated συμβαίνει:

> '29 John Law obit
> As you may read in San Moisé, in the pavement,
> SUMBAINAI
>
> 100/734[11]

Law, while failing in his personal financial life, is praised by Pound for attempting to create order and harmony in the public sphere.

The last occurrence of the Greek word is in *Thrones* in Canto 109, the final of the three Cantos devoted to Sir Edward Coke (1552–1634), the English lawyer who fought against royal prerogative, and championed the legal and just administration of taxes. He is presented by Pound as an enlightened man translating his vision of the good into practice. In Canto 109, Pound summarizes his achievements as:

> Coke
> συμβαίναι
> in the 43rd of Elizabeth
>
> 109/792

Yet Pound in the last years of his life felt that 'splendour' and 'order' would not be his personal reward, as made clear by perhaps the most famous example of the use of the key phrase of *Women of Trachis* in *The Cantos*. In the last complete Canto, Canto 116, drafted in the summer of 1959, Pound referred to *The Cantos* as 'the palimpsest', 'a little light / in great darkness', and used the image of a triumphant Herakles as an inverted self-portrait:

> I have brought the great ball of crystal;
>   who can lift it?
> Can you enter the acorn of light?
>   But the beauty is not the madness
> Tho' my errors and wrecks lie about me.
> And I am not a demigod,
> I cannot make it cohere.
>
> 116/815–16

Although Pound personally 'cannot make it cohere', he is still confident the 'Cosmos' 'coheres all right / even if my notes do not cohere' (817). The saving grace of the Universe and the unifying theme of *The Cantos* is Love and Charity, which, although the poet feels he 'cannot make it flow thru', is 'like a rushlight / to lead back to splendour' (817). In this sense, Canto 116 constitutes a perfect gloss on and coda to *Women of Trachis*, exemplifying the significant place Pound's translation of this Greek work occupied in the context of his oeuvre.

Notes

1 As we have seen in the analysis of *Elektra*, Pound in Canto 87 would conflate words from lines 676–77 from the *Trachiniae* with the words πρὸς κακοῖσι taken from what he regarded as the key line (S l. 351) of *Elektra*, 'Need we add cowardice to all the rest of this filth?' (*E* ll. 400–01), in a denouncement of modern civilization:

> The pusillanimous wanting all men cut down to worm size.
> Wops, maggots, crumbled from simple dishonesty.
> διάβορον ... ἐδεστὸν ἐξ αὐτοῦ φθίνει πρὸς κακοῖσι ...
>
> 87/590

2 The allusion to 'the twelfth year' may at first seem confusing as in earlier lines (ll.44–45, 164ff.) the period of time mentioned is fifteen months. Yet there is no contradiction here: the latter period refers to the duration of Herakles' (latest) absence at this time, while the mention of 'the twelfth year' specifies when the oracle at Dodona was given. Both periods of time have now simultaneously come to an end. On the presentation of the oracle in the play, see Davies 268–69, Appendix A: 'The Flexibility of the Oracle in the *Trachiniae*'.

3 I see *phoniai nephelai* as proleptical; the 'cloud of death' was a common image in Greek poetry; see, e.g., *Iliad* 16.350 and 20.417, and Pindar *Nem.* 9.37.

4 In a letter to Michael Reck of 17 May 1955, Pound himself commented on the translation of *chamaikoitoon* as an adjective qualifying the Selloi: 'NOT necessary to translate adjectives (epithets) by adjectives./ Note Selloi, in TRAX/ chaps sleep there on the ground./ or something like that./ rather than the onthegroundsleeping' (Reck 83).
5 David Moody quotes from a letter written by Pound to T. S. Eliot in 1951: 'When he finds the destiny FITS, Herakles exults' (302).
6 For seeing this as an example of 'tragic weaving' or 'prophetic fulfilment', see Griffiths 221–23.
7 Mason argues that Pound 'has systematically omitted the lines which show the tension between father and son and the extreme reluctance with which the son yields to the father's inhuman will' (Mason 309).
8 See Liebregts 2004, 341–42.
9 For a reading of this very Neoplatonic Canto, see Liebregts 204, 304–11.
10 See Canto 91/631, 99/715, 104/764, 111/803.
11 Pound also used the phrase λαμπρὰ συμβαίνει in an unpublished draft for the *Rock-Drill* Cantos in the early 1950s; see Bacigalupo 154.

Bibliography

Ezra Pound – Publications

ABC of Reading. London: Faber, 1961.
The Cantos. London: Faber, 1987.
The Classic Anthology Defined by Confucius. New York: New Directions, 1959.
Collected Early Poems, ed. Michael John King. London: Faber, 1977.
Confucius: The Unwobbling Pivot, The Great Digest, The Analects. New York: New Directions, 1969.
Confucius to Cummings: An Anthology of Poetry, ed. Ezra Pound and Marcella Spann. New York: New Directions, 1964.
Gaudier-Brzeska: A Memoir. New York: New Directions, 1970.
Guide to Kulchur. London: Peter Owen, 1952.
'H.D. Choruses from Euripides', *Little Review* 5/7 (November 1918), 16–20.
'Hellenist Series VI', *The Egoist* 6/2 (March–April 1919), 24–26.
'The Island of Paris: A Letter. November 1920', *Dial* 69/6 (December 1920), 635–39.
Literary Essays of Ezra Pound, ed. T. S. Eliot. London: Faber, 1954.
Machine Art and Other Writings, ed. Maria Luisa Ardizzone. Durham and London: Duke University Press, 1996.
'Paris Letter. February, 1923', *Dial* 74/3 (March 1923), 273–80.
Personae: The Shorter Poems, ed. Lea Baechler and A. Walton Litz. New York: New Directions, 1990.
Posthumous Cantos, ed. Massimo Bacigalupo. Manchester: Carcanet Press, 2015.
Selected Prose 1909–1965. Ed. William Cookson. London: Faber, 1973.
Sophocles: Elektra, a version by Ezra Pound and Rudd Fleming, ed. Richard Reid, London: Faber, 1990.
Sophocles: Women of Trachis. London: Faber, 1969.
The Spirit of Romance. London: Peter Owen, 1952 (rev. edn of 1910).
Translations. London: Faber, 1970.

Ezra Pound – Correspondence

Ezra Pound and James Laughlin: Selected Letters, ed. David M. Gordon. New York and London: Norton, 1994.

Ezra Pound to His Parents. Letters 1895–1929, ed. Mary de Rachewiltz, A. David Moody, and Joanna Moody. Oxford: Oxford University Press, 2010.

Pound/Lewis: The Letters of Ezra Pound and Wyndham Lewis, ed. Timothy Materer. London: Faber, 1985.

Selected Letters 1907–1941, ed. D. D. Paige. New York: New Directions, 1971 (1950).

Works about Pound

Adams, Stephen J. (1988), 'The Metrical Contract of *The Cantos*'. *Journal of Modern Literature*, 15/1, 55–72.

Bowra, C. M, F. R. Earp, Richmond Lattimore, and Frederic Peachy (1955), '*The Women of Trachis*: A Symposium'. *Pound Newsletter* 5, 3–8.

Bush, Ronald (1989), *The Genesis of Pound's CANTOS*. Princeton, NJ: Princeton University Press.

Carpenter, Humphrey (1988), *A Serious Character: The Life of Ezra Pound*. London: Faber.

Carter, Thomas C. (1957), 'That Hard Sophoclean Light'. *Kenyon Review* 19, 458–61.

Cole, Thomas (1987), 'Ezra Pound and *Imagi*'. *Paideuma* 16/3, 55–57.

Davenport, Guy (1954), 'Pound and Frobenius', in *Motive and Method in the Cantos of Ezra Pound*, ed. Lewis Leary. New York: Columbia University Press, 33–59.

Davidson, Peter (1979), 'HERACLES & m'la calata.' *Paideuma* 8/3, 413–14.

Dick, Bernard F. (1961), 'Sophocles Com-Pounded'. *The Classical World* 54, 236–37.

Edwards, Barry S. (1998), '"The Subtler Music": Ezra Pound's Prosody'. *Paideuma* 27/1, 31–53.

Ehrenpreis, Irvin (1976), 'Love, Hate, and Ezra Pound'. *New York Review of Books* 23/9, 6.

Flack, Leah Culligan (2015), *Modernism and Homer: The Odysseys of H.D., James Joyce, Osip Mandelstam, and Ezra Pound*. Cambridge: Cambridge University Press.

Flory, Wendy Stallard (1989), *The American Ezra Pound*. New Haven/London: Yale University Press.

Fleming, Rudd (1972), 'A Reminiscence'. *Sunday Star and Daily News* (Washington, DC), 12 November 1972.

Gainor, J. Ellen (1987), '*Elektra* . . . The Classic Stage Company [production], November 1–20, 1987'. *Paideuma* 16/3, 127–31.

Gallup, Donald (1986), 'Ezra Pound's "An Opening for *Agamemnon*"'. *Paideuma* 15/2&3, 117–20.

Hall, Donald (1977), 'E.P.: An Interview', in *Writers at Work: The Paris Review Interviews*, ed. George Plimpton. Harmondsworth: Penguin, 35–59.

Ingber, Richard (1978), 'Ezra Pound's *Women of Trachis*: A Song for the Muses' Garden'. *Amerikastudien* 23, 131–46.

Kenner, Hugh. (1972), *The Pound Era*. London: Faber.

Kindellan, Michael (2017), *The Late Cantos of Ezra Pound: Composition, Revision, Publication*. London/New York: Bloomsbury.

Laughlin, James. (1989), *Pound as Wuz: Recollections and Interpretations*. London: Peter Owen.

Liebregts, Peter (2004), *Ezra Pound and Neoplatonism*. Madison: Fairleigh Dickinson University Press.

Liebregts, Peter (2015), 'Wrestling with Verbiage: Ezra Pound, Thomas Stanley and Aeschylus', in *Ezra Pound and London: New Perspectives*, ed. Walter Baumann and William Pratt. New York: AMS Press, Inc., 95–109.

Marsh, Edward (1939), *A Number of People: A Book of Reminiscences*. London: Heinemann.

Marsh, Alec (2000), 'Letting the Black Cat Out of the Bag: A Rejected Instance of "American-Africanism" in Pound's *Cantos*'. *Paideuma* 29/1&2, 125–42.

Marsh, Alec (2011), *Ezra Pound*. London: Reaktion Books.

Marsh, Alec (2015), *John Kasper and Ezra Pound: Saving the Republic*, London/New York: Bloomsbury.

Mason, H. A. (1970), '*The Women of Trachis* and Creative Translation'. *Arion* 2/1 (1963), 59–81, repr. in a revised version in *Ezra Pound*, ed. J. P. Sullivan. Harmondsworth: Penguin, 279–310.

Mihálka, Reka (2013), 'He Do Elektra in Different Voices: Pound and Fleming's Translation of *Elektra*', in *ROMA/AMOR: Ezra Pound, Rome, and Love*, ed. William Pratt and Caterina Ricciardi. New York: AMS Press, 197–213.

Moody, A. David (2015), *Ezra Pound: Poet*, Volume III: *The Tragic Years 1939-1972*. Oxford: Oxford University Press.

Norman, Charles (1969), *Ezra Pound*. New York: Minerva Press.

Polten, Orla (2017), 'To Break the Hexameter: Classical Prosody in Ezra Pound's Early Cantos'. *Modern Philology*, 115/2, 264–88.

Powell, James A. (1979), 'The Light of Vers Libre'. *Paideuma* 8/1, 3–47.

Rachewiltz, Mary de (1971), *Discretions*. New York: New Directions.

Rattray, David (1957), 'Weekend with Ezra Pound'. *The Nation* 185, 343–49.

Reck, Michael (1968), *Ezra Pound: A Close-Up*. New York: McGraw-Hill.

Redman, Tim (1986), 'Pound's Library: A Preliminary Catalog'. *Paideuma* 15 2/3, 231–37.

Stergiopoulou, Katerina (2014), 'Towards a Modernist Hellenism: Ezra Pound, H. D., and the Translation of Greece' (PhD diss., Princeton University).

Stergiopoulou, Katerina (2015), '"And a Good Job"? Elektrifying English at St. Elizabeths'. *Journal of Modern Literature* 39/1, 87–111.

Surette, Leon (1979), *A Light from Eleusis: A Study of Ezra Pound's 'Cantos'*. Oxford: Clarendon Press.

Syros, Christine (1994), 'Beyond Language: Ezra Pound's Translation of the Sophoclean *Elektra*'. *Paideuma* 23/2&3, 107–39.

Terrell, C. F. (1993), *A Companion to The Cantos of Ezra Pound*. Berkeley & Los Angeles: University of California Press.

Tryphonopoulos, Demetres P. (1992), *The Celestial Tradition: A Study of Ezra Pound's 'The Cantos'*. Waterloo, Ontario: Wilfried Laurier University Press.

General Bibliography

Barnard, Mary (1984), *Assault on Mount Helicon: A Literary Memoir*. Berkeley/Los Angeles/London: University of California Press.

Bassnett, Susan (2014), *Translation Studies*. London and New York: Routledge.

Camps, W. A. (1966), *Propertius: Elegies Book III*. Cambridge: Cambridge University Press.

Carne-Ross, D. S. (1979), 'Deianeira's Dark Cupboard: A Question from Sophocles', in *Instaurations: Essays In and Out of Literature, Pindar to Pound*. Berkeley/Los Angeles/London: University of California Press, 61–115.

Davies, Malcolm (1991), *Sophocles: Trachiniae*, Oxford: Clarendon Press.

Dryden, John (2012), 'From the Preface to *Ovid's Epistles*', in *The Translation Studies Reader*, ed. Lawrence Venuti. London and New York: Routledge, 38–42.

Earp, F. R. (1944), *The Style of Sophocles*. Cambridge: Cambridge University Press.

Easterling, P. E. (1982), *Sophocles: Trachiniae*. Cambridge: Cambridge University Press.

Easterling, P. E. (1989), 'Sophocles', in *The Cambridge History of Classical Literature, Volume I, Part 2: Greek Drama*, ed. P. E. Easterling and B. M. W. Knox. Cambridge: Cambridge University Press, 43–64.

Eliot, T. S. (1969), *The Sacred Wood: Essays on Poetry and Criticism*. London: Methuen & Co.

Eliot, T. S. (2009), *The Letters of T. S. Eliot*, Vol. I: 1898–1922, ed. Valerie Eliot and Hugh Haughton. London: Faber and Faber.

Golden, Leon (1983), 'Aristotle: Poetics' (translation), in *Classical and Medieval Literary Criticism: Translations and Interpretations*, ed. Alex Preminger, Leon Golden, O.B. Hardison Jr., and Keven Kerrane. New York: Frederick Ungar.

Griffiths, Eric (2018), *If Not Critical*. Edited by Freya Johnston. Oxford: Oxford University Press.

Gross, Harvey (1964), *Sound and Form in Modern Poetry*. Ann Arbor: The University of Michigan Press.

Haynes, Kenneth (2003), *English Literature and Ancient Languages*. Oxford: Oxford University Press.

Jebb, Sir Richard C. (1907), *Sophocles: The Plays and Fragments. Part VI. The Electra*. Cambridge: Cambridge University Press.

Jebb, Sir Richard C. (1908), *Sophocles: The Plays and Fragments, Part V: The Trachiniae*. Cambridge: Cambridge University Press.

Kells, J. H. (1973), *Sophocles: Electra*. Cambridge: Cambridge University Press.

Kitto, H. D. F. (1950), *Greek Tragedy: A Literary Study*. London: Methuen.

Lloyd-Jones, Hugh (1994), *Sophocles: Antigone, The Women of Trachis, Philoctetes, Oedipus at Colonus*. Cambridge, Mass./London: Harvard University Press (Loeb Classical Library).

MacKenna, Stephen (1991), *Plotinus: The Enneads*. Harmondsworth: Penguin.

Michelini, Ann (1987), *Euripides and the Tragic Tradition*. Madison, WI: The University of Wisconsin Press.

Nida, Eugene (2012), 'Principles of Correspondence', in *The Translation Studies Reader*, ed. Lawrence Venuti. London and New York: Routledge, 141–55.

North, Michael (1994), *The Dialect of Modernism: Race, Language, and Twentieth-Century Literature*. New York/ Oxford: Oxford University Press.

Sommerstein, Alan H. (2008), *Aeschylus: Oresteia*. Cambridge, MA/London: Harvard University Press (Loeb Classical Library).

Stanley, Thomas (1663), *Aischylou tragodiai epta Aeschyli tragoediae septem : cum scholiis Graecis omnibus : deperditorum dramatum fragmentis / versione & commentario Thomae Stanleii*. Londini: Typis Jacobi Flesher, prostant verò apud Cornelium Bee.

Steiner, George (1998), *After Babel: Aspects of Language and Translation*. London, Oxford and New York: Oxford University Press.

Storr, F. (1913), *Sophocles: Ajax, Electra, Trachiniae, Philoctetes*. London: William Heinemann/New York: The Macmillan Co. (Loeb Classical Library).

Venuti, Lawrence (1995), *The Translator's Invisibility: A History of Translation*. London and New York: Routledge.

Venuti, Lawrence (2012), 'Introduction', in *The Translation Studies Reader*, ed. Lawrence Venuti. London and New York: Routledge, 1–9.

Weir Smyth, Herbert (1926), *Aeschylus: Persians. Seven Against Thebes. Suppliants. Prometheus Bound*. Cambridge, Mass.: Harvard University Press/London: William Heinemann, Ltd. (Loeb Classical Library).

Williams, William Carlos (1951), *Autobiography*. New York: Random House.

Williams, William Carlos (1992), *Paterson*, ed. Christopher MacGowan. New York: New Directions.

Yeats, William Butler (1990), *The Poems*, ed. Daniel Albright. London: J. M. Dent.

Index

Achelous (Acheloös; Akheloös) 154, 162, 164, 174–75, 202, 204–05, 208n.1, 219
Achilles 34, 39, 57
Actaeon 38, 44
Adams, Stephen J. 13
Aegisthus (*see also* Aigisthos) 81, 150–51
Aeneid (Virgil) 6
Aeschylus vi, vii, 8–11 *passim*, 17, 18, 21–31, 34–42, 45–46, 46n.3, 48, 53, 54–55, 56, 64, 67, 68, 73, 90, 101, 102, 140, 143, 146, 153, 158, 239
Agamemnon 23–24, 30, 39, 41, 43, 44, 46n.10, 67, 70, 74, 77, 78, 79, 81, 82, 84–87 *passim*, 90, 91, 98, 104, 106, 111, 112, 117, 119, 125, 131, 143, 145, 146, 148, 151, 239
Agamemnon (Aeschylus) vi, vii, 9, 10, 18, 21–28, 30–46, 46n.3, 47, 51, 111, 143, 148, 158, 229
Aigisthos (*see also* Aegisthus) 38, 39, 59, 62, 68, 77, 78, 81, 84, 85, 86, 90, 94, 97–99, 108, 113, 119, 121, 125, 131, 135, 142, 145–47, 151
Ajax (Sophocles) 63, 65n.14, 153, 212
Alcmaeon 117
Alcmene (Alkmena) 150, 178–79, 210, 233
Alexandria 17, 58
Alkestis (Euripides) 15–16
Amphiaraus 117
Antigone 60, 64
Antigone (Sophocles) 19n.2, 63, 153, 169
Aphrodite (*see also* Venus) 15, 154, 169, 202–03, 204, 221–23
Apollo 43, 67, 68, 69–70, 76, 114, 139–40, 190–95, 210
Aquinas 114
Ara 83, 144

Ares (*see also* Mars) 81, 82, 140, 141, 144, 211
Arion 156
Aristotle 21, 46n.3, 133, 167
Arnold, Matthew 11
Artemis (*see also* Diana) 44, 112, 134, 190–94, 209, 243
Athena 45, 67, 146
Athens 45, 54, 55
Atossa 8
Atreus 33, 36, 105, 124, 125, 147
Auvergnat 38–39, 46n.7

Bacigalupo, Massimo 247n.11
Barnard, Mary 18, 156
Barry, Iris 1, 6, 7, 8, 9, 10, 14, 51, 174
Bassnett, Susan 4–5
Beckwith, Osmond 58
Beinecke Library viii, 21, 31, 34, 38, 39–40, 41, 47, 48, 50, 53, 54, 55, 58, 64n.7, 112, 156, 157–61 *passim*, 171, 223, 235
Bellotti, Felice 28
Bird, Otto 165
Bohn, Henry George 28
Borgia, Giovanni 39
Bowra, Sir Maurice 155–56
Brer Rabbit 47–48, 49
Bridges, Robert 48, 160
Browning, Elizabeth Barrett 23
Browning, Robert 11, 22, 23–24, 36
Brunnenburg vi, 7, 47, 71, 72, 73, 155
Buckley, Theodore Alois 28
Bunting, Basil 37
Bush, Ronald 28–29
Butler, Samuel 22

Cabestanh, Guillems de 38
Cadmus 184–86
Cairns, Huntington 165
Camps, W.A. 214
Capaneus 21–22, 40

Carlyle, Thomas 4
Carne-Ross, D.S. 157, 164
Carpenter, Humphrey 61
Carter, Thomas C. 156
Cassandra 43–44
Cavalcanti, Guido 244–45
Chapman, George 6
Checkhov, Anton 32
Chêng-ming 75
Choephoroi (Aeschylus) 21, 67, 68
Chorus (*Agamemnon*) 39, 40
Chorus (*Elektra*) 80, 84–92, 97, 99, 100, 104, 105–09, 113, 115–18, 121, 123–24, 126, 128, 131, 133, 140, 141, 142, 143, 145, 147, 149
Chorus (*Oedipus Rex*) 50, 173
Chorus (*Women of Trachis*) 102, 154, 164, 165, 168, 169, 170, 171, 178, 180, 183, 184, 186–87, 188–90 *passim*, 194, 207, 208, 209–13, 214, 216, 218, 220–24 *passim*, 226–29, 232, 236, 237
Christ 214, 219, 228
Chrysothemis 62, 67, 73, 78, 99–105, 118–21, 123, 124, 134, 146, 149
Cicero, Marcus Tullius 2
Circe 244
Classical World, The 156
Cocteau, Jean 63–64, 171
Coke, Sir Edward 245
Cole, Thomas 51, 59
Colonus 19n.1
Confucius (*see also* Kung) vii, 48, 52, 61, 62, 74, 75, 79, 102, 114, 238, 240
Creon (Kreon) 50, 64
Cyclops 51

Daimon 119, 130, 231
Daniélou, Abbé Jean 171
Dante 22, 53, 64n.5, 114
Darius 8–9
Davenport, Guy 53, 54, 55
Davidson, Peter 233
Davies, Malcolm 173, 193, 206, 231, 246n.2

Dean, James 170
Deianeira 102, 153, 154, 155, 156, 160, 162, 163, 164, 167, 169, 173–77, 180–84 *passim*, 186–88 *passim*, 188–90, 195–96, 198, 199–200, 201–02, 204, 206, 207–08, 209, 211–13 *passim*, 213–14, 215, 216, 220, 221, 222, 224, 225, 226, 231, 232, 233, 236, 237, 243
Delphi 69, 76, 149
Dial, The 16, 19, 25, 31, 63
Diana (*see also* Artemis) 44
Dick, Bernard F. 156
Dikè (*see also* Justice) 69–70, 78, 105, 106, 107, 111, 121, 132, 215
Dionysus (*see also* Zagreus) 190–94
Dodona 176, 233, 234, 235, 246n.2
Doolittle, Hilda (H.D.) 7, 11, 30, 171
Douglas, Gavin 6
Drake, Sir Francis 44
Dryden, John 2–3, 5
Duncan, Robert 37
Duncan, Ronald 171n.6

Earp, F.R. vi, vii, viii, 54–56, 64n.6, 64n.7, 68–69, 70, 73, 100, 109, 110, 112, 118, 132, 140, 148, 153–54, 155, 157–61, 163, 175, 190, 201, 210, 214, 225
Easterling, P.E. 53, 171n.1, 188, 190, 196–97, 225, 226, 230, 232, 237, 238
Edwards, Barry S. 12, 19n.5
Egoist, The vii, 21
Ehrenpreis, Irvin 62
Eleanor of Aquitaine 25
Elektra 59, 60, 61, 62, 65n.13, 67–70, 73, 78, 79–80, 82–94, 97–104, 105, 110–22, 122n.2, 123–27 *passim*, 128–39, 142, 143, 145–46, 147, 149, 150–51, 154
Elektra (Euripides) 67, 68, 94n.1, 170
Elektra (Sophocles) vi, vii, viii, 2, 52, 56, 57, 58, 61, 67–70, 72, 73, 76, 94n.1, 102, 104, 118, 122n.2, 132, 153, 155, 165, 173, 239, 246n.1

Eliot, T.S. 7, 11, 21, 30, 31, 46n.2, 47–48, 51, 53, 64n.1, 159, 247n.5
Eliot, Valerie 31
Elizabeth I 44, 245
Ellendt, Fridrich 72, 98, 107, 120, 139, 142, 155
Enneads (Plotinus) 242–43
Epistles (Ovid) 2
Erebus 150
Erinys (Fury; *see also* Eumenides) 45, 67, 68, 69, 83, 98, 108–09, 120, 125, 140, 215–16, 224, 231, 232
Eris 27–28
Eros 199, 202
Eros 154, 225, 236, 237, 244
Espey, John 53
Eteokles 21, 60
Euboea 180
Eumenides (Aeschylus) 21, 45–46, 101, 102, 146
Eumenides (Furies; *see also* Erinys) 45, 46n.11
Euripides 7, 10–12, 14–16, 17, 53, 55, 61, 67, 68, 69, 94n.1, 158, 159, 170
'Euripides and Professor Murray' (Eliot) 7, 11, 30
Eurytus 162, 163, 196–98, 199, 201

Fenollosa, Ernest 28–30, 59, 165–67
Fitts, Dudley 51
Fitzgerald, Edward 5
Fitzgerald, Robert 51
Flack, Leah Culligan 51–52, 64n.2, 64n.3
Fleming, Mary ('Polly') 56, 57, 60
Fleming, Rudd vi, vii, 56–60, 64n.8, 64n.9, 65n.10, 65n.12, 69, 71, 72, 76, 77, 89, 91, 104, 105, 106, 107, 115, 122n.3, 134, 135, 137, 165
Flory, Wendy Stallard 61, 101, 243–44
Four Pages 37, 101

Gainor, J. Ellen 65n.13
Gallup, Donald 31, 32
Geryon 25
Goacher, Denis 170
Golden, Leon 133

Golding, Arthur 6
Goodwin, W.W. 72
Griffiths, Eric 247n.6
Gross, Harvey 13
Grosseteste, Robert 164

Hades 83, 88, 117, 174, 184, 185, 203
Hall, Donald 166
Hamilton, Edith 156
Hardy, Thomas 24
Harris, Joel Chandler 47
Haughton, Hugh 31
Haynes, Kenneth 14, 19n.6
Helen 9, 25, 26, 27, 38, 40
Helios 179–80
Henry II of England 25
Hephaestus 40
Hera 170
Herakles 61, 63, 102, 153, 154, 155, 156, 159, 160, 162, 163, 164, 165, 168, 169, 170, 173, 175, 176, 178, 180, 181, 183, 184, 185, 188–90, 196–202 *passim*, 204, 207–16 *passim*, 218–23 *passim*, 225, 226, 228, 229–44, 246n.2, 247n.5
Hermes 83, 140–41, 207, 244
Hesse, Eva 171
Heydon, John 235
Heymann, C. David 61
Hippodameia 110
Hippolytus (Euripides) 14
Homer 4, 6, 9, 10, 11, 12, 14, 22, 25, 28, 32, 46, 51, 56, 57, 58, 60, 67, 68, 83, 90, 129, 149, 150, 153, 155, 158, 194, 202, 203
Hsin 101
Hudson Review 52, 60, 155, 161
Hugo, Victor 42
Hydra 219
Hygdrassil 239
Hyllus (Hyllos) 153, 164, 170, 177, 214–16, 225, 229, 232, 233, 237–42

Ibsen, Henrik 11, 32
Iliad (Homer) 6, 9, 10, 25, 39, 246n.3
Imagi 51
Inachus 74
Inferno (Dante) 22

Ingber, Richard 64n.6
Ino 51
Io 74
Iocaste 50
Iole 62, 154, 163, 164, 195, 197, 199, 200,
    201, 208, 220–24 *passim*,
    237–39 *passim*
Ion (Euripides) 7
Iphigeneia 111, 113
Iphigeneia Among the Taurians (Euripides)
    11
Iphitus 162, 196–98
Ismene 60
Ithaca 244
Ito, Mishio 168, 169
Itys 38, 82, 86, 87

James, Henry 29
Jankowski, Stanislaw Victor 157
Jebb, Sir Richard C. vi, vii, viii, 7, 18–19n.1,
    63, 67–68, 69, 71, 72, 74, 77,
    78, 84, 88, 90, 94n.1, 98, 101,
    108, 113, 117, 119, 120, 123,
    125, 132, 133, 134, 135, 136,
    137, 142, 144, 145, 153, 163,
    164, 190, 200, 201, 213, 218,
    224, 231, 232, 236, 242
Jefferson, Thomas 41
Jerome 2
Johnson, Lionel 160
Joyce, James 64n.9
Julian 65n.14
Jupiter (*see also* Zeus) 34
Justice (*see also* Dikè; Themis) 23, 43, 45,
    61, 62, 64, 67–68, 69–70, 78,
    105–06, 107, 111, 215–16
Justinian 114

Kasper, John 170
Katuo, Kitasono 169
Kells, J.H. 68, 69, 76, 77, 92, 93, 94n.1, 99,
    108–09, 113, 115, 121, 133,
    135, 151n.1
Kenner, Hugh 62–63, 64n.5, 65n.10
Kenyon Review, The 156
Kindellan, Michael 171n.2
Kitto, H.D.F. vii, 69–70
Klytaimnestra 23, 24, 33–37, 38, 39, 42, 44,
    46n.5, 59, 62, 68, 69, 70, 77, 78,
    84–85, 86, 90, 94, 97, 98, 99,
    102, 104–08 *passim*, 110–16,
    119, 125, 134, 135, 139, 142,
    143, 145, 146, 149, 151
Kuanon 169
Kung (*see also* Confucius) 52
Kronos (Chronos) 186–87

Lattimore, Richmond 155
Laughlin, James 2, 171
Law, John 245
Leda 148
Lekakis, Michael 60, 65n.11
Lewis, Wyndham 170
Lichas 189, 190, 191, 195–202, 207–09
    passim, 214, 215
Liddell-Scott Greek-English Dictionary 72,
    77, 83, 107, 155, 183, 203,
    205, 208
Liebregts, Peter 19n.3, 46n.1, 122n.5,
    171n.3, 171n.4, 247n.8,
    247n.9
Lilly Library 57, 58, 59, 60, 64n.8, 65n.12,
    71, 72, 165
Little Review, The 11
Lloyd-Jones, Hugh 181
Loeb Classical Library 2, 51, 53, 63
Louis VII of France 25
Lowell, Robert 3
Lydia 197–97

MacKenna, Stephen 242–43
Macon, Nathaniel 63
Maensac, Pieire de 38, 46n.7
Malatesta, Sigismondo 233
Malis 209–10
Mars (*see also* Ares) 141, 144, 145, 211
Marsh, Alec 41–42, 46n.6, 46n.9, 65n.11,
    102, 170
Marsh, Edward 1
Marshall, Judge 44, 112
Mason, H.A. 156, 247n.7
Mazzini, Giuseppe 112
McLuhan, H.M. 65n.10
Medici, Alessandro di 39, 114
Medici, Lorenzo di 39
Mencius 234
Menelaus 38, 40
Messenger (*Elektra*) 115, 119, 149

Messenger (*Women of Trachis*) 160, 189–90, 196, 197, 199, 200, 201
Metamorphoses (Ovid) 6
Micheline, Ann 19n.4
Mihálka, Reka 122n.4
Monorou 166, 169, 170
Moody, David A. 46n.6, 47, 61, 62, 64n.4, 64n.5, 65n.10, 165, 171n.6, 245, 247n.5
Moore, Frank Ledlie 59–60
Moore, Thomas 138
Morell, Thomas 22
Morris, William 4
Morrison, Toni 41
Morshead, E.D.A. 46n.5
Murray, Gilbert 6–7, 11, 53, 55, 156, 160–61, 170
Mussolini, Benito 26, 46n.10, 101, 243–44, 245
Mycenae 36, 74, 88, 104, 115
Myrtilus 110

Neoplatonism viii, 150, 157, 164, 165, 167–68, 242–43
Nessus 102, 154, 164, 207–09 *passim*, 213, 214, 218–19, 221, 234, 236, 237
New English Weekly 63
Nicomachean Ethics (Aristotle) 46n.3
Nida, Eugene 4
Nietzsche, Friedrich 11, 19n.3
Niobe 86, 87
Nishikigi 104
Noh viii, 29, 58, 59, 63, 64, 104, 119, 165–70, 231
Norman, Charles 2
North, Michael 47–48, 64n.1
Nurse (*Women of Trachis*) 161, 169, 170, 177, 224, 225

Odysseus 25, 51, 52, 150, 175, 244
Odyssey (Homer) 1, 6, 14, 46, 51, 57, 67, 68, 150, 175
Oechalia 154, 196–97, 221–23 *passim*
Oedipus 10, 48, 49, 50, 51, 60, 154, 167
Oedipus at Colonus (Sophocles) 18n.1, 63
Oedipus at Colonus (Yeats) 63
Oedipus Rex (Sophocles) vii, 7, 48, 50, 51, 57, 63, 173
Oedipus Rex (Stravinsky) 171
Oedipus Rex (Yeats) 63, 156
Oeta (mountain) 190, 209, 223, 237, 239, 240
Oineus 162, 232
Orcus 184, 185–86
Oresteia (Aeschylus) vii, 21, 46n.5, 67, 156
Orestes 45, 59, 62, 67, 68–70, 73–74, 75–79, 84, 86, 87, 88, 89, 98, 99, 104, 113, 115–20 *passim*, 128–39, 140, 142, 145, 146, 147, 149
Orestes (Euripides) 69
Ortygia 191, 192, 194
Ovid 2

Paedagogus (*Elektra*) 73–74, 75, 77, 78, 79, 115, 116, 139, 149
Paige, D.D. 31
Parcelli, Carlo 57
Paris 28, 34, 38
Paris Review 166
Paterson (W.C. Wiliams) 53
Peachy, Frederic 250
Peisistratus 28
Pelops 74, 110, 146
Perloff, Carey 59
Persephone 83, 150
Persians (Aeschylus) 8–9
Philoktetes 154
Philoktetes (Sophocles) 63
Philomela 125–26
Phocis 74, 115
Phoebus (Sun) 178, 180, 181, 194
Phoenissae (Euripides) 15, 16
Pindar(us) 107, 246n.3
Pisa vii, 42, 44, 52, 56, 114
Plotinus 2, 235, 242–44
Plutarch 55
Poetics (Aristotle) 21, 133
Polten, Orla 18, 19n.5
Polyneikes 21, 60
Pope, Alexander 6
Poseidon 51, 150, 203
Possum (T.S. Eliot) 31, 47–48
Potter, Robert 22
Pound, Ezra
    and classical metre (general) 12–18, 57–58
    and Greek tragedy (general) 6–12
    and knowledge of Greek 1–2, 72

and *melopoeia* vi, 12, 13–14, 16–17, 18,
    56–58, 83, 94, 98, 128, 136,
    142, 149, 151, 165, 170, 193,
    206, 216
and theme of Amor (Eros) viii, 25, 44,
    154–55, 163, 221–23, 225, 236
and theme of *directio voluntatis* 62,
    114, 154
and theme of (restoration of) order 30,
    42, 45, 52, 61–62, 75, 78, 105,
    111, 128, 144, 146, 150, 151,
    165, 245
and theme of 'splendour' viii, 44, 91,
    168, 181, 190, 214, 227–28,
    229, 236, 237, 242–46
and theme of Usura (Usury) 25, 26, 105
and translation studies 2–6
and use of Afro-American speech
    41–42, 47–51
and use of *Agamemnon* in *The Cantos*
    38–45, 61, 114, 142
Works:
ABC of Reading 6, 9–10, 13, 17, 28, 53
A Lume Spento 46n.11, 167
Analects, The 52, 114
'Anima Sola' 46n.11
'Apparuit' 16
Cantos, The vi, vii, viii, 6, 9, 21, 25,
    28–29, 38, 40, 42, 45, 46n.7,
    44, 62, 65n.14, 75, 79, 94, 101,
    105, 150, 154, 155, 165, 171,
    244, 245, 246
    Canto 1 6, 25, 129
    Canto 2 [Canto 8] 21, 25, 31
    Canto 4 25, 38, 87, 229
    Canto 5 21, 25, 38–40, 41, 114, 142,
        143
    Canto 7 21, 25
    Canto 9 233
    Canto 13 79
    Canto 17 244
    Canto 21 41–42
    Canto 23 46n.7, 72
    Canto 39 90
    Canto 46 25–26
    Canto 47 244
    Canto 49 74
    Canto 51 94n.2
    Canto 58 23–24, 42
    Canto 60 94n.2
    Canto 66 94n.2
    Canto 68 94n.2
    Canto 73 244–45
    Canto 77 43, 75
    Canto 78 26, 43, 87
    Canto 81 57, 114
    Canto 82 25, 42–43, 44, 87
    Canto 83 171n.3
    Canto 85 45, 101, 150
    Canto 86 45, 101, 150
    Canto 87 102, 150, 168, 171n.2,
        234–35, 243–44, 246n.1
    Canto 88 63
    Canto 89 44–45, 45–46, 65n.14, 112
    Canto 90 viii, 150–51
    Canto 91 44, 243, 247n.10
    Canto 93 171n.3
    Canto 95 171n.3, 235
    Canto 96 171n.3
    Canto 99 247n.10
    Canto 100 171n.3, 245
    Canto 101 208n.1
    Canto 104 247
    Canto 105 2
    Canto 109 245
    Canto 111 247n.10
    Canto 116 245–46
    Pisan Cantos vii, 42, 52, 56, 61, 62,
        75, 78, 87, 165
    Posthumous Cantos 247n.11
    Section: Rock-Drill de Los Cantares
        44, 45, 62, 78, 101, 112, 150,
        165, 242, 244, 247
    Thrones de los Cantares 62, 78, 165,
        244, 245
Canzoni 167
Cathay 5
'Cavalcanti' 164–65
*Chinese Written Character as a
    Medium for Poetry, The* 29
*Classic Anthology Defined by Confucius,
    The* 48, 52, 74
Confucius to Cummings 37, 53, 166
'Dr Williams' Position' 10
Elektra vii, 44, 56, 57, 58–62, 63, 65n.13,
    69, 70, 71–95 *passim*, 97–151
    passim, 155, 161, 165, 231,
    243, 246n.1

Prologue (S ll. 1–120;
    E ll. 1–140) 73–84
Parodos (S ll. 121–250;
    E ll. 141–305) 84–94
First Episode (S ll. 251–471;
    E ll. 306–534) 97–105
First Stasimon (S ll. 472–515;
    E ll. 535–88) 105–10
Second Episode (S ll.
    516–1057; E ll. 589–1194)
    110–22
Second Stasimon (S ll.
    1058–97; E ll. 1195–1257)
    123–28
Third Episode (S ll. 1098–
    1383; E ll. 1258–1624)
    128–40
Third Stasimon (S ll. 1384–97;
    E. ll. 1625–33) 140–42
Exodos (S ll. 1398–1510;
    E ll. 1634–1802) 142–48
Elektra and Noh 104, 119
general comparison Sophocles and
    Pound's version 73
Line 351 100–02, 150
Pound's annotations in and use of
    the Loeb *Elektra* vi, vii, 63,
    71, 72, 75, 78, 79, 84, 86, 90,
    93, 95n.6, 97, 98, 99, 100, 104,
    105, 107, 110, 111, 112, 115,
    116, 119, 120, 121, 122, 123,
    127, 128, 132, 134, 135, 138,
    140, 142, 143, 146, 147, 243
Pound's method of translation
    71–73
style of Pound's version 148–51
themes of Pound's version:
    justice 61–62, 64, 78, 80, 83, 86,
        93–94, 95, 99, 101, 102,
        105–07, 109, 111, 112, 113,
        121–22, 124, 125, 128, 144,
        145, 150–51
    purgation 74, 76, 77, 78, 98,
        113
    restoration of order 61, 70, 75,
        78, 105, 111, 128, 144, 146,
        165
    words versus deeds 74–75, 76,
        79, 114, 138–39

See also Agamemnon, Aigisthos,
    Chorus, Chrysothemis,
    Elektra, Klytaimnestra,
    Messenger, Orestes, Pylades
Exultations 160
'A Few Don'ts by an Imagiste' 17,
    167
Gaudier-Brzeska 6, 167
Great Digest, The (Ta Hio) 52, 61–62
Guide to Kulchur 6–7, 24, 30, 31, 32, 37,
    46n.3, 48, 51, 52, 64
'H.D. Choruses from Euripides' 11
'Hell' vi
'Hellenists' 57–58
'Hellenist Series' 21, 28
'Hellenist Series V: Aeschylus'
    [='Translators of Greek',
    LE 267–75] vii, 21–30, 36, 42,
    43, 46n.1, 46n.5, 51, 111
'Hellenist Series VI' 28
Homage to Sextus Propertius 5, 27, 160,
    214
How to Read 6, 9, 10, 14
'How to Write' 14
Hugh Selwyn Mauberley 9, 21–22, 30,
    40
I Gather the Limbs of Osiris 18
Instigations 21
'The Island of Paris' 16
'Ité' 10
'Jean Cocteau Sociologist' 63–64
Make It New 164
'Noh' or Accomplishment 165–67
'Oedipus Rex' (unpublished typescript)
    vii, 48–51
'An Opening for *Agamemnon*' 21,
    30–37, 47, 48, 51, 61
'Paris Letter' 19n.2, 30, 31–32, 63
Personae 160
Poems 1918–21 25
'The Return' 16–17, 27
'Re Vers Libre' 16, 17–18
Ripostes 16
'The Seafarer' 5
'Song fer the Muses' Garden' 48, 51
*Sonnets and Ballate of Guido
    Cavalcanti, The* 13
Spirit of Romance, The 18–19n.1, 22
'The Tradition' 12, 14–16, 17

'Translators of Greek' 1, 7, 21, 28, 43, 143
Unwobbling Pivot, The 52, 75
'A Visiting Card' 6
Women of Trachis viii, 52, 56, 59, 60, 63, 72, 102, 104, 119, 122n.1, 155, 156, 157, 158, 160, 165, 168, 169, 170, 171, 173–247 *passim*
    Prologue (S ll. 1–93; WT pp. 25–28, ll. 1–74) 173–78
    Parodos (S ll. 94–140; WT pp. 28–29, ll. 75–108) 178–88
    First Episode (S ll. 141–496; WT pp. 29–41, ll. 109–453) 188–202
    First Stasimon (S ll. 497–530; WT pp. 41–43, ll. 454–94) 202–07
    Second Episode (S ll. 531–632; WT pp. 43–46, ll. 495–598) 207–08
    Second Stasimon (S ll. 633–62; WT pp. 46–48, ll. 599–629) 209–13
    Third Episode (S ll. 663–820; WT pp. 48–53, ll. 630–788) 213–16
    Third Stasimon (S ll. 821–62; WT 53–55, ll. 789–832) 216–23
    Fourth Episode (S ll. 863–946; WT 55–58, ll. 833–915) 224–25
    Fourth Stasimon (S ll. 947–70; WT 58–59, ll. 916–38) 226–29
    Exodos (S ll. 971–1278; WT pp. 59–71, ll. 939–1242) 229–42
    contemporary reception of Pound's version 155–57
    influence of Noh 165–70
    line 1174 236–38, 247n.11
    line 1174 and Neoplatonism 242–46
    performances of Pound's version 170–71
    Pound and F.R. Earp
        correspondence on the play (general) 157–61 (*see also* Earp)
    Pound's annotations in and use of the Loeb *Trachiniae* vi, 63, 155, 158, 161, 164, 165, 173, 177, 178, 188, 189, 193, 195, 196, 199, 201, 202, 207, 209, 212, 213, 216, 224, 226, 229, 230, 236, 238, 239
    Pound's general approach/style 155, 161–63
    themes of Pound's version viii, 163–65, 181, 195, 208 (*see also* Pound and theme of Splendour)
    See also Achelous, Chorus, Deianeira, Herakles, Hyllus, Iole, Messenger, Nurse
Powell, James A. 15, 19n.5
Priam 35
Princeton 52, 71, 148, 192, 199, 236
Procne 82, 86, 87, 228–29
Prometheus 39–40, 55
Prometheus Bound (Aeschylus) 8, 10, 21, 22, 23, 28, 30, 39–40
Propertius, Sextus 214
Proteus 175
Pylades 74, 77, 78, 79, 128, 139, 142, 145

Rachewiltz, Mary de 122n.2
Rattray, David 2
Reck, Michael 2, 56, 59, 65n.11, 168–70, 171n.5, 247n.4
Redman, Tim 73
Reese, Gustave 57
Reid, Richard 71, 94n.2, 114, 138, 142
Reiss, Katharina 4
Richard of St Victor 157
Rossetti, Dante Gabriel 36
Rouse, W.H.D. 1, 51–52
Rudge, Olga 61, 62

Sacred Wood, The (Eliot) 7
St Elizabeths Hospital 2, 10, 37, 44, 52, 53, 56, 61, 63, 122n.2, 151, 156
Sappho vi, 1
Scheria 244
Schleiermacher, Friedrich 3

Schliemann, Heinrich 158
Selloi 234–35, 247n.4
Seven Against Thebes (Aeschylus) 21–22, 57, 60
Shakespear, Dorothy 60, 62
Shang, Chinese dynasty of 45
Shaw, George Bernard 11
Sheppard, J.T. 69, 70
Simois 27–28
Simpson, Dallam (a.k.a. Dallam Flynn) 37–38, 46n.6, 101
Siracusa vi
Skopos theory 4
Sommerstein, Alan H. 23
Sophocles vi, vii, viii, 2, 7, 8, 10, 11, 18n.1, 19n.2, 44, 47, 48, 49, 50, 52–56, 62, 63, 64n.5, 67–71, 73, 74, 76, 77, 78, 82, 84, 85, 87, 90, 93, 94n.1, 98, 99, 101, 102, 103, 104, 105, 107, 110, 111, 112, 114, 115, 116, 118, 120, 121, 124, 125, 127, 128, 129, 131, 136, 143, 145, 146, 148, 153–55, 156, 157, 158, 159, 161, 162, 168, 169, 171, 173–77, 180, 181, 183, 184, 185, 187, 189, 190, 193, 194, 198, 200, 203, 204, 206, 210, 211, 212, 213, 217, 218, 221, 225, 233, 236, 237, 238, 242
Spearman, Neville 60
Stanford, W.B. 23
Stanley, Sir Thomas 22, 23–28, 42, 43, 46n.1
Steiner, George 3
Stendhal 8
Sterglopoulou, Katerina 46n.10, 80, 83, 95n.5, 95n.8, 129, 131, 141, 229, 235
Storr, F. vi, viii, 63, 71, 76, 77, 78, 79, 84, 88, 90, 95n.6, 97, 98, 100, 101, 103, 104, 105, 107, 111, 119, 120, 123, 127, 133, 135, 138, 141, 142, 143, 144, 145, 155, 161, 162, 163, 173, 175–76, 177, 179–80, 181, 182–85, 187, 189, 193, 196, 199, 203, 205, 208, 212, 215, 218, 223, 227, 231, 232, 233, 239, 240
Stravinsky, Igor 171
Suppliants (Aeschylus) 54–55
Surette, Leon 38, 150
Syros, Christine 95n.10, 149, 151n.2
Sweeney Agonistes (Eliot) 48
Swinburne, Algernon 14, 42

Tê 62
Tereus 82
Terrell, Carroll F. 39, 65n.14, 102, 111
Thebes 21–22, 162, 185, 204
Themis 124
Thermopylae 209–10
Thucydides 1
Tierci, Bernard de 38, 46n.7
Tiresias 50
Trachiniae (Sophocles) vi, vii, viii, 56, 57, 61, 62–63, 72, 73, 102, 153–55, 161, 163, 165, 166, 173, 175, 203, 205, 234, 235, 236, 237, 238, 239, 242, 243, 246n.1
Trachis 176, 178
Translation Studies 2–6
Trojan War 25, 29, 30, 34
Trova, Ernest 59
Troy 33–35, 36, 38, 39, 40, 43, 45, 46n.7, 81
Tryphonopoulos, Demetres P. 151n.3
Tyro 150

Uncle Remus (Harris) 47–49

Venus (*see also* Aphrodite) 169
Venuti, Lawrence 3–4
Vermeer, Hans 4
Verona Program 101–02
Vidal, Perre 38
Virgil 4

Washington, George 41
Watchman (*Agamemnon*) 31, 32–35, 38, 42, 43, 51
Weir Smyth, Herbert 8
Williams, William Carlos 11, 37, 53

Xerxes 8–9

Yasuo, Fujitomi 168
Yeats, William Butler vi, 63, 64n.9, 148, 156, 183

Zagreus (*see also* Dionysus) 192–94
Zephyrus 26–27

Zeus (*see also* Jupiter) 22, 34, 37, 40, 46n.3, 87, 88, 91, 124, 127, 128, 150, 161, 175, 180, 187, 188, 190, 197–98, 203, 204, 205, 210, 217, 227, 229–30, 233, 234, 235, 236, 238, 239, 242

www.ingramcontent.com/pod-product-compliance
Lightning Source LLC
Chambersburg PA
CBHW050323020526
44117CB00031B/1684